# Philosophy and Politics - Critical Explorations

Volume 27

The purpose of Philosophy and Politics - Critical Explorations is to publish high quality volumes that reflect original research pursued at the juncture of philosophy and politics. Over the past 20 years new important areas of inquiry at the crossroads of philosophy and politics have undergone impressive developments or have emerged anew. Among these, new approaches to human rights, transitional justice, religion and politics and especially the challenges of a post-secular society, global justice, public reason, global constitutionalism, multiple democracies, political liberalism and deliberative democracy can be included. Philosophy and Politics - Critical Explorations addresses each and any of these interrelated yet distinct fields as valuable manuscripts and proposal become available, with the aim of both being the forum where single breakthrough studies in one specific subject can be published and at the same time the areas of overlap and the intersecting themes across the various areas can be composed in the coherent image of a highly dynamic disciplinary continent. Some of the studies published are bold theoretical explorations of one specific theme, and thus primarily addressed to specialists, whereas others are suitable for a broader readership and possibly for wide adoption in graduate courses. The series includes monographs focusing on a specific topic, as well as collections of articles covering a theme or collections of articles by one author. Contributions to this series come from scholars on every continent and from a variety of scholarly orientations.

Beatrice Okyere-Manu • Stephen Nkansah Morgan
Ovett Nwosimiri
Editors

# Contemporary Development Ethics from an African Perspective

## Selected Readings

Springer

*Editors*
Beatrice Okyere-Manu
Applied Ethics
University of KwaZulu-Natal
Pietermaritzburg, KwaZulu-Natal
South Africa

Stephen Nkansah Morgan
Department of Philosophy and Classics
University of Ghana
Accra, Ghana

Ovett Nwosimiri
Ulster University
London, UK

African Centre for Epistemology
and Philosophy of Science
University of Johannesburg
Johannesburg, South Africa

ISSN 2352-8370 ISSN 2352-8389 (electronic)
Philosophy and Politics - Critical Explorations
ISBN 978-3-031-32897-8 ISBN 978-3-031-32898-5 (eBook)
https://doi.org/10.1007/978-3-031-32898-5



This Springer imprint is published by the registered company Springer Nature Switzerland AG
The registered company address is: Gewerbestrasse 11, 6330 Cham, Switzerland

# Preface

One of the growing fields in development studies is Development Ethics. This field of study highlights the ethical challenges and moral responsibilities as a result of human advancement. There is no doubt that the world is undergoing changes due to technological development, climate change, migration, globalization, and socio-economic and political changes. The implications of these changes include numerous benefits and opportunities that they present. Despite the positive benefits, these changes also present a number of ethical conundrums in the whole world of which Africa has not been spared. These challenges need to be addressed for proper development to take place.

Among the major challenges particularly in Africa is how to ensure that development is equitable and sustainable. This is because development programs and projects have a significant impact not only on the lives of individuals, but communities, the continent, and natural resources. In many cases, development has not been inclusive, leaving behind most marginalized and vulnerable communities, and exacerbating existing inequalities. In addition, development in Africa has often been unsustainable, causing harm to the environment and depleting natural resource, thus contributing to current environmental crisis.

While there are many publications on Development Ethics from the Western standpoints, very little has been published from African perspectives, and more so, it is difficult to come across a single reader that brings all the developmental and ethical concerns together in one volume. This volume, therefore, seeks to fill in that gap by bringing together in one book reflections and discussions on questions, issues, and approaches of Development Ethics that takes into consideration African beliefs and values.

The book would be a valuable resource for anyone working in development, as well as for students, academics, and anyone interested in exploring the ethical dimensions of development in Africa.

A development ethics from an African perspective book would explore the ethical dimensions of development and provide a framework for critically examining development practices on the continent. The book would examine topics such as poverty, human rights, environmental sustainability, socio-cultural diversity, and the responsibilities of governments, corporations, and individuals in the development process.

Poverty and human rights are among the most pressing issues facing Africa today. Development ethics should address the issue of poverty and work toward creating a continent where people have access to basic needs such as food, shelter, and healthcare, something that this book would explore and challenge governments, corporations, and individuals to address poverty, and the ethical implications of various poverty reduction strategies.

In terms of human rights, some of the authors of the book examined women's rights implications of development policies, programs, and projects and explored how development can be made more inclusive and respectful of human rights.

Environmental sustainability is another key aspect of African development ethics. The book challenges governments, corporations, and individuals to protect the environment and ensure sustainable development. The book would also explore the ethical implications of various environmental protection strategies, such as conservation, renewable energy, and sustainable agriculture.

In conclusion, the volume provides a comprehensive overview of the ethical challenges and responsibilities arising from human advancement. It would provide a framework for critically examining development practices and for making ethical decisions in the field of development. Doing this successfully is not easy. We can hardly hope that we have been successful in overcoming all difficulties. It is our hope that this volume will inspire development practitioners in Africa.

University of KwaZulu-Natal
Pietermaritzburg, South Africa — Beatrice Okyere-Manu

University of Ghana
Accra, Ghana — Stephen Nkansah Morgan

Ulster University
London, UK — Ovett Nwosimiri

University of Johannesburg
Johannesburg, South Africa

# Acknowledgement

The completion of this project is due to the support of a number of people. We wish to thank all the contributors to this volume for their hard work and expertise in making this project a success. Many thanks go to the reviewers and editors, particularly Christopher Wilby and Floor Oosting. Thank you so much Arun Santhosh Kannan for your professional expertise in shaping the manuscript.

# Contents

**Part I Development Ethics in the African Context**

**Introduction: Exploring Development Ethics in an African Context** . . . . . . 3
Beatrice Okyere-Manu, Stephen Nkansah Morgan, and Ovett Nwosimiri

**African Ethics as a Conduit to Development** . . . . . . . . . . . . . . . . . . . . . . . . 15
Emmanuel Musoke Mutyaba

**Part II Theories and Approaches to Development Ethics in Africa**

**Neo-Liberalism and the Ethics of Pan-African Development Governance in Sub-Saharan Africa** . . . . . . . . . . . . . . . . . . . . . . . . . . . . . . . . 33
Kizito Michael George

**An Anatomy of Neoliberalism's Subversion of Development and Democracy in Africa** . . . . . . . . . . . . . . . . . . . . . . . . . . . . . . . . . . . . . . . . . 51
Peter Osimiri

**Development Theories and Governance Ideologies Conundrums in Africa: An Observable Disconnects Between Values and Practices** . . . . . 65
Stephen Nkansah Morgan and Beatrice Okyere-Manu

**The Moral Dimension of Development in Zimbabwe** . . . . . . . . . . . . . . . . . 79
Nomatter Sande

**Part III Environment and African Development**

**African Ethics and Sustainable Development Goals: Towards Achieving the SDGs in Africa** . . . . . . . . . . . . . . . . . . . . . . . . . . . . 95
Ovett Nwosimiri

**"Environmental Crisis or Environmental Retaliation": Reflections on the Nexus Between the Manyika People and the Environment in Post-colonial Zimbabwe** . . . . . . . . . . . . . . . . . . . . 107
Silindiwe Zvingowanisei and Sophia Chirongoma

**Part IV Gender, Ethics and Socio-economic Development in Africa**

**A Blessing or a Curse: An Exploration of Zimbabwe's Plight in the Global Village** ... 131
Isaac Mhute

**African Development and Disruptive Innovations: An Ethical Implication of the e-Hailing Services on the Metered Taxi Industry in South Africa** ... 143
Beatrice Okyere-Manu

**Women's Rights: A Precursor for African Development** ... 155
Faith Matumbu

**The Economic Foundation of Racism** ... 165
Emmanuel Ifeanyi Ani

**Part V Migration and African Development**

**Medical Brain Drain and Healthcare Delivery in Africa: Beyond Restrictive Migration Policies** ... 183
Damilola Victoria Oduola

**Part VI Education and African Development**

**Epistemic Decolonisation in African Higher Education: Beyond Current Curricular and Pedagogical Reformation** ... 197
Husein Inusah

**Educational Challenges to Africa's Development: The Imperative of Epistemic Decolonisation** ... 213
Victoria Openif'Oluwa Akoleowo

**Part VII Politics and African Development**

**"A Model Without Plenty"? A Critical Assessment of the "Winner Takes All" Concept in Zimbabwean Politics 1980–2021** ... 231
James Hlongwana

**Zimbabwean Politics and Development: An *Ubuntu* Perspective** ... 243
Tobias Marevesa and Esther Mavengano

**Integrity, Public Accountability, Ethical and Exemplary Leadership Models as Imperatives for Resolving the Problem of Leadership in Africa** ... 257
Peter Wilfred Naankiel, Robert Odey Simon, and Ghulam Abbas

# About the Editors

**Beatrice Okyere-Manu** is a Professor in the Applied Ethics department at the University of KwaZulu-Natal in Pietermaritzburg. Her research interests cover the following areas: HIV and AIDS, Ethical issues Affecting African Women, AIKS, Ethics of Technology, and Environmental Ethics. She has written a number of journal articles and book chapters in these areas. She recently edited a book on "African Values, Ethics, and Technology: Questions, Issues, and Approaches" which provides critical and ethical reflections on technology from an African perspective. She co-edited a book on "Intersecting African Indigenous Knowledge Systems and Western Knowledge Systems: Moral convergence and divergence".

**Stephen Nkansah Morgan** is currently a lecturer with the Department of Philosophy and Classics of the University of Ghana where he teaches a wide range of philosophy and ethic courses at both graduate and undergraduate levels. Stephen holds a PhD in Ethics Studies from the University of KwaZulu-Natal in South Africa, and a Master of Philosophy and Bachelor of Arts degrees in Philosophy both from the University of Ghana. He has research interests in Environmental and Animal Ethics, Ethics of Technology, Social and Political Philosophy, and African philosophy broadly construed. He has previously taught at the University of Kwazulu-Natal in South Africa.

**Ovett Nwosimiri** has a PhD in Philosophy from the University of KwaZulu-Natal where he also lectured Applied Ethics. He also lectured Philosophy at St. Joseph's Theological Institute Cedara, South Africa. He was a Post-Doctoral Research Fellow at the African Centre for Epistemology and Philosophy of Science (ACEPS), University of Johannesburg. His research interest is in African Philosophy, African Epistemology, Philosophy of Race, Applied Ethics Epistemology and Existentialism. He is currently at Ulster University, Business School, London campus. He is a Research Associate at the African Centre for Epistemology and Philosophy of Science, University of Johannesburg.

# About the Editors

# Part I
# Development Ethics in the African Context

# Introduction: Exploring Development Ethics in an African Context

**Beatrice Okyere-Manu, Stephen Nkansah Morgan, and Ovett Nwosimiri**

**Abstract** The word 'development' can mean different things to different people. It is one of the most elusive concepts to define, alongside the concept of modernization. Often and perhaps due to its elusive nature, people tend to rely on an economic definition of development where definite parameters and indices can be used to assess and determine levels of development 'objectively'. Thus, a nation's development is measured in terms of its Gross Domestic Product (GDP), Gross National Income (GNI), Per-Capita Income and Foreign Exchange Reserves. But does the attainment of these economic parameters really translate into development qua development? Historical and current development predicaments of many sub-Saharan African nation points to a negative response to the question. How, then, do we define or approach development that encompasses all the relevant development factors? Is there anything like an ideal definition of development at all or do we need to contextualize what development should mean for each society, culture, or nation? What does development ethics in an African context look or should like? This chapter explores these questions at an introductory level.

B. Okyere-Manu (✉)
Applied Ethics, University of KwaZulu-Natal, Pietermaritzburg, KwaZulu-Natal, South Africa
e-mail: okyere-manv@ukzn.ac.za

S. N. Morgan
Department of Philosophy and Classics, University of Ghana, Accra, Ghana

O. Nwosimiri
Ulster University, London, UK

African Centre for Epistemology and Philosophy of Science, University of Johannesburg, Johannesburg, South Africa



B. Okyere-Manu et al. (eds.), *Contemporary Development Ethics from an African Perspective*, Philosophy and Politics - Critical Explorations 27,
https://doi.org/10.1007/978-3-031-32898-5_1

# 1 Introduction

What is wrong with Africa's development agenda, and why does it look like she is lagging? Many may want to blame Africa's developmental woes on her wholesale attempt to model her development in the manner of the West or Europe when clearly, she has different histories and aspirations. Others will prefer to lay the blame at the doorsteps of leadership rather than on a specifically chosen development agenda. Such persons perceive development as a scientific model, which, when followed carefully would lead to a similar outcome for all irrespective of their histories or ambitions. They believe that Africa's failed developmental pursuit is mainly due to the greed and selfishness of her leaders, who despite knowing what is best for their citizens, rather pursue undertakings that are not necessarily meant to correct the developmental needs of their people but rather to fill their pockets. Yet, others think Africa's developmental challenges is a conceptual problem. African leaders are yet to understand what development is or should be and which approaches are best suited for their peculiar needs. Of course, there is also the influences from external global players who stand to benefit from Africa's current development turmoil and would do anything to keep the status quo.

How then should development be properly defined? What are some conceptual challenges faced by existing definitions for development? Given Africa's unique slavery and colonial history and violent struggle for independence, should she have a unique approach to development? If so, what manner should such an approach take? The chapter looks at these questions from a purely conceptual level. We understand ethics to be the study of right and wrong actions and behaviour, the dos and don'ts of society and the study of what makes for a just society. Thus, it becomes imperative for ethical theories of development to demonstrate how they could ensure a fair and just society rather than tilting wealth towards a few oligarchs or bourgeoisie. We also understand that the pursuit of these development agendas is not an easy task given the nuances and complexities on the ground and the scarce resources that are becoming more and more scarce every day. However, it appears there is something the African continent is not doing or getting right that makes it continue to grapple with high unemployment, poverty, low literacy rate, hunger, predicament of women, poor housing, poor infrastructure, wars, conflicts and violence, and general below-average standard of living.

Answers to the above-raised questions cannot be answered by one person. Thus, in this collection, various authors have attempted to tackle various aspects of Africa's developmental woes. Before we look at the synopses of each chapter, we will do a critical exploration of some existing definitions of development and some conceptual and practical challenges they face. Next, we explore a description of what development ethics from an African perspective could look like and why there is a need for such an approach.

## 2 Defining Development

The starting point for getting development right is having a clear understanding of the concept. This will help in determining what issues are important and what are not, and also to know whether one is making progress or failing. However, pinning down a 'suitable' definition for such an open-textured word like development is no easy task. Many existing definitions come with some conceptual or practical challenges, mostly because the concept remains very broad and expansive (Haaften 1997).

Often and perhaps due to its elusive nature, people tend to depend on an economic definition of development where definite parameters and indices can be used to assess and determine levels of development 'objectively'. However, historical experiences have taught us that development is not entirely an economic phenomenon but instead a multi-dimensional process. Thus, the attempt to measure a nation's development based on its Gross Domestic Product (GDP), Gross National Income (GNP), Per-Capita Income, and Foreign Exchange Reserves does not quite capture a holistic understanding of development. Amartya Sen (1988), therefore, rightly points out the inadequacy in measuring development by using the purely economic approach. He was of the view that such an approach leaves out important factors such as the question of the *fairness* of the distribution of the GNP among a nation's population and items that do not come with price tags attached to them. GNP, for example, does not measure health, education, equality of opportunity, the state of the environment, and the rule of law. He asserts that "It is, of course, possible for a country to have an expansion of GNP per head, while its distribution becomes more unequal" (Sen 1988: 13). Sen was basically questioning what is taken to be a straightforward connection between material prosperity and welfare.

Given that an economic definition of development does not give us a holistic understanding of the term, how else can development be analysed? According to Woutervan Van Haaften:

> The term "development" is a member of the family of change-words. Other terms are "actualization," "growth," "maturation," "evolution," and the recently trendy "self-realization." All these members of the family have certain semantic features in common. For instance, they all refer to a form of change which requires some time to come about (1997: 15).

There is a lot to unpack in Haaften's description of development above. Firstly, we note that development involves a change, presumably a positive and an incremental or forward-looking (progressive) change. All the other terminologies mentioned by Haaften similarly alludes to some change of a sort, that is, actualization, growth, maturation, and evolution. However, actualization, maturation, and self-realization tend to suggest and endpoint to development. Perhaps this allusion to an end goal is part of the reason why some nations are referred to as developing nations while others are referred to as developing. However, others who find this classification problematic. Lansana Keita (2011), for instance, thinks that the use of the word 'developed' gives the impression of a completed or finished process, while 'underdeveloped' tends to imply stasis or lack of progress. For him, a look at where European societies were some decades ago and the technological and economical advancements they have made, makes it absurd to use the term 'developed' to describe them, especially when they are still making advancements. He states: "Thus, the idea that European societies are 'developed' is obviously questionable. European societies are in the process of development just as other societies deemed 'undeveloped' or 'developing' (Keita 2011: 116).To him, the obviously confirmable difference between contemporary developing European societies and those of Africa is that the former societies are the producers and users of more novel forms of technology than the latter (Keita 2011: 117).

Given the above notwithstanding, it does appear that the notion of development involves some form of change, a change that is not negative or retrogressive or backwards-looking but rather positive, forward-looking, and progressive. Perhaps, it is this kind of change that Haaften refers to as 'qualitative change'. He writes that:

> In short, we take qualitative change as the main definitional criterion for "development." Combined with some of the more obvious criteria it shares with other members of the change-family, we may then say that "development" means (a) a process of (b) more or less gradual (c) change, (d) resulting in (what can be reconstructed as one or more qualitatively different stages for which (e) the prior stages are necessary conditions. (Haaften 1997: 18)

It is evident from the above that development involves not just any change but a qualitative change. This qualitative change is perhaps the reason for the inadequacy of the economic definition of development. Because while there could be a change or growth or increase in a nation's GDP or GNP or foreign exchange reserves, such changes are only quantitative and not qualitative. In other words, they do not capture the qualitative standard of living of the people. Sen again puts it better in the following words: "Even though an expansion of GNP, given other things, should enhance the living conditions of people, and will typically expand the life expectancy figures of that country, there are many other variables that also influence the living conditions, and the concept of development cannot ignore the role of these other variables" (1988: 13).

The indicative qualitative change as critical within the concept of development is important to ensure that countries do not make balancing the financial numbers and statistics their priority as a mark of development. Development should be all-encompassing and must reflect in the daily lives of the people and not just on paper. Sen refers to this approach to development as 'the capability approach', which when done right can take care of what he refers to as the 'functions of a person'. These 'functions of a person' are supposed to be the things that individuals in every society aim to achieve or do, of which development, when properly done right, must give the people access. He posits that:

> Insofar as development is concerned with the achievement of a better life, the focus of development analysis has to include the nature of the life that people succeed in living… People value their ability to do certain things and to achieve certain types of beings (such as being well nourished, being free from avoidable morbidity, being able to move about as desired, and so on). These "doings" and "beings" may be generically called "functioning" of a person (Sen 1988: 15).

Development as a qualitative change will therefore improve the standard of living of the people, improve social service delivery, including healthcare and education, to ensure an improved better life of the people.

## 3 Reflections on Development Ethics from an African Perspective

Kwesi Kwaa Prah (2011: 156) notes that: "in the fifty years or so of post-colonialism in Africa, no single obsession has been as overriding in the preoccupations of Africa's intellectuals as the question of development." He refers to development as "the single, most obsessive object of all governments and ruling elites in Africa." He is not far from the truth. It is a well-known fact that sub-Saharan African nations have failed in their pursuant of development despite having so many natural resources. This is the predicament of the African continent and there is a constant need to persistently reflect on how Africa can do better.

The field of development ethics raises moral questions about the following: governance, leadership, equality, gender justice and social and environmental justice and Technology. It points our minds to the challenges of development and how to ensure a fair and just society for all particularly African women who are among the most vulnerable on the continent. It is its preoccupation to reflect on what a fair and just society ought to look like and which approaches are the most equitable way to do so. It is a daunting task and yet must be embarked on head-on. Perhaps a contributing factor to African developmental woes is the fact that development ethics has over the years been approached from a Eurocentric perspective. As a result, one of the central presumptions of development ethics has been the idea that European cultures have universal validity and applicability. In other words, there is the presumption that European or Western cultures and ideals are global and superior to others and as such must be embraced and adopted by all. For this reason, Des Gasper asked the question: "Can development ethics avoid presuming that European cultures have universal validity and yet also avoid treating every distinct culture as sacrosanct and beyond criticism?" (1996: 627). This question is of utmost importance because of the Eurocentric and universalist posture that development ethics has assumed. European cultures do not have universal validity because different cultures have their own ways of doing things, and these cultural differences and identities have an important role to play in their development. Eurocentric perspectives to development have been the monotonous way and the ideal way/form of theorising and engaging development for many people in different continents, including Africa for some time now.

Development ethics must consider the cultural differences and the plurality of values across the world. Africans cannot, as a result, pick and use the approaches of the West on a wholesale without subjecting them to critical evaluation. African problems need African solutions. Ideas may be borrowed but even so, they must be contextualized. Therefore, at this point in history, Africa needs to ethically assess her developmental agenda, partly to disentangle herself from the Eurocentric impositions or acquisitions, and partly to seek justice and a better life for her people.

More promising development ethics for Africa would recognize and integrate positive and progressive values and practices that are founded upon the African ways of life. It will, for example, consider an individual as "part of the whole, being close, sharing a way of life, belonging and being bound up with others, and, on the other, there is 'exhibiting solidarity' with them, i.e., achieving the good of all, being sympathetic, advancing the common good, serving and being committed to others' good" (Metz 2017: 118). This is, indeed, a reflection of the good old philosophy of *Ubuntu* and African communalism. It is, therefore, an imperative that Africans find a way to make the philosophy and ethics of *Ubuntu* relevant to modern society and modern needs. How to do this on a continent that is day by day becoming individualistic is a daunting task for African thinkers.

Africa today is a heterogeneous continent that is made up of people from different communities. Because of this, her development agenda must seek to integrate her different cultures, ethics, and moral values and balance these with the positive values and ideals from elsewhere that have unavoidably also become part of her reality. Despite the many infiltrations of foreign cultures, African cultures have stood the test of time and would still be relevant going into the future. James K. Kigongo, thus rightly notes that:

> The viability of the African [culture], however, can be justified in the sense that we can still talk of a continuity of the African cultural content despite the change, though the essence and intensity of this content cannot be established with certainty. In fact, African culture and ethics did not collapse. Instead, they lost their intrinsic importance in people's thinking and assumed a peripheral role in the event of colonization and its attendant cultural impingement (2002: 37).

Thus, there does seem to be a sense of hope for Africa if she plays her cards right in forging an ethical development agenda.

It is also worth noting that: "the moral values of a people determine their economic and political behaviour. It is in this sense that the moral beliefs and values of a society cannot be completely detached from their political and economic attitudes and performance" (Tosam 2014: 41). Development ethics from an African perspective should then take into consideration the experience, culture, and history of Africans to make sense of the people's experiences through critical and rigorous reflection. Development ethics from an African perspective must consider the moral assessment of the ends and means of societal change in Africa, with its connection with policy formation, institution, nation-building, economics, etc.

Perhaps, it will do some good for African leaders to take insight from understanding the concept of development as discussed in the previous section. Development implies positive, progressive, and forward-looking change, a qualitative change. It is not about balancing the books to look good with the IMF or World Bank or so-called 'development partners' to secure the next big loans or grants. It is about ensuring a better quality of life for the people and increasing their access to basic needs, wants, and freedoms. It is, therefore, imperative for African scholars to reflect on these matters deeper than we have in the past and come out with a more practical approach to help the continent attain a genuine qualitative change for the benefit of current and future generations alike.

Today, young Africans particularly women have lost hope in their leaders and have assumed that there is no hope for them should they remain on the continent. Hence, we see a mass exodus of young African skilled workers and professionals into Europe for a better future for themselves and their families. Some go on government scholarships to study and never return in contravention of their scholarship contracts. They will rather endure the hardship and discrimination out there than come back home where there are no opportunities. This current reality of the African continent must change and it is the role of development ethics to conceptualize a practical solution for these and other predicaments she is facing.

Perhaps African leaders could further take a clue from Michael Paul Todaro and Stephen Smith's three values of development. Todaro points out that development must firstly raise peoples' living levels, i.e., incomes and consumption, levels of food, medical services, education through relevant growth processes. Secondly, development must create conditions conducive to the growth of people's self-esteem through the establishment of social, political, and economic systems, and institutions that promote human dignity and respect. Thirdly, development must increase peoples' freedom to choose by enlarging the range of their choice variables, e.g., varieties of goods and services (Todaro and Smith 2012). African scholars and leaders need to constantly reflect on how they can attain these three objectives for their people in a bid to transform the current outlook of the continent. These are some of the reasons why there is a need for reflections on what development ethics should mean for Africa. They are also why this book comes in handy.

## 4 Chapters of the Book

In the first chapter, "*Introduction – Exploring Development Ethics in an African Context*?" Beatrice Okyere-Manu, Stephen Nkansah Morgan, and Ovett Nwosimiri explore the concept of development from an African perspective. They engage with how African ethical values are relevant to the concept of development and development ethics. The chapter highlights some conceptual problems to do with defining the term development and makes some suggestions on how an African development ought to look like.

Emmanuel Musoke Mutyaba, argues in chapter "*African Ethics as a Conduit to Development*" that African ethics is important in establishing effective and a holistic development agenda. He specifically highlights community and fraternity found in African ethics as important virtues that can produce good character that is needed in any holistic development. To him, these virtues stand against vices such as egoism, corruption, embezzlement, theft, cheating, laziness, violation of human dignity, etc. He further posits that these vices hinder the overall wellbeing of people. It is with this backdrop that he encourages African communities to revisit these community and fraternity virtues in the attainment of individual and social progress.

The next chapter, "*Neo-Liberalism and the Ethics of Pan-African Development Governance in Sub-Saharan Africa*" is by Kizito Michael George. In it, he argues that African neo-colonies are still trapped in the Western racist paradigm of development conceptualisation and management. To him, neo-liberalism has fundamentally paralysed ethical Pan-African development governance by relegating development to the whims of the positivistic market, which is deterministic and scientific. This is what the chapter labours to unpack.

In chapter "*An Anatomy of Neoliberalism's Subversion of Development and Democracy in Africa*", Peter Osimiri provides an analysis of the several subtle and non-subtle ways by which the wholesale imposition and embracement of the neoliberal ideology and its accompanying prescriptions and practices are facilitating the subversion of democracy and undermining the possibility of authentic and autochthonous development on the continent of Africa. It concludes that radical engagement remains an essential part of an integrated strategy for breaking the stranglehold of neoliberalism on African societies.

In chapter "*Development Theories and Governance Ideologies Conundrums in Africa: An Observable Disconnects Between Values and Practices*", *the authors,* Stephen Nkansah Morgan & Beatrice Okyere-Manu, assess why African nations continue to grapple with the same old challenge of poverty, human rights abuses, lack of clear political ideology, moral and political corruption, and political and tribal conflicts among others amidst various ethical, philosophical, political, and development theories fashioned on tradtional African values and practices. The authors attempt to make sense of the conspicuous disconnection between theories that are built on indigenous African values and the practices and ways of life of the African people that do not reflect these values. The paper concludes by making recommendations on how we can, perhaps, bridge this gap.

Nomatter Sande, in chapter entitled "*The Moral Dimension of Development in Zimbabwe*", explores the moral ethos that defines development, including ethical judgement for a good life, good society, and good relationships. The study concludes that for meaningful development in Africa, the focus should be on African indigenous knowledge systems, culture, philosophy, and spirituality. It further adds that rather than implementing Western scientific development strategies only, it is also essential to integrate Western science with African values and ethics.

In the next chapter, "*African Ethics and Sustainable Development Goals: Towards Achieving the SDGs in Africa*", Ovett Nwosimiri examines how African ethics can help in achieving Sustainable Development Goals (SDGs) in Africa. He argues that the recognition and integration of African ethics together with the SDGs will help Africa move to a sustainable trajectory. Drawing upon insights from Thaddeus Metz discussion on African ethics, he reflects on how SDGs can be fully achieved if they integrate African ethics, thus welfare-based and community-based African ethics.

In chapter, ""*Environmental Crisis or Environmental Retaliation*"*: Reflections on the Nexus Between the Manyika People and the Environment in Post-Colonial*

*Zimbabwe*" by Silindiwe Zvingowanisei and Sophia Chirongoma, the authors argue for the need to engage and deploy indigenous environmental ethics and methods to mitigate the impact of the environmental crisis. Using the phenomenological method for its theoretical framework, the They explore how Manyika traditional conservation methods have been overlooked by Western approaches and concludes that an appraisal and recognition of the essence of traditional leadership and efficacy of indigenous environment strategies is imperative if environmental problems are to be curtailed.

In chapter "*A Blessing or a Curse: An Exploration of Zimbabwe's Plight in the Global Village*", Isaac Mhute explores the political, economic and socio-cultural fate of Zimbabwe in the globalized world. He purposively sampled Zimbabwean experiences and analysed them in light of the theory of constructivism to determine the extent to which globalization is impacting on the nation. The chapter concludes that just like Zimbabwe, most developing countries are going nowhere in as far as proper development is concerned and advocates for a closer look at how the limited developmental opportunities in these countries could be improved for the betterment of the entire global village.

In chapter "*African Development and Disruptive Innovations: An Ethical Implication of the e-Hailing Services on the Metered Taxi Industry in South Africa*", Beatrice Okyere-Manu acknowledges the presence of disruptive innovation in Africa. She explores the benefits of these disruptive innovations on the African development landscape. She argues that a closer look at the ethics of these innovations raises a number of moral concerns for the incumbent businesses in South Africa. She argues that these innovations are developed and owned by rich Individuals and multi-Million companies from different cultural settings. This, for her, raises a number of ethical questions for Africa. Through the lens of the political theory of consensus by Kwame Gyekye, she argued for a consensus through dialogue by all stakeholders involved.

Chapter "*Women's Rights: A Precursor for African Development*" is by Faith Matumbu. In this chapter, the author explores what the term development means from women's perspective. Through the lens of the ethical theory of consequentialism, Matumbu interrogates whether women's rights are recognized in practical terms. She argued that a gap exists in the area of women's rights in women's quest to make a claim in the development of the continent. She further posits that for the continent to tap into women's potential to the fullest, an enabling environment has to be created.

In chapter "*The Economic Foundation of Racism*", Emmanuel Ifeanyi Ani exposes the connection between economic inequality and racism. He argues that racism is predicated on the economic superiority of the racist. Ani concludes that the relationship between racism and economic inequality is more significant than the relationship between racism and skin colour. He further proposed how races at the receiving end of racism should respond to racism.

Chapter "*Medical Brain Drain and Healthcare Delivery in Africa: Beyond Restrictive Migration Policies*", Damilola Victoria Oduola argues that Africa continues to witness enormous shortages of health-care workers as a result of "medical brain drain". To him, to successfully combat medical brain drain, African countries need to address the underlying factors that are responsible for bad health outcomes and also adopt viable health and public policy approaches which are considerate of individual liberty and at the same time sympathetic to the "plight" of developing African countries.

Husein Inusah in chapter "*Epistemic Decolonisation in African Higher Education: Beyond Current Curricular and Pedagogical Reformation*", underscores the importance of the study of non-cognitive factors in the curriculum development and transformation effort by connecting it with the resources in virtue epistemology, educational psychology, and paremiology to emphasize the teaching of epistemic virtues in Akan proverbs to provide a comprehensive approach to the concerns of decolonising knowledge in Africa.

The next chapter, entitled: "*Educational Challenges to Africa's Development: The Imperative of Epistemic Decolonisation*" is by Victoria Openif'Oluwa Akoleowo. The chapter builds on the notion of 'colonial legacy' as an insidious challenge to Africa's development. Utilising the analytic and synthetic methodologies, the author avers that epistemic decolonisation is an essential factor in development ethics.

In chapter, ""*A Model Without Plenty": A critical Assessment of the "Winner Takes All" Concept in Zimbabwean Politics 1980–2021*", James Hlongwana looks at Zimbabwe's governance system between 1980 and 2021 and argues that Zimbabwean politics and economics have receded into the doldrums. In view of the challenges, emanating from the "winner takes all" political paradigm, Hlongwana argues for the adoption of coalition democracy in Zimbabwe because it will arguably promote national unity and macro-economic fundamentals that favour economic development.

In chapter, "*Zimbabwean Politics and Development: An Ubuntu Perspective*", Tobias Marevesa and Esther Mavengano-Marevesa explore the essentials of Ubuntu/Unhu philosophy as an ethical framework which helps to frame arguments for a possible 'rebirth' of the nation after the demise of the late president Mugabe to pave way for national development. The authors argue that political conflict and sanctions should be carefully examined to unpack the complex dynamics of the present-day Zimbabwean politics. They conclude that political stasis and sanctions require immediate solutions to pave way for national development in post-coup Zimbabwe.

Chapter "*Integrity, Public Accountability, Ethical and Exemplary Leadership Models as Imperatives for Resolving the Problem of Leadership in Africa*" authored by Peter Wilfred Naankiel, Robert Odey Simon, and Ghulam Abbas, offers sustainable ideological and pragmatic solutions to leadership issues in Africa. Using qualitative approach and secondary data with text-content analysis, the chapter discusses, with examples, how the integrity criterion and public accountability of ethical and exemplary leadership models (IPACEEL Models) could aptly address leadership issues in contemporary Africa. The authors conclude that institutionalising the IPACEEL Models would ideologically and pragmatically resolve most leadership issues, such as bad governance, mismanagement and underdevelopment, in Africa.

## 5 Conclusion

This book has upcoming and established scholars all over Africa take on different aspects of the continent's developmental ethical challenges either on general issues that affect the continent in general or on issues unique to a particular African nation. We hope that this collection of current ethical reflection of old and new developmental challenges faced by the African continent can offer newer, practical, and workable solutions and insights that would propel Africa into a new age of ethical leadership and positive quantitative development.

## References

Gasper, D. 1996. Culture and development ethics: Needs, Women's rights, and Western theories. *Development and Change* 27: 627–661.

Keita, Lansana. 2011. Philosophy and development: On the problematic African development – A diachronic analysis. In *Philosophy and African development: Theory and practice*, ed. Lansana Keita, 115–138. Dakar: Council for the Development of Social Science Research in Africa.

Kigongo, James K. 2002. The relevance of African ethics to contemporary African society. In *Ethics, human rights and development in Africa*, ed. A.T. Dalfovo, K. James, J. Kigongo, G. Kisekka, E. Tusabe, et al., 51–66. Washington, DC: The Council for Research in Values and Philosophy.

Metz, T. 2017. Replacing development: An afro-communal approach to global justice. *Philosophical Papers* 46 (1): 111–137.

Prah, Kwesi Kwaa. 2011. Culture: The missing link in development. In *Philosophy and African development: Theory and practice*, ed. Lansana Keita, 156–168. Dakar: Council for the Development of Social Science Research in Africa.

Sen, Amartya. 1988. The concept of development. In *Handbook of development economics*, ed. H. Chenery and T.N. Srinivasan, vol. 1, 10–24. Elsevier Science Publishers B.V.

Todaro P, Michael and Smith C. Stephen. 2012. *Economic development*, 12th edn. Cape Town: Pearson.

Tosam, M.J. 2014. The relevance of Kom ethics to African development. *International Journal of Philosophy* 2 (3): 36–47.

Haaffen, Wouter Van. 1997. The concept of development. In Philosophy of development: Reconstructing the foundations of human development and education, ed. Wouter Van Haaffen, Michiel and Thomas Wren, 13–30. Springer-Science+Business Media, B.Y.

**Beatrice Okyere-Manu** is a Professor in the Applied Ethics department at the University of KwaZulu-Natal in Pietermaritzburg. Her research interests cover the following areas: HIV and AIDS, Ethical issues Affecting African Women, AIKS, Ethics of Technology, and Environmental Ethics. She has written a number of journal articles and book chapters in these areas. She recently edited a book on "African Values, Ethics, and Technology: Questions, Issues, and Approaches" which provides critical and ethical reflections on technology from an African perspective. She co-edited a book on "Intersecting African Indigenous Knowledge Systems and Western Knowledge Systems: Moral convergence and divergence".

**Stephen Nkansah Morgan** is currently a lecturer with the Department of Philosophy and Classics of the University of Ghana where he teaches a wide range of philosophy and ethic courses at both graduate and undergraduate levels. Stephen holds a PhD in Ethics Studies from the University of KwaZulu-Natal in South Africa, and a Master of Philosophy and Bachelor of Arts degrees in Philosophy both from the University of Ghana. He has research interests in Environmental and Animal Ethics, Ethics of Technology, Social and Political Philosophy, and African philosophy broadly construed. He has previously taught at the University of Kwazulu-Natal in South Africa.

**Ovett Nwosimiri** has a PhD in Philosophy from the University of KwaZulu-Natal where he also lectured Applied Ethics. He also lectured Philosophy at St. Joseph's Theological Institute Cedara, South Africa. He was a Post-Doctoral Research Fellow at the African Centre for Epistemology and Philosophy of Science (ACEPS), University of Johannesburg. His research interest is in African Philosophy, African Epistemology, Philosophy of Race, Applied Ethics Epistemology and Existentialism. He is currently at Ulster University, Business School, London campus. He is a Research Associate at the African Centre for Epistemology and Philosophy of Science, University of Johannesburg.

# African Ethics as a Conduit to Development

**Emmanuel Musoke Mutyaba**

**Abstract** The objective of this work is to contribute to the existing literature, a theoretical argument that, African ethics can help in effecting a holistic development. African ethics with its emphasis on the common good and guided by the two cardinal virtues of community and fraternity, can lead to the improvement of people's quality of life as those virtues are vital in effecting progress in meeting economic, social and environmental betterment. Such a communitarian and fraternal ethics emphasizes good character for all members thereby mal practices like: egoism, corruption, embezzlement, theft, cheating, laziness, violation of human dignity, etc. which hinder the overall wellbeing of people, are detested. Instead, good practices such as accountability/reliability, hard work for sustainability, innovativeness, charity, cooperation, responsibility for fellow human beings and nature at large, and good governance are encouraged which leads to the attainment of social progress and the achievement of a holistic well being for all. African ethic's principle of participation where all members participate in the matters of their community which is the gist of democracy is of great help in building democratic states. As a way forward, this chapter encourages African communities to revisit African ethical values for their relevancy in the attainment of individual and social progress. The method used in writing this chapter was a desk study research method that was purely qualitative in approach.

**Keywords** African ethics · Community · Fraternity · Holistic and development

E. M. Mutyaba (✉)
Uganda Martyrs University, Kampala, Uganda
e-mail: emutyaba@umu.ac.ug



B. Okyere-Manu et al. (eds.), *Contemporary Development Ethics from an African Perspective*, Philosophy and Politics - Critical Explorations 27,
https://doi.org/10.1007/978-3-031-32898-5_2

## 1 Introduction

Some writers have argued that traditional Africans regulate their conducts by means of superstitions and magical sanctions rather than appealing to reason. Therefore, there is no moral sense or behavioral guiding principles in traditional Africa which can be properly termed as ethics (Fanon Frantz 1998: 305). This chapter used a desk study research method to present a purely qualitative study in defense of the existence of African ethics and more so that, this ethics is fundamental to a holistic form of development.

This chapter is organized into four parts. Part one clarifies on the concept of ethics in general. Part two proves by way of argument, that ethics exists and very much upheld in traditional Africa. Part three constitutes the main idea of the chapter; it shows that African ethics can lead to holistic development. The fourth part consists of the conclusion in which the way forward is also suggested.

In short, this chapter attempts to respond to three concerns whereby the main one is as to whether African ethics can effect development. But to do that, it had to first investigate whether African ethics exists at all. Yet, that could not be done before clarifying what ethics is. The questions implied therein are; what is ethics? Is there African ethics? Can African ethics effect development? And if yes, which kind of development?

## 2 The Concept of Ethics in General

Ethics is an English word which is translated from a Greek word *ethike*. *Ethike* is derived from *ethos* which is directly translated into English as character. In point of fact, what is today called ethics, an ancient Greek philosopher Aristotle, called it, *he ethike* meaning, the study of character (Robinson Mairi and George Davidson 1999: 1ff). Aristotle stressed the practical importance of developing excellence of moral character (in Greek, *ēthikē aretē*), as the way to achieve a happy life. Aristotle in Nicomachean Ethics, 1.13, spoke of a good moral character as a human excellence (Aristotle 2009).

Like Aristotle, Kevin Timpe (1995) too, links between virtues and moral character. He argues that one's moral character is primarily a function of whether s/he has or lacks virtues. And according to him, the virtues that comprise one's moral character are to be understood as dispositions to behave in a certain way in a given circumstance. He gave an example that, one who has a virtue of honesty, is disposed to telling the truth at all times. Having considered the arguments of those two thinkers, one can say that, generally speaking, virtues/excellences are the qualities that make a human being to be of a good character. Marcia Homiak (2019) also bonds virtues to character as he defines virtues as admirable moral character.

Actually, there are many other contemporary thinkers who tend to define ethics in terms of character. For example, John Murray (1891: 1–4) and John Muirhead

(1892:4) conceive ethics as a science of moral character. Even in the Islamic moral philosophy the word used for ethics is *akhlaq* which literally means character (Milton Cowan 1994) and (John Esposito 2003).

Basing on the above observations, one may conclude that the notion of moral character forms the central aspect of ethics or that ethics is all about the formation of moral character of individuals. Let us now move to the question as to whether ethics as considered above exist in traditional Africa or in a purely African setting so that we can talk of African ethics.

## 3 Does the Notion of Ethics Exist in Traditional African Cultures?

Some Western thinkers thought that Africans have no moral sense, that Africans have no behavioral patterns which can be properly termed as ethics. They argue that traditional Africans regulate their conducts by means of superstitions and magical sanctions rather than appealing to reason. For example, Fanon Frantz (1998:305ff) argues that George William Fredrick Hegel, a German philosopher (Fredrich Hegel 2001: 10ff), a French philosopher, Jean Jacques Rousseau, a British philosopher, David Hume, and some others, affirmed that Africans have a sub-critical or a pre-logical mentality and their conducts have no rational basis.

The claims of the above-mentioned authors and some others, have given a false idea that life in a purely African setting is simply emotional and superstitious, incapable of any moral rationality. This led to people like Rudyard Kipling to describe an African as half devil and half child who needs the anodyne of brutality or physical violence to make him/her truly human (Thoman Eliot 1962: 143).

Conversely, African scholars/philosophers strongly believe that, African societies, as organized and functioning communities, could not have failed, not to develop ethical systems of values, principles and rules that guide interpersonal and individual-society relationships. More-so, we have seen that ethics/*ethike* is derived from *ethos* which means character, yet the notion of a good character is present and very much emphasized in traditional African societies. For instance, when look at the *Itaŋikom* language of the Kom people of West Africa, Cameroon in particular, we find an expression, *nchini kom* which literary means the Kom character; thus, the Kom ethics (John Mbith 2014: 37–38). Likewise, when come to East Africa, among the Baganda of Uganda (my tribe), have words like *empisa* which means character from which *enneeyisa* which refers to behavior is derived. It can be argued that, *mpisa* comes from the verb *kuyita* which means “to pass by”. *Mpisa* is the causative form of *kuyita*, meaning “to make something pass”. *Enneeyisa*, which comes from the same root, *–yisa,* means “the way one makes oneself pass by”. This is passing through life, living in society. A human being has an inner self which is made explicit through actions. This inner self, this bundle of inner qualities, is what the Baganda called character.

Ethics very much uses the concepts of good and bad to evaluate people's character as good or bad and these concepts are present in traditional African vocabulary and they are very much used in evaluating people's character among others. Good character is the essence of African ethics. Bad character that leads to corruption, embezzlement, theft cheating, laziness, etc. which are detrimental to overall wellbeing are detested. African moral maxim is about the formation of good character. The Yoruba have a proverb that says, character is the person's guide (Kwame Gyekye 2011: 2ff). According to John Mbith (2012: 209), the Kom expression for good and bad are: *njuŋ ni mbi* where *njuŋ* refers to good, right, happiness, joy, pleasure and beauty and *mbi* stands for bad, wrong, evil, painful, ugly, disgusting and distasteful. To tell someone that you are ethical in the *Itaŋikom* language of the Kom, you say that, *wa kel nchini injuŋ* which is literally translated as you have a good character. Being of a good character is one of the main obligations of a human being in Kom culture. The expression used to refer to one as good, is the very one used for one who is ethical/one with good character. This means that a moral man/woman is the good man/woman. To be good, one has to necessarily be ethical/of good character. According to Malcolm Guthrie (1971: 18–126), the root of the proto-bantu word for good is *dong'g* which later became *dung'g*. In line with Guthrie, Edward Kanyike (2003: 156) explains that, it was *dung'g* which evolved into various current bantu languages as the word for good such as Luganda's *lungi*, Runyoro, Runyankole and Rukiga's *rungi*, Samya's *lai*, Tchiluba's *lenga*, etc., which refers to goodness of character, beauty, and it is also used to refer to the quality of a performance. But the baganda's expression muntu *mulungi*, has strictly a moral sense; it is translated as, s/he is of a good character. So *muntu mulungi* in this way signifies one of good character/an ethical person. One who has bad character is referred to as *muntu mubi*; *bi* signifies bad. This is similar to what Mbith teaches that in *Itaŋikom* language, to say that *wa kel wi nchini injuŋ* means that you do not have character/ you are unethical/you are a bad human being (John Mbith 2012: 209).

In other words, the notion of character which is associated with ethics as seen above is very much present in African cultures. Segun Gbadegesin (1991: 79), traces this concept in various African cultures. He says that, in the Akan language, *onni suban* means that he has no character, and in Ewe the same phrase is expressed as *nonmo mele si o* and in the Yoruba language, the word for character is *iwa*. In the Igbo language of Eastern Nigeria, the word for character is *agwa* so much so that the statement *onwe ghi ezi agwa* means he has bad character. The Shona language of Zimbabwe has *hunhu* for character where *haana hunhu* means he has no character. In South Sotho language of Lesotho and in Sourthern language of Zimbabwe (Matebeleland), *maemo* refers to character so that *maemo a mabe* means, he has a bad character. When one behaves well, they say s/he has a good character but using the word *lokileng* or *boitswaro,* both of which meaning good behavior. In Akan, *pa* or *papa* signifies good and *bone* refers to bad or evil. The expression *onipa bone* points to a bad human being that is one with a bad character hence unethical, and *onni suban* means that s/he has no character therefore unethical (Gbadegesin 1991: 79).

It is worth mentioning that, in African ethics, only one with good character qualifies to be called a person. Personhood is a normative term in African tradition (Kwame Gyekye 1997b: 42; Steve Biko 2004; Kwame Gyekye 1992: 111; Kwasi Wiredu 2009; Thad Metz 2009: 52–84; Ifeanyi Menkiti 1984: 176; Mogobe Ramose 2009: 302; Kwame Gyekye (2010: 1ff) observes that this idea of personhood as a normative term is found in all Bantu cultures. In the traditional African mentality, this personhood is communicated by one's good character. For instance, the Kom people, to say that, you are a person, they say that, *wag hi wul* which literary means that you have a good character; *wag hi wi wul* which is directly translated as you are not a person, means that you are of a bad character (John Mbith 2014: 38). Ifeanyi Menkiti (1984: 176) asserts that,

> It is the carrying out of one's moral obligations that transforms one from the it-status of the early child-hood, marked by an absence of moral functions, into the person-status of later years, marked by a widened maturity without which personhood is conceived as eluding one.

This means that an individual can be a human being without being a person. The Baganda talk of *muntu nsolo*; where *muntu* means a human being and *nsolo* refers to an animal or a beast. So *muntu nsolo* connotes a human being with the behaviors of a beast. The Akan's *onnye onipa* and Yoruba's *ki i se eniyam,* both mean s/he is not a person; so refers to a human being who lack the quality of personhood (Segun Gbadagesin 1991: 26). The Baganda also talk of *omuntu mulamu where omuntu is a human being and mulamu* means "s/he is alive". *Mulamu* is derived from *bulamu* which means life. This is because, good acts communicate life; they sustain life, improve on the quality of life. So the person who performs good acts is associated with life; since his or her actions are life-centered, s/he is morally alive.

In a nut shell, since the term ethics points to the study of character as we have seen above, yet the formation of good character is key in traditional Africa, then it is plausible to say that ethics exists in traditional Africa. One's character is reflected in his or her conduct. This is why Mbiti, argues that, African morality is a morality of conduct rather than of being in that, one is, because of what s/he does rather than, s/he does what s/he does because of what s/he is (John Mbiti 2012: 209.

Surely there are differences but also similarities in the way character is conceived in the various African societies, but all those make what today we term as African ethics. An ethical trend of thought to be African does not need to be practiced by all Africans just as Virtue ethics originated by Plato and Aristotle is western yet it is not followed by all western people. Not even Immanuel Kant's deontological ethics or Jeremy Bentham and John Stuart Mill's utilitarian ethics which are western ethical thoughts convince all people in the west. Therefore, an ethical trend of thought is African if it originates from and practiced by a given African ethnic group living in Africa. Basing on the above views, it can, therefore, be affirmed that truly African ethics exists. Having ascertained that, the discussion shifts to explore whether African ethics can lead to African development.

## 4 Can Traditional African Ethics Lead to Development?

In development ethics, development is understood as a process of change from one state to another, pursuing a particular moral ideal, like well-being (Nigel Dower 2008). In its simplest sense, development that is talked of in this work, refers to growth, betterment, improvement, or a positive change towards the overall wellbeing of a given group of people. The wellbeing intended in this work, is the improved people's physical, social, spiritual and economic situation. It has been observed that, development in traditional African sense is about people, attaining the best of life deserved of human beings. It is considered in terms of life-economy not so much in sophisticated sciences and technologies which may not necessarily be at the service of bettering human wellbeing.

Unfortunately, most of the world development analysts have mistaken the concept of development by tying it to economic and technological progress only; the spiritual, social and psychological dimensions are neglected. They consider a partial, not a holistic, type of development. Fine, (2009) asserts that, historically, much of the discourse on development has been interpreted within the dominating discipline of economics. He singles out development studies which are historically dominated by economics. In Kwasi Wiredu's perception, the western world is just relatively developed since it has only developed technological sophistication which is just an aspect of development. He maintains that development in traditional Africa is considered in a humanistic and holistic sense (Kwasi Wiredu 1980: 63). Gyekye supports Wiredu's view when he says that,

> I support the view that the humanist essence of African culture…ought to be maintained and cherished in the attempt to create a postcolonial modernity. It must be realized that technology alone cannot solve deep-rooted problems such as poverty, exploitation, economic inequalities and oppression in human societies unless it is underpinned and guided by some basic moral values, technology can in fact create other problems, including environmental problems. Social transformation, which is an outstanding goal of the comprehensive use of technology moves under the aegis of basic human values. (Kwame Gyekye 1997a: 42)

The above authors seem to consent to the fact that, the kind of development that is suggested by traditional African ethics is a holistic one. The Cambridge dictionary defines the term holistic as dealing or treating not just a part but the whole of something or someone (Colin McIntosh 1999).

Reading through African ethics, we see that the kind of development emphasized is holistic that seeks to uplift the entire person in his/her four (already mentioned) dimensions and it is not individual but communal. This explains why African ethics is centered on good character. This is because s/he who has good character can contribute to the well being of society in which individual well being depends since for the single part to be okay, the whole must be okay.

The Nso of North West Cameroon have an expression that, wir wo júŋ, dze ye júŋi, meaning that, one with good character, loves, cherishes and promotes truth, peace, uprightness, compassion, s/he relishes in the wellbeing of all (Christian Mofor

2008: 208). Still Mofor informs us that, the Nso also have the expression that, lii wo bi, which refers to a man/woman, of bad character; it denotes a dishonorable, worthless personality. In other words, we are saying that, traditional African ethics insists on good character of everyone, in its search for the wellbeing of all, which is the essence of development. Once people are of good character: honest (they do not embezzle, are not corrupt, not easily bribed, do not cheat or steal), they have a sense of responsibility, accountability, hard working, community minded/not egoist, creative, as African ethics suggests can attain social progress and achieve a holistic well being for all members. African ethics does not insist on good character for its sake, but for the purpose of wellbeing which is a good desired by human beings in common. This brings us to the idea of the common good in African ethics.

## *4.1 The Notion of the Common Good as Pertinent to African Ethics*

In the African sense, the common good is that which is essentially good for human beings as a whole for the fulfillment of their lives. This notion of the common good is the purpose of African ethics which aims at the wellbeing for all. A traditional African ethical person considers all human individuals as having a common ultimate interest, which is good life (Kwame Gyekye 1998: 317–336). The Temne people express this common interest in a proverb, *se yigboagant ginse yi skera kin*, translated as, we are all in one tree but different branches (Abou Bai-sharka 1986: 121). This one tree can be interpreted to mean humanity which we share in common, whereas the branches are the various people with their various endowments, opinions, and ambitions in life and other individuating factors. The common good points to the universal desire we have as human beings, not as individuals, is wellbeing. According to Wiredu, this common good, is expressed in the art pontiff of two crocodiles with only one stomach (Kawsi Wiredu 2000: 1ff).

Like the preceding Temne proverb, this art pontiff can be understood as a teaching in a community, where people have different opinions and aspirations in their heads, but all have the same basic human need, which is wellbeing. Human beings are different in many ways but humanity and the desire for the fundamental human good (good life) is shared in common by all. So it is the common good that we all strive for. The art pontiff also points to the fact that, the wellbeing of an individual is attained in communion with others that is why crocodiles are said to have a common stomach. Therefore, each individual should use his or her giftedness like intelligence, hard work, innovativeness, inventiveness, etc. for the wellbeing of all. The Akan have a saying that, *onipa yieye firi onipa,* meaning that the wellbeing of a man depends on the wellbeing of his fellow men. They also say that, *onipa nye abe na ne ho ahyia ne ho*, meaning that man is not a palm-tree that is complete/self-sufficient (Kwame Gyekye 2010: 10ff). So for an individual to attain wellbeing, s/he needs to work and plan together with others, alone s/he cannot have all the necessary capacities to fulfill his or her life, socially, economically, spiritually, psychologically and emotionally. Therefore, African ethics requires that each individual cooperates with others for his or her own fulfillment. If one wants progress, in his or her social, physical, psychological and economic aspects, s/he has to practice the value of mutual help, good will, reciprocity and others, which are fundamental to society's and in return to individuals' progress.

There is a Kom proverb which says, *wul nin ghi wul bôm wul* (a person is a person through other persons), to express the reciprocal responsibility of each member of the community which stems in the strong fraternal bond. The Baganda say that, *agali awamu gegaluma ennyama,* meaning that the teeth have to be together in order to bite a piece of meat. The same expression is found in the Akan language and it goes as follows, *wo nsa nifa hohorow benkum, na benkum nso hohorow nifo*, meaning that the right hand washes the left arm and the left arm washes the right arm (Peter Ikechukwu 2014: 123). The Akan also say that, *obra ye nnoboa,* translated as, life is mutual aid (Kwame Gyekye 2010: 1ff). The Akan ethics detests being indifferent to others' situations by saying that, *wo yonko da ne wo da*, translated as, your neighbors' situation is your situation. While the Baganda express the same as, *omuliraano gwokya bbiri*. This means that when your neighbor's hut catches fire, do not remain indifferent, help in extinguishing the fire because soon it will reach your hut too.

The above proverbs indicate that African ethics discourages being apathetic towards other's suffering, and encourages mutual help, mutual progress. The achievements or failures of an individual are taken to be achievements or failures of the whole. Since African ethics promotes mutual progress, it is clear then that, it condemns the enemies of development which are: envy, embezzlement, corruption, theft, cheating, etc., which enriches a few whiles impoverishing the majority. In that way, it is clear that, according to African ethics, development is measured in terms of how a given society progresses in the achievement of wellbeing for all.

In summary, we have seen that African ethics is development oriented; being intensely humanistic (Kwasi Wiredu 1998), it stresses very much improving the overall human welfare, not only in economic sphere but also in social, psychological and spiritual arena; so it advocates for a holistic kind of development. Gyekye says that, human welfare constitutes the hub of the African axiological wheel (Kwame Gyekye 2010). John Mbith (2014: 32–44), too, confirms that, human wellbeing is at the foundation of all moral traditions. The Kon have a proverb which states that, *nchi wul misong nin chow nchi nyamsi* which means that, being concerned of human beings is more gracious than caring for animals.

### 4.2 Traditional African Ethics as an Ethics of Responsibility

Unlike Western ethics which is centered on rights of individuals, African ethics is an ethics of responsibility (Kwame Gyekye 2010: 1ff). African ethics being communitarian and fraternal, where each individual is expected to contribute for the wellbeing of the community on which the wellbeing of each individual rests, involves one in some form of responsibilities (Kwame Gyekye 2010). The two cardinal virtues of community and fraternity stem in the fact that for a traditional Africa, all creatures have a common parenthood. Chika (2015) argues that, the Igbo talk of the common motherhood, *ala* (earth or land), who gave rise to us and feeds us. From the concept *ala*, derives the *anyaala*, which is literary translated as the "earth eye". This implies that, wherever you are, you are on earth/land, so behave because mother *ala* sees whatever you do. Therefore, this *anyaala* (earth eye), came to express the fundamental principle of Igbo morality which advocates diligence, caution, knowledge, gracefulness, respect and so forth, and these virtues are relevant for good living. *Anyaala* is opposed to *anyaelu*, which expresses carelessness, indecency, ignorance, inarticulate, uncoordinated and the like, and these are vices which jeopardize development/ wellbeing of the individual and of the community.

Edward Kanyike (2003: 81–83) teaches that, the bantu has the concept *bandi/bene/bendi* which exists in various bantu languages. *Bandi/bene/bendi* refers to the other but in its non-discriminative sense where it is applied to all creatures (humans and non-humans alike), points to the great other/God. In that way it points to the fact that, all creatures (humans and none-humans alike) belong to God. For example, the Baganda talk of *omuntu wa bandi* = the human being of *bandi*, *ekinyonyi kya bandi* = the bird of *bandi*, *omuti gwa bandi* = the tree of *bandi*, *olwazi lwa bandi* = the rock of *bandi*, *ennyanja ya bandi* = the lake of *bandi*, etc. everything that is, belongs to *bandi* which in this case symbolizes God, the creator and owner of everything. From the idea of a common belonging of all creatures, a virtue of fraternity emerges, from which other derivative virtues arise such as, charity/sharing, humour, equality, etc. Since our beings are communicated by one being (*bandi/bene/bendi*) in whose being creatures participate, by participating in his being, we participate in the being we creatures too participate in the being of each other, hence we humans have a natural responsibility of minding about the wellbeing of all creatures since our wellbeing is influenced by their wellbeing by virtue of our participation in each other's being (African sense of ecosystem). This is why Tangwa, G characterized African ethics as an eco-bio-communitarian ethics Godfrey Tangwa (2000: 39–43) and Godfrey Tangwa (1996a: 183–200). This sense of responsibility which necessitates respect and care for the environment minimizes the impacts on climate change, increased water scarcity, biodiversity and ecosystem loss, desertification and the low resilience to natural disasters, which would jeopardize the attainment of overall human wellbeing/development.

Much as the notion of fraternity encompasses all creatures, it is used in the primary sense between human beings. From this virtue of fraternity which binds us together as of a common belonging, emerged the virtue community, from where those virtues necessary to uphold the communion among us are derived like: truthfulness, honesty/sincerity, braveness, hardworking, intelligence, justice, moderation, forgiveness/reconciliation, respectfulness, responsibility, etc. (Emmanuel Mutyaba 2018: 24–27). The culmination of this argument on oneness is found in Mbiti's claim that a traditional African can only say that, "I am because we are and because we are, therefore I am" (John Mbiti 1969: 108ff). The Kon people too have the same expression, *wul nin ghi wul bôm wul,* which means that, a person is a person through other persons. For the Nso, say, *wir dze wir bi wir*, meaning that man is man by other men (Jerome Mbith 2014: 37–38). The Kon say that, *ninyiŋ nin jofi kisi àvɨŋà,* which associates self-alienation or aloofness with wizardry. The Chikewa, *Kali kokha ndi kanyama,* transalated as one who dissociates him/her self from others is an animal. The Kon also have proverbs like, *awu àmi'a ka'kɨ bû lœ kul ibu'*, which means, one hand cannot tie a bundle. This means that human beings, by our nature, are not self sufficient, but interdependent; life is about mutual support (Jerome Mbith 2014: 37–38). This is why, Dugald observed that, in Africa, a native will give his best house and his evening meal to a guest, without the slightest thought that he is doing anything *extraordinary* (Dugald Campbell 1922). Julius Nyerere (1968) too talks of that universal hospitality Kaunda K, too talks of a traditional African character of opening up to strangers in conservation, and get to know each other. This is not an intrusion into the other's life but an expression of a belief that, we are wrapped up together in the same bundle of life (Keneth Kaunda 1966).

Therefore, a traditional African feel that s/he is meant to live in a fraternal community in which life is a shared good; hence a responsibility for one's life involves the responsibility of others' lives. This is why things that enhance life such **as** food and medicine, are almost free of charge in traditional Africa because life is more valuable than money. For instance, in the case of an outbreak of an epidemic disease, traditional healers mobilized their technical know-how and served others free of charge. They believed that, medicine is revealed by ancestors to save human life which is beyond price (John Mbith 2014). The Akan have a proverb that says, *onipa yefe sen sika,* translated as, a human being is more valuable than gold (Kwame Gyekye 2011). Such ethics which puts at the forefront the enhancement of the quality of life which development is all about, is highly developmental.

Indeed, creating a fraternal community is fundamental to development/improvement of people's lives, Saccheri, argues that it is the best way to read social problems, define the action to take and to organize people for action. Only organized people can affect social progress. He goes and says that, in such communities, members operate with reciprocity and they evaluate views from other communities by their values, laws, traditions and collective interests (Tulia Saccheri 2005). Ferdinand Tönnies (1887) and Emille Durkheim (1893) too recognize that a community creates a high degree of personal social cohesion, and stability due to the common values and laws with eliminate conflicts. And that, in a communitarian way of life, resources are easily mobilized. Pierre Lévy (1994), and Giuseppe D'Agostino (2002), also think that, policy makers who aim to start a territorial sustainable development have to enhance the idea of community. Even Amitai Etzioni (1995) sees community as essential in enhancing sustainable development network.

This work suggests the promotion of traditional African ethical values in African societies in order to attain a holistic development. Below are the suggestions of who should play the role of inculcating these values and how that can be done.

## 5 Parents, Teachers, Religious Leaders and Social Workers as Having a Role to Play in Promoting Traditional African Ethical Values

In my view, the dissemination of traditional African values can be done through education, persuasion and inspiration particularly of the young generation by their parents, teachers, religious leaders, media, and so forth. Parents play a very important role in inculcating values in their children during their early formative years. These parents should be helped by their religious and community leaders through preaching, seminars, conferences, social groups etc., to sensitize them about these traditional African ethical values and their responsibility to inculcate them into their children and persuading them to follow them. Religious leaders and social workers could create groups and gatherings aimed at promoting these values. Academia both at lower and higher levels of learning, too need to collaborate in this effort of promoting traditional African ethical values that Africa needs for a holistic development. Traditional African ethics should be included in curriculums and staff members should teach these values both in theory and in practice outside class; they should be exemplary in living these values in order to inspire those they teach to do the same. I believe that once all that is done, Africans' attitude towards themselves and towards reality in general, will be transformed characterized by the will to strive for their betterment.

## 6 Is Traditional African Ethical Perspective All Perfect?

While striving to return to traditional African ethics in our endeavor to attain a holistic development for Africa, we need to be aware of the fact that, not all what traditional African ethics teaches is accepted today as good. As we return to it, we should guard ourselves against its loopholes which can instead hinder us from attaining the development we are striving for. Bujo (1990: 102–111) warns us that, much as traditional African ethics contains many good things, it has weaknesses too. For instance, the basis of traditional African moral codes are the ancestors who vary from tribe to tribe. We need to find a common ground of unifying these tribal moral codes or else, the first loyalty will continue to be given to tribal leaders as the ancestral moral codes demand than to the heads of states and their cabinets which cherishes tribalism. Tribalism is an enemy of a nation's development since it divides people than uniting them. Besides that, this ancestral-based morality compels people to behave well, do the right thing and avoid evil simply because of fear of the ancestors' wroth rather than because it is right to do good and avoid evil.

There is also a need of widening traditional African sense of community and fraternity, to go beyond one's own ethnic group to embrace the whole humanity. As far as it stands, in traditional African morality, what is right or wrong is confined only to one's own ethnic group (Yusufu Turaki 1997: 68–71; Douglas Waruta 1992:

134; Philip Steyne 1989: 186–186). With this kind of mentality, favoritism, cheating, stealing, embezzlement of national funds to enrich one's own group is not considered bad but seen as a sense of a community spirit or fraternity by the members of his group. Many leaders in Africa are labeled as bad leaders simply because they have concentrated on working for the nation as a whole rather than using national funds to enrich their own ethnic group; we hear of questions like, "he has been a leader for long, but what has he done for his own people (village mates or tribe mates)?"

Another weakness of traditional African ethics that we need to correct as we decide to revive this ethical trend of thought for African development is that, being communitarian, traditional African morality teaches that, a healthy relationship is better than truth. This makes whistle blowing hard in Africa a thing that allows many evils to go on without coming to public which is detrimental to a nation's development. People feel that it is a good thing to keep quiet at a wrong done by a relative, a friend, a village mate and so forth, than disclosing it which may bring enmity between the discloser and the one disclosed. In traditional Africa, a need to maintain a good relationship at times causes dishonesty especially where telling the truth point blank may lead to trouble among friends, relatives, village mates, and so on. For instance, if one's father in law asks him for a goat which he is not willing to give, he keeps telling him lies that he is still looking for it, till he gets tired of asking for it. This too puts in question the virtue of reliability which is vital for a nation's development.

## 7 Conclusion

The first part of this chapter clarifies that, the term ethics is got from a Greek word *ethike* which was derived from *ethos* which refers to character. For that matter, since traditional African societies stress very much the formation of individuals' character as presented in part two of this chapter, implies that ethics exists in traditional Africa so we can rightly talk of African ethics in that respect. Part three reveals that, this character-based African ethics detests bad character which influences bad behaviors such as: egoism, hatred, intolerance, abuse of human rights, dehumanization, exploitation, authoritarianism, corruption, embezzlement, poverty, oppression, murder, etc., which are the vices that hinder achievement of overall human wellbeing for all which is the essence of development. Instead, African ethics upholds as cardinal virtues, community and fraternity from which all other virtues needed for overall human wellbeing are derived like; fraternal concern, hard work for sustainability, responsibility of oneself and of the community as well as of the environment, cooperation, reliability, mutual respect, transparence, fear of God, care for nature at large, and others. This show that African ethics is quite developmental and it stresses overall development of a human being in his/her integral being, physical, social, psychological, economical and spiritual dimensions. Hence, African ethics leads to a holistic development of a personal within his/her community. For example *Ubuntu* ethics which emphasizes a peaceful relationships among people, and respect for human life and human dignity indeed echoes human progress and the improvement of people's quality of life, since it effect progress in meeting economic, social, psychological, physical of betterment of people which are the indicators of development in general.

As a way forward, we should not abandon African ethics hoping to be developed by imported moral values from the west without our own. Chiedozie Okoro (2011) argues that they are the traditional norms, myths and principles that help in re-adaption or indigenization of alien ideologies which could be incorporated to effect a holistic development. Kwasi Wiredu (1980) too thinks that, it is better to blend the borrowed positive values of sciences and technologies with our African humanistic ethos, a society that abandons its cultural norm, deteriorates and can easily yields to egoism with its consequences such as corruption, embezzlement, theft, cheating and so forth, which hinder society's progress.

The African idea of community founded on the principle of participation, where members actively involved in decision making in matters regarding their community based on the principles of tolerance and acceptance of each other, can lead to the democratization of Africa.

African ethics' idea of extending fraternal concern to all creatures, is very much needed in our time of deforestation, destruction of swamps, mindlessness of the ecosystem, replacement of natural crops and domestic animals with the genetically modified ones, global warming and the rest, which cause negative climatic changes and other havocs to humanity like, health, social, psychological challenges and others such as floods, droughts, poverty, loss of biodiversity and medicinal plants. However, as we return to traditional African ethics, we need to guard ourselves against some of its weaknesses seen above, that cherish tribalism, nepotism and some forms of segregation.

## References


Aristotle. 2009. *The Nicomachean ethics*. Trans. W.D. Ross. Oxford: Oxford University Press

Bai-sharka, Abou. 1986. *Temne names and proverebs*. Free Town: People's Educational Association of Siera Leone.

Bénézet, Bujo. 1990. *African Christian morality at the age of inculturation*. Nairobi, Kenya: St. Paul Publications-Africa.

Biko, Steve. 2004. *Some African cultural concepts*. Johannesburg: Picador Africa.

Campbell, Dugald. 1922. *In the heart of Bantuland: A record of twenty-nine years in Central Africa among the Bantu peoples*. London: Seely Service and Co.

Cowan, Milton. 1994. *The Hans Wehr dictionary of modern written Arabic*. 4th ed. UK: Snowball Publishing Co.

D'Agostino, Giuseppe. 2002. *Fare Comunità: Documento di Sintesi of Laboratory: Principi e Strumenti dell'agire locale per uno Sviluppo inclusive*. Napoli: SLST.

Durkheim, Emille. 1893. *De la Division du Travail Social*. Paris: Alcan.

Eliot, S. Thomas. 1962. *A choice of Kipling's verse*. Atlanta: A Cappella Books.

Esposito, John. 2003. *The Oxford dictionary of Islam*. Oxford, Oxford University Press.

Etzioni, Amitai. 1995. *The new communitarian thinking: Persons, virtues, institutions and communities*. Virginia: University Press of Virginia.

Frantz, Fanon. 1998. Racism and culture. In *African philosophy: An anthology*, ed. C. Emmanuel Eze. Oxford: Blackwell Publishers Ltd.

Gbadegesin, Segun. 1991. *African philosophy: Traditional Yoruba philosophy and contemporary African realities*. New York: Peter Lang.

Guthrie, Malcolm. 1971. *Comparative Bantu 1-1V: An introduction to the comparative linguistics and prehistory of Bantu languages*. Westmead: Gregg International Publishers Ltd.

Gyekye, Kwame. 1992. Person and community in Akan thought. In *Person and community: Ghanaian philosophical studies*, ed. Wiredu Wwasi and Gyekye Kwame. Washington, DC: The Council for Research in Values and Philosophy.

———. 1997a. Philosophy, culture and technology in the postcolonial. In *Postcolonial African philosophy*, ed. E. Eze Chukwudi. Cambridge: Blackwell.

———. 1997b. *Tradition and modernity: Philosophical reflections on the African experience*. Oxford: Oxford University Press.

———. 1998. Person and community in African thought. In *Philosophy from Africa: A text with readings*, ed. H. Peter Coetzee. Johannesburg: International Thompson Publishing.

Ikechukwu, O. Peter. 2014. *African traditional medicine: Autonomy and informed consent*. New York: Springer.

Kanyike, Edward. 2003. *The principle of participation in African cosmology and anthropology*. Balaka: Montfort Media.

Kaunda, D. Keneth. 1966. *A humanist in Africa*. London: Longmans.

Lévy, Pierre. 1994. *L'intelligence Collective: Pour une Antropologie du Cyberspace*. Paris: La Découverte.

Mairi, Robinson, and Davidson George. 1999. *Chambers 21st century dictionary*. Edinburgh: Harrap Publishers Ltd.

Mbith, T. Jerome. 2014. The relevance of Kom ethics to African development. *International Journal of Philosophy* 2 (3): 36–47.

Mbiti, S. John. 1969. *African religion and philosophy*. London: Heinemann.

———. 2012. *Concept of god in Africa*. Nairobi: Action Publishers.

Menkiti, Ifeanyi. 1984. Person and community in African traditional thought. In *African philosophy: An introduction*, ed. Adupa Richard, 3rd ed. Lanham: Wright University Press of America.

Metz, Thad. 2009. African moral theory and public governance. In *African ethics: An anthology of comparative and applied ethics*, ed. M. Felix Murove. Scottsville: University of Kwa-Zulu-Natal Press.

Mofor, Christian. 2008. *Plotinus and Africa concepts of evil: Perspectives in multicultural philosophy*. Bern: Peter Lang.

Muirhead, H. John. 1892. *The elements of ethics: An introduction to moral philosophy*. New York: Charles Scribner's Sons.

Murray, C. John. 1891. *An introduction to ethics*. Boston: De Wolf, Fiske & Co.

Mutyaba, M. Emmanuel. 2018. *Ontological foundation of traditional African morality*. Nairobi: Pauline Publications for Africa.

Nyerere, K. Julius. 1968. *Ujamaa: Essays on socialism*. Oxford: Oxford University Press.

Ramose, Mogobe. 2009. Towards emancipative politics in Africa. In *African ethics: An anthology of comparative and applied ethics*, ed. F. Murove. Pietermaritzburg: University of Kwa-Zulu Natal Press.

Saccheri, Tulia. 2005. *Sviluppo e Trasformazione della Comunità*. Napoli: Liguori.

Steyne, M. Philip. 1989. *Gods of power; A study of the beliefs and practices of animism*. Houston: Houston Touch Publications.

Tangwa, B. Godfrey. 1996a. *The traditional African perception of a person: Some implications for bioethics*. Hastings Center Report 30, N° 5.

———. 1996b. *Bioethics: An African perspective*. Cambridge: Cambridge Scholars Publishing.

———. 2000. The traditional African perception of a person: Some implications for bioethics. *Hastings Center Report* 30 (5): 39–43.

Tönnies, Ferdinand. 1887. *Gemeinschaft und gesellschaft*. Leipzig: Reisland.
Turaki, Yusufu. 1997. *Tribal gods of Africa; Ethnicity, racism, tribalism and the Oospel of Christ*. Lagos: Crossroads Media Services.
Waruta, W. Douglas. 1992. Tribalism as a moral problem in contemporary Africa. In *Moral and ethical issues in African Christianity*, 1992. Nairobi: Initivatives.
Wiredu, Kwasi. 1980. *Philosophy and an African culture*. Cambridge: Cambridge University Press.
———. 1998. The moral foundation of an African culture. In *Philosophy from Africa: A text with readings*, ed. Peter Coetzee. Johannesburg: International Thompson Publishing.

## *Internet Source*

Chika, J. B Gabriel. 2015. The re-birth of African moral traditions as key to the development of sub-Saharan Africa: The Igbo paradigm. *Journal of international Education and Leadership* 5 (1) http://www.jielusa.org
Dower, Nigel. 2008. The nature and scope of development ethics. *Journal of Global Ethics* 4 (3) www.reaserchgate.net.
Gyekye, Kwame. 2010. *African ethics*. http://plato.stanford.edu/entries/african-ethics/# HumfouafrMor.
———. 2011. African ethics. In *The Stanford encyclopedia of philosophy*, ed. E.N. Zalta. http://plato.stanford.educ/archives/fall2011/entries/african-ethics/.
Hegel, W. Fredrich. 2001. *The philosophy of history*. Trans. S.J. Ontario. Batoche Books. https://socserv.mcmaster.ca/econ/ugcm/3ll3/hegel/history.
Homiak, Marcia. 2019. Moral character. In *The Stanford encyclopedia of philosophy*, ed. E.N. Zalta. https://plato.stanford.edu/archives/sum2019/entries/moral-character.
McIntosh, Colin. 1999. *The Cambridge dictionary*. Cambridge: Cambridge University Press. https://dictionary.cambridge.org/dictionary/english/holistic.
Okoro, Chiedozie. 2011. *Philosophy and the recultivation of African culture*. https://www.project-topics.org/journals/22980-philosophy-and-the-recultivation-of-african-culture.html.
Timpe, Kevin. 1995. *The internet encyclopedia of philosophy*. IEP. https://iep.utm.edu/moral-ch/.
Wiredu, Kwasi. 2000. *Polygon: Forum for intercultural philosophy*. them.polylog.org/2/fwk-en.htm.
———. 2009. *An oral philosophy of personhood: Comments on philosophy and orality, research in African literatures*. Indiana: Indiana University Press. https://www.jstor.org/stable/30131182. Retrieved on 6 July 2021.

**Emmanuel Musoke Mutyaba** holds a PhD in Philosophy from the Pontifical Gregorian University of Rome. He is a Lecturer of Ethics at Uganda Martyrs University.

# Part II
# Theories and Approaches to Development Ethics in Africa

# Neo-Liberalism and the Ethics of Pan-African Development Governance in Sub-Saharan Africa

**Kizito Michael George**

**Abstract** Pan-Africanism is a philosophy that postulates that African ideas and practices about development, economics, politics, art, religion, law, morals, science and technology are as equally valid as Western ones. Although Pan-Africanists do not condemn the democratic influences of African culture from Western culture, they detest and denigrate the treatment of African social realties as barbaric and inferior to the Western lot. In the 1950s, Pan-Africanists like Kwame *Nkrumah* and Patrice Lumumba embarked on the campaign to emancipate Black Africans from neo-colonialism. They argued that although the colonialists had physically left and allowed native Africans to take over the governments of newly independent states, the new states were still trapped in the racist politics and economics of the imperialists. They therefore advocated for socialism as an appropriate system for African development governance due its close affinity to African communitarianism. This chapter argues that African neo-colonies are still trapped in the Western racist paradigm of development conceptualisation and management. The chapter contends that neo-liberalism has fundamentally paralysed ethical Pan-African development governance by relegating development to the whims of the positivistic market which is deterministic and scientific. Consequently, neo-liberal capitalism has transformed a number of African leaders from Pan-Africanists to neo-liberal oligarchs.

## 1 Introduction

Development ethics (DE) is a normative evaluation of development theories and practices. It questions the ethicalities of means and ends of local, national and global development (Dower 1988; Crocker 2008). DE aims at promoting human flourishing by situating the human person at the centre of his or her development. Accordingly, the human person is an agent and not a patient in the process of

K. M. George (✉)
Department of Religious Studies and Philosophy, Kyambogo University, Kampala, Uganda





B. Okyere-Manu et al. (eds.), *Contemporary Development Ethics from an African Perspective*, Philosophy and Politics - Critical Explorations 27,
https://doi.org/10.1007/978-3-031-32898-5_3

development. This implies that the human person is a dignified being endowed with fundamental human rights that shouldn't be violated for the sake of economic efficiency. Development ethicists make normative and analytical judgments "about the good life, the just society, and the quality of relations among people" (Goulet 1997). Development ethicists "agree that the moral dimension of development theory and practice is just as important as the scientific and policy components" (Gasper 2012).

The rise of Pan-African consciousness as far back as the 1940's was an explicit rejection of the development ethos the colonizers had imposed on Africa. Imperialism not only denigrated African development perspectives but also excluded the endogenous African concepts of development, wellbeing and progress. Pan-Africanism is a struggle against the racist tendency to regard African perspectives on issues like development as untenable. Pan-Africanists loathe racist and imperialist perceptions of Africans as persons who are incompetent to govern their development and offer anything useful to the rest of 'civilized humanity' (Western world).

Although the white colonialists declared African states theoretically independent, they left behind 'leaders' who would perpetuate the enslavement and oppression of Africans (Ayittey 2006, pp. 459–506). These post independence 'leaders' continued to interpret African development and wellbeing using Eurocentric lens. They persistently bragged about African economic progress using alien concepts like Gross Domestic Product (GDP), Gross National Product (GNP) and Economic growth. These concepts made little sense to traditional native Africans but were used by African leaders to propagate the deception of African endogenous development. The existence of organised capitalism at the time however, gave the state some minimal discretion to directly intervene in improving social and economic rights.

However, Pan-African voices spearheaded by the prominent Pan-Africanists like Julius Nyerere, Kenneth Kaunda and Milton Obote in the 1970's and early 80's faded with the introduction of neo-liberal reforms on the African continent. A new breed of neo-liberal African rulers emerged. These neo-colonial rulers were instructed by the World Bank(WB) and International Monetary Fund(IMF) to retrench fellow Africans from public service jobs in thousands, impose recruitments bans in the public service and enforce cost sharing in health and education.

The above neo-liberal austerity measures pushed thousands of Africans into abject poverty and despair. Neo-liberal structural adjustment measures were projected as scientifically inevitable because they were perceived as stimulants of markets and economic growth. Neo-liberal reforms were generally imposed without consulting the native Africans at the bottom of the societal ladder. This was a violation of the principles of development ethics because Africans were treated as objects and patients of Western development.

This chapter is an ethical criticism of the impasse of ethics-less development propagated by neo-liberalism in Sub-Saharan Africa. The chapter uses critical discourse analysis, critical historical analysis and emancipatory criticism as methodological frameworks to situate the need to expunge neo-liberalism from the African development milieu through a re-awakening of Pan African ethical development governance.

## 2 Ethics of Pan-African Development Governance

Pan Africanism is an ideology that aims at emancipating and integrating the black race (Ola 1979, p.67). It aims at liberating Africans from the forces of colonialism and neo-colonialism that have alienated and denigrated African culture, politics and development. African integration aims at uniting Africans on the African continent and in the diaspora to resist all forms of imperialism that stand in the way of self-determination. Du Bois argues that "Pan Africanism is an aid to the promotion of national self-determination among Africans under Africa leadership for the benefit of Africans themselves" (Nantambu 1998, p. 561).

During the 1960's, Pan-African leaders like Kenneth Kaunda and Julius Nyerere envisaged ethical development basing on the full belly thesis. This means that social and economic rights such as food, water, health and education took precedence over civil and political rights like voting, freedom of expression and freedom of assembly. Nyerere for instance argued that the right to vote was meaningless to somebody with an empty stomach (Howard 1983, p. 467). The obliviousness to the interconnectedness of economic and social rights with civil and political rights is responsible for turning Pan-African post-independence governments into single party dictatorships. Similarly, the prioritization of scientific development governance by neo-liberal African governments explains the crisis of ethical Pan-African development governance.

Development governance refers to the practice of achieving development through the lenses of certain ideologies or paradigms such as developmentalism(economic liberalism), neo-liberalism and human development. Ethical Pan African Development Governance (EPADG) entails putting in place African human development paradigms that prioritise the dignity of all Africans in the development process. EPADG is premised on the imperative that all Africans are possessors of social, economic, cultural, civil and political rights that ought to take precedence over instrumental development goals such as economic growth and economic development. This chapter argues that neo-liberalism is at variance with EPADG because it prioritises scientific development governance over Pan-Africanism and human development.

## 3 Pan Africanism and the Endogenisation of African Development

One of the major purposes of Pan-Africanism was to endogenise African development. This meant that development would be conceived from an African point of view. In fact the term development comes from the Latin word *veloper* which means to unwrap from within. This implies that genuine development should be endogenic rather than exogenic. African leaders ought to liaise with the intelligentsia to derive concepts of progress, wellbeing and success that are in tandem with Pan-African values, epistemologies and metaphysics.

As already intimated, for a long time Africans have come to understand themselves using Western concepts such as income poverty, GDP and economic growth. These concepts do not make sense to even many modern Africans. For example, a number of African states have persistently bragged about high economic growth rates amidst social injustices such as: massive unemployment, land grabbing, corruption, torture and development induced displacements. Economic growth amidst social and structural injustices should be characterized as unethical or pseudo development. David Crocker (2001) argues that the descriptive understanding of development in terms of economic growth has caused more harm than good. He therefore urges development ethicists to focus on normative questions on good, authentic and ethically justifiable development.

Colonialism was able to entrench development economics as the only science of development in Africa. This led to thousands of Africans to cherish offering degrees in economics in order to be able to address the development challenges in Africa. A number of African economists understand poverty in terms of the International Monetary Fund(IMF) and World Bank(WB) standard i.e. living on less than a dollar a day or two dollars a day. The Pan-African movement has failed to endogenise development perspectives in Africa so that it is not a replica of the IMF and WB neo-liberal imperialism.

Due to the upsurge of neo-liberalism, Africans views on development are situated on epistemic injustice and hermeneutic injustice. Epistemic injustice refers to the treating of the perspectives of others as inferior. Hermeneutics injustice on the other hand implies regarding the interpretations of others as less credible (Fricker 2007, p. 1). The *scientification* of development by neo-liberalism has rendered African endogenous development perspectives unscientific and implausible.

Rajeeve Bhargava argues that:

> epistemic injustice is a form of cultural injustice. It occurs when the concepts and categories by which a people understand themselves and their world are replaced or adversely affected by the concepts and categories of the colonizers….. epistemic injustice takes at least three distinct forms. First, an imposed change in the content of epistemic frameworks. Second, a forced alteration in basic epistemic frameworks. Finally, damage to or loss of the capacity to sustain, retrieve or develop one's own epistemic frameworks. (Bhargava 2013, p. 414)

## 4 Socialism and Ethical Pan African Development Governance

After attaining independence, a number of African leaders such as Modibo Keita of Mali and Léopold Sédar Senghor of Senegal opted for socialism as an alternative to capitalism because they believed that it was analogous to African communitarianism. A number of African leaders made alliances with Russia in order to make African socialism a reality. Unlike capitalism which promoted individualism, socialism like African communitarianism emphasized the common good. Capitalism was repugnant to Africa because it promoted greed and selfishness. African socialists also believed that socialism promoted a classless society unlike capitalism which enhanced a wide gap between the rich and poor. Pan Africans such as Kwame Nkrumah praised Karl Marx for adequately analysing the evils of capitalism and articulating the tenets of socialism and communism (Nkrumah 1980, p. 75–77).

African leaders greatly misinterpreted Karl Marx's analysis of socialism. Marx "saw his work as a science, even as a positive science…" (Mullick 1978, p. 56). Raymond Aron argues that Marx was too scientifically oriented to admit that his interpretation of capitalism had moral implications (Aron 2019, p. 155). According to Marx, society evolves dialectically from primitive communalism to slavery, feudalism, capitalism, socialism and consequently communism. There are blind material forces or scientific social laws that determine the evolution society from one mode of production to another. Marx argued that what causes change from one social mode to another is the conflict between the factors of production and the relations of production. In every mode, those who control the factors of production and relations of production will also control the law, policies and institutions of government. For instance under feudalism, the laws, policies and state institutions are in the interests of the landlords and under capitalism, they are in the interests of the bourgeoisie or owners of capital.

Marx also argued that capitalism had to break its neck because of the over exploitation of the workers. He contradicts his positive economic philosophy by advocating for a revolution against the exploitative tendencies of capitalism. He opined that, at one time, the workers will become conscious of their exploitation and this will trigger a revolutionary transition from capitalism to socialism. Socialism is a preparation to transit to communism. Under communism, there is a stateless but not chaotic state. There is no law, no army, no police and no classes because the causes of conflict have been eliminated. Since a communist society is too wealthy, everybody has the necessary material amenities for sustenance and does not need to struggle against the others over these resources.

Therefore, only states which had evolved into nations with substantive material wealth and resources were candidates for socialism and communism. Under socialism and communism, resources are owned in common and every one finds happiness in working for the good of all (Singer 2000, p. 57). This means that there is no personalization of resources such as land, water, electricity, houses etc. Thus, there was no way in which African peasant societies that had just attained independence would become socialist and communist states. African leaders like Kwame Nkrumah therefore erred greatly in associating the ethics of Pan-African development governance with Socialism and Communism.

Although a number of Pan-Africanists tried to differentiate African socialism from Marxist Scientific socialism by contending that Africa has always exuded socialist tenets like egalitarianism, communal ownership of property, social cooperation and social obligation (McCain 1974, p. 22), there is a lack of consensus on how African socialism is different Marxian scientific socialism. African socialism is therefore an ambiguous concept that can never constitute a painstaking paradigm for ethical pan African governance. Walter Rodney (1972), clarifies the communalistic dimension of Nyerere's so called socialist *Ujaama* project as follows:

> Tanzanian *Ujamaa* is not 'African Socialism'... *Ujamaa* villages seek to recapture the principles of joint production, egalitarian distribution and the universal obligation to work which were found within African communalism. Socialism emerged as an ideology within the capitalist society...For Marx, 'Scientific Socialism' is quite simply socialism that is scientific...

## 5 From Pan Africanists to Neo-Liberal Oligarchs

Although African leaders such as Modibo Keita and Ahmed Sékou Touré of Guinea confused African communitarianism with socialism and communism, the 1960s and 1970s can be characterized as the golden age of Pan-Africanism. During this time, African Universities were buzzing with debates and discourses on Pan-African development and governance. There were also ubiquitous discourses on African literature, fashion, music and art. However, the transition of a number post- independence African governments into single party military dictatorships became one of the crevices for the entry of neo-liberal imperialism. In the 1980s and 1990s, a number of African countries made a paradigm shift from organised capitalism to neo-liberalism or disorganized capitalism. Organized capitalism gave the state a great lee way to manage development in order to improve the wellbeing of the people. Neo-liberalism on the other hand evicted the state and the people out of the development process and surrendered it to the market. The market was envisaged to be a scientific mechanism to distribute opportunities for wellbeing.

Under the rulership of the World Bank and International Monetary Fund, African leaders in Uganda, Nigeria, Zambia and Kenya among other countries unleashed Anti-Pan-African development policies that were never known in the history of the above countries. These pro-market Structural Adjustment Programmes (SAPs) unleashed poverty and terror on the people. Thousands were retrenched from work and quality education and quality health care became entitlements for only the rich.

Ekanade (2014, p. 6) elucidates the transition to neo-liberal capitalism in Nigeria as follows:

> As a major oil-producing nation, Nigeria enjoyed almost a decade of unprecedented revenue boom arising from the petroleum price increases of the 1970's. One remarkable characteristic of Nigeria's expenditure during this period was its "welfarist" orientation with government domestic investments and concentrated provision of a massive transport system, road networks, public buildings, and health infrastructure. Employment rates soared, coupled with increases in subsidies on food, transport, health, fuel, and education. The Shehu Shagari regime (1979–1983) systematized the subsidized sale and distribution of specific commodities known as essential commodities to Nigerians. These included rice, milk, beef, and sugar, among other items. These products were imported by the Nigerian government through the Nigerian National Supply Company and sold to Nigerians at rates below prevailing market prices. These subsidies remained all through the Shagari era but terminated with the introduction of SAPs in 1986...

Neo-liberalism signaled the end to Pan-African development. Unlike Pan-Africanism that looked at the Africans as ends of development, neo-liberalism turned Africans into objects of the development process. As *thingfied* objects, Africans people could be dehumanised, alienated from their land and even killed for the sake of neo-liberal economic efficiency. The neo-liberal oligarchs in black skins turned African economies into slave states of the American neo-liberal empire. They invested a lot of energy in helping the neo-colonialists have a firm grip on the mineral resources in the African continent. The neo-liberal imperialists rewarded the black neo-liberal oligarchs with immunity from prosecutions for gross human rights abuse. They also funded the neo-liberal dictatorships with police and military training as well as military paraphernalia in terms of guns, bullets, tear gas, anti-riot gear and armored vehicles.

Interestingly, neo-liberal African dictators persistently envisioned themselves as Pan-Africanists and patriots. For example, despite the institutionalization of neo-liberal tyranny in Uganda, Museveni brags of being a Pan-Africanist and patriot and has threatened to crush anyone who stands in his way of modernizing the economy using the neo-liberal ideology. According to President Museveni:

> the ideology of the NRM right from the early days, is based on 4 principles: Patriotism – love Uganda; Pan-Africanism – love Africa; Social – economic transformation – (from peasantry to middle and skilled working classes); and democracy (power of the people, by the People, for the people). This love for Uganda (anti-sectarianism) and love for Africa (Pan-Africanism) is not a fashion or mere slogans. It is because that is the only way we can guarantee the prosperity of each of us by creating big markets for our products. Currently, we have surplus sugar, surplus milk, surplus maize, surplus bananas etc. In some parts of Africa, they have need for these products. That is why the NRM always works for the integration of Africa – both economic and political. (The New Vision 2020)

## 6 From Washington Consensus to Post Washington Consensus

The Washington consensus refers to a set of policy proposals that were derived by John Williamson in 1989 as strategies for economic transformation in Latin America. These proposals were later recommended by the World Bank, International Monetary Fund and the US Treasury as strategies for neo-liberal reform in the developing countries of Africa and Asia (Williamson 1990). The neo-liberal Structural Adjustment proposals that were proposed by the three Washington based institutions are; retrenchment, recruitment bans in the public service, cost sharing in education, health etc., privatization, liberalization and financial deregulation. These,

> policy recommendations were nothing else but neoclassical economics espousing a firm belief in the market's "invisible hand," the rationality of economic actors' choice, and a minimalistic vision of the states' regulation of economies. (Lopes 2012, p. 40)

John Williamson has accused the International Financial Institutions (IFIs) of diverting from his previous policy proposals especially when it comes to the implementation of SAPs in developing countries (Williamson 2005, pp. 200–201). Stiglitz, a former consultant of the World Bank from 1997–2000 has also criticized the above neo-liberal policy proposals of IFIs as a one size fits all. According to him, these market fundamentalist proposals did not produce substantive economic growth in a number of developing countries (Stiglitz and Schoenfelder 2003). It must be emphasised that:

> the social impact of these reforms was devastating for Sub-Saharan Africa. Many economists recognized that the difficulties associated with the promotion of economic stability and liberalization had a disproportionate impact on the poor, leading to greater poverty and unequal income distribution. (Lopes 2012, p. 40)

Krugman provided a scathing critique of the neo-liberal scientism that was used to defend SAPs by sarcastically opining that "the economics profession went astray because economists, as a group, mistook beauty, clad in impressive-looking mathematics, for truth" (Lopes 2012, p. 75 cited in Krugman 2009, p. 36).

The neo-liberal Structural Adjustment Programmes from the Washington based institutions are some of the most Anti-Pan African economic strategies that were imposed on Africans by neo-colonial imperialists. Thousands of Africans languished in poverty due to retrenchment from work and public health facilities were left in a sole state due to underfunding. Doctors and nurses were also greatly demotivated due to meager salaries, lack of drugs, long working hours and lack of medical equipment (Gatwiri et al. 2020). In Uganda, some Doctors in rural health facilities carried out surgical operations on mothers in labour with Kerosene lamps due to lack of electricity. Some medical personnel were forced to use polythene bags due to lack of medical gloves (CEHURD 2011). As the sanitation conditions deteriorated in public health facilities due to increasing numbers of poor lads seeking for medical treatment, the rich neo-liberal aristocrats flew their wives, children and relatives to Western nations for first class treatment (Kagaba 2013).

Neo-liberalism challenged the patriarchal status quo in a number of African societies where males are supposed to be the bread winners of the family. The biting poverty occasioned by the stringent SAPS lured a number of men to abandon their wives and children due to poverty. More so, the increasing unemployment led a number of African youths to opt for enslavement in Middle East countries such as: Saudi Arabia, Oman, Qatar, Bahrain, United Arab Emirates, Iraq and Afghanistan where some were killed and sexually exploited (Lirri 2017). These labour migrants come from Uganda, Ethiopia, Kenya, Ghana, Nigeria, Tanzania and Zambia among other countries (Nkirote 2018).

Neo-liberalism created a paradigm shift in our conception of slavery. In the past the Arab and European colonialists came to Africa to capture slaves. However, the introduction of neo-liberal structural reforms forced Africans to enslave themselves to Arab slave masters. Also, several American and European companies recruited poor Africans to fight in the so called war against terror in Iraq and Afghanistan. In addition, a number of Africans also lost their lives in these neo-liberal oil wars. For instance, former child soldiers from the civil war in Sierra Leone were used as cheap military labor by private American and British companies in the 2003 Iraq war (Hoyle 2017).

The criticisms of the dire misery created by the implementation of Structural Adjustment Programmes in Africa perfunctorily led to a re-evaluation of the austerity measures embedded in neo-liberal reforms. This culminated into the so called post Washington consensus which was a mere paper gimmick bereft of a fundamental paradigm shift from neo-liberal policy prescriptions. In 1999, the World Bank and IMF created the concept of Participatory Poverty Reduction Strategy Papers (PRSPs) as a new condition for access to debt relief and their concessional loan programmes(through International Development Association(IDA) and the IMF's Poverty Reduction and Growth Facility (PRGF) as a response to the criticism that policies were being forced upon countries(World Development Movement 2005, p. 7–8). More so, in 2000, the World Bank published its famous publications titled, *Voices of the Poor*. The WB used the Voices of the Poor research project to direct countries in Africa to derive Poverty Reduction Strategy Papers (PRSPs) based on the voices of the poor and other stakeholders in the country. This has come to be known as the post-Washington consensus (Hahn 2008, p. 152).

Although a number of countries solicited the voices of the poor and other stakeholders in the drafting of PRSPs, these views were largely ignored in the final PRSPS. These PRSPs remained fundamentally neo-liberal in their interpretation of development and social progress (Shah 2013). This implies that they ignored human development notions such as human rights and social justice as well as Pan-African nuances like Ubuntu ethics. The post Washington consensus did not alter neo-liberal policy prescriptions such as: the imposition of recruitment bans in the public service, cost sharing in education and health, privatization of water and electricity, export dumping and denial of farmers agricultural subsidies(World Development Movement 2005, p. 7–8).

In practice, it was extremely difficult, if not impossible, for the poorest countries to truly determine their own development because the content of PRSPs was influenced by pre-existing World Bank and IMF programme conditions. Secondly, the PRSPs had to be endorsed by the Joint Boards of both the IMF and World Bank which ensured that austere neo-liberal prescriptions were pririotised (World Development Movement 2005, p. 7–8).

In both the Washington and post Washington consensuses, neo-liberal regimes have prioritized rich, innovative and entrepreneurial Africans who contribute to economic growth. The majority of less enterprising Africans according to neo-liberal postulations were regarded as less useful. Consequently, a number of Africans were socially alienated through land grabbing and development induced displacements as the neo-liberal states paid a deaf ear to the plight of their citizens.

Osimiri (2013, p. 62) opines that:

> If development was designed to serve the interest of human beings, the practice of Washington consensus failed woefully in Africa; not only did it fail to deliver growth and prosperity that has been part of the standard promises of neo-liberalism, it has also led to deepening of poverty, inequality, and political instability. It is for this reasons that Africa must jettison neo-liberalism and scout for an alternative model of economic development that pays the needed attention to issues of social welfare, justice and human development. To extricate herself from the crises of underdevelopment, Africans must initiate the process

from inside-out. First, we must reconstruct the post colonial state into one that is accountable, transparent and development oriented, secondly, African intellectuals, states men and all other progressive forces on the continent must transform society into a more democratic and egalitarian one.

## 7 Neo-Liberalism and the Entrenchment of Corruption, Cronyism and Indebtedness

Harrison (2019, p. 274) argues that "authoritarian neo-liberalism in Africa is a failed strategy of capitalist trans-formation". He defines neo-liberalism as "a universal social project pursued in the name of free markets", and authoritarianism as "a specific state-form that emerges in countries in which the bourgeoisie is weak and capitalist development requires centralized and forcible state action" (Harrison 2019, p. 277). Gentle (2020) avers that "neo-liberal capitalism breeds institutionalised corruption and is nothing less than a political victory of the super-rich over the working class and poor".

In September, 2020, The UN Commission on Human Rights exposed the misappropriation of "$36 million since 2016 in South Sudan, the world's youngest fragile nation. Most of the embezzlement was done by senior politicians and government officials with the aid of international corporations and multinational banks" (Sooka 2020). This fraud transpired in the Ministry of Finance and Economic Planning as well as the National Revenue Authority. South Sudan's National Revenue Authority divulged that "approximately $300 million US dollars were "lost" in just three months", while the Economic Crisis Management Committee reported that "$3.1 million US dollars was "missing" at the Directorate of Nationalities, Passport, and Immigration" (Sooka 2020).

It must be emphasized that the implementation of neo-liberalism in Sub-Shaharan Africa led to unprecedented levels of corruption and patronage in a number of states because it prioritized greed and avarice at the expense of ethical and social justice led development. This led to the creation of pseudo bourgeoisie capitalist class that enriched itself through robbery and fraud. For example, Uganda's privatization in the 1990s was marred by malpractice and nepotism.

In November 1998, a parliament select committee decried how powerful families closely associated with President Museveni were manipulating the privatisation process. The committee recommended the prosecution of President Museveni's brother General Salim Saleh and the ministers for privatization and investment, Matthew Rukikaire and Sam Kuteesa (Tangri and Mwenda 2001). The president however took no strong action against these culprits. The former Managing Director of Greenland Bank, Dr. Sulaiman Kiggundu divulged that president Museveni and top government officials had endorsed particular corruption deals (Tangri and Mwenda 2001).

In 2005, the World Bank threatened to withdraw its funding for privatisation in Uganda if President Museveni continued to directly influence the process of privatization of Uganda Dairy Corporation (UDC). The World Bank declined to extend its financial and technical support for Uganda's privatisation process when it lapsed in January, 2006 (Tangri 2010, p. 84). The Uganda neo-liberal state headed by Museveni has looted the country's resources through buying junk military equipment, personalizing privatized public enterprises and apportioning the largest share of the national budget to security. Museveni used corruption to cement loyalty between him and the cadres of the National Resistance Movement which consequently entrenched him in power (Tangri and Mwenda 2003).

The excess corruption by politicians in African neo-liberal states trickled down to civil servants, the private sector and consequently to the peasants at the bottom of the social ladder. The Pan- African altruistic concern for the other African neighbor as person with dignity was replaced by the capitalistic zeal for greed, super profits, wealth and splendor. Corruption therefore became a social system where almost everyone was entangled. One needed to bribe to get a job, to see a doctor, to pass an exam, to see a patient in the hospital, to secure a suspect under police custody, and to avoid a traffic fine. In addition, a number of young women were forced to use sex bribery in exchange for jobs, promotions and examination marks.

According to Ani et al. (2014, p. 218):

> The most shocking part of the widespread corruption in Nigeria is the fact that it is not anymore within the parameters of how Transparency International defines corruption; it is no longer limited to politicians or the public servants. It has become very common within every section of the society at every level. It is prevalent not only among the rich who are greedy in spite of possessing enough but also among the poor. The fact is that a huge population of Nigerians is now involved in corrupt practices in one way or the other, either due to greed or due to the so called unethical compulsion to amass public wealth. People have gone to the extent of adulteration of food-stuffs such as milk, life-saving medicines, motor tires and food supplements.

In 2018, Ugandans were shocked to learn that a number of the meat and food vendors across the country, especially those dealing in meat, chicken, fish and *nsenene(grasshoppers) were using dangerous chemicals to* make foodstuffs look deceptively fresh (Etukuri 2018). Formaldehyde, a chemical used to preserve dead bodies in hospitals was one of the chemicals being used. This was exacerbated by lack of proper monitoring from the institutions tasked with supervision, such as Kampala Capital City Authority (KCCA), Ministry of Health, Ministry of Agriculture and Uganda National Bureau of Standards (UNBS) (Etukuri 2018).

There were fears that hundreds of lives could have been exposed to ailments, such as cancer, due to the excessive consumption of large amounts of illegal chemicals used in the preservation of meat and fish. Wilfred Emeku, a veterinary pathologist at Makerere University opines that "consuming chemicals, such as formaldehyde, can be extremely toxic for the human body" (Yiga 2018). According to him,

> the chemical can cause damage to the digestive tract, right from the mouth to the lower parts. It can also lead to symptoms like abdominal pain, vomiting, and diarrhea and in severe cases even death. Formaldehyde, can destroy human tissue, or even damage the nucleus of the cells and if this occurs, cancers can develop (Yiga 2018).

## 8 Neo-Liberal Greed and Debt Sustainability in Africa

Corrupt neo-liberal states in Africa continue to borrow money from International Financial institutions (IFIs) in order to promote economic development that is measured by the increase in economic growth. However, most of the borrowed funds are embezzled by politicians, civil servants or contracted private firms and corporations. Although loans from IFIs are wasted through the corruption stratagems of the neo-liberal states, the ordinary citizens both born and unborn must bear the burden of paying back these loans. The World Bank Estimates that Uganda looses 500 billion Shillings annually in procurement-related corruption. A government Instituted inquiry into the road sector also revealed that the country lost 4 trillion shillings to corruption in the road sector over a period of 4 years (Uganda National NGO Forum 2016).

Although Nigeria celebrated its 60th independence anniversary on October 1, 2020, its debt had accumulated to an astounding \$85.9 billion. This is the highest debt level in the country's history (Momoh 2020). The pressure on the economy caused an 8.31 per cent increase in debt owed from the total of \$79.3 billion recorded in March 2020. By December 2005, Nigeria was rated as one of the most heavily indebted countries, owing \$33.9 billion (Momoh 2020). According to "the Debt Management Office (DMO), the increase by \$6.593 billion was caused by the \$3.36 billion budget support loan from the International Monetary Fund, new domestic borrowing to finance the revised 2020 Appropriation Act, including the issuance of Sukuk and Promissory Notes to settle claims of exporters"(Momoh 2020). Former Vice President Atiku Abubakar accused government "of mortgaging the future of Nigerians and having nothing to show for amassing such debt" (Momoh 2020).

On 1st September 2020, government revealed that Uganda's public debt is projected to hit 47.5 per cent of the Gross Domestic Product (GDP) which is Shs150.267 trillion in the Financial Year 2020/2021. This was occasioned by increased borrowing and expenditure to counteract the Covid-19 pandemic on the economy (The Monitor 2020). According to expert economists, the projected rise in public debt implies that the country is not collecting enough domestic taxes to meet the ever increasing government expenditure, and that it also puts a lot of pressure on the government to service the debt (The Monitor 2020).

Patrick Tumwebaze, the Executive Director of Uganda Debt Network (UDN) articulates the Uganda Debt Crisis as follows:

> We are heading into a point where we shall be borrowing just to pay debt – meaning, we shall be digging a pit to cover another pit. We don't want to be in such a situation. According to World Bank, Uganda loses about \$300 million (Shs1.1 trillion) in wasteful expenditure annually. When you consider this with the dwindling revenue streams we are experiencing, you see that we are headed for disaster. According to World Bank estimates, about 60 per cent of funds we get in loans are wasted. We did a research that we are yet to publish and we found that 40 per cent of the loans for mostly roads were behind schedule. This is because of mainly corruption and issues around delay of counter funding by government. (Ladu 2020)

## 9 Market Fundamentalism and the Demise of Ubuntu Ethics in African Development

The concept of Ubuntu in African development is precedented on harmonizing development interventions with the dignity and worth of individuals and communities (Mupedziswa et al. 2019). The promotion and protection of social justice and the common good are also central to Ubuntu development ethics. Ubuntu ethics therefore gives development a human face by advocating for treating human beings as ends in themselves and never as a means to an end. Ubuntu also promotes the dictums of consideration, generosity and humanness towards others (Sekuda 2019; Nyaumwe and Mkabela 2007). According Osei-Hwedie (2014), "Ubuntu emphasises norms for interpersonal relationships that contribute to social justice, such as; reciprocity, selflessness and symbiosis".

Neo-liberalism has prioritized markets, economic growth, private property and private sector led development over the dignified treatment of human persons (ubuntu) hence treating African people as cogs or instruments in the development process. Neo-liberalism has also valorized the rich, innovative and enterprising in terms of business acumen at the expense of the poor, 'lazy' as well as those with low business and investment IQ.

Neo-liberalism is anchored on the Social Darwinistic science that propagates the survival of the fittest individuals in the market place. According to this flawed science, development is an arena where the rich (pure breed) will be separated from the poor (residues) by natural selection. Neo-liberalism therefore condemns the poverty of the poor on their lack of business innovation. A number of neo-liberal states have advocated for minimal and contradictory social protection measures for the poor (*residualist* approach) aimed at helping the poor transit into a pure breed. Yash Tandon opines that the neo-liberal capitalist-imperialist system of production and wealth distribution is inherently flawed. This is because it not only divides people between the rich and the poor but also compounds this division over time since the market rewards the rich and penalises the poor (Tandon 2019).

## 10 Pan African Development Ethics and the Neo-Liberal Tragedy of the Commons

The Tragedy of the Commons refers to a situation where shared resources or resources protected for the sake of the common good (van Laerhoven and Ostrom 2007) of all individuals in society are privatized or individualized. These common resources include; schools, health facilities, forests, grazing grounds, lakes, rivers, wells and the atmosphere (Hardin 1968; Ostrom 1990). Neo-liberalism prioritizes the protection of private property over the common good. Also, the fraudulent capital accumulation 'dialectic' fostered by neo-liberalism has led to not only the destruction or pollution of the Commons but also the individualization or corporatization of the same.

Wichterich (2014, p. 348–349) argues that:

> Commoning is away to protect commons and public goods from privatization, commercialization and speculation; otherwise private capital owners and the rules of the market would decide about the common good and the enforcement of human rights. Commons break with the logic of private property as root cause of individual greed for prosperity and accumulation, and open up space for more democratic decision making, economic activity in solidarity and redistributive justice.

Neo-liberal regimes in Sub-shaharan African have embraced modernization as a way forward for African development. Modernization is interpreted as embracing science and an industrial ethic. In an effort to promote economic development in African countries, a number of African countries are striving to increase their economic growth even at the expense of safeguarding the Commons. In Uganda, Museveni has laughed off environmental activists who are critical of the government's overtures to give away Uganda's protected forests to investors. Museveni has persistently called environmentalists economic saboteurs who need to be reminded that the future of Uganda lies in modernization and industrialization.

For instance, in December 2020, a Court of Appeal judge "allowed the destruction of 22 Square miles of the disputed Bugoma Central Forest Reserve in order to pave way for sugarcane growing by Hoima Sugar Limited" (Kasozi 2019). Justice Frederick Egonda Ntende "dismissed with costs, an application in which the National Forestry Authority (NFA) had sought to temporarily halt the implementation of the orders of the High Court" (Kasozi 2019).

The Bugoma Forest is a protected tropical forest that is situated southwest of Hoima and northeast of Kyenjojo town, and east of Lake Albert, in the Hoima district of western Uganda. It was gazetted in the 1930s and came under the mandate of the National Forestry Authority in 2003 (Okiror 2020). The forest is crucial for the development of tourism in Uganda. It is home to over 500 endangered and internationally protected chimpanzees as well as thousands of primate species like the endangered Mangabeys. Hoima Sugar Limited, one of the newly established Sugar Plant is targeting the denudation of 8000 hectares of forest cover which is about 20% of the entire Bugoma Forest (Okiror 2020).

Under "the 1998 Land Act, forest reserves like Bugoma are held in trust for the common good of the citizens of Uganda and may not be leased out or sold by the government"(Lewton 2020). However, "in August 2016, the Bunyoro-Kitara Kingdom, one of five traditional kingdoms which hold autonomous powers from the central government in Kampala, successfully claimed 5700 hectares (14,100 acres) of Bugoma forest as ancestral land. Just 4 days later, the kingdom transferred the title to this land to Hoima Sugar Limited" (Lewton 2020).

The Ugandan case above is a microcosm of the Tragedy of the Commons in a number of African countries that embraced neo-liberal capitalism at the expense of social justice and the common good. In order to ameliorate the dilemma embedded in the tragedy of the Commons in Sub-Saharan Africa, it is pertinent to make a paradigm shift from promoting economic efficiency to fostering economic sufficiency. The former focuses on economic growth and economic development while the later prioritizes de-growth, human development, social justice, ecological justice, climate justice and commoning.

## 11 Conclusion

Neo-liberalism has rendered a terrible blow to Pan-African development governance in Sub-Saharan Africa. It not only decimated Ubuntu development ethics but also greatly obliterated the African Communitarian spirit. The disorganised capitalism embedded in neo-liberal transformation also annihilated the specs of ethical altruism in African social cohesion which were replaced by the dictums of individualism, greed and avarice. African societies were transformed from man care about man societies to man prey on man and man plunder man societies. Hundreds and sometimes thousands of peasant Africans lost land to neo-liberal land grabbers through the so called development induced displacements. Others lost assets, monies and properties through the fraudulent capital accumulations ruses of Ponzi scheming companies. Neo-liberalism created a sham bourgeoisie class that thrived on fraud and banditry. This created a corrupt social system which entangled virtually every one. The rights to health, education, social security and a decent standard of living became a prerogative for the rich and middle class Africans. Neo-liberalism also transformed African leaders and states men from Pan-Africans to neo-liberal oligarchs who reinforced and crystallised the understanding of African development using Western economic growth model. Consequently a true African citizen according to the neo-liberal stance was one who promoted economic growth even at the expense development ethics, human rights and social justice. Since Pan-Africanism is at total variance with neo-liberalism, there is a need to reawaken the Pan-African consciousness against the onslaught of neo-liberalism through peaceful social disobedience, social *conscientisation* interventions and development endogenisation.

## References


Ani, K.C., E.M. Izueke, and I.F. Nzekwe. 2014. Public sector and corruption in Nigeria: An ethical and institutional framework of analysis. *Open Journal of Philosophy* 4: 216–224. https://doi.org/10.4236/ojpp.2014.43029.

Aron, R. 2019. *Main currents in sociological thought*. New York: Routledge.

Ayittey, G. 2006. *Indigenous African institutions*. Leiden: Brill-Nijhoff.

Bhargava, R. 2013. Overcoming the epistemic injustice colonialism. *Global Policy* 4 (4): 413–417.

CEHURD. 2011. *The sick hospital system in Uganda*. Viewed 16 July 2021. http://www.cehurd.org/2011/10/the-sick-hospital-system-in-uganda/.

Crocker, D. 2008. *Ethics of global development*. Cambridge: Cambridge University Press.

Croker, D.A. 2001. *Globalisation and human development: Ethical approaches*. Viewed 18 April 2020. www.pass.va/content/dam/scienzesociali/pdf/acta7/acta7-crocker.pdf.

Dower, N. 1988. 'What is development? A philosopher's answer'. *Centre for development studies occasional paper series*. University of Glasgow, no.3.

Ekanade, O.V. 2014. The dynamics of forced neo-liberalism in Nigeria since the 1980s. *Journal of Retracting Africa* 1 (1): 1–24.

Etukuri, C. 2018. Butchers treating meat with drugs meant for dead bodies. *The new vision*, 4 January.

Fricker, M. 2007. *Epistemic injustice: Power and the ethics of knowing*. New York: Oxford University Press.

Gasper, D. 2012. Development ethics – Why? What? How? A formulation of the field. *Journal of Global Ethics* 8 (1): 117–135. https://doi.org/10.1080/17449626.2012.672450.

Gatwiri, K., J. Amboko, and D. Okolla. 2020. The implications of neoliberalism on African economies, health outcomes and wellbeing: A conceptual argument. *Social theory & health: STH* 18 (1): 86–101. https://doi.org/10.1057/s41285-019-00111-2.

Gentle, L. 2020. *Corruption and neo-liberalism: We are caught between those who have captured the state and those who want to*, 28 September. Viewed 26 July 2021. https://www.thejournalist.org.za/spotlight/corruption-and-neoliberalism-we-are-caught-between-those-who-have-captured-the-state-and-those-who-want-to/.

Goulet, D. 1997. Development ethics: A new discipline. *International Journal of Social Economics* 24 (11): 1160–1171.

Hahn, N.S.C. 2008. Neoliberal imperialism and pan African resistance. *Journal of World Systems Research* 13 (2): 142–178.

Hardin, G. 1968. The tragedy of the commons. *Science* 162 (3859): 1243–1248.

Harrison, G. 2019. Authoritarian neoliberalism and capitalist transformation in Africa: all pain, no gain. *Globalizations* 16 (3): 274–288. https://doi.org/10.1080/14747731.2018.1502491.

Howard, R. 1983. The full-belly thesis: Should economics rights take priority over civil and political rights? Evidence from sub-Saharan Africa. *Human Rights Quarterly* 5 (4): 467–490.

Hoyle, C. 2017. *How former African child soldiers ended up fighting in the Iraq war*, 16 March. Viewed 25 June 2021. https://muftah.org/former-african-child-soldiers-ended-fighting-iraq-war/#.Wi5u83lRXIU.

Kagaba, C. 2013. Corruption? What corruption? In Uganda impunity reigns supreme. *The black star news*, 7 September.

Kasozi, E. 2019. Court okays razing Bugoma forest for sugarcane growing. *The monitor*, 7 December 2019.

Krugman, P. 2009. How did economists get it so wrong?. *New York Times*, 6 September, p. MM36. Viewed 23 July 2021. http://www.nytimes.com/2009/09/06/magazine/06Economic-t.html?pagewanted=all.

Ladu, I. 2020. Cancel debt for economy to recover, says UDN boss. *The monitor*, 29 September.

Lewton, T. 2020. *Uganda environment authority greenlights clearing of Bugoma Forest*, 5 November. Viewed 16 June 2021. https://news.mongabay.com/2020/11/uganda-environment-authority-greenlights-clearing-of-bugoma-forest/.

Lirri, E. 2017. *Ugandan domestic workers stuck between poverty wages at home and extreme exploitation abroad*, 16 June. Viewed 16 July 2021. https://www.equaltimes.org/ugandan-domestic-workers-stuck?lang=en#.X4md5HVRWqY.

Lopes, C. 2012. Economic growth and inequality: The new post-Washington consensus. *RCCS Annual Review*, no.4, https://doi.org/10.4000/rccsar.426 . Viewed 6 June 2021. http://journals.openedition.org/rccsar/426.

McCain, J. 1974. Personality and culture: A case of African socialism. *Ufahamu: A journal of African studies*. https://doi.org/10.5070/F751017513. Viewed 21 June 2021. https://escholarship.org/uc/item/1ch2c75g

Momoh, M. 2020. Record-breaking $86bn debt leaves Nigerians stunned., *The East African*, 5 October.

Mullick, M. 1978. On Marx's conception of a positive science. *Social Scientist* 6 (9): 55–66.

Mupedziswa, R., M. Rankopo, and L.K. Mwansa. 2019. Ubuntu as a pan-African philosophical framework for social work in Africa. In *Social work practice in Africa*, ed. J.M. Twikirize and H. Spitzer. Kampala, Uganda: Fountain Publishers.

Nantambu, K. 1998. Pan-Africanism versus Pan-African nationalism: An Afrocentric analysis. *Journal of Black Studies* 28 (5): 561–574.

Nkirote L. 2018. *A job at any cost': Experiences of African women migrant domestic Workers in the Middle East*. Global Alliance against traffic in women (GAATW), viewed 10 June 2021, https://gaatw.org/publications/Africa_Domestic_Work_Consolidated_regional_report.pdf.

Nkrumah, K. 1980. *Consciencism*. New York: International Publishers.

Nyaumwe, L.J., and Q. Mkabela. 2007. Revisiting the traditional African cultural framework of ubuntuism: A theoretical perspective. *Indilinga: African Journal of Indigenous Knowledge Systems* 6: 152–163.
Okiror, S. 2020. 'A shame for the world': Uganda's fragile forest ecosystem destroyed for sugar. *The Guardian*, 18 June.
Ola, O. 1979. Pan-Africanism: An ideology of development. *Présence Africaine Nouvelle série* 4 (112): 66–95.
Osei-Hwedie, K. 2014. Afro-centrism: The challenge of social development. *Social Work/ Maatskaplike Werk* 43: 106–116.
Osimiri, P. 2013. An ethical critique of neoliberal development in Africa. *Covenant Journal of Politics and International Affairs (CUJPIA)* 1 (1): 62–71.
Ostrom, E. 1990. *Governing the commons: The evolution of institutions for collective action*. Cambridge: Cambridge University Press.
Singer, P. 2000. *Marx: A very short introduction*. Oxford: Oxford University Press.
Rodney, W. 1972. Tanzanian *Ujamaa* and scientific socialism. *African Review* 1 (4): 61–76.
Sekudu, J. 2019. Ubuntu. In *Theories for decolonial social work practice in South Africa*, ed. A.D. Van Breda and J. Sekudu. Cape Town: Oxford University Press South Africa.
Shah, A. 2013. *Structural adjustment—A major cause of poverty*, viewed 21 June 2021. https://www.globalissues.org/article/3/structural-adjustment-a-major-cause-of-poverty.
Sooka, Y. 2020. *Statement by chair of the UN Commission on human rights on South Sudan to the human rights council*, 23 September. Viewed 23 July 2021. https://www.ohchr.org/EN/HRBodies/HRC/Pages/NewsDetail.aspx?NewsID=26281&LangID=E#_ftn1.
Stiglitz, J., and L. Schoenfelder. 2003. Challenging the Washington consensus'. *The Brown Journal of World Affairs* 9 (2): 33–40.
Tandon, Y. 2019. *Common people's Uganda*. Nairobi: Zand Graphics.
Tangri, R. 2010. Executive manipulation and corruption in Uganda's public governance. *In 7th IDEA international conference proceedings in ethics and international development*, ed. A.B. Rukooko. Nairobi: Law Africa.
Tangri, R., and A.M. Mwenda. 2001. Corruption and cronyism in Uganda's privatisation in the1990s. *African Affairs* 100 (398): 117–133.
———. 2003. Military corruption and Ugandan politics since the late 1990s. *Review of African Political Economy* 98: 365–378.
The Monitor. 2020. Uganda debt nears crisis level. *The monitor*, 2 September.
The New Vision. 2020. *Museveni responds to hostile, negative, arrogant people*, 6 April. Viewed 21 June 2021. https://www.newvision.co.ug/news/1524173/museveni-responds-hostile-negative-arrogant-people.
Uganda National NGO Forum et al. 2016. Open letter to the president of the World Bank. *The daily monitor*, 16 September.
van Laerhoven, F., and E. Ostrom. 2007. Traditions and trends in the study of the commons. *International Journal of the Commons* 1 (1): 3–28.
Wichterich, C. 2014. Occupy development – Towards a caring economy. *Development* 56 (3): 348–349. https://doi.org/10.1057/dev.2014.12.
Williamson, J., ed. 1990. *Latin American readjustment: How much has happened*. Washington, DC: Peterson Institute for International Economics.
———. 2005. The strange history of the Washington consensus. *Journal of Post Keynesian Economics* 27 (2): 195–206.
World Development Movement. 2005. *One size for all: A study of IMF and World Bank poverty reduction strategies*. Viewed 16 June 2021. https://www.globaljustice.org.uk/sites/default/files/files/resources/onesizeforeall01092005.pdf.
Yiga, F. 2018. Uganda: Meat contaminated by toxic chemicals. *DW.com*, 11 January 11. Viewed 21 June 2021. https://www.dw.com/en/uganda-meat-contaminated-by-toxic-chemicals/a-42110782

**Kizito Michael George** is a Lecturer at the Department of Religious Studies and Philosophy, Kyambogo University. He holds a Master of Philosophy Degree in Gender and Development from the University of Bergen (Norway) and obtained a PhD in Development Ethics from Makerere University in 2019. Kizito is a member of the American Philosophy Association (APA) and the International Development Ethics Association (IDEA). His research interests include Development Ethics, Pan-Africanism, White Saviorism, Human Rights, Poverty Eradication, Gender, Jurisprudence and African Philosophy.

# An Anatomy of Neoliberalism's Subversion of Development and Democracy in Africa

**Peter Osimiri**

**Abstract** This paper seeks to provide an analysis of the several subtle and non-subtle ways by which the wholesale imposition and embrace of the neoliberal ideology and its accompanying prescriptions and practices are facilitating the subversion of democracy and undermining the possibility of authentic and autochthonous development on the continent of Africa. It argues that the hegemonic ascendance of neoliberalism or market fundamentalism in Africa has substantially reversed the democratic gains made after the third wave of democracy in the eighties and is increasingly impeding the quest for collective welfare. It specifically demonstrates that while the rhetoric typically promoted by the International Financial Institutions such as the World Bank (WB) and International Monetary Funds (IMF), bristles with an apparent concern for democracy and development, the combination of the logics of unbridled market capitalism, reckless state apparatus and hostile international environment only deepens Africa's governance and development crisis. The paper considers the nature of politics that is conducive to the implementation of socio-economic policies that are likely to deepen democratic governance and the enhancement of people-centred economic transformations. It concludes that radical engagement remains an essential part of an integrated strategy for breaking the stranglehold of neoliberalism on African societies.

**Keywords** Neoliberalism · Democracy · Development · Africa

---

P. Osimiri (✉)
Department of Philosophy, University of Lagos, Lagos, Nigeria
e-mail: posimiri@unilag.edu.ng



B. Okyere-Manu et al. (eds.), *Contemporary Development Ethics from an African Perspective*, Philosophy and Politics - Critical Explorations 27,
https://doi.org/10.1007/978-3-031-32898-5_4

## 1 Introduction

Central to the appeal of neoliberalism is an avowed capacity to create socio-economic conditions conducive to the maximisation of individual freedom and economic growth. In the last 40 years, however, it has become increasingly clearer that there is a glaring disconnect between the theoretical postulates of neoliberalism and its practical import for the African continent. In fact, the socio-economic conditions on the African continent today, after decades of experimentation with neoliberal economic prescriptions, are in sharp contrast with the promises of the IMF and the World Bank. Whereas the advocates of neoliberalism promised development, peace and prosperity (Scholte 2008, p. 38), most neoliberalising African countries have suffered economic decline, incessant conflicts stemming from resistance to austerity measures and a general fall in the standard of living. The agents of neoliberalism did not only gloat about the capacity of neoliberalism to maximise individual freedom, they also insisted on political conditionality which required the liberalisation of national political spaces as a precondition to access much needed credit for financially distressed countries. As it turned out, most of the "neoliberal democracies" thereby created were quasi-democracies with evident democratic deficits (Osimiri 2020; Jeff Haynes 2001). For these democracies, periodic multiparty electoral competitions were a smokescreen that conceals the authoritarian and patently antidemocratic tendencies of neoliberalism.

In the wake of the realization that the Structural Adjustment Programmes (SAPs) – the package of economic prescriptions by which neoliberalism found its way to Africa- have failed abysmally, the World Bank (1994, pp. 1–2) argued that nothing is inherently wrong with neoliberal prescriptions. In other words, the failure of SAPs is only explicable in terms of the lack of institutional capacity on the part of implementing states.

A major objective of this essay to analyse of the several subtle ways by which the wholesale imposition and embrace of the neoliberal ideology and its accompanying prescriptions and practices facilitate the subversion of democracy and undermine the possibility of autochthonous development on the continent of Africa. This paper debunks the claim that SAPs failed to deliver due to poor implementation. In other words, the results would not be different if the SAP package were fully implemented. Aside from the introduction and conclusion, the essay is organised into four sections. The first attempts an explication of the concept of neoliberalism. The second and third sections deal with the issue of how neoliberalism subverts democracy and development respectively. The final part suggests that an integrated strategy to break the dominance of neoliberalism in Africa would require radical political engagement with national governments across the continent.

## 2 Conceptualising Neoliberalism

Neoliberalism is an essentially contested concept which has become extremely popular both in the academic and policy circles in the last four decades (Briebricher 2018). Approaching the status of a buzz word, neoliberalism as an idea is embedded in conceptual confusion partly because the word could apply to things such as a *body of thought, anacademic theory* or even a *set of policy prescriptions*. This is due to the fact that the discourses on neoliberalism are often conducted by individuals with divergent ideological leanings and persuasions. Without minimising the fact that neoliberalism stands in the danger of lapsing into conceptual incoherence, it may be argued that the idea has a conceptual core which might be elucidated by a few select number of definitions and an elaboration of the central features of neoliberal theory and practice.

As a first step towards capturing neoliberalism's core, we might begin with Vilde Wikan (2015) conceptualization of neoliberalism as an economic theory and an ideological conviction that that supports the reduction of state intervention in the economy and promotion of laissez-faire capitalism in order to foster economic efficiency personal freedom and human well-being. Wikan's definition certainly shed some light on the nature of neoliberalism but the concept is more nuanced than the definition allows. Neoliberalism goes beyond an economic theory and ideology; it is also has political moral and cultural dimensions(Giroux 2008; Biebricher 2018).

Secondly, the idea that neoliberal theory supports reduction in the state intervention in the economy is not entirely correct. This is because, as shown in the body of this essay, the institutionalization of the neoliberal orthodoxy in any society, especially in those of the global South, requires an authoritarian state operating as an active agent of the market. In other words, it is unlikely, that the neoliberal regime would be successfully imposed without a strong interventionist state that could dismantle the constraints to the operation of the markets in order to unleash its potentials (Purcell 2008; Harvey 2005). David Harvey's now famous definition of neoliberalism appears to overcome some of the shortcomings of the preceding one. In his Words,

> Neoliberalism is in the first instance a theory of political economic practices that proposes that human well-being can best be advanced by liberating individual entrepreneurial freedoms and skills within an institutional framework characterized by strong private property rights, free markets, and free trade (2005: 22).

Scholte (2008, p. 38) corroborates the vision inherent in neoliberal self-understanding when he asserts that neoliberalism is an ideology based on the conviction that market forces will deliver prosperity, liberty, democracy and peace to the whole of mankind. From the above conceptualisations, it is clear that central to the neoliberal theory is a strong emphasis on the idea of free markets, (and individual freedom) which is in tandem with its neoclassical roots. The profoundly influential neoliberal thinkers, such as Hayek and Friedman in their various writings expressed a strong antipathy towards centrally planned economies and, therefore, advocated for the "rolling back" of the state as well as the creation of societies governed by markets mechanism (Mcleavy 2016, p. 254). Aside from the contention that free markets is conducive to the maximization of individual freedom and democracy, these neoclassical thinkers are also of the view that free markets are more efficient than governments in the allocation of resources. Thus, compared to any alternative economic arrangement, the market system is in the best position to engender the economic growth necessary for the enjoyment of a good life.

Popular definitions of neoliberalism tend to emphasize the rise of free markets as an evidence that neoliberalism is patently anti-statist and, therefore, is typically associated with "rolling back" the state. This certainly is a misunderstanding or misrepresentation of the neoliberal theory because it is not necessarily anti-statist. Instead, neoliberals and requires the construction of the state apparatus that will play an active role in the facilitation and construction of a competitive market order (Cahill et al. 2018, p. xxix).

At this junction, it important to raise the question: "how did the neoliberal economic model become the dominant paradigm in Africa?" The introduction of the Structural Adjustment Programmes- a set of economic prescriptions inspired by the neoliberal ideology- may be traced to what is known in development circles as the debt crisis of 1980. Closely connected to this crisis was the oil shock of 1973 when the price of oil quadrupled in the global market as a result of an embargo mounted by OPEC. Thus, oil-producing states such as Saudi Arabia, Kuwait and Abu Dhabi came into possession of vast financial resources (Harvey 2005, p. 127). Responding to the oil embargo, the US allegedly threatened the oil rich Arab countries who had benefited from the oil windfall with military action, if they fail to deposit their new-found petrol-dollars into Wall Street investment banks (Hickel 2012). Since the US economy was distressed at that time, the Wall Street banks chose to lend the "confiscated" deposits at high interest rates to selected countries in the global South. Incidentally, these loans were issued in dollars and any considerable increase in the interest rate would push vulnerable countries into default (Harvey 2005, p.29) This eventually happened in the early 1980s when floating interest rate was introduced, leading to a sharp rise in the value of the Third World debt stock (Hoogvelt 2001, p.180). This development precipitated the debt crisis. Confronted with a bloated debt stock, Mexico declared bankruptcy and other indebted countries in the Third World followed suit. Sensing the imminent collapse of the Wall Street and the destruction of the international financial system, the US waded in by dispatching the IMF and the World Bank "to the frontiers of the global economy to exact payments from and supervise the credits to the Third World" (Ibid., p. 180).

This, in sum, is how the IMF and the Word Bank leveraged on the debt crisis to dominate the process of economic management on the African continent. In managing the crisis, the IMF insisted that financially distressed African countries who desire debt rescheduling or fresh loans sign up to a package of policies that more or less reflects the neoliberal agenda encapsulated by the Structural Adjustment Programmes (Kiely & Marfleet 1998, p. 33).

With this brief effort at clarifying the meaning of neoliberalism and the manner of neoliberalism's entry into Africa, we will now proceed to the analysis of how neoliberal ideology and its accompanying prescriptions and practices have led the subversion of democracy and undermined authentic development on the continent.

## 3 Neoliberalism and the Subversion of Democracy

In order to proceed systematically and for analytical simplicity, the succeeding discussion will separate how the neoliberal doctrine subverts democracy from how it impedes development. It must be noted, however, that in the empirical world of the network of forces and causation, things are much more complex. On the surface, it would appear that IMF and the World Bank are engaged in the promotion of democracy, particularly if we focus on their rhetoric and the fact that at some point they introduced political conditionality which requires the liberalisation of national political spaces as a condition for loans. A deeper examination however reveals the implementation of neoliberalism reinforced tyrannical rule across the continent.

Neoliberalism in whatever guise, whether presented as structural adjustment or the Washington consensus remains a veritable threat to democracy anywhere. In the African experience, the anti-democratic character of neoliberalism was palpably demonstrated by the manner in which it was imposed on the continent. In the wake of the oil shock in 1970s, many African countries sought for loans, which were granted at agreed interest rate. Few years down the lane, the United States Federal Reserve, in what is now known as the Volcker Shock unilaterally increased interest rates which ultimately raised the debt stock of the Third World countries and precipitated the debt crises in the 1980s (Harvey 2005, p. 23). As already highlighted above, the IMF and its collaborators seized the opportunity to impose the Structural Adjustment Programmes on indebted African states. So widespread was the imposition that as far back as 1986, close to 40 African countries have "embraced" the Structural Adjustment Programmes (Chazan et al. 1999, p.337). If the imposition of SAPs requires coercion and subterfuge, the implementation of its neoliberal economic prescriptions in diverse ways further endangers and undermines democracy which in many parts of Africa is at its embryonic stage. In the discussion that follows, the diverse ways in which the SAPs erode democratic ethos and practices will be explored.

First, it is now a well-established position in literature that under the conditions of widespread poverty and inequality, SAPs could only be successfully implemented by a strong, authoritarian government (Abrahamsen 2000; Mafeje 2002; Akpopari 2001; Harvey 2005). It is therefore, misleading to suppose that neoliberalism supports the emergence of a minimalist state. The reality is that in practice, it takes an aggressively authoritarian state to impose and implement the unpopular neoliberal economic policies which ultimately further impoverishes whole populations.

Gill (2008) buttresses the point about authoritarian neoliberalism in the following terms:

> ...a pure market system is an utopian abstraction and any attempt to construct it fully would require an immense authoritarian application of power through the state. This would raise doubts about the viability of a minimal or 'night-watchman' state, as portrayed in the liberal ideology. Indeed, it can be shown that many of neoliberal forms of state have been authoritarian. In some case this involved a considerable coercive power to destroy opposition and eliminate the possibility of a third way... (p. 147).

The conflation of authoritarianism with neoliberalism is rather paradoxical, given that one of the justifications touted by the advocates of neoliberalism is that in contrast with centrally planned economies, the neoliberal arrangement is capable of maximising individual freedom and liberty. But after decades of practicing the coercively imposed neoliberalism, the term "authoritarian neoliberalism" has been added to the lexicon of political theory. Tansel (2018, p. 199) conceptualised authoritarian neoliberalism as:

> ... a mode of governance that operates on twin principles. These are (1) establishing a disciplinary statecraft which closes off key decision-making processes to popular pressures, public input and non-partisan auditing mechanisms – particularly, but not exclusively, with a view to protecting the circuits of capital accumulation, and (2) deploying the coercive, legal and administrative state apparatuses to marginalise democratic opposition and dissident social groups.

Anyone sceptical about the notion of authoritarian neoliberalism need not look too far: the authoritarian credential of neoliberalism which has largely undermined the emergence of genuine democracy in Africa is there for everyone to see. Beyond the violent imposition of neoliberal policies on already pauperised populations, the radical free market system encapsulated in Structural Adjustment Programmes truncate democracy in other ways.

Closely related to the immediately preceding point, is that neoliberalism tends to generate adversarial, conflictual politics, creating a permanent state of instability which is hardly conducive to the entrenchment of democratic ethos. The implementation of harsh adjustment policies such currency devaluation and the retrenchment of welfare subsidies often worsen the declining living standards in adjusting countries. For that reason, the ruling class in such countries are pitched against an army of the impoverished who periodically ventilate their frustration by embarking in sporadic riots and violent protest, leaving the state in permanent state of political turmoil and instability. Unfortunately, the typical response of the ruling elite to the agitations over biting austerity measures is to roll out the security apparatus of the state -the police and military forces- to suppress what is perceived as popular rebellion. By provoking this cycle of mass agitation and state suppression, structural adjustment generates adversarial politics which ultimately undermines democracy. In the word, of Claude Ake (1996, p. 94), in such situations, societies become "effectively fragmented, incoherent and unstable".

In her book *Disciplining Democracy*, Abrahamsen (2000, pp. 117–118) refers to the phenomenon of "irreconcilable constituencies" and how it contributes to undermining democracy in countries implementing SAPs. According to her, adjusting governments are caught on the horn of a dilemma because they must jostle to retain the support of two constituencies, namely, the domestic majority and external creditors. The problem, however, is that the demand of the two constituencies are irreconcilable. The domestic constituency continues to demand for improved living standards which may lead to the abandonment of austerity measures, whereas the foreign creditors insist on the continued implementation of SAPs. Should the government heed to the call of the domestic constituency, it risks losing critical funding from the external constituency. If, on the other hand, it accedes to the demand of the external constituency, it risks being voted out. To resolve this dilemma, most African countries pander to the external creditor and donors and then engage in massive manipulation of the electoral process to stay in power. This way, neoliberalising societies in Africa remains mere electoral democracies, lacking in any serious democratic substance. They are reminiscent of societies that Zakaria (1997) has dubbed illiberal democracies.

Another dimension to the neoliberal subversion of democracy in Africa is that the implementation of SAPs leads to loss of sovereignty and self-determination on the part of adjusting countries (Held 1995, 2010; Abrahamsen 2000). A fundamental postulate of conventional political theory is that a democracy is premised on the congruity between a territorially bounded community and locus of power which is internal to the community. Should an external power exercise authority over the affairs of such a community, it loses its democratic autonomy (Held 1995). In hijacking the traditional prerogative of governments to govern their own economic affairs, the IMF and the World Bank effectively compromised the democratic autonomy of adjusting countries. This amounts to loss of sovereignty on the part of the states in question, because an area as crucial as economic self-determination has been ceded to the unelected officials of the international financial institutions, resulting in a democratic deficit described by Held (2010, p. 36) as an arrangement where "decision makers" are not elected and nor answerable to "decision takers." Hickel (2016) describes the hijack of economic decision making by the IFIs in the following terms.

> Structural adjustment represented a serious attack on democracy in the global South. It meant that key decisions over economic policy were made not by national parliaments, but rather by bankers and technocrats in Washington and New York. It operated as a new kind of coup: a way for Washington to impose its economic agenda without the bloodshed, torture, and overt dictatorship that marked the Chile experiment. Furthermore, most citizens would never know it happened; they would continue to believe that their elected representatives held power, when, in fact, power … had been shifted abroad (p. 146).

To sum up this section, it is not surprising that in spite of the democratic gains that Africa made in the third wave of democracy at least in terms of the sheer number of transitions to nascent democracies, many of those democracies are not consolidating, and in some cases, have regressed back into authoritarianism. In the next section will focus on how neoliberalism undermines authentic development in Africa.

## 4 Neoliberalism and the Subversion of Development in Africa

Development is an extremely difficult concept to define but for our purposes here, we will adopt Goldemberg (1993) characterisation of the concept. This serves to illuminate what might be considered an authentic form development. According to him,

> development is a process of self-reliant growth, achieved through the participation of the people acting in their own interests as they see them, and under their own control. Its first objective must be to end poverty, provide productive employment, and satisfy the basic needs of all the people, any surplus being fairly shared (p. 240).

From this definition, the key questions to ask in order to determine when development is authentic are: (1) is the process of development self-reliant? (2) Is it based on the participation of the people, acting in their own interest? (3) Is the objective to end poverty and satisfy basic needs? Interestingly, with regard to SAPs, none of the above questions can be answered in the affirmative. From the discussion so far, SAPs are not based on any self-reliant strategy and their implementation is heavily dependent of external creditor and donors. In addition, SAPs are not premised on popular participation activated by self-interest, if anything the SAPs are likely to protect the interest of external creditors and perhaps the indigenous ruling elite. Harvey, for instance, has argued that the objective of neoliberalisation is to "re-establish the conditions for capital accumulation and to restore the power of global economic "elites" (Harvey 2005, p. 19). Clearly, this is a violation of the Rawlsian difference principle which demands that social and economic inequalities are to be arranged to the greatest benefit of the least advantaged (Rawls 1999). Neoliberal economics is designed to advance the hegemony of an already privileged class. And to the last question, is the objective, to end poverty and satisfy basic needs? Of course, defenders of SAP and Neoliberalism in general are wont to invoke the trickle-down "theory" on the basis of which poverty will be eliminated in the long run, but if the experience of SAP in African nations was anything to go by, the verdict is clear: forty years of the practice of neoliberalism have resulted in the deepening of poverty and the intensification of inequality. This verdict will be further unravelled by analysing how neoliberalism thwarts development on the African continent. But first we need to examine the fact and figures which point to the impact of neoliberalism on African economies.

After the first years of the implementation of SAPs in Africa, here in an outline are some of the outcomes:

- Though the earlier decade was riddled with economic crisis, Africans were poorer in the 80 s because SAPs brought about a 20% reduction in the average income in Sub-Saharan Africa (Harrison 2010, p. 39).
- Roughly within the same period, the per capita income in developing countries declined to about half of the previous levels, that is, from 3 to 1.7% (Hickel 2016, p. 146).

- Between 1981 and 2001, the number of the extremely poor, that is, those who live on less than $1 a day doubled, reaching $313 million. (Harrison 2010, p. 39).
- The GNP of the average country in Sub-Saharan Africa contracted by 10% between the 1980s and the 90s (Hickel 2016, p. 146).
- By the year 2004 the foreign debt stock of Sub-Saharan African countries had exceeded $250 billion, but due to debt relief that was granted in 2006 by the G7 the outstanding debt crashed to $170 billion. However, by the end of 2018, the debt stock had accumulated to over $580 billion (Bond 2021, p. 135).

With these the depressing figures on the impact of neoliberalism in Africa, we may now deal with the issue of why the neoliberal economic paradigm will deepen, rather than ameliorate, the crisis of development in Africa and other parts of the global South. It is important here to reiterate a point which was made earlier: a holistic explanation of the failure of development in Africa must pay attention to the combined role of neoliberalism, the rapacious ruling elite and the unjust global economic order. An exclusive focus on either internal or external factors, will proffer an incomplete explanation which will *Ipso facto* yield ineffective recommendations about the way forward. Given the constraint of space, however, the discussion that is to follow would focus primarily focus on the neoliberalism's contribution to the forging of Africa's current development impasse. Specifically, I will highlight three points, namely, how neoliberalism creates and promotes the debt crisis; the inappropriateness of neoliberal prescriptions for developing countries and how the neoliberal ideology diverts attention away from other factors responsible for the crisis of development in Africa.

The narrative around the debt crisis in the 1980s is rather instructive on how the unilateral increase in interest rate by creditors could precipitate a crisis of global proportions, on the basis of which indebted countries were railroaded into adopting and implementing neoliberal economic programmes as precondition for accessing external loans. The big challenge with this arrangement, as elucidated in our analysis, is that African nations have been further pauperised by neoliberal policies. Paying back the loans, therefore, becomes increasingly impossible or excruciatingly difficult. The import of this is that neoliberalised Heavily Indebted Poor Countries (HIPCs) will have to prioritize debt repayment over essential social services, which would force them scamper for fresh loans just stay afloat (Wengraf 2018: p. 42). Ultimately, these countries may be trapped in the vicious circle of debt and dependency. Bond (2021, p. 136),for instance, assert that as at 2016, Nigeria and Angola expended 66 and 60 per cent of their annual revenues respectively on debt servicing, and according the recent figures released by Nigeria's Debt Management Office, debts servicing gulped a whopping 97 per cent of Nigeria's revenue in 2020 (Chizea 2020).Unless something drastic happens, the massive debt overhang and the consequent strangulating debt servicing obligations are sure to stymie the development of HIPCs and keep them trapped in the neoliberal cul-de-sac.

Another reason why neoliberalism may constitute an impediment to development in Africa is the inappropriateness of the policy of total economic liberalisation to countries at the earliest stage of industrial take off. Central to the neoliberal paradigm is the policy of economic liberalisation which is always recommend because it is good for growth and development (Kiely 2005). The typical neoliberalising country is required to implement a collection of prescriptions which include the promotion of free trade, deregulation, the elimination of subsidies and the downsizing or privatization of public enterprises. According to neoliberals, once these policies are in place, the country stands to enjoy comparative advantage, the inflow of Foreign Direct Investment and unprecedented economic prosperity. To be sure, economic liberalisation looks good on paper but for virtually all the adjusting countries in Africa, the promises never materialised, and the reasons are obvious. Firms located in the industrial North are better able to take the advantages of international trade. In addition, liberalisation may open the floodgates for cheaper imports which inundate the markets of the neoliberalising states, resulting in the collapse of infant industries and the contraction of the economy. The probability that a country in the global South would enjoy the advertised benefits is further reduced by the protectionist strategies which are deployed by developed countries. Indeed, it has been pointed out that the latter attained their current status by the systematic deployment of protectionist trade and financial policies. It for this reason that Chang (Cited in Kiely 2005, p. 41) argues that imposing liberalisation on the economies of developing countries is akin to 'kicking away the ladder' and "undermining the development strategies that enabled the 'advanced' countries to develop in the first place." In the end, it appears that the journey towards prosperity since the establishment of Bretton Wood institutions require a total breach, or the selective deployment, of economic liberalisation. Developing countries can certainly learn from the Chinese model. Byres (2005, p. 90) opines that:

> The Chinese case is instructive. China has not adopted anything resembling a neoliberal policy package. Privatisation of industry, the embracing of the market and so on have proceeded relatively slowly and been pursued with due caution. Moreover, and critically, the Chinese state has not withdrawn. It has been an actively interventionist, growth-promoting state.

Another major way neoliberalism stifles development in Africa is that as the hegemonic orthodoxy in the development discourse, it misdiagnoses the root causes Africa development crisis, and therefore, impedes an effective response to the crisis. In other words, the neoliberal emphasis on economic liberalisation and market-based development strategies effectively conceal, and deflect attention away from the structural imbalances in the global economic system, the asymmetric economic relations between the global North and South which continues to perpetuate poverty and underdevelopment in the global South. Inherent within every development theory is some explanation about why economies fail to achieve growth and development. As far as the neoliberal orthodoxy is concerned the prevalence of strong interventionist state and the presence of other internal factors such as corruption and ineptitude on the part of the indigenous ruling classes are responsible for the economic underdevelopment in most of Africa. As already intimated in this essay, this explanation fails to bring into view the full range of factors responsible for development crisis in Africa. These include the reckless state apparatus manned by morally and politically bankrupt elites as well as an unjust global economic order that is skewed against developing countries. Thus, a neoliberal development strategy which requires wide ranging market reforms elides the fact that the unjust global economic system plays a significant role in the underdevelopment of African countries. Incidentally, the subtle imposition of the neoliberal economic model on Africa is indeed part of the ground rules which according to Pogge (2008, p. 118) "foreseeably and avoidably reproduces severe and wide spread poverty." Economic liberalisation, for instance, negatively affects the industrial growth and the economic diversification of developing countries due to the fact that infant industries are exposed to undue competition from multinationals. Currency devaluation which is another neoliberal prescription, tends to have similar effect for developing nations. Devaluation erodes the value of the average income of citizens, precipitates an inflationary spiral that shoots prices of local and imported goods beyond the roof, and significantly increases the production cost for manufacturing concerns. Ultimately, many industries collapse and the economy contracts.

The preceding discussion over how the neoliberal ideology impede development in Africa brings to the fore the need to address the continent's development malaise with an integrated approach which tackles the problem at its different nodes. In other words, breaking out of underdevelopment in Africa will require construction of responsible developmental state, the adoption of economic policies cut to the specificities of the African predicament and the emergence a of a more equitable global economic order. None of these, however, is likely to happen without a concerted struggle, given the powerful forces and classes that benefit from the status quo. The last part of this essay addresses the issue of the nature of politics that will promote genuine democracy and emergence of people-centred development aimed at enhancing human flourishing on the continent. First the point must be made that extricating Africa from neoliberal imperialism and the institution of a developmental state and people democracy will not be a top-down but bottom-up event, if the hierarchies of power established by the Wallenstein's world system approach were anything to go by, Africa's salvation will not come from the metropole, neither will it come from their collaborators, the ruling class in the periphery (2004). This leaves us with the masses that bear the brunt of the misgovernance characteristic of many societies in Africa. Mahmood Mamdani (2012) hints at the locus of a possible African renaissance when he wrote:

> The antidote to the market was never the state but democracy. Not the state but a democratic political order has contained the worst fallout from capitalism over the last few centuries. The real custodian of a democratic order was never the state but society. The question we are facing today is not just that of market failure but of an all-round political failure.

The social mobilisation of the masses aimed at the expansion of popular participation is crucial to addressing the neoliberal underdevelopment and the all-round political failure occasioned by the misgovernance foisted on African societies by an ideologically and morally bankrupt political elite. As long as Africa remains constrained by neoliberal strictures, authentic and equitable development would elude the continent in perpetuity. From all indices, the neoliberal model, at best, can only deliver economic growth and radical inequality, but for reasons which are already discussed in the essay, economic growth in Africa remains a remote possibility. This why beyond sporadic protests and demonstrations against harsh economic conditions, the African masses must rise up to the occasion and organise themselves for the purpose of concerted and consistent political engagement of their respective governments in order to orchestrate the shifting of power back to the people, particularly with respect to the governance of the economy. One of the unfortunate fallouts of the imposition of the neoliberal doctrine on African societies is the removal of the governance of the economy from popular control. If Africa must generate just and human centred development, the arena of economic decision making must be subject to popular oversight.

In *the Wretched of the earth*, Fanon (1963) has argued that a revolutionary transformation of the African condition lies in the strategic alliance between the intelligentsia and the oppressed classes. The role of the intelligentsia is particular crucial in this quest. It must provide the intellectual leadership to the teeming masses and continuously deconstruct the neoliberal economic paradigm to supplant its hegemony in the development discourse until the masses become aware that neoliberalism is a major source of their economic predicament. It is with this alliance between the intelligentsia and the masses that, hopefully, popular forces within Africa can mount the politics of subversion to break the stranglehold of neoliberal ideology over the continent.

## 5 Conclusion

The main objective of this essay has been to demonstrate that contrary to dominant rhetoric and appearances, the imposition and uncritical implementation of the neoliberal ideology in many ways undermining genuine democracy and authentic development in Africa. In particular, an attempt was made to show the machinations that accompanied the process by which financially distressed African countries were mandated to implement Structural Adjustment Programmes, a one-size-fit-all basket of economic prescriptions, fails to pay adequate attention to the specificities of the various economies on which they were imposed. It is not surprising therefore, that the SAP and subsequent adaptations of the neoliberal economic paradigm failed to deliver on the promise of economic growth or even genuine democracy. Of course, the World Bank argued that Structural Adjustment Programmes failed because they were shabbily implemented, it should become clear from the analysis here that given the current development stage of most African countries, the neoliberal prescriptions were inappropriate and therefore could not have engendered development or democracy. More importantly, for the discerning, it is obvious that the development of adjusting countries have never been on the agenda. The spread of neoliberalism to Africa was rather motivated by the need to consolidate the project of global capitalist domination. It is for this reason, that an alliance involving the intelligentsia and masses must mobilise the politics of subversion to overthrow the dominance of neoliberalism over the economic affairs of the African peoples. Admittedly, this may not be sufficient for attainment of an authentic African development but it is a necessary first step.

## References


Abrahamsen, R. 2000. *Disciplining democracy*. London: Zed.

Ake, C. 1996. *Democracy and development in Africa*. Washington, DC: The Brookings Institute.

Akokpari, J.K. 2001. Meeting the challenges of sustainable democracy. In *Globalization, democracy and development*, ed. T. Assefa, A. Ahmed, A, and M. Severine, 83–100. Addis Ababa: OSSREA.

Biebricher, T. 2018. *Thepolitical theory of neoliberalism*. California: Stanford Press.

Bond, P. 2021. Neoliberalism, authoritarianism, and popular resistance in Africa. In *The global rise of authoritarianism in the 21st century crisis of neoliberal globalization and the nationalist response*, ed. B. Berberoglu, 133–158. New York: Routledge.

Byres, T.J. 2005. Neoliberalism and primitive accumulation in less developed countries. In *Neoliberalism: a critical reader*, ed. A. Saad-Filho and D. Johnston, 83–90. London: Pluto.

Cahill, D., et al. 2018. Introduction. In *The sage handbook of neoliberalism*, ed. D. Cahill, M. Cooper, M. Konings, and D. Primrose. London: Sage.

Chazan, N., P. Lewis, R. Mortimer, D. Rothchild, and S.J. Stedman. 1999. *Politics and society in contemporary Africa*. Boulder, CO: Lynne Rienner.

Chizea, B. 2020. Nigerian economy and fiscal sustainability. *This DayOnline,* viewed 21 August 2021. https://www.thisdaylive.com/index.php/2020/12.

Fanon, F. 1963. *The wretched of the earth.* Trans: C. Farrington. New York: Grove Press.

Gill, S. 2008. *Power and resistance in the new world order*. New York: Palgrave.

Giroux, H. 2008. *Against the terror of neoliberalism*. London: Paradigm Publishers.

Goldemberg, J. 1993. The 'leap-frogging' approach to national development. In *Facing the challenge: Responses to the report of the south commission*, 240–245. London: South Centre.

Harrisson, G. 2010. *Neoliberal Africa*. London: Zed.

Harvey, D. 2005. *A brief history of neoliberalism*. Oxford: Oxford University Press.

Haynes, J. 2001. *Democracy and political change in the "Third World"*. New York: Routledge.

Held, D. 1995. *Democracy and the global order*. California: Stanford University Press.

———. 2010. *Cosmopolitan ideals and realities*. Cambridge: Polity Press.

Hickel, J. 2012. *Ashort history of neoliberalism (and how we can fix it),* viewed 19 August 2021. www.newleftproject.org.

———. 2016. Neoliberalism and the end of democracy. In *The handbook of neoliberalism*, ed. S. Springer, K. Birch, and J. MacLeavy, 142–152. London: Routledge.

Hoogvelt, A. 2001. *Globalisation and the post-colonial world: The new politics of development*. Hampshire: Palgrave.

Kiely, R. 2005. Capitalist expansion and the imperialism–globalization debate: Contemporary Marxist explanations. *Journal of International Relations and Development* 8 (27): 38–57.

Kiely, R., and P. Marfleet. 1998. *Globalisation and the third world*. New York: Routledge.

Mafeje, A. 2002. Democratic governance and new democracy in Africa: Agenda for the future. In *NEPAD: A new path?* ed. P. Anyang Nyong'o, A. Ghirmazion, and D. Lamba, 72–87. Nairobi: Heinrich Boll Foundation.

Mamdani, M. 2012. The state, private sector and market failures: A response to Prof Joseph Stiglitz. *Pambazuka News 595*, viewed 19 August 2021. https://www.pambazuka.org/global-south/state-private-sector-and-market-failures.

Mcleavy, J. 2016. Neoliberalism and welfare. In *The handbook of neoliberalism*, ed. S. Springer, K. Birch, and J. MacLeavy, 252–261. London: Routledge.

Osimiri, P. 2020. Globalisation and the search for an authentic African democracy. *AMAMIHE: Journal of Applied Philosophy* 18 (9): 112–127.
Pogge, T. 2008. *World poverty and human rights. Cosmopolitan responsibilities and reforms.* Cambridge: Polity Press.
Purcell, M. 2008. *Recapturing democracy: Neoliberalization and the struggle for alternative urban futures.* New York: Routledge.
Rawls, J. 1999. *A theory of justice.* 2nd ed. Cambridge: Harvard University Press.
Scholte, J.A. 2008. *Globalization: A critical introduction.* 2nd ed. New York: Palgrave.
Tansel, C.B. 2018. Authoritarian neoliberalism and democratic backsliding in Turkey: Beyond the narratives of progress. *South European Society and Politics* 23 (2): 197–217.
Wallerstein, I. 2004. *World-systems analysis: An introduction.* 7th ed. Durham: Duke University Press.
Wengraf, L. 2018. *Extracting profit imperialism, neoliberalism, and the new scramble for Africa.* Chicago: Haymarket Books.
Wikan, V. 2015. *What is 'neoliberalism', and how does it relate to globalization?*, viewed 20 August 2021. https://www.e-ir.info/2015/03/21/.
World Bank. 1994. *Adjustment in Africa: Reforms, results and the road ahead.* Washington, DC: World Bank.
Zakaria, F. 1997. The rise of illiberal democracy. *Journal of Democracy* 76 (6): 22–43.

**Peter Osimiri** is a Senior Lecturer at the Department of Philosophy, University of Lagos. He specialises in Political Philosophy and Ethics, while his research interest straddles the subfields of Environmental Philosophy, Bioethics and Neoliberalism.

# Development Theories and Governance Ideologies Conundrums in Africa: An Observable Disconnects Between Values and Practices

**Stephen Nkansah Morgan and Beatrice Okyere-Manu**

**Abstract** For many decades, African theorists and ideologists have made it a preoccupation to discover values, ideas, models, and principles that are born out of African traditional and cultural ontologies—values of which, in their view, can and ought to be adopted as a better alternative solution to the political and social miseries facing contemporary African nations. Resultantly, the values of *Ubuntu* and African humanism dominate. These values found in indigenous African communitarian societies are not only employed by African scholars as a litmus paper to test the viability of prevailing theories and practices but have also become the foundational grounds upon which new theories are propounded as solutions for effective governance. These theories cover different fields of study ranging from religion and ethics to politics and economics. Based on this preoccupation, theories and ideologies such as African socialism, consensual democracy, African relational ethics, eco-bio-communitarianism, and African feminism, and many others, have emerged. Despite the above theorization based on traditional African values, African nations continue to grapple with the same old challenge of poverty, human rights abuses, lack of clear political ideology, moral and political corruption, and political and tribal conflicts among others. Through conceptual examination, the chapter does not only assess what could account for their failure but also makes sense of the conspicuous disconnect between these theories that are built on indigenous African values and the Africans' ways of life which do not reflect these values. The paper concludes by making recommendations on how we can, perhaps, bridge this gap.

S. N. Morgan
Department of Philosophy and Classics, University of Ghana, Accra, Ghana

B. Okyere-Manu (✉)
Applied Ethics, University of KwaZulu-Natal, Pietermaritzburg, KwaZulu-Natal, South Africa
e-mail: Okyere-manv@ukzn.ac.za



B. Okyere-Manu et al. (eds.), *Contemporary Development Ethics from an African Perspective*, Philosophy and Politics - Critical Explorations 27,
https://doi.org/10.1007/978-3-031-32898-5_5

## 1 Introduction

What is the African vision? Is there an African vision at all? Many African countries, decades after independence, continue in the struggle to find political and economic stability. The term good governance has become for many African countries a phantasm and for many African citizens an all-too-common aphorism flung at them by the numerous and ever-growing politicians anytime they mount a political stage. Whatever the notion of good governance is conjectured to mean, it appears that the African has not been able to properly make it work as made evident in the many socio-political quandaries confronting the people of the continent. As Uwaezuoke Precious Obioha and Godwin Okaneme correctly point out:

> Today Africa is certainly confronted with challenges of social unrest, general human life abuses and frustrations such that many years after independence of most African nations, much has not changed in the socio-humanistic experiences of Africa and Africans. Poor governance or bad governance and ineptitude leadership have become synonymous with most African states (2017:43).

To help grapple with the numerous struggles besetting the continent, African political theorists, nationalists, economists, and ethicists have formulated theories and models that they believe to be the best antidotes for the continent's predicaments. One can call this their postulation of the 'African vision'. In their effort to formulate a solution tailor-made to meet the challenges head-on, these theorists have formulated solutions premised on indigenous values and beliefs of the African people themselves. As Obioha and Godwin (2017:44) indicate: "Our philosophy must find its weapons in the environment and living conditions of the African people." For them, values within the African culture and belief systems are very relevant molding solutions to African problems. One of such solutions, according to Obioha and Okaneme, is found in what they consider to be an important constituent of African culture, that is, 'African humanism'. Similarly, the South African anti-apartheid activist, Stephen (Steve) Biko, in line with this approach of finding a solution to the African problem based on the people's own indigenous values asserted that:

> We must seek to restore to the black man the great importance we used to give to human relations, the high regard for people and their property and for life in general; to reduce the triumph of technology over man and the materialistic element that is slowly creeping into our society. These are essential features of our black cultures to which we must cling (Biko 2002:84).

The idea behind these attempts to discover or formulate theoretical and practical solutions that are born out of the people's own ontology, traditional practices, and indigenous value systems are perhaps based on two identifiable reasons; the first reason is to bring about a solution or envisage an African vision that can easily resonate with the African people themselves. Secondly, it is considered an attempt to move the African people away from the influences of Western values. In the words of Steve Biko (2002:84), "black culture above all implies freedom on our part to innovate without recourse to white values."

Resultantly, the indigenous value and principle of *Ubuntu*, communalism, the common good, or African humanism has dominated the African scholarly literature. The ethical values that are said to be found in African communitarianism have not only been employed by African scholars as a litmus paper to test the viability of prevailing theories and practices but have also become the foundational grounds upon which new theories are propounded as solutions for effective governance, social cohesion, and ethical living. Despite these attempts by the African theorists, not only have their proposed African-based solutions failed to make the necessarily impact but a conspicuous disconnect is observable between the ideals formulated in these theories presented as solutions and the way of life of the people. Olatunji Alabi Oyeshile (2007:235) notes this and posits that "the sense of community in Africa today is not only at its lowest ebb, it is also fast disappearing." It does, therefore, appear that African theorists are engaged in ivory-towerism, a state where there is a disconnect or a mismatch between values proposed in theories and values subscribed to by the people on the ground.

African leaders themselves are culprits of this disconnect between values and practice. They preach virtue and practice vice. African leaders have on several occasions pledged to uphold democracy yet held on to power and altered national constitutions to cement their grips on power. They pledge freedom of speech and free media in their countries but are alleged to trump down on the opposing press and intimidate citizens or opposition parties who speak against them. African leaders will call for probity and accountability of public officials and yet again have plenty of allegations of corruption and embezzlement levelled against them. They will promise their people good governance and rule of law and an all-inclusive government yet will before long be doing the very opposite. On this matter, Christopher Clapham (1970) correctly notes that there seem to be some acute problems in the connection between the actual practice of politics and the language that its practitioners use to describe it.

Thus, despite the many theorizations based on traditional African values, African nations continue to grapple with the same old challenge of poverty, human rights abuses, lack of clear political ideology, moral and political corruption, and political and tribal conflicts among others. The goal of this paper is, first, to assess why theories and ideologies that are based on indigenous African values fail to make anticipated impact. Second, to explore the reason for the disconnect between values that form the bases of theories and the ways of life of the African people that do not reflect these values. The paper does these by first exploring some conceptualizations of the African vision that were premised on traditional African values and communal structures and yet failed to make the anticipated impact. This will be followed by an exploration of the African values of humanism and *Ubuntu* as the main indigenous African values and how they manifest in African theories. Next, the chapter explores some likely reasons for the disconnect and failures of these theories and ideologies. Finally, the paper concludes by making recommendations on the way forward.

## 2 Visualizations of an 'African Vision'

The problems confronting the African continent are myriad, this is a given. It is also a given that there have been numerous attempts to find a way out of these conundrums. African nations, individually and collectively as regional and continental organizations, have since independence chartered an African vision that they want for themselves. From the writings and speeches of nationalists like Kwame Nkrumah, Jomo Kenyatta, Leopold Senghor, and Julius Nyerere to the works of professional academics, Charters, and policy documents of governments, regional, and continental organizations, one can perceive that there is at least some amount of genuineness in the desire to attain a better situation for the African people.

The 'African vision' for the African nationalists then was for an Africa free of imperialism. As Issa G. Shivji (2003) notes, the core objective of the African nationalists was anti-imperialism. Theirs was a demand and struggle against the denial of humanity, the denial of respect and dignity, and the denial of the 'Africanness' of the African. Shivji calls it the struggle for the "re-Africanisation of minds (2003:3)." Relatedly, the African nationalists also shared the pan-African vision which meant to express the identity or the Africanness of the African people and was considered a global movement to unite Africa and its people, both on the continent and in the Diaspora, against racial oppression and exploitation associated with Western and European dominations (Kah 2016; Shivji 2003). Kwame Nkrumah's primary vision, for example, was to see a breakdown of colonialism in Africa. In addition, he wanted to see "the restoration of the dignity that was lost as a result of slavery and colonialism to enable the African to function freely in the coming unified world society as an equal player and partner" (Dodoo 2012:79). A vision which the African continent is still in pursuit today. Furthermore, the pan-African vision included the call for an African continental unity, a United States of Africa pioneered by Nkrumah and Nyerere (Kah 2016; Shivji 2003). Nkrumah and Nyerere, together with some of their contemporaries, believed strongly that a united Africa would facilitate the liberation struggle from imperialism and neo-colonialism and strengthen solidarity among the African people, a feat yet to be attained in its proper sense to date.

Since its creation in May of 1963, the Organization of African Unity (OAU), now the African Union (AU), has come up with its own envisaged vision for the continent through agreements, charters and agendas. Some of these agreements include the Lagos Plan of Action (1980), Africa's Priority Programme for Economic Recovery (1986–1990), the African Alternative Framework to Structural Adjustment Programme (1989), the African (Arusha) Charter for Popular Participation and Development (1990), the Abuja Treaty (1991), and the Cairo Agenda (1994). The most recent one is the African Agenda 2063 which was proposed in May of 2013 when African leaders converged in Addis Ababa to commemorate the 50th anniversary of the founding of the OAU. The vision of this Agenda 2063 reads: "the continent re-dedicated herself to the attainment of the Pan-African Vision of an integrated, prosperous and peaceful Africa, driven by its own citizens, representing a dynamic force in the international arena (African Union Commission 2015a:11)."

The individual goals of Agenda 2063 are spelt out under seven different chapters as follows:

1. A prosperous Africa based on inclusive growth and sustainable development
2. An integrated continent, politically united and based on the ideals of Pan-Africanism and the vision of Africa's Renaissance
3. An Africa of good governance, democracy, respect for human rights, justice and the rule of law
4. A peaceful and secure Africa
5. An Africa with a strong cultural identity, common heritage, shared values and ethics
6. An Africa whose development is people-driven, relying on the potential of African people, especially its women and youth, and caring for children
7. Africa as a strong, united and influential global player and partner (African Union Commission 2015b:2)

Beyond the AU, there are also regional blocks like the Economic Community of West African States (ECOWAS) in West Africa, the East African Community (EAC) in East Africa, and the Southern African Development Community (SADC) in Southern Africa, among others. These regional organisations have also articulated their own agendas alongside those of the African Union. ECOWAS, for example, adopted the Vision 2020 resolution in June 2007. The ECOWAS Vision 2020, according to the ECOWAS website, is aimed at setting a clear direction and goal to significantly raise the standard of living of the people through conscious and inclusive programmes that will guarantee a bright future for West Africa and shape the destiny of the region for many years to come (ECOWAS.INT n.d.). The SADC Vision 2050 also aims to position the SADC region in a context of emerging global and continental issues such as climate change, the democratisation of the United Nations and increasing financial instability (Ngwawi 2012)."

Furthermore, we have individual countries articulating their own development plans. Thus, we can speak of the South African National Development Plan 2030 which seeks to eliminate poverty and reduce inequality by 2030. It also aims to create a South Africa where everybody feels free yet bounded to others; where everyone embraces their full potential and proud to be a community that cares. There is also Zimbabwe's vision 2030 announced by President Emmerson Mnangagwa last year aimed to ensure that Zimbabwe becomes an upper-middle-class economy by the year 2030.

A prima facie assessment of these envisioned visions for the African continent shows the thoughtfulness and usefulness of their goals and objectives. However, a good retrospection of past agendas and visions and the failure to attain their set objectives may bring one to doubt the possibility of the future successes of these new visions. Amadu Sesay (2008:27), for instance, notes concerning the OAU that one of its major failures was its inefficiency to bolster economic development, democracy, good governance, and rule of law in its Member States and as a result Africa continues to be the most economically deprived continent in the world. Similarly, Alhaji Ahmadu Ibrahim (2016:3) points out that when the OAU, regarded then as a "toothless bulldog" that did not have the wherewithal to hurl the continent to greatness, was transformed into the African Union, it was anticipated that there will be a structured and well-established systemic reforms that will propel prodigious gains however, the results are much more unsatisfactory. In reference to SADC, Anne Hammerstad states that on paper, SADC can be considered as a momentous force in the economic, political and security dynamics of the Southern African region, yet in reality, the picture is quite different. Furthermore, "almost since the birth of SADC in 1992, the gap between protocols signed and their implementation is big and widening, creating a credibility problem for the organisation" (Hammerstad 2003:1–2). It is, therefore, important for us to come to an understanding of why many of these programmes, agendas, and visions fail.

In the section that follows, we will explore the indigenous African values of humanism and *Ubuntu* and how they feature as the bases of many conceptualized African theories. This will be followed by an assessment of the potential causes of the disconnect and failures of these theories.

## 3 Indigenous African Values in Theories and Ideologies

As was mentioned in the introduction, in a bid to address the problems of the continent and create a prosperous future for the African people, scholars and politicians alike have hypothesized and employed varied theories and ideologies that they perceive can effectively get the job done. Most of these theories and political ideologies are built on and from the traditional values and socio-religio-cultural practices of traditional African people. The theorists and politicians presume and postulate that their proposals or strategies to be the right solutions because they believe that theories or policies founded on the beliefs and practices of their people maintains their Africanness in character and can better resonate with the people than those based on foreign values. In this section, we look at some of these theories and the African values that they are derived from.

The African value of humanism is the most dominant theory in the literature on African values though they may be expressed with different terminologies such as *Ubuntu, Boto, Ukama, Umundu, Bumuntu* communalism or the common good, depending on which part of Africa you are or who is writing. African humanism is associated with the communal values and customs of the traditional African ethnic community. It is considered a philosophy which seeks to promote the good of the human person in general and as such making the welfare of people the central objective of policies (Eleojo 2014:298; Pietersen 2005:54).

Obioha and Godwin (2017:47) note that the philosophy of African humanism stands on three major values. There is first, an expression of a strong aversion for absolute individualism, the kind which could lead to a harmful and excessive rivalries and intrapersonal conflicts, and personal enrichment of public officials. Secondly, African humanism supports a community-based society which augments the virtues of social well-being, synergy, solidarity, cooperative togetherness, interdependence and reciprocal obligation, values that are regarded as promotive of social justice. Thirdly, African humanism has a theistic underpinning which brings a spiritual dimension to its understanding. This theistic underpinning is said to complement and satisfy humans' spiritual needs and longings and help humans to treat each other well because created we are created in God's own image. Obioha and Okaneme were positive that a blend of these values found in African humanism can lead to "practical consequences that will concretize the reality of wholesome human relationship which is necessary for the actualization of life's aspirations both for the individual and for the community at large" (2017:47).

Rob Gaylard correctly points to the centrality of the value of African humanism in, for example, the ideologies of the African nationalists. He asserts that:

> In seeking to construct an alternative value system to that imposed on them through colonialism, African thinkers and political leaders have asserted or appealed to an African humanism in one form or another – Nkrumah's "Conscientism", Nyerere's "Ujamaa", Kaunda's "African Humanism", Biko's "Black Consciousness" (2004:267).

It is common knowledge that underpinning Nkrumah's major works on political philosophy that pointed to the dangers in neocolonialism and imperialism and Nkrumah's guide towards socioeconomic transformation in a united Africa were core values found in traditional African societies. These included African ethics, African humanism, and communalistic ethos (Botwe-Asamoah 2005:41). Nkrumah pushed for a political ideology he labelled 'African socialist'. Nkrumah was convinced that this African socialist ideology was a derivative of the communal set up of traditional Africa, that is, in term of its institutions such as the clan and the emphasis on the equality of all and the responsibility of many for one (Botwe-Asamoah 2005:42). Deji Adesoye further notes that:

> The central theme in African socialism is African communalism. African communalism maintains that the central values of Africans in the traditional societies were communal rather than individualistic. Individualism belongs to the West while communalism belongs to Africa. It is believed that traditional African society had shared values wherein every man and woman lived as in a family. Therefore, the guerrillas of Africa socialism regarded socialism as a direct metamorphose of communalism (2017:3).

Despite this, as Bernard Matolino (2012) points out, African socialism did not record any notable achievement on the African continent, instead, the various leaders who were either convinced or motivated by it led their respective countries into serious problems. Some nations, Matolino notes, based on the adoption of this African socialism ideology became stagnated or even saw a decline in their economic status while others turn into a one-party autocracies "where the citizens were alienated from all ideals that the humanism of socialism was supposed to represent and bring" (2012:116).

Relatedly, *Ubuntu* as another expression of this African humanism is used to express an African outlook of life and the world in which people share and treat each other as humans, based on an underlying 'universal brotherhood' of Africans (Eliastam 2015:2). Mogobe B. Ramose (2002) describes *Ubuntu* as the root and basis of African philosophy, the wellspring flowing with African ontology and epistemology. Attributes associated with *Ubuntu* in the literature are myriad and include acting humanely towards others, having harmonious relations with others, sharing identity with the community, and the show of solidarity with others. Rob Gaylard (2004:271) notes that *Ubuntu* has rather become a term that readily assumes different forms and has been appealed to or used in many different fields including religion, education, ethics, jurisprudence, and business management.

Similarly, Matolino and Wenceslaus Kwindingwi (2013) point us to what they call the 'commercialisation' of *Ubuntu* in South Africa. Thus, one can find the Ubuntu School of Philosophy (Pretoria), Ubuntu Security Company (Pietermaritzburg), Ubuntu Security Alarm Systems (Gauteng), Ubuntu Education Fund and Ubuntu Centre (Port Elizabeth), among many others. Gaylard (2004) adds that there are also Ubuntu Food Distributors, Ubuntu Cash Loans, and Ubuntu Training and Management Consultants. For Gaylard, perhaps *Ubuntu* is incorporated in these businesses as an instrument to increase productivity or promote the company's brand. He, however, questions the effectiveness of this.

In reference to democracy, Daniel Osabu-Kle (2000) relies on the presupposition that Africa had an indigenous political culture which was essentially democratic and consensual to propose that for modern Africa to attain favourable political conditions that can facilitate needed development, it needs to adopt a democracy that is well-matched with the African cultural environment. In light of this attempt to Africanize democracy, many African scholars have been attempting to conceptualize for the African continent the idea of a consensual democracy as a better alternative to the majoritarian democracy we are used to. Consensual democracy, defined generally as the participation of all who matter in the decision making of the state through extensive deliberation of issues until a consensus is reached, has been argued by most of these scholars to be a derivative of African humanism and African indigenous political communal structure. (See, for example, Ajei 2016; Wiredu 1996). Outside politics, African humanism has been proposed as a tool for business management and effective business interactions. As Barbara Nussbaum (2009:249) saw it, "*Ubuntu* can help to foster the human qualities of humility over arrogance, co-operation over domination and generosity over greed, not only within but between companies and in their relationships with stakeholders in other countries." In the area of good environmental practices and sustainable environmental practices in Africa, the likes of Segun Ogungbemi, Godfrey Tangwa, Thaddeus Metz, Felix Murove, Kevin Behrens, and others have also immensely relied on African indigenous practices to propose various theories that they consider viable to address the environmental challenges of the continent. Ogungbemi's (1997), for example, proposed the ethics of nature-relatedness, which he argues can lead to a peaceful coexistence between humans and nature. Tangwa's (2004) proposed eco-bio-communitarian ethic is meant to recognize the interdependency of humans and nature. These two environmental theories were derived from the African indigenous communal relationship with the natural environment. Relatedly, the proposed African environmental justice theory referred to as eco-collective responsibility theory proposed by Ssebunya et al. (2019) was mainly centered on the communal character of traditional African societies.

Similar arguments have, of course, been advanced in the areas of healthcare and sciences as well as in various aspects of the human life including the proposal to employ moral principles of *Ubuntu* as a tool for the moral regeneration of today's African societies. Thus, it suffices to say that African humanism and *Ubuntu* have been employed in all sectors in the attempt to charter or forge a prosperous African vision. However, much of these old visions have failed to yield the expected fruits and as a result, placing doubts on the viability of these emerging theories and proposals that are also embedded in African indigenous values.

## 4 Assessing the Reason for the Disconnect and Failures

The many attempts in the past decades to forge the African vision based on indigenous African values and belief systems and the little impact these attempts have made should make anyone wonder why this has been the case. The incessant and common-place use of African humanism and *Ubuntu* as a bedrock for most African ideologies and theories and the modicum of impression they have on the ordinary person, again, cause one to wonder whether these concepts do not in the process become devalued. John L. B. Eliastam was, for instance, positive that: "the notion of *Ubuntu* appears to have been eroded to the extent that it currently seems unable to play a meaningful role in nation building" (2015:1). More scepticism is expressed by Herman Johan Pietersen (2005) that despite the encouraging empirical research done in Africa to date, these researches do not offer strong indications as to the deeper nature, function, or impact of African humanism in the South African workplace.

Perhaps Christoph Marx and Pietersen give a hint on one possible reason for the inability of these theories and ideologies to make a significant impact. Marx describes *Ubuntu* as "an invented tradition, whose task it is to minimise historical chasms and fractures" and also as a form "a cultural essentialism" (2002: 59). Pietersen notes that the literature on African humanism tends to be "monocular, conceptually muddled and utopian" (2005:54). We agree with Marx and Pietersen on the score that the literature on African humanism presents an appearance of the existence of a single monotonous and ubiquitous values in indigenous Africa. One is made to believe that nearly everyone in traditional Africa subscribed to this monolithic value of African humanism or *Ubuntu*. Meanwhile, it is very likely and not implausible, as Matolino and Kwindingwi (2013) also thought, for there to have been other values in traditional African societies, albeit not dominant. Again, in concordance with Matolino and Kwindingwi, the fact that these alternative values or modes of being African do not receive similar attention as *Ubuntu* or African humanism does not imply that they were or are any less African or any less authentic (Matolino and Kwindingwi 2013:201).

This point is very relevant because the inability to recognise the existence of multiple values is made worse by the inability of African theorists and ideologists to recognise the plurality and validity of other values subscribed to by the African person today, values of which some may or may not have any derivation from indigenous African values. The possibility of this, of course, should not be difficult to conceptualize giving the extensive impact of globalization and fortunately or unfortunately, Westernization and Europeanization on the African continent. Thus, much of Africa today is cosmopolitan in character at different intensities; cosmopolitan in terms of the conglomeration of different people from different part of the world working and living on the continent or in terms of the influence of ideas, cultures, values and practices from different part of the world on the way of life of the African people. This, evidently, is propelled by the growth and expansion of the internet and technology in general. Resultantly, the African today are given lots choices when it comes to values and cultures to pick from.

It is, therefore, possible that while African theorists and ideologists engage traditional African values to harness positive principles to address African challenges of today, the ordinary African is out of touch with these traditional values and as a result participating in a different set of values that are entirely incongruent with these African values—to such an extent that the theories that emerge from the engagement of the traditional African values, at the end of the day, fail to work because the people cannot relate or associate with them. Thus, the inability to recognise the plurality of values, in spite of traditional African values, that exist for the African today is a possible explanation to why theories and ideologies fail.

Furthermore, even if we are to accept that African humanism or *Ubuntu* was the prevailing value in traditional Africa, the attempt to repackage it as the best solution for African moral, social, political, economic, and even religious woes today may miss the mark. Relatedly, Matolino and Kwindingwi (2013:201) refer to what they call "revivalism", which they describe as the attempt to see everything African to be found in the pristine state of Africa prior to slavery and colonialism. We are, however, referring to the false illusion that only solutions based on the indigenous values and practices of traditional Africa are capable of solving Africa's present predicament. This illusion gives the impression that indigenous Africa, prior to its contact with the West, was, because of the spirit of *Ubuntu* or humanism, living in an idyll state that was conflict-free, lack of impoverishment, crimeless, and classless. It is this impression that, perhaps, Marx had described as "an invented tradition" and Pietersen calls a "utopian".

The act of falling on African indigenous values and practices every time to solve all the modern challenges of Africa today misses the mark because rural traditional Africa, as we know it, was predominantly conservative while the Africa we have today is noticeably becoming liberal by the day. As a result, traditional practices that were encouraged then, such as arranged and forced marriages, though sparsely exist today, are no more popular occurrences. Today, most of us will generally frown upon these practices. In the spirit of *Ubuntu*in traditional communal society, resources and benefits were more likely to be available to all members of the society (Obioha and Godwin 2017). However, this cannot be said of African societies today. The economic conditions, the depletion of natural resources, and high population numbers today make these impracticable. Today, even sustaining ties and maintaining solidarity with the extended family, which hitherto was an essential feature of traditional Africa, is a challenge, not because there is no desire to do so, but largely because of prevailing living economic conditions that require family members to travel far and near in search of work. Thus, perhaps, there is a need for ideologists and theorists to put this into account in the visualizations of the new African vision.

Another crucial point worth pointing to is how the literature on African theories and ideologies often antagonize traditional African values with Western values. Thus, it is usually made to look like African and Western values are mutually exclusive, that is, to appropriate Western values is to reject one's Africanness and to embrace African values is to reject Western values in toto. This is not the case and need not be the case at all. Again, it is possible for one to adhere to a multiplicity of values, values whether from Africa or elsewhere without any contradiction or a lessening in the effectiveness of that value to deal with an African challenge. This is not to be understood as a call to reject African values but instead, a call to appreciate that while these African values may exist, there are in existence other values as well, values that arguably may be more familiar with the people than those of their remote ancestors.

## 5 Recommendations and Conclusion

The goal of the paper is not to argue that indigenous African values and socio-cultural practices ought not to be regarded in modern theories, policies, or ideologies but rather to assess why despite decades of theorizing and ideologizing based on these indigenous African values and socio-cultural practices there have not been much positive progress on addressing the African predicaments. As Martin Trump tacitly puts it: "The central tension in black South African writing is between the violence of the society and the sense of communalism in the black communities" (Trump 1988:34 as cited by Gaylard 2004:276). Thus, we have tried to come to some understanding of this disconnect that exists between values that are expressed in theories and ideologies and way of life of the African people that do not reflect these values.

It is common for a typical theory based on African communalism to place more emphasis on community goals and interests over that of the individual, yet as Pietersen points out, "both individualist and collectivist views of humans are necessary but insufficient explanations of the reality of human nature" (2005:59). Implicatively, African theorists and ideologists must take this into cognisance and put across theories that do not entirely engulf the individual interest into the interest of the community. Kwame Gyekye (1997) had, perhaps, pointed us to this in his advocate for 'moderate communitarianism', which balances group responsibility with individual rights.

Nevertheless, it appears that African theorists, have placed very little emphasis on the important implication of this in terms of advancing appropriate theories and ideologies that harness some of the advantages of individualism—for certainly there are some merits to be found in individualism such as its promotion of individual creativity and initiatives. It is therefore essential that this features in the theorizing of the African vision and in the proposed solutions to the African challenges. Pietersen, again, is accurate in expressing that "self and society may be juxtaposed intellectually but is, in reality, an inseparable whole and can neither component ever be disregarded or abolished, without consequently attenuating any meaningful discussion of the human condition" (2005:59).

Beatrice Okyere-Manu (2018) notes that a dilemma faced by African theorists and other stakeholders today is how to practically integrate African indigenous knowledge with that of the West. In light of the plurality of values for the modern day African, values which include those that are African and those that are not, the goal of African theorists and ideologists should not be focused only on finding a theory that is necessarily based on indigenous African values but in finding a solution that works. As Gyekye (2004:41) indicates, all things or activities are valuable only insofar as they enhance human well-being and as a result, human well-being ought to be made the common measure by which cultures can be evaluated. Thus the focus should be placed in finding solutions that work and not necessarily in solutions that are African.

In any event, if we are to maintain that the solutions to the African problems lie in theories based in indigenous African values then there is a need for these African values to be made relevant in the everyday practical affairs of the people. Principles of *Ubuntu* or African humanism must be taught to the people as part of their early childhood education so that it is imprinted in their moral psychology as they grow. When this happens, ideologies and philosophies that are built on *Ubuntu* or African humanism will not appear utopian or based on some ivory-towerism because, this time, the people can relate accordingly.

## References

Adesoye, D. 2017. African socialism in Nkrumah and Nyerere. *Philosophy Pathways* 216: 1–11.

African Union Commission. 2015a. *Agenda 2063: First ten-year implementation plan 2014–2023*. Available at: https://www.un.org/en/africa/osaa/pdf/au/agenda2063-first10year implementation.pdf. Accessed 17 June 2019.

———. 2015b. *Agenda 2063: The African we want*. Popular edition. Available at: https://www.un.org/en/africa/osaa/pdf/au/agenda2063.pdf. Accessed 17 June 2019.

Ajei, M.O. 2016. Kwasi Wiredu's consensual democracy: Prospects for practice in Africa. *European Journal of Political Theory* 15 (4): 445–466.

Biko, S.B. 2002. Black consciousness and the quest for a true humanity. In *The African philosophy reader*, ed. P.H. Coetzee and A.P.J. Roux, 2nd ed., 79–86. New York: Routledge.

Botwe-Asamoah, K. 2005. *Kwame Nkrumah's politico-cultural thought and policies: An African-centered paradigm for the second phase of the African revolution*. New York: Routledge.

Clapham, C. 1970. The context of African political thought. *The Journal of Modem African Studies* 8 (1): 1–13.

Dodoo, V. 2012. Kwame Nkrumah's mission and vision for Africa and the world. *The Journal of Pan African Studies* 4 (10): 78–92.

Ecowas.int. n.d. Vision 2020. Available at: https://ecowas.int/about-ecowas/vision-2020/. Accessed 20 July 2020.

Eleojo, E.F.E. 2014. Africans and African humanism: What prospects? *American International Journal of Contemporary Research* 4 (1): 297–308.
Eliastam, J.L.B. 2015. Exploring Ubuntu discourse in South Africa: Loss, liminality and hope. *Verbum et Ecclesia* 36 (2): 1–8.
Gaylard, R. 2004. Welcome to the world of our humanity: (African) humanism, *Ubuntu* and black South African writing. *Journal of Literary Studies* 20 (3–4): 265–282.
Gyekye, K. 2004. *Beyond cultures. Perceiving a common humanity*. Accra: Ghana Academy of Arts and Sciences.
———. 1997. *Tradition and modernity: Philosophical reflections on the African experience*. Oxford: Oxford University Press.
Hammerstad, A. 2003. *Defending the state or protecting the people? SADC security integration at a crossroads*. Braamfontein: The South African Institute of International Affairs.
Ibrahim, A.A. 2016. African union and the challenges of underdevelopment in contemporary Africa. *British Journal of Education, Society & Behavioural Science* 14 (4): 1–10.
Kah, H.K. 2016. Kwame Nkrumah and the panfrican vision: Between acceptance and rebuttal. *Austral: Brazilian Journal of Strategy & International Relations* 5 (9): 141–164.
Marx, C. 2002. Ubu and Ubuntu: On the dialectics of apartheid and nation building. *South African Journal of Political Studies* 29 (1): 49–69.
Matolino, B. 2012. Democracy, consensus, and Africa: An investigation into consensual democracy's contribution to African political philosophy. *Philosophia Africana* 14 (2): 105–124.
Matolino, B., and W. Kwindingwi. 2013. The end of Ubuntu. *South African Journal of Philosophy* 32 (2): 197–205.
Nussbaum, B. 2009. Ubuntu and business: Reflections and questions. In *African ethics: An anthology of comparative and applied ethics*, ed. F.M. Murove, 238–258. Scottsville: University of KwaZulu-Natal Press.
Ngwawi, J. 2012. Vision 2050 SADC ponders future. *SADC Today* 14 (4): 1–2. Available at: https://www.sardc.net/editorial/sadctoday/documents/v14n3.pdf. Accessed 19 June 2019.
Obioha, U.P., and O. Godwin. 2017. African humanism as a basis for social cohesion and human Well-being. *Africa International Journal of Humanities Social Sciences and Education (IJHSSE)* 4 (5): 43–50.
Ogungbemi, S. 1997. An Africa perspective on the environmental crisis. In *Environmental ethics: Readings in theory and application*, ed. L.J. Pojman, 2nd ed., 265–270. Belmont, CA: Wadsworth Publishing Company.
Okyere-Manu, B. 2018. The paradox of adoption and adaption of African indigenous knowledge and Western knowledge systems. In *Intersecting African indigenous knowledge systems and Western knowledge systems: Moral convergence and divergence*, ed. B. Okyere-manu and H. Moyo. Pietermaritzburg: Cluster Publications.
Osabu-Kle, D. 2000. *Compatible cultural democracy: The key to development in Africa*. Toronto: University of Toronto Press.
Oyeshile, O.A. 2007. Sense of community and its sustenance in Africa. *Human Affairs* 17: 230–240.
Pietersen, H.J. 2005. Western humanism, African humanism and work organizations. *SA The Journal of Individual Psychology* 31 (3): 54–61.
Ramose, M.B. 2002. The philosophy of *Ubuntu* and *Ubuntu* as a philosophy. In *The African philosophy reader*, ed. P.H. Coetzee and A.P.J. Roux, 2nd ed., 230–238. New York: Routledge.
Sesay, A. 2008. The African union: Forward march or about face-turn? In *Claude Ake memorial papers no. 3. Department of peace and conflict research*. Uppsala: Uppsala University & Nordic Africa Institute. Available at: http://nai.diva-portal.org/smash/get/diva2:278874/FULLTEXT01.pdf. Accessed 21 May 2019.
Shivji, I.G. 2003. *The rise, the fall, and the insurrection of nationalism in Africa*. Keynote Address to the CODESRIA East African Regional Conference held in Addis Ababa, Ethiopia, October 29–31, 2003.

Ssebunya, M., S.N. Morgan, and B.D. Okyere-Manu. 2019. Environmental justice: Towards an African perspective. In *African environmental ethics. The international library of environmental, agricultural and food ethics*, ed. M. Chemhuru, vol. 29. Cham: Springer.

Tangwa, G.B. 2004. Some African reflections on biomedical and environment ethics. In *A companion to African philosophy*, ed. K. Wiredu, 387–395. Oxford: Blackwell Publishing Ltd.

Trump, M. 1988. Black South African short fiction in English since 1976. *Research in African Literatures* 19 (1): 34–64.

Wiredu, K. 1996. *Cultural universals and particulars*. Bloomington: Indiana University Press.

**Stephen Nkansah Morgan** is currently a lecturer with the Department of Philosophy and Classics of the University of Ghana where he teaches a wide range of philosophy and ethic courses at both graduate and undergraduate levels. Stephen holds a PhD in Ethics Studies from the University of KwaZulu-Natal in South Africa, and a Master of Philosophy and Bachelor of Arts degrees in Philosophy both from the University of Ghana. He has research interests in Environmental and Animal Ethics, Ethics of Technology, Social and Political Philosophy, and African philosophy broadly construed. He has previously taught at the University of Kwazulu-Natal in South Africa.

**Beatrice Okyere-Manu** is a Professor in the Applied Ethics department at the University of KwaZulu-Natal in Pietermaritzburg. Her research interests cover the following areas: HIV and AIDS, Ethical issues Affecting African Women, AIKS, Ethics of Technology, and Environmental Ethics. She has written a number of journal articles and book chapters in these areas. She recently edited a book on "African Values, Ethics, and Technology: Questions, Issues, and Approaches" which provides critical and ethical reflections on technology from an African perspective. She co-edited a book on "Intersecting African Indigenous Knowledge Systems and Western Knowledge Systems: Moral convergence and divergence".

# The Moral Dimension of Development in Zimbabwe

**Nomatter Sande**

**Abstract** Regardless of the availability of gold, diamonds, platinum and arable land, Zimbabweans experience abject poverty because of poor resource management. In Africa, most politicians and elite religious actors are guilty of corruption, greed, cheating, violation of human rights and individual amassing of wealth. Such behaviour by African leaders disrupt the Africa's traditional development ethos bundled in communalism and collectivism. Besides arguing that morality is a fundamental principle which substance development, this paper explores moral ethos that defines development, including ethical judgement for a good life, good society, and good relationships. The paper concludes that African Indigenous Knowledge Systems, culture, philosophy and morality are toolkits for development in Africa.

**Keywords** African traditional religion · Indigenous knowledge systems · Culture · Ubuntu · Moral ethos for development · Zimbabwe · African spiritual-moral theology

## 1 Introduction

The term development is broad and complex, and in this paper, I define the term development as a process of enhancing human lives through addressing issues of political, economic, social, cultural and the empowerment of people. Some African thinkers have ascribed slavery and colonialism are the cause of underdevelopment in Africa (Mawere 2017). In view of Mawere's argument, regardless of the end of slavery and colonisation Africa is not developing. Therefore, development in Africa should be unpacked using the problems within African context. It is helpful to heed the call that development in Africa calls for "concerted effort from all stakeholders"

N. Sande (✉)
Research Institute for Theology and Religion (RITR), College of Human Sciences, University of South Africa (UNISA), Pretoria, South Africa



B. Okyere-Manu et al. (eds.), *Contemporary Development Ethics from an African Perspective*, Philosophy and Politics - Critical Explorations 27, https://doi.org/10.1007/978-3-031-32898-5_6

(Sande and Denga 2019:267). For instance, development in Africa must focus on promoting social justice, equality and economic growth.

Further, I advance the notion that morality is a critical component of development in Africa. In the African sense, morality embeds the intrinsic values that emanate from the family and community values. According to Marchand (2003), it is the actions of the community which produce knowledge. Accordingly, African societies are responsible for defining what is morally right and codes that define these parameters, for instance Africans encourages mutual progress and discourages being apathetic towards other's suffering. Thus, to understand morality in African thought, it is helpful to peep into how Africans acquire knowledge. Africans acquire knowledge from the experiences of elders. Therefore, the elders demonstrated how to live and respect others. Morality is about distinctions between good or right and wrong or evil. Such principles give morality an authoritative code about how people conduct themselves. African morality, ethics and value systems are the glue to the social and economic transformation, especially how people view good life, good society, and good relationships. I suggested that development ethics should include reflections stemming from colonisation, post-second war development policies and strategies.

The claims of Croaker and others who link development only to issues of colonisation and anything related to the West is misleading because it takes away the role of African leadership in issues of development. Unfortunately, world development analysts have tied the concept of development only to economic and technological progress neglecting the moral dimension. African spirituality has a role in development, especially when one considers issues of morality. African spirituality is the moral campus of the indigenous society. It is worth mentioning that African spirituality lenses has a potential to articulate how Africans understand the concept of development. I strongly believe that while scientific approaches have been the focus to deal with underdevelopment issues, but it is high time to think about the moral dimension of morality to Zimbabwe. Accordingly, Ruben (2011:225) argued that "the basic foundations for development studies precisely lies in ethical concerns about persistent poverty and marginalisation of poor countries and the exclusion of poor people upon decolonisation". As a point of departure, there are differences between the West and indigenous culture notions of development. Notions of development from the western context is an offshoot of secularism and secularisation (Gunda 2020). The western scientific approach to development concentrates on developing 'good policies' and 'good institutions' as controls for economic development. These policies seem to bring good results in the West. Subsequently, the developed world exerts enormous pressure on the developing countries to demonstrate good democracy, an independent judiciary and governance.

The question that is taking long to be answered African scholars is whether these recommended Western policies and institutions are appropriate to the contemporary African context. Curiously, it is possible that people find it hard to accept that most scientific methods have not successfully influenced Africa's development. If this position is anything to go by, then it is areality that the most plausible scientific approach to development has created disruptions and dilutions to African worldviews of development to a greater extent. The idea that anything emerging from the West is special needs to be tested again in the twenty-first century. I put the motion that development is closely linked to morality. Morality has also to be considered from indigenous culture, traditions, and value system. Since development involves human contribution, the place of Africans' perspectives about development issues is critical. African spirituality has remained the epitome force that permeates all aspects of life, enhancing peoples' morality, well-being by paying attention to rituals and spiritual dispositions. From an African spiritual-moral theology perspective, this chapter explores moral ethos that defines development, including ethical judgement for a good life, good society, and good relationships.

## 2 Challenges of Development in Zimbabwe

While there are many factors that hinder development, but the main culprit is the lack of considering the role of morality to development. Accordingly, to put this study in context Zimbabwe, there is a gap to explore the role of the moral dimension of development to alleviate corruption, greedy, human misery, and environmental crisis. The reason for this status quo is the lack of morality. For instance, the presence of resources, which includes but is not limited to gold, diamonds, platinum and arable land, is a blessing to which all Zimbabweans can benefit. On the contrary, most Zimbabweans live in abject poverty, with political elites and their subordinates' realising dividends of wealth generated from natural resources. Those who escape poverty are linked to people in echelons of power who have a better political influence. The political influence has also become one of the sources which trigger rampant corruption in Zimbabwe. Mostpoliticians and some religious actors are guilty of corruption, violation of human rights and act above the confines of the rule of law. The unequal distribution of resources is the source of corruption and violence as people seek to survive or grab something from the few hands amassing wealth for themselves. In my view, to ease guilty conscience against the poor, the politicians blame colonial legacies as the main culprit. During the colonial period, Africans indeed embraced the Western ideology and philosophy of living an individualistic life. In this way, wealth is accumulated by individuals, not a community. Individualism is Western, whereas African ethos zeroes on communalism which cultivates Ubuntu among communities. According to Sjostrom et al. (2017), the West uses individualistic pedagogical philosophy of empowerment.

Iblame the impact of colonisation on Zimbabwe, but there is more to the failure of development in Zimbabwe than the arrival of the colonisers. It is correct to accept that there was a notable development in Zimbabwe during the rule of the colonial regime. Kristof (2017) argued that Robert Gabriel Mugabe destroyed all the economy that Rhodesia built. Beyond, 1980 independence it is not an overstatement to think that development has not moved much past the colonial leadership. Instead of progressing with the established development frameworks from the colonial era, nationalists through socialism chose to spoil Zimbabweans with free services. These services were free education, health, and many subsidies that were not complemented by better developmental policies. A possible explanation for this is that politicians felt obligated to honour their promises to the people. According to Gunda (2020:37),"Zimbabwe has been described as having been the "breadbasket" of Africa at independence in 1980, that gradually deteriorated to becoming the "basket case" of Africa". Further, the Fast-Track Land Reform was a haphazard ransacking of the farming sector, one of the significant streams of economic stability in Zimbabwe. To a greater extent, the Fast-Track Land Reform was a reactionary political project against the rising opposition party Movement for Democratic Change (MDC). The MDC was viewed as a project of the wealthy white commercial farmers together with the Western nations. In essence, proper indigenous developmental methods were not used.

## 3 Connections Between African Spirituality and Development in Zimbabwe

The theme of spirituality is gaining traction in modern life and the academic level. The study uses African spirituality as conceptual lenses to understand how Zimbabweans formulate notions of development. I define African spirituality as a belief about the holistic permeation of religion to all aspects of life including but not limited to the social, economic and political spheres. The use of the connectivity of African spirituality to development issues is a departure from the current western categorisation of development which stems from rationalism. African epistemology about development stems from the deep-rooted spirituality which moulds the total person and their behaviour towards development. It can be suggested that development in African should be considered in a humanistic and holistic sense. Also, the link between African Spirituality and development involves how Africans know things. McNabb (2019:1) argued that religious epistemology is responsible for "how epistemic concepts relate to religious beliefs and practices". Accordingly, this can be distinguished from the Western scientific approach, which uses cognitive lenses to develop policies and development strategies. The use of African spirituality in this study helps to appreciate that Africa's development's core problem is the subjugation of African moral ethics by scientific ideologies. The western paradigms of epistemology disenfranchise existing African Indigenous knowledge systems (Ntuli 2012). Therefore, it is possible to argue that development in Africa should consider the role of morality.

Basing on the above observations, since African spirituality permeates the socio-economic and political sphere it is important to use emphasis morality as the starting point of development. Morality in African communities is a reasonable practice that pleases the ancestors, living beings and God the creator. By seeing development is seen through moral lenses, means that the starting point of development is the humans. Instead of thinking about the western scientific means of development, the problem in Zimbabwe is behavioural. To be more precises it is difficult for a nation to upload policies which enhances development is themselves lack morality. For instance, elevating moral values like respect and loving one another are building pillars to development.

It follows therefore that instead of focusing on political, economic and technological development, there is a need to revisit African spirituality as a vanguard of morality. In the context of Zimbabwe, development should stem from Afrocentrism. The sense of community helps to increase participation, involvement in decision making and tolerance to each other. In fact. Owusu-Ansah and Mji (2013:2) opined that anything that is Afrocentric must have "at its core the understanding of the African identity as rooted, centred and located in the African culture in all aspects-spiritual, social, political and economic dimensions".

Appropriately, intentional use of African spiritual-moral theology as theoretical lenses for development can promote ethos for protecting and managing natural resources management to promotes peace and sustainable development. Accordingly, the moral dimension of development in helps to influence positive mindset to emerging issues of global warming, poverty and migration. Hence, this study advances that the African spiritual-moral theology holds together the social cohesion, norms and values which collectively culminate into sustainable development.

Therefore, it is not far-fetched to argue that development in Africa relies heavily on African spiritual-moral theology. Musasiwa (2020:49) asked the question "how can we explain the unfortunate paradox that Africa, a continent with the largest percentage of Christians, and the fastest-growing church, is riddled with problems of governance, corruption, disease, poverty and ethnic tensions?" In the same vein, Ojore (2008) noted the paradox of Africa that it is notoriously religious and infested with poverty and violence. Therefore, whether vocalised or subconsciously, religion is a critical tool to issues of development. African religiosity has also suffered syncretic infiltrations of western and foreign religious practises, thereby demeaning the essence of African spirituality. While it is prudent in the postmodern world to grapple with global ethics of development, it pays dividends to take few steps back to rethink how the notions of development were constructed from the indigenous context of Zimbabwe. The thrust is to unpack the ethical judgement for a good life, good society, and good relationships as precursors for sustainable development in Zimbabwe.

## 4 Towards a Moral Dimension to Development in Zimbabwe

Development in Zimbabwe can be enhanced by indigenous moral values and revisiting what has worked in past generations. What worked in past generations developmental contexts are critical pillars of indigenous knowledge systems. In African, morality remains a fundamental value. Therefore, continuous articulations of the African spiritual, moral theology of development can potentially guide sustainable ethic of development.

## 4.1 Ethical Judgements of a Good Life

African spiritual-moral theology perspectives about a good life. A traditional African moral person considers all human individuals as having a common ultimate interest, which is good life. In this case, a good life is a by-product of good morals which directly contribute to development. Commenting on developing countries, Smirzai (2005) argued that the low living standards of the people are a key issue in development. Development has to do with how people perceive good life. The grand output of development is promoting a good life for the people. Within the African spiritual, moral theology, the source of the good life comes from the relationship between the Supreme Being, ancestors and the living human community. The parameters of a good life are broad in African indigenous culture. For instance, a good life has both a spiritual and materialistic connotation. The materialistic includes but is not limited to having significant business success, having children, and seeing them getting married without problems, being free from evil people and their machinations. It could be concluded that a good life is characterised by comfort and success. A cordial relationship with one's ancestors is the fountain from where everything good supposedly springs from. The Shona proverbs *chawawana idya nehama midzimu haipe kaviri* (whatever you find, eat with relatives because ancestors do not give twice) illustrate the providence of ancestors to people. A good life is living without fear, sickness, wealth, many wives, no enemies, good rains, and a good relationship with *Mari* (Supreme Being) in the Shona language and ancestors. The Shona people argue that to live a good life does not happen but comes from the spiritual world, a blessing from the ancestors. *Vadzimu* (ancestors) are the source of good living and misfortune (Bourdillon 1998). The Shona worldview of a good life is about being obedient to ancestors, living elders, and God. Furthermore, the Shona worldview "emphasises responsibility rather than right… personal and individual interests tend to be submerged in the common will, and responsibilities become more important than individual rights" (Bennett and Patrick 2011: 227). Appeasing the ancestors results in a good life. Ancestors are central intermediaries between the living and *Mwari* (God).

Good life is enhanced by employing divine abilities from the ancestors. For instance, the Shona people use hunting skills for both providences. Success is a gift from the divine. As noted by Bourdillon (1998: 243) the Shona people believes that "in some cases, all skills are associated with alien spirits". The Shona spirits responsible for these skills are called *mashavi* (alien spirits). Hunters who possessed certain *shavi* (alien spirit) called *hombarume* (huntsman). Other highly skilled were called *mhizha* (blacksmith). These skills were responsible for the production of livelihoods in which people made a good life. The spirits were vanguards of development, nothing simply happens without the power of the supreme being. However, the spirit periodically requires rituals, rites and ceremonies to be performed by communities to attract more blessings. According to Kazembe (2011), the spirit medium of Chaminuka was responsible for prosperity and rain. I believe that such claims make sense within the Shona people because of how they see spirit medium as acting on behalf of the Supreme Being. Further, in the traditional perspective the spirit medium of Chaminuka is regarded to be responsible for protecting the Shona people against other ethnic attacks.

Those who were struggling to make it in society were helped by working together *nhimbe* (working together as a community). Some of the tasks included but were not limited to harvesting, weeding fields, and constructing a house. *ZundeRamambo* (King's granary) was established to support the vulnerable of the community with food. According to Ringson (2017:54), "the *Zunde*also played important religious, economic, social and political functions. Members of the society would take turns to participate in the planting and harvesting of crops. Both men and women normally did harvest. People would collectively come together and do the work". There is much that the government can learn from *Zunde Ramambo* concept to alleviate poverty in Zimbabwe. Involving people to work together, as espoused in *Zunde Ramambo* ensure development for the nation.

While the Shona people encourage a relationship with the Supreme Being and hardworking for success, this should be done humanely. Greediness and *consumeristic* issues are not allowed. In the Shona indigenous moral theology, good behaviour is obtained from societal socialisation; it is the society that moulds the whole person (Mararike 2012). Those who would use other means to attain a good life were detested by society. For instance, some family members bought *zvikwambo* (goblins) to increase their wealth. The route of using *zvikwambo* is detestable because it involves human sacrifices like killing family members for the goblins to get them wealth. Acquiring goblins for wealth creation, is nothing short of a spirit of greediness. Chitando (2020) explained that global economic players interested in satisfying their whims use corrupt internal elites to exploit oil, minerals, and arable land.

Further, acquiring *zvikwambo* (goblins) is like cheating to obtain wealth through evil means. It replaces hard working which also a key component to development. The Shona people have means to rebuke and look down to people who amass wealth through unconventional means. People with *zvikwambo* are considered shameless and do not consider and value others because of the human scarifies. Failure to take responsibility is called *munhu asina musoro/rombe* (senseless, insensitive, and lousy person (Sande 2021). From the Shona people's perspective, a good life is the ability to relate with the Supreme Being and to be responsible one's behaviour.

## 4.2 *The Ethos of Good Relationships in Society*

African spiritual-moral theology perspectives about good relationships are critical to the moral dimension of development. The moral dimension of development should be framed by values that enhances personhood. Zimbabweans must relate to one another using the "concept of *unhu* (cardinal values, belief systems)" (Sande 2021:249). From a normative perspective, personhood is not a virtue that one is born with, but it is a commitment and internalisation of societal values. Therefore, by fostering morality or providing behavioural guidelines to the Zimbabweans indirectly impacts development since people value and respect others. According to Samakange and Samukange (1980), social relationships are a by-product of personhood. The person's *unhu*, helps to resolve conflict and build a society full of harmony. Basing on the above ethos of good relationships, one may conclude that Zimbabweans have moved away from valuing good relationships. For instance, the violations of human rights by the Zimbabwe National Patriotic Front (ZANU-PF) impacted the economy. In 2020 alone, over 70 critics of the Mnangagwa governments were abducted and tortured by unidentified assailants (Mavhinga 2020). Security forces under the instruction of the President commit arbitrary arrests, violence assaults and other abuses. Such behaviour dishonours the President as someone without democratic leadership.

To further understand the role of the ethos of good relationships to development, one can learn how the Shona people deal with corrupt and bad people in society. For the Shona people, someone who abuses others or is mean is frowned upon by society as *munhupasina* (useless person). The actions of those in the ruling power in Zimbabwe show the absence of *hunhu* and they are *vanhupasina* (useless people). A true African communitarianism maxim can be summed as "I am because we are, and since we are, therefore I am" (Mbiti 1969:214). Therefore, there is no communitarianism when politicians and those in power are doing corruption and embezzlements.

In addition, ethos of good relationships requires observing the rights of others. On the contrary to this, the Zimbabwean government is guilty of violating human rights. For instance, the report by Reuter (2019) argued that besides the position that African Union and Southern Africa Development Community (SADC) have been tolerant to ZANU-PF regime's politics, the United States and European Union increased sanctions on Zimbabwe because of human rights abuses. Instead of owing up for violating human rights President Mnangagwa blames the West for the lack of development because of sanctions and describes sanctions as cancer destroying the nation. The assertion by President Mnangagwa to blame the West in everything is a true reflection of leaders who lacks introspection about how he deals with other people. Therefore, simply put having good ethos of relationship is a pillar to development because development in traditional African sense is about people, attaining the best of life deserved of human being.

Unfortunately, the above claims of sanctions by President Mnangagwa for the lack of development in Zimbabwe is denied by the West. The European Union asserted that "Zimbabwe is not where it is because of the so-called sanctions, but years of mismanagement of the economy and corruption" (Mushava 2019). In the same vein, the United States ambassador argued that "any responsibility for the catastrophic state of the economy and the government's abuse of its citizens" (Gerald 2019). If Gerald's statement is anything to go by, then president Mnangagwa should not abuse his citizens, a sure sign that he does not relate well with the people he leads. Therefore, building good relationships helps to avoid violence perpetrated by the ruling party.

The strength of using the ethos of good relationship to development is that it requires politicians to exhibit *hunhu* that make the populace respect them. *Unhu* is "a higher level of consciousness" (Rukuni 2007:17). The highest development consciousness in Zimbabwe must be providing opportunities for everyone to benefit from the natural resources. Accordingly, this is echoed by The African Union Agenda for 2063 that "Africa shall be a prosperous continent, with the means and resources to drive its development, with sustainable and long-term stewardship of its resources…" (African Union 2015:2). The Shona people view the life development and progress of individuals as communal. What this suggests is that ethos of good relationships is tied to development because of the intrinsic *hunhu* makes people humanely depend on each other (Mboti 2015). Communalism and the ethos of good relationships are pillars to enhance development. Rethinking this communalism model can recalibrate the contemporary ruling party's governance system and intensify the socio-cultural ethos.

## 4.3 Beacons of What Constitute a Good Society

African spiritual-moral theology perspectives about a good society are critical to the moral dimension of development because good character can contribute to the wellbeing of society. African spirituality has moral campus which develops individuals to search for the wellbeing of all and not individuals. Therefore, beacons of a good society are a fundamental pillar which contributes to development by making sure that human beings as a whole (society) are fulfilling their lives. If one develops in their social, physical, psychological, economic, and spiritual inevitably results in a good society.

Indeed, politics plays a role in society. Politics is a fundamental pillar of development because it ascertains how power is shared in society. The political context has affected the development of Zimbabwe. The long service of Robert Mugabe left the country plunged into an economic and political crisis. In 2017, the military replaced Robert Mugabe from power, putting Emmerson Dambudzo Mnangagwa (Mackintosh 2017). To revamp the economy, President Mnangagwa declared that Zimbabwe is "open for business" and stated that "we look forward to playing a positive and constructive role as a free, democratic, transparent and responsible member of the family of nations" (Mnangagwa 2018). This statement implies a link between Zimbabwe foreign relations and the local economic policy, which are responsible for creating disruptions and dilutions to African worldviews of development to a greater extent.

Subsequently, the developed world exerts enormous pressure on the developing countries to demonstrate good democracy, an independent judiciary, corporate governance. The underdevelopment in Zimbabwe questions whether the nation is independent or not. Independence implies that Zimbabweans are now responsible for developing the nation. Yes, in 1980, Zimbabwe celebrated independence but to what extent has this culminated into the development. According to Gunda (2009),

Africans are not independent of dictatorial leaders. Dictatorial leadership does not promote development, it is a sign of selfishness. Transformational leadership which promotes development should not be based on fear but mutual understanding and respect. The Shona proverbs says, *gudo guru peta muswe kuti vadiki vakutye* (older people should be dignified for them to be respected by the younger ones). The failure to appreciate that a good society is the one which people have a voice in creating their society militants against development.

Whenever molarity is not emphasised as a key component of development there is a danger of the spread of corruption and violence. Potentially, this explains why there is poverty in rural places and people in urban cities experience ill-health, poor living standards and pollution. In most cities in Zimbabwe, people always live-in fear, anxiety, isolation, crime, and helplessness. In Zimbabwe, corruption is the order of the day permeating all institutions. Togarasei (2020: 103) argued that people were proverbially expressing it in such statements as "*mbudziinodyapayakasungirwa*" (a goat grazes around where it is tied). This proverb means that it is normal to enjoy the benefits of the place they are situated. However, without guiding moral principles people always abuse their privileges.

A society free from oppression breeds the quality-of-life which development is all about which is highly developmental. In Zimbabwe and across Africa, politicians are still struggling to remove the colonial regalia of oppression. According to Mana (1992), explaining the context of the Democratic Republic of Congo, noted that there is no independence in Africa but a change of foreign oppressors and even internal oppression by their brothers and sisters. I agree to the assertion by Mana above, because for four decades post-independence Zimbabweans have suffered more under the fellow black leaderships than the white colonisers. Besides the lack of molarity of the leadership in Zimbabwe, politicians have focused on changing taskmasters (economic colonisers). The land redistribution programs introduced by Zimbabwe made the West to put sanctions on Zimbabwe (Mkodzongi and Lawrence 2019). From the British coloniser (West), Zimbabwean leadership has moved to China (East). In the year 2000 onwards, Zimbabwe has forced people to adopt the 'look East policies' where the Chinese replaced the space once invaded by Britons. Currently, Zimbabwe is dealing with Chinaas a development partner. The relationship between Zimbabwe and China serves a few elites in the Zanu-PF government (Chipaike and Bischoff 2019). A society with only a few benefiting economic resources is not a good society. The African moral ethos of togetherness opens a space of sharing, hence a responsibility of everything to take care of others. Development at its highest level is about how resources in society are shared for the benefit of everyone.

Oppressive leadership is weakened when people believe that it is their moral responsibility to create a better society. According to Gunda (2009), oppressive leadership in Zimbabwe is dealt by the reconstruction of the political system. While on one his assertion by Gunda relates to development at a strategic level, but on the other hand it does incorporate the role of morality in the lives of the politicians. It is correct to assume that Zimbabwean leaders' oppressive and corrupt nature is perpetuated by the individualistic legacy of the West, which emphasises individual's accumulation of wealth. The impact of Western individualised society is summarised by Togarasei (2020: 105) that "Zimbabweans compete to drive the latest and most expensive cars, to own the largest and most beautiful houses, to send children to the most expensive schools, and so on. Although I find nothing wrong in working hard to beone's best, the problem is doing so in a selfish way. Togarasei's finding indicates that drifting from the African philosophy of *hunhu/Ubuntu* has undermined development issues in Zimbabwe.

From the foregoing discussion, it can be concluded that the Ubuntu philosophy is framed on moral values which are needed in development. *Ubuntu/hunhu* philosophy is similar in many African countries, expresses in a different language, for instance, in South African vernacular language, *umuntungumuntungabantu* (a person is a person through other persons (Okyere-Manu and Konyana 2018). In a society where people value others, it evokes good life and indirectly impact development. For instance, *Ubuntu*, encourages "that a person gives to another: kindness, courtesy, compassion, consider and friendliness in the relationship between people; a code of behaviour, an attitude to other people and life" (Samkange and Samkange (1980:39).

So, the moral maxim in development is about the formation of good character and a good society. The failure of or forgetting *Ubuntu* values results in a flawed society which struggle to develop. Masoka and Mamvura (2017:31) were correct to suggest that development is "where people of African countries live under just, equitable and humane conditions". The moral theology of *hunhu/Ubuntu* has traits that foster a sense of community, hospitality, compassion, and integration. The role of personhood from the African moral thought is to focus on communalism instead of the West, which promotes individualism (Mofele 2016). The Shona peoples never regard someone as an individual but a community. Therefore, issues of development start on how people are socialised in a community. The Shona people socialisation process is "in accordance with the expectations of his society—whole person/*munhuanehunhu* … a result of deliberate and purposeful socialisation" (Mararike 2012).

## 5 Conclusion

This chapter argued that morality is a fundamental principle which sustains development. Development is this paper is as a process of enhancing human lives through addressing issues of political, economic, social, cultural and the empowerment of people. The moral ethos that defines development, includes but not limited to ethical judgement for a good life, good society, and good relationships. The Zimbabwean traditional perspective of development ethos is framed upon communalism and collectivism. For meaningful development in Africa, the focus should be on understanding African indigenous culture, philosophy, and spirituality, rather than implementing scientific development strategies only. Scientific ideologies for development subjugate the African moral dimension of development. It is essential to integrate African spirituality as a panacea to development. African moral ethics like *unhu/Ubuntu*, indigenous culture brings positive worldviews of a good life. In Africa, there is a direct link between African morality and development; for instance, African spirituality has remained the epitome force that permeates all aspects of life, enhancing peoples' morality, well-being, and spiritual dispositions. So, the spiritual and moral theology especially paying attention to the social cohesion, norms and values collectively culminate into sustainable development.

## References


African Union. 2015. *Agenda 2063: The Africa we want. The popular version*. Addis Ababa: The African Union.

Bennett, Tom W., and James Patrick. 2011. Ubuntu, the ethics of traditional religion. In *TraditionalAfrican religions in south African law*, ed. Tom W. Bennett, 223–242. Cape Town: UCT.

Bourdillon, M.F.C. 1998. *The Shona peoples: Ethnography of the Contemporary Shona, with special reference to their religion*. Gweru: Mambo Press.

Chipaike, R., and P.H. Bischoff. 2019. Chinese engagement of Zimbabwe and the limits of elite agency. *Journal of Asian and African Studies* 54 (7): 947–964.

Chitando, E. 2020. The bible as a resource for development in Africa. In *Religion and development*, ed. Ezra Chitando, Masiiwa Ragies Gunda, and Lovemore Togarasei, 401–418. Bamberg: University of Bamberg.

Gerald, C. 2019. *Zimbabwe's anti-sanctions march: Much ado about nothing?* Retrieved 18 July 2021 from https://www.aa.com.tr/en/analysis/zimbabwe-s-anti-sanctions-march-much-ado-about-nothing/1652712.

Gunda, M.R. 2009. African theology of reconstruction: The painful realities and practical options! *Exchange* 38 (1): 84–102.

———. 2020. Rethinking development in Africa and the role of religion. In *Religion and development*, ed. Ezra Chitando, Masiiwa Ragies Gunda, and Lovemore Togarasei, 37–58. Bamberg: University of Bamberg.

Kazembe, T. 2011. Divine Angels and Vadzimu in Shona Religion, Zimbabwe. *The Rose + Croix Journal* 8: 89–98.

Kristof, N. 2017. *How Mugabe has destroyed Zimbabwe after inheriting a prosperous country from Rhodesia, Zimbabwe Today*.

Mackintosh, E. 2017. *Zimbabwe's military takeover was the world's strangest coup*. Retrieved 17 July 2021 from https://edition.cnn.com/2017/11/20/africa/zimbabwe-military-takeover-strangest-coup/index.html.

Mana, K. 1992. *FoiAfricaine et Reconstruction de l'Afrique*. Lomé: HAHO/CETA.

Mararike, C.G. 2012. Developing the whole person: Education based on Concepts drawn from culture. In *Rediscoursing African womanhood in the search for Sustainable renaissance: Africana Womanism in multi-disciplinary approaches*, ed. I. Muwati, Z. Mguni, T. Gwekwerere, and R. Magosvongwe, 8–16. Harare: College Press.

Marchand, T.H.J. 2003. A possible explanation for the lack of explanation: Or "Why the master builder can't explain what he knows": Introducing informational atomism against a "definitional" definition of concepts. In *Negotiating local knowledge. Power, identity and development*, ed. J. Pottier et al., 30–50. London: Pluto Press.

Masoka, Angeline, and Zvinashe Mamvura. 2017. African philosophy of development as Expressed in Shona proverbs. *International Journal of Arts & Humanities* 6 (2): 28–40.

Mavhinga, D. 2020. Mnangagwa's broken human rights promises two years on. *Zimbabwe independent*. Retrieved 24 July 2020 from https://www.hrw.org/news/2020/09/04/mnangagwas-broken-human-rights-promises-two-years.

Mawere, M. 2017. *Theorising development in Africa*. Cameroon: Langaa.

Mbiti, J.S. 1969. *African religions and philosophy*. London: Heinemann.

Mboti, N. 2015. May the real Ubuntu please stand up? *Journal of MediaEthics* 30 (2): 125–147.

McNabb, T.D. 2019. *Religious epistemology: Elements philosophy of religion*. Cambridge: University Printing House.

Mkodzongi, G., and P. Lawrence. 2019. The fast-track land reform and agrarian change in Zimbabwe. *Review of African Political Economy* 46 (159): 1–13.

Mnangagwa, E.D. 2018. *Inauguration speech by the incoming president of the Republic of Zimbabwe, comrade Emmerson Dambudzo Mnangagwa*. Retrieved 17 July 2021 from https://www.zimcitizenswatch.org/static/documents/Inauguration%20Speech.pdf.

Molefe, M. 2016. Revisiting the Menkiti-GyekyeDabate: Who is a radical communitarian? *Theoria* 149 (63): 37–54.

Musasiwa, R. 2020. Theology and social democratisation. In *Religion and social marginalization in Zimbabwe*, ed. Lovemore Togarasei, David Bishau, and Ezra Chitando, 49–58. Bamberg: University of Bamberg Press.

Mushava, E. 2019. *"We are not moved by march: EU, US" Newsday*. Retrieved 17 July 2021 from https://www.newsday.co.zw/2019/10/we-aint-moved-by-march-eu-us/.

Ntuli, P.P. 2012. Indigenous knowledge systems the African renaissance. In *Indigenous knowledge and the integration of knowledge systems*, ed. C.A. Odora Hoppers, 53–67. Claremont, Cape Town: New Africa Books.

Ojore, A. O. 2008. *The role of the Catholic Church in the democratization of Africa*. www.tangaza.org/classnotes/depaul/DePaulLectureThree.doc.

Okyere-Manu, B. D., and E. Konyana. 2018. Who is Umuntu in Ngumuntu Ngabantu? Interrogating moral issues facing Ndau women in polygyny. *South African Journal of Philosophy* 37 (2): 207–216.

Owusu-Ansah, F.E., and G. Mji. 2013. African indigenous knowledge and research. *African Journal of Disability* 2 (1): 1–5.

Reuters. 2019. *Trump extends U.S. sanctions against Zimbabwe by a year.* Retrieved 17 July 2021 from https://www.reuters.com/article/us-usa-zimbabwe-sanctions-idUSKCN1QM01Q.

Ringson, J. 2017. Zunde Ramambo as a traditional coping mechanism for the care of Ophans and vulnerable children: Evidence from Gutu District, Zimbabwe. *African Journal of Social Work* 7 (2): 52–58.

Ruben, Ruerd. 2011. Can religion contribute to development? The road from 'truth' to 'trust'. *Exchange* 40: 225–234.

Rukuni, M. 2007. *Being Afrikan: Rediscovering the traditional Unhu-Ubuntu-Botho pathways of being human*. Johannesburg: Mndala.

Samkange, S., and T.S. Samkange. 1980. *Hunhuism/Ubuntuism: A Zimbabwean indigenous political philosophy*. Harare: Graham Publ.

Sande, N. 2021. The impact of technologies on African religions: A theological perspective. In *African values, ethics, and technology*, ed. B.D. Okyere-Manu, 247–261. Cham: Palgrave Macmillan.

Sande, N., & B. Denga. 2019. Reconstructing the Nexus of Pentecostalism, Politics and Development in Zimbabwe: Political Voices from the Apostolic Faith Mission (AFM), In *Religion and Development in Southern Africa*, ed. James N. Amanze, Maake Masango, Lilian Siwila, and Ezra Chitando. vol. 2, 267–286.

Sjöström, J., N. Frerichs, V.G. Zuin, and I. Eilks. 2017. Use of the concept of Bildung in the international science education literature, its potential, and implications for teaching and learning. *Studies in Science Education* 53 (2): 165–192.

Smirzai, Adam. 2005. *"Developing countries and the concept of development", TheDynamics of socio-economic development: An introduction*, 1–34. Cambridge: CambridgeUniv. Pr.

Togarasei, L. 2020. Reconstruction theology and the Church's role in post-crisis Zimbabwe. In *Religion and social marginalization in Zimbabwe*, ed. Lovemore Togarasei, David Bishau, and Ezra Chitando, 49–58. Bamberg: University of Bamberg Press.

**Nomatter Sande** holds a PhD in Religion and Social Transformation from the University of KwaZulu Natal (South Africa). Nomatter is a Practical Theologian. He is a Research Fellow at the Research Institute for Theology and Religion (RITR), College of Human Sciences, University of South Africa (UNISA). His research interests include disabilities studies, Pentecostal theology, religious violence, peace and gender.

# Part III
# Environment and African Development

# African Ethics and Sustainable Development Goals: Towards Achieving the SDGs in Africa

**Ovett Nwosimiri**

**Abstract** This chapter examines how African ethics can help in achieving the Sustainable Development Goals (SDGs) in Africa. I argue that the recognition and integration of African ethics together with the SDGs will help Africa move to a sustainable trajectory. Drawing upon insights from Thaddeus Metz's discussion on African ethics, I reflect on how SDGs can be achieved in Africa if it integrates African ethics—welfare-based and community-based African ethics.

**Keywords** Africa · African ethics · Recognition and integration · Sustainable development goals

## 1 Introduction

African ethics is associated with African moral systems (moral life and thought)—the notions of the ethics of duty and common good. African ethics is embedded in African moral life and thought—the beliefs and ideas about what is morally right or wrong, what is good or bad, and about community harmony for the wellbeing and development of the community. Talking about wellbeing and development, when compared with other continents or considered on its own, much of Africa is faced with underdevelopment, poverty, famines, crisis, and drought etc. In 2000, leaders from 189 countries of the world came together to discuss a way forward in dealing with the above issues. With the awareness of the perpetual problems (poverty, famines, plagues, wars, and drought) of the world, they decided to set a plan that can help them eradicate these problems, especially that of their countries. These leaders from these countries created a plan called the Millennium Development Goals (MDGs) that will begin from 2002 to the targeted date of 2015.

O. Nwosimiri (✉)
Ulster University, London, UK

African Centre for Epistemology and Philosophy of Science, University of Johannesburg, Johannesburg, South Africa



B. Okyere-Manu et al. (eds.), *Contemporary Development Ethics from an African Perspective*, Philosophy and Politics - Critical Explorations 27,
https://doi.org/10.1007/978-3-031-32898-5_7

After the expiration of the Millennium Development Goals came the Sustainable Development Goals (SDGs)[1] adopted by the United Nations General Assembly (UNGA) in September 2015 that need to be achieved by the year 2030. According to Jeffrey D. Sachs (2012), some of the millennium development goals were not met. This can be seen as a failure on the path of these leaders. Thus, one can rightly infer from this that the failure to meet all the MDGs necessitated the SDGs Agenda 2030. Hence, there would be no need for the SDGs had it been all the MDGS were met. To this, Sachs suggests that "between 2015 and 2030, the world should aim not merely to achieve the MDGs where they have not been met, but to carry on with the task initiated at the very start of the UN itself (and represented in the Universal Declaration of Human Rights)" (2012: 2208). In view of the aforementioned, I will like to assert that the reason for the failure to meet all the MGDs was because the United Nations appear to have used a one size fits all strategy. This strategy is a predetermined idea of the West that demands that Africa must use its strategy to solve its problem. Such strategy downplays the importance of African ethics and values because it forces Africa to substitute her ethics and values with ideas that represent a continuation with and affirms the basic principles of the Western. So, given that Sub-Saharan Africa (and possibly other countries) failed to achieve the MDGs in 2015, I think that the reason(s) for their failure to achieve or meet these goals might possibly affect its SDGs of 2030. Thus, for the SDGs to avoid the same fate as the MDGs, there is a need for the recognition and integration of African ethics together with the SDGs in whatever strategic plan that has been put in place to achieve the goals in Africa.

In this chapter, I examine how African ethics can help in achieving Sustainable Development Goals (SDGs). In the first section, I will briefly discuss African ethics. In the second section, I will briefly discuss the Sustainable Development Goals. In what follows, I will discuss the need for the recognition and integration of African ethics with the SDGs. Here, I argue that the recognition and integration of African ethics together with the SDGs will help Africa move to a sustainable trajectory. In the fourth section, drawing upon insights from Thaddeus Metz discussion on African ethics, I show how African Ethics—welfare-based and community-based African ethics—can help to achieve the SDGs in Africa.

## 2 On the Term 'African Ethics'

The term 'African ethics', according to Kwame Gyekye, is used to refer to both the moral beliefs and presuppositions of people living in Sub-Saharan Africa, as well as the philosophical clarification and interpretation of such beliefs and presuppositions (2011 § 1). According to Motsamai Molefe, African ethics can be defined in two

[1] I will be making use of Sustainable Development Goals and its abbreviation, SDGs, interchangeably.

facets. "Firstly, it defines it by invoking commonly shared moral beliefs and presuppositions by people below the Sahara" (Molefe 2016: 106). "Secondly, it refers to the intellectual reflections and deliberations on these moral intuitions" (Molefe 2016: 106). He further avows that the "definition does not presuppose that there is absolute agreement about African moral thought, but to mean that there are sufficient commonalities among the peoples below the Sahara that warrant and justify the use of this phrase to capture a body of work attempting to critically reflect on these (commonly) held moral beliefs" (Molefe 2016: 106).

According to Thaddeus Metz, 'African ethics' "principally mean work done by contemporary moral theorists that is significantly informed by features salient amongst the beliefs and practices of the indigenous black peoples below the Sahara desert (thereby excluding peoples of Arab, Indian or European descent and culture)" (2017: 62). Elsewhere he defined 'African ethics' as "values associated with the largely black and Bantu-speaking peoples residing in the sub-Saharan part of the continent" (Metz 2007: 321). As a well-structured and functional human communities, I think that Africa as a continent has evolved ethical systems, which consist of ethical ideas and norms meant to govern cultural and ethical (moral) conducts in the community. In Africa, the ethics of the community are deep-rooted in how people think about what is right and wrong, and what defines bad and good behaviour. Thus, African ethics can be seen as African moral principles that guides the behaviours of those in the community.

Gyekye explicates that "African ethics is, thus, a character-based ethics that maintains that the quality of the individual's character is most fundamental in our moral life" (2011 § 3). A person, in African societies, is morally evaluated and judged based on his/her character—good or bad character. Talking about 'character—*iwa*', Segun Gbadegesin explains that, for the Yoruba, "perhaps the most important moral concept. A person is morally evaluated according to his/her *iwa*—whether good or bad" (1991: 79). To this, when a person is honest and empathetic, he/she is considered a decent person, which means he/she has a good character. Also, a person is considered to have bad character when he/she is seen to be dishonest and cruel. Gyekye further explicates that "good character is the essence of the African moral system, the linchpin of the moral wheel" (2011 § 3). Regarding moral conduct, he asserts that all that a society can do is to impart moral knowledge to its members. In this case, making them become aware of the moral values and principles that are accepted by the society (Gyekye 2011 § 3). In Africa, there are moral principles and rules of the society that can help a person to have a good character. An example is that it is wrong to insult an elder. The person may fail to apply this rule to a particular situation; the person is, thus, not able to effect the transition from knowledge to action, to carry out the implication of his/her moral belief (Gyekye 2011 § 3). This is why Gyekye explains that:

> In the Akan and other African moral systems, such a moral failure would be put down to the lack of a good character (*suban pa*). In other words, the ability to act in accord with the moral principles and rules of the society requires the possession of a good character. Thus, in the context of the activities of the moral life—in our decisions to obey moral rules, in the struggle to do the right thing and to avoid the wrong conduct, in one's intention to carry out

> a moral duty, the quality of a person's character is of ultimate consequence. It is from a person's character that all his or her actions—good or bad—radiate: the performance of good or bad acts depends on the state of one's character. Wrong-doing is put down to a person's bad character. Thus, the Yoruba maxim (proverb): 'Good character is a person's guard' (Gyekye 2011 § 3).

The above simply shows the formation of character. It also shows that a person is responsible for the state of his/her character. It is important to highlight that society instils moral conduct and knowledge in its members through making them become aware of it, by educating them on the community's recognized moral norms and ideals. Similarly, this moral conduct and knowledge can be taught through storytelling and folktales with moral values to its members. This moral conduct and knowledge are preserved through these values embedded in African ethics. But the individual is still responsible for his/her character because character results from the habitual actions of the individual. The reason is that "one is not born with a bad 'head', but one takes it on from the earth. …that a bad habit is not an inborn characteristic; it is one that is acquired" (Gyekye 2011 § 3). Thus, it would be worthless for an individual "to embark on moral instruction through moral proverbs and folktales, as it is done in African societies, if our character or habits were inborn. But the belief is that the moral narratives would help the *individual* to acquire and internalize the moral values of the society, including specific moral virtues, embedded in those ethical narratives" (Gyekye 2011 § 3; *my emphasis*).

Metz (2013) in his article "*Two Conceptions of African Ethics*", presented what he deemed as the two conceptions of African ethics. These two conceptions are the 'welfare-based and community-based conceptions of African ethics'. According to Metz, in the welfare-based African ethics, "the ultimate aim of a moral agent should be to improve people's quality of life, which she can reliably do by supporting the community in certain ways" (2013: 142). While the community-based African ethics should "be valued for its own sake, with the enhancement of welfare being morally relevant only insofar as it is part of that" (2013: 142), it is important to note that both conceptions are not completely unrelated. According to the welfare-based theory,[2] "one should share one's wealth, time, labour and so on at the bottom because doing so is likely to make others' lives better" (2013: 151). And in contrast, the community-based theory "prescribes helping others ultimately because doing so would be part of what it is to enter into community with them, or perhaps to foster communal relationships among them" (2013: 151). Thus, in view of these, it is important to underscore that as much as both theories/conceptions appear to be different, they are not completely unrelated. The relatedness of both theories and conceptions is evident in the fact that they both focus on helping an individual or a community. They also focus on caring for the well-being of an individual. What this implies is that they appreciate the idea of bettering the lives of others. These, at least to some degree show how they are related. Hence, both theories/conceptions are important because they focus on the well-being of individuals in the community.

[2]For both welfare-based and community-based conceptions/theories, I would like to note that I will be making use of theory and conception interchangeably.

## 3 Sustainable Development Goals

The idea of SDGs, according to Sachs, "gain ground because of the growing urgency of sustainable development for the entire world" (2012: 2206). Sustainable Development Goals is a universal set of goals that will be used as a basis to oversee political policies and agendas for fifteen years. Sustainable Development Goals aim to "end poverty and set the world on a path of peace, prosperity and opportunity for all on a healthy planet" (United Nations 2020: 2). There are 17 Sustainable Development Goals, and these goals build on the Millennium Development Goals. These 17 SDGs are broader in scope than the MDGs. SDGs address issues like (1) poverty, (2) hunger, (3) good health and well-being, (4) quality education, (5) gender equality and women empowerment, (6) clean water and sanitation, (7) and clean energy, (8) economic growth and decent work, (9) infrastructure, industrialization and innovation, (10) reduce inequality within and among countries, (11) sustainable cities and human settlements, (12) sustainable consumption and production, (13) climate change, (14) conserve life below waters, (15) protection of life on land, (16) promote peace, justice and strong institutions, and (17) global partnership[3] (ICSU and ISSC 2015; United Nations 2020). It is worth noting that the above goals apply to all countries, and they cover and embrace the three dimensions of human wellbeing which are: economic development, social inclusion and environmental sustainability (Sachs 2012: 2206). According to the United Nations, "the 17 Sustainable Development Goals (SDGs) demand nothing short of a transformation of the financial, economic and political systems that govern our societies today to guarantee the human rights of all" (2020: 2).

While the United Nations are hoping that the SDGs will be a success when they "accelerate responses to the world's gravest challenges – from eliminating poverty and hunger to reversing climate change" (2020: 3), there has been criticism levied against the SDGs. Scholars like Asa Persson, Nina Weitz and Mans Nilsson state that some actors consider the implementation of the SDGs to be "unrealistic and sprawling goals with no clear definition of sustainability guiding them" (2016: 59). The reason for this is because the goals are "so broad and all-encompassing that it is difficult to define discrete implementation processes and responsibilities" (Persson et al. 2016: 59). Because of its broadness, Palash Kamruzzaman (2016) argued that the SDGs did not identify probable challenges that could deter countries from meeting the target in 2030. And even if these goals can be met, the possibility of meeting all the targets is not viable, as there will be some problems during implementation. This is why Sachs proposed that SDGs should have been organized in a way that "all the world's people will have access to safe and sustainable water and sanitation, adequate nutrition, primary health services, and basic infrastructure, including electricity, roads, and connectivity to the global information network" (2012: 2208).

[3] I would like to note that these goals are all paraphrased.

Aside from the fact that achieving the SDGs has been proven to be challenging and difficult, achieving these goals during the current crisis – Covid-19 Pandemic – will be more challenging, given that the Covid-19 pandemic has ravaged humanity resulting in the massive loss of livelihoods (Nwosimiri 2021a: 3). United Nations affirms this when it explicates that:

> One third of the way into our SDG journey, the world is not on track to achieve the global Goals by 2030. Before the COVID-19 outbreak, progress had been uneven, and more focused attention was needed in most areas. The pandemic abruptly disrupted implementation towards many of the SDGs and, in some cases, turned back decades of progress (2020: 3).

The above shows the challenge faced by SDGs even before the global pandemic. But, even if the SDGs are progressing in some developed countries, the same cannot be said about some underdeveloped countries. Thus, this clearly shows that underdeveloped continents like Africa actually do need help in achieving SDGs. Also, considering the current covid pandemic, it would be interesting to see if the goals will be achieved by 2030. Nevertheless, in order to achieve the SDGs in Africa, there is a need to recognize and integrate African ethics—welfare-based and community-based African ethics together with the SDGs.

## 4 The Need for the Recognition and Integration of African Ethics with the Sustainable Development Goals

The reason for the inability of Africa to develop is due to the refusal by Africa to acknowledge some of its principles, like moral principles, that reflect the lives of its people that can help in its development. To this, I think that the recognition and integration of her principles can go a long way in achieving SDGs in Africa. The United Nations SDGs target Africa in a one-dimensional approach or 'one style fits all' approach. They failed to look at the possible inclusion of African principles, more specifically African ethics (which includes African moral beliefs, thoughts, cultural practices and values) to achieve its aims. Hence, I think that there is a need for the recognition and integration of African ethics with the SDGs. This suggests the need for a two-dimensional approach. I am aware that the SDGs apply to all countries but knowing how to successfully implement the SDGs in each UN member country should be pivotal, as there are principles in each country that if not recognized and integrated will hinder the success of SDGs.

I believe the recognition and integration of African ethics with the SDGs will help Africa move to a sustainable trajectory. To achieve this there is a need to approach the SDGs in accordance with the African ethics and tenets of the African people. We must not concentrate only on the one-dimensional approach—one style fits all, we must also bring in other approaches—a two-dimensional approach—to achieve these goals. Therefore, African leaders must engage with their citizens, to recognize and integrate African ethics (principles) together with the SDGs in order to move to a sustainable trajectory. Even if we were to acknowledge that the SDGs can help in the development of Africa, what can we say about the strategy of achieving it? As a response to this question, I think that one thing we need to acknowledge is the fact that the SDGs cannot be achieved independent of the recognition and integration of African values. Thus, there is a need for the recognition and integration of African ethics.

Africa has always been an innovative place with novel ideas. These innovations and novel ideas have always been achieved with the recognition and integration of the communitarian values of African community. In traditional societies for example, things have always been done in recognition and integration of the communitarian nature and values of the community for the survival of the society (Nwosimiri 2021b: 94). Without the recognition and integration of the community values and the needs of the people, these innovations and novel ideas would not have been possible. The recognition and integration of African ethics together with the SDGs will enable the opening of Africans to collectively respond to SDGs through their communal way of living. They will take responsibility for their current state of affairs and apply their moral beliefs, thoughts, principles and rules that guide the behaviours of the community to make sure the SDGs are achieved. This will be tactical in finding African ways of overcoming whatever obstacles that will stop them from not achieving the SDGs. If we take into cognisance African ethics and allow citizens to make choices about everything that affects their community, lives and their destinies, it will help Africa move to a sustainable trajectory that is capable of transform African society for the better. This will be possible as Africans will seek inventive and appropriate processes that will help achieve SDGs in Africa – the integration of knowledge. To this end, "Africa will have to participate significantly in the cultivation and promotion of this aspect of human culture, if it is to benefit from it fully" (Gyekye 1997: 36). African ethics and the SDGs can be integrated in such a way that they will serve their purpose, which is helping the community to grow. In this case, one would complement the other to help individuals in the community. In this way, they will have a great relevance and impact on the social life of the people, given that they will both quickly meet the demands of the community. Thus, the integration of both will deal with specific problems of human survival because, when integrated, they can immediately be seen (Nwosimiri 2021b: 97) "as having direct connections with societal problems and as being appropriate to meeting certain basic or specific needs" (Gyekye 1997: 37–38).

## 5 Achieving Sustainable Development Goals in Africa

When the desire to develop Africa is informed by Western pre-determined and hegemonic ideas of what Africans lack and need, that desire will not succeed because the ethics, values, culture, practices etc. of the African people are not considered. This will pose a huge challenge to the success of SDGs in Africa. Because the applicability of the SGDs framed by the United Nations within the strategy of one size fits all or a one-dimensional approach will not achieve its aims if it neglects the ethics, values, culture, practices and tradition of the African people. Thus, for the SDGs to be achieved in Africa, they must be integrated together with African ethics to provide a practical and social solution that is in accordance with the ethical milieus of the African people. The integration of African ethics to SDGs is essential for the development of Africa because it will help to reconceptualize and re-theorize the views, ideas and strategies that the SDGs have in place for African development. This integration will properly help in addressing the needs of African people. The integration of African ethics to SDGs will help illuminate our understanding of the lived experiences and realities of the African people as implementing the SDGs alone will be faced with more problems of achieving its aims and satisfying the needs of the people.

Let's take for example SDGS 4 (quality education) and 17 (global partnership). Here, I am referring to the dominance of Western education and ideas in Africa. These goals still involves pre-determined ideas of the West that demands that Africa must use its strategies to solve its problem. Such strategy downplays the importance of African ethics and values because it forces Africa to substitute her ethics and values with ideas that represent a continuation with and affirms the basic principles of the Western. This is not promising because it sees Africa through the lens of the West. Africa cannot use this strategy to solve her problem. Because this strategy is one among many strategies that can be used. African problems need an African solution. This is why the idea of decolonization—the idea of dismantling epistemic violence and Eurocentrism in Africa is currently the topic of discussion. Educational curriculum and ideas remains largely rooted in Western worldviews and epistemological traditions, and it continues to reinforce Western dominance and privilege. Thus, the SDGs needs the integration of African ethics in order for Africa to move to a well sustainable trajectory.

In light of the above, one might possibly argue that the United Nations is also made up of African representatives, as such its view is not entirely informed by Western pre-determined and hegemonic ideas. This is possibly true, but one thing we should be aware of is that the Western pre-determined and hegemonic ideas have dominated the views of many continents, including Africa. So, whether Africans are members of the United Nations, the chances of adopting the pre-determined and hegemonic ideas are high, given that many, if not all of the African representative in the United Nations, have been indoctrinated into the Western pre-determined and hegemonic ideas brought about through colonialism. Colonialism and the Western imperial dominion have shaped the makings of the modern world.Many Africans tend to copy and assimilate the ways of life of the colonizers through education, hence abandoning their own native values and principles. Though African countries have gained independence, Western values still remain the required mode of living. Africans want to do things as their colonizers, tagging or seeing it as a proper and a better way of living (Nwosimiri 2015: 10–11). African people should not take a sort of cultural pride in the Western pre-determined and hegemonic ideas. In view of this, I think that Africa need both the welfare-based theory and the community-based theory. This is because, given the current state of Africa, I am inclined to think that Africa can really do with the help of moral agents that will improve the quality of life of the African people. This moral agents can support the community in different ways and at the same time value the community for what it is.

To ensure that the SDGs are achieved, firstly, there is a need for the integration of African ethics—welfare-based—thereby enabling individuals with a strong moral value to determine ways that will assist in improving people's quality of life—"something one can often do by *means* of entering into community" (Metz 2013:149) with others. By this integration, the SDGs will be achieved "through a network of social relations ruled by a strong sense of unity and caring" (Masolo 2010: 216), and it will make the individual and the community "feel that they are in an atmosphere of positive relations with other members of society or neighbourhood" (Masolo 2010: 250). Nevertheless, for the individual to fully succeed in his or her pursuit to improve the quality of life for the people, the individual needs to posit the existence of others as an essential part to achieving his or her goals, such that realizing his or her personal aim of improving the quality of life for the people is done in recognition of the communal life of the people. By recognizing the communal life of the people, the individual will give "the well-being of others equal consideration consequent to imagining what it would be like to be them" (Metz 2013: 150). And by so doing, the individual will be able "to create humane conditions that, at least, enhance the community's ability to reduce unhappiness and suffering" (Masolo 2010: 250; see also Metz 2013: 150). Thus, through the integration of SDGs and African ethics—welfare-based theory—what makes the behaviour or character trait of the individual a virtue towards achieving SDGs "is that it reliably improves people's quality of life" (Metz 2013: 150).

To ensure that the SDGs are achieved, secondly, there is a need for the integration of African ethics—community-based—the understanding of the moral value of the community—which will enable the community to determine ways that will assist them in planning and implementing feasible programmes and initiatives to address the SDGs in line with their ethics. The feasibility of these programmes and initiatives could be assessed in terms of how they sustainably address the SDGs in line with their ethics for the development of their community. This is essential because community-based theory creates harmony in the community and a caring relationship that promotes human well-being among people in the community (Metz 2013). The SDGs cannot be achieved independent of, or in opposition to the ethics and interests of the community. The community-based "prescribes helping others ultimately because doing so would be part of what it is to enter into community with them, or perhaps to foster communal relationships among them" (2013: 151). Hence, to achieve the SDGs there is a need to integrate them with community-based ethics. And the understanding of this ethics is significant in achieving the SDGs. Given that the SDGs are supposed to address the needs of the community, the question that comes to mind is: how would the SDGs address the needs of the community when it has no understanding of the ethics of the community? To this, the ethics of the community needs to be taken into consideration first. This is because the community best understands the ways to care for the well-being of her people.

It is imperative to accentuate that as much as both conceptions of African ethics, to some extent, seem to be pursuing different motives, they are not completely unrelated. Both conceptions can be employed in order to achieve a particular aim, which in this case is to achieve the sustainable development goals in Africa. Both conceptions are two sides of the same reality. As such, none of these conceptions should be favoured over the other as they stem from one source: 'African ethics—African'. They are fundamental to the African people. Hence, "there is no contradiction as to which value is fundamental; rather they belong together side by side, as aims that are often compatible" (Metz 2013: 152). Taking as one ethics, SDGs can be achieved in Africa if it integrates welfare-based and community-based African ethics in its goals or in the process of achieving its goals. As much as they can possibly prescribe divergent decisions, thereby providing divergent outcome of the SDGs to the community, what is important is the fact that they are both two logical parts that forms African ethics. So, where one conception or theory cannot account for the full achievement of the SDGs, the other can be applied. Both views have their implications, but when logically viewed as one—African ethics—they will help in achieving the SDGs in Africa. Thus, when the SDGs has been integrated with African ethics—welfare-based and community-based African ethics—then it will be understood by the community as 'African SDGs', that is, SDGs that recognizes and integrates African ethics.

## 6 Conclusion

What I have shown in this chapter is that for SDGs to be achieved in Africa, they should be integrated with African ethics—welfare-based and community-based African ethics. SDGs are principles that were generated by United Nations. To overcome underdevelopment and the financial, economic and political systems that govern our societies today, and to embraces economic development, social inclusion and environmental sustainability, they came up with principles that will aid their process of development. These principles can be characterized as a progressive step. Like I have already shown, the SDGs target Africa in a one-dimensional approach, in the sense that it presumed that one size would fit all. It fails to take into consideration the idea that countries are different. It failed to recognize the cultural structure of Africa and the inclusion of its culture to achieve its aim. To this, I showed that unless SDGs is integrated together with African ethics, it will not be its aims in Africa.

The fact that Africans are communitarian in nature and that the community-based theory is more characteristically African than the welfare-based does take away from the fact that Africaneeds both theories in order to achieve the SDGs in Africa. These theories are fundamental to the full achievement of SDGs in Africa. These theories will not only help African people achieve the SDGs and grow beyond their (existential) problems, but they will also help address whatever problem they might possibly face in the future. These theories will help facilitate growth and development in all facets of their endeavours as any (future) problem would be approached and addressed through the recognition and integration of African ethics and the collective effort of the African people.

## References


Gbadegesin, S. 1991. *African philosophy: Traditional Yoruba philosophy and contemporary African realities*. New York: Peter Lang.

Gyekye, K. 1997. Philosophy, culture, and Technology in the Postcolonial. In *Postcolonial African philosophy: A critical reader*, ed. E.C. Eze, 25–44. Massachusetts: Blackwell Publishers Inc.

———. 2011. African ethics. In *The Stanford encyclopedia of philosophy,* ed. E.N. Zalta, Fall 2011 edn. Available from https://plato.stanford.edu/archives/fall2011/entries/african-ethics/. Accessed 15 April 2021.

ICSU and ISSC. 2015. *Review of the sustainable development goals: The science perspective*. Paris: International Council for Science (ICSU).

Kamruzzaman, P. 2016. A critical note on poverty eradication target of sustainable development goals. *European Journal of Sustainable Development* 5: 87–110.

Masolo, D.A. 2010. *Self and Community in a Changing World*. Bloomington: Indiana University Press.

Metz, T. 2007. Towards an African moral theory. *The Journal of Political Philosophy* 15 (3): 321–341.

———. 2013. Two concepts of African ethics. *Quest: An African Journal of Philosophy* 25: 141–161.

———. 2017. An overview of African ethics. In *Themes, issues and problems in African philosophy*, ed. I.E. Ukpokolo, 61–75. Cham: Springer Nature.

Molefe, M. 2016. African ethics and partiality. *Phronimon* 17 (1): 104–122.

Nwosimiri, O. 2015. *Rethinking the concept of Race's conundrums in African philosophy*. MA. Thesis: University of Kwa-Zulu Natal.

———. 2021a. Covid-19 and job losses: Should affirmative action and preferential hiring still be applicable in South Africa? *Filosofia Theoretica: Journal of African Philosophy Culture and Religions* 10 (1): 1–18.

———. 2021b. African cultural values, practices and modern technology. In *African values, ethics and technology: Questions, issues and approaches*, ed. B. Okyere-Manu, 89–120. Cham: Palgrave Macmillan.

Persson, Å., N. Weitz, and M. Nilsson. 2016. Follow-up and review of the sustainable development goals: Alignment vs. internalization. *Review of European, Comparative and International Environmental Law* 25: 59–68.

Sachs, J.D. 2012. From millennium development goals to sustainable development goals. *Lancet* 379: 2206–2211.

United Nations. 2020. *The sustainable development goals report*. Retrieved from: https://unstats.un.org/sdgs/report/2020/The-Sustainable-Development-Goals-Report-2020.pdf. Accessed 19 July 2021.


**Ovett Nwosimiri** has a PhD in Philosophy from the University of KwaZulu-Natal where he also lectured Applied Ethics. He also lectured Philosophy at St. Joseph's Theological Institute Cedara, South Africa. He was a Post-Doctoral Research Fellow at the African Centre for Epistemology and Philosophy of Science (ACEPS), University of Johannesburg. His research interest is in African Philosophy, African Epistemology, Philosophy of Race, Applied Ethics Epistemology and Existentialism. He is currently at Ulster University, Business School, London campus. He is a Research Associate at the African Centre for Epistemology and Philosophy of Science, University of Johannesburg.

# "Environmental Crisis or Environmental Retaliation": Reflections on the Nexus Between the Manyika People and the Environment in Post-colonial Zimbabwe

**Silindiwe Zvingowanisei and Sophia Chirongoma**

**Abstract** The ecological crisis is one of the greatest threats faced by nations worldwide. The future of planet Earth poses many developmental challenges for our generation, more than ever before. Overpopulation, rapid industrialisation, heightened consumerism, unrestricted technologies and other human activities are affecting every region of land and water resulting in unprecedented environmental degradation. The ecological crisis has not only resulted in climate change and radical undermining of life, but it is also triggering a mass extinction of species (including humanity) as well as putting future generations in a predicament. The situation is deplorable, but arguably religion and spirituality can contribute to the challenge. African countries in general and Zimbabwe in particular, employed westernized methods of environmental conservation and these failed to yield meaningful results. Yet, in Africa, the entire relationship between humans and nature, including activities such as land use, has deep religious and spiritual underpinnings. Religion is central to many decisions people make about their own communities' development. Using the phenomenological method for its theoretical framework, our chapter explores how Manyika traditional conservation methods have been sucked by Western philosophical approaches such as egoism and selfism. In the first section, we outline how the Manyika people's cosmology shapes their environmental ethics. We also argue that when the environment is disturbed by human actions, it reacts harshly to the onslaught. What humanity calls the environmental crisis, therefore, is in fact, the environment's way of retaliating. The next segment elucidates how the Manyika women tap into their indigenous knowledge systems in order to responsibly and sustainably interact with the environmental. Here, we proffer that there is need to engage and deploy the indigenous environmental ethics and methods to

S. Zvingowanisei
Department of Philosophy, Religion & Ethics, University of Zimbabwe, Harare, Zimbabwe

S. Chirongoma (✉)
Faculty of Arts and Humanities, Religious Studies and Ethics Department, Midlands State University, Gweru, Zimbabwe


B. Okyere-Manu et al. (eds.), *Contemporary Development Ethics from an African Perspective*, Philosophy and Politics - Critical Explorations 27,
https://doi.org/10.1007/978-3-031-32898-5_8

mitigate against the impact of the environmental crisis. The chapter concludes by reiterating that an appraisal and recognition of the essence of traditional leadership and efficacy of indigenous environment strategies is imperative if environmental problems are to be curtailed.

**Keywords** Crisis · Ecology · Environment · Manyika indigenous environmental ethics · Retaliation · Shona · Post-colonial Zimbabwe

## 1 Introduction

Environmental woes are worsening day after day in the Zimbabwean society in general and the Shona-Manyika community in particular. Siltation of rivers, gullying, rise in temperatures, droughts, bare grounds, wanton cutting down of trees and eutrophication of water reservoirs are a common sight in most Zimbabwean communal and urban areas. The major environmental challenges in Zimbabwe bear the imprint of human actions. There is reason to argue that environmental challenges for the Manyika community today stem from the fact that humanity is failing to treat the environment in a responsible and protective manner.

Our objective in this chapter is not to present the traditional Manyika community as ethically pure in relation to the environment. Instead, our chapter's thrust is to demonstrate how the Manyika people have been affected by the ecological crisis as well as to illustrate how their behaviour affects the environment. We argue that the main culprit in environmental woes can be described as the skewed social, political and economic setup that in turn tamper with the environmental conservation beliefs and practices of the indigenous Manyika people. The chapter also illustrates how the Manyika attitudes to nature are strongly influenced by their religiosity and belief systems. We contend that the balance between humanity and the environment that existed in the Manyika traditional society was disturbed through interaction with the colonial capitalistic ideology whose approach to the environment is aggressive and arrogant. The colonial masters demonised indigenous conservation systems as well as the communal living setup of the Manyika people. Consequently, the Manyika attitudes and their understanding of the environment has become blurred. The harmony with nature that existed in pre-colonial Zimbabwe has been grossly contaminated. A new profit- oriented and selfish mind-set germinated among the Shona people and it focuses on self-satisfaction as the primary goal of life. Humanity became so pre-occupied with the need to open new frontiers while turning a blind eye to the effects of such a mind-set on the environment. It is our conviction that nature can be an agent of action in the ecological crisis. Given the connection between nature and the spiritual realm, there is a reason to argue that nature can retaliate against an onslaught on it. The chapter also posits that humanity's talk about the environmental crisis is a display of the self-centred nature of this species. What is referred to as the environmental crisis by the human community is not a crisis for the environment but for humanity as the environment responds negatively to humanity's onslaught on it.

Our chapter therefore seeks to answer questions such as: (1) How did the traditional Manyika society maintain ecological balance between nature and the human activities? (2) Were the Manyika concerned about the well-being of the environment before getting into contact with the West? (3) How did colonialism and the advent of a new approach to life disregard traditional environmental conservation methods of the Manyika people? (4) How can the Manyika religio-cultural environmental conservation strategies be harnessed and utilised to mitigate against the impact of the environmental crisis in Zimbabwe?

## 2 The Manyika People

The Manyika people who have been selected in this research as the reference point are a branch of the broader Shona speaking people in Zimbabwe and they are mainly situated in Manicaland province. The Manyika people have been selected as the reference point mainly because the first missionaries who later turned colonialists established their first mission stations in Manicaland province in the 1890s, for example, St Augustine's Mission of the Anglican Church and Old Mutare Mission of the Methodist church *inter-alia.* This has motivated the researchers to hold that the Manyika people have been in contact with the colonial ideology for some time as compared to other Shona speaking people. With this in mind, our general assumption is that the Manyika people's traditional environmental conservation methods and their attitudes to nature have suffered a long period of colonial aggression in all spheres of life ranging from the social, economic, political, religious and environmental among others. The impact of colonialism or westernisation on the traditional conservation systems is thus, so manifest. We therefore feel that the impact of the Manyika people can give a hint on what happened and is happening to other Shona communities in Zimbabwe. As such, the term Shona and Manyika will be used interchangeably in this chapter.

Scholars like Tatira (2000), Masaka and Chemhuru (2010) and Taringa (2014) have discussed environmental ethics among the Shona people in light of *mitupo* (totems) and *zvieraera* (taboos). They argue that these are instrumental tools in fostering environmental conservation among the Shona people. Though these scholarly works have been presented, in this chapter, the researchers feel that there is need to go beyond highlighting the ethical relevance of Shona traditional values, taboos and totems. Our chapter adds to the ongoing discussions and it focuses on investigating how and why Zimbabwe continues to face environmental challenges despite the attractive traditional environmental conservation strategies of the Shona people. We take note of the fact that despite the positive attitudes of the Shona people to the environment as presented by scholars like Masaka and Chemhuru (2010), Mapara (2009), Muguti and Maposa (2012), Muyambo (2017), Taringa (2014) and Tanyanyiwa (2019), the Shona societies are still writhing in pain today under unprecedented environmental doldrums. In this vein, our chapter contends that the rich environmental conservation techniques of the traditional Manyika society have been suppressed by the colonial mentality. Mental colonisation took a roost in the midst of the Shona people's environmental ethic to the extent that they now regard the imported western knowledge as superior and their own indigenous knowledge systems as inferior. Hence, we are advocating for a return to the traditional environmental conservation practices which sustained the environment in the past. It is our conviction that traditional environmental conservation strategies are nearer to the indigenous people as compared to some of the imported scientific approaches.

## 3 Phenomenological Approach

The phenomenological approach provides a platform for the researched community to speak for themselves whilst the researcher refrains from judging or evaluating the phenomena under study. Using the phenomenological method, our chapter analyses Shona people's attitudes to nature, with particular reference on the Manyika. It examines the interplay between religion and ethics in traditional Shona society in relation to environmental conservation. We also investigate how the fragile balance between human activities and the environment was disturbed through interaction with the west. Mawere (2013) explored the effects of colonization on indigenous Zimbabwean environmental conservation methods in light of causing pressure on resources, for instance, through the Land Apportionment Act and the Creation of Tribal Trust Lands. Mawere (2013) succeeded in highlighting that colonial legislation and the Land Tenure Act caused pressure on resources through land policies. Drawing insights from the field research conducted among the Manyika people in chief Mutasa's community in July 2019, we argue that there is more to colonisation than causing pressure on resources through land policies. Our discussion therefore goes beyond Mawere's (2013) observation into unravelling how colonialism changed the economic system of the traditional Manyika people. We take note of for instance, how the study participants decried the submersion of the communalistic mentality of the Manyika people based on the underlying ethical principle of *Ubuntu/hunhu/ unhu*, by the colonial ideology and the germination of a profit oriented, capitalist mind-set triggered in a general ignorance of environmental conservation practices. This inevitably provided fecund ground for a 'survival of the fittest' mode of existence. Stampede for natural resources through legal and illegal means in order to make profit became manifest. Westernisation therefore, caused discord in the Shona people's environmental management systems. Using the Manyika people as a case study, our chapter analyses the way in which a capitalistic economy created poverty, caused pressure on resources, created ignorance about environmental management as people strive for survival and are preoccupied with amassing wealth for themselves without concern for the environment.

## 4 The Manyika People's Cosmology and How It Sharpens Their Environmental Ethic

The concept of being among the Manyika people is not partial, but all-encompassing and total. *Being* is so diverse in its manifestation and there is solid unity in that diversity. Etim (2013:15) posits that in African cosmology, "No being exists in isolation but ontologically in connection and interaction with other beings (both animate and inanimate)." In concurrence, an African can realise himself/herself in the midst of the hierarchy of beings; some above and some below (both animate and inanimate). In this sense, it can be noted that among the Africans in general and the Shona people of Zimbabwe in particular, there is unity of beings, there is unity in diversity among beings. Unlike the western culture that values the "I" ignoring the "we", the Manyika people have a communal approach to life. The underlying Manyika philosophy is, "*Tiripo nokuda kwenyu, muripo nekuda kwedu.* (We are because of you, you are because of us)" (Interviewee 1, 2019). The "we" encompasses even the spiritual entities and even the inanimate beings for these are believed to be the habitat of the ancestors. Anthropocentric attitudes to the environment are an import and an anterior to the Shona culture. The ontological connection and interaction are described by Momoh (2000) as communal spiritualism implying that the spirit of the whole community is harnessed in one unity for the benefit of the individual. The physical grouping of beings is understood as nothing but simply a reflection of the ontological order and harmony in the universe. Given this value ascribed to the unity of being, the traditional Manyika people of Zimbabwe found themselves compelled to promote and maintain harmony with the environment.

As such, the holistic and interrelated profile of the African worldview manifests itself in Manyika society. Respect for all creation manifests itself among the Manyika people. It is common to hear of "rain snakes", "lions of the ancestors", sacred animals, trees, groves, pools etc., showing that humanity approaches the environment with ingrained respect. Ancestors, spirit mediums and territorial spirits are indispensable entities of the Shona cosmology (Muguti and Maposa 2012). These spirits facilitate communication between the visible and the invisible worlds (Cox 2006:107). African cosmology exists in a hierarchical structure which is designed in accordance with seniority. As noted by Mapara (2009), the order in the hierarchy can be illustrated as follows:

1. God/ The Supreme being (*Mwari*)
2. Ancestors (*Midzimu*)
3. Territorial spirits (*Mhondoro*)
4. Alien spirits (*Mashavi*)
5. Nature spirits
6. Human beings (*Vanhu*)
7. Nature (*Zvisikwa*)

## 5 God/The Supreme Being (*Mwari*)

As shown above, the first in the hierarchy of beings is the supreme being/God (*Mwari*), who is understood to be the overseer of all human activities. Among the Shona, *Mwari* is all-powerful and has the capacity to bless or curse the living whenever they misstep (Taringa 2014). Mbiti (1969) notes that the Shona people have the name *Nyadenga* (the owner of the sky). *Mwari* is also called *Musiki* (Creator). He is the Creator and sustainer of the whole cosmos (Bourdillon 1976). Hence, according to the Shona people's worldview, since *Mwari* is the giver of rain, the fecundity of the Earth is dependent on him. *Mwari* can withhold the heavens such that no rains fall on the ground if people continuously sin. One of the reasons that triggers *Mwari* to withhold the rains is *hutsinye kumhuka* (cruelty to animals). *Mwari* is therefore understood as a God who punishes the living for any sins committed whether against Him, animals or inanimate beings or even among people themselves. For this reason, *Mwari* is understood as the principal overseer of environmental conservation management (Muyambo 2017).

## 6 Ancestors/(*Midzimu*)

In the hierarchy of being, God is followed by the ancestors (*midzimu/madzitateguru*). According to Gelfand (1973), ancestors are understood by the Shona people as the spirits of the deceased forefathers/foremothers who are active in the lives of their living descendants. Ancestors occupy a strategic position in the relationship between human beings and the Supreme Being. They occupy the spiritual realm, thus, giving them an edge over the living. The Shona believe that *Madzitateguru* are nearer to the creator *Musikavanhu*. Assuch, they act as the conveyor belt between the living and God. These ancestors are believed to be the guardians of the land (Bourdillon 1976). The forests, mountains, groves, rivers, pools, caves and other natural phenomena are all believed to be the habitat of the ancestors. Ancestors always safeguard these areas since they are their habitat. The fear of ancestral wrath among the Shona therefore triggers the emergence and valuing of taboos, myths and reverence of sacred places (Muguti and Maposa 2012).

Taringa and Sipeyiye (2013:57) support this standpoint by arguing that the living are the custodians of the resources for the future generation within the kinship social group. In this sense, being is not an isolated entity among the Shona people. Everything was created for a purpose. Even the unintelligent beings like insects and animals want to preserve their bodies in a warm, comfortable way and avoid suffering. This was explicated by Interviewee 2 as follows:

> *Chinhu chose chakasikwa naMwari chine chakakosha uye chine basa rechakasikirwa. Hapana chinhu chakasikwa chisina basa. Kunyangwe masvosve chaiwo akakosha uye haatodiwo kufa.* (Everything which was created by God is important and it serves a purpose.

> There is nothing which was created which is useless. Even ants are also important and they also fear death (Interviewee 2, 2019).

For the Africans in general and the Shona people in particular therefore, being forms an intricate nexus of reality. It is the holistic interconnection that exists among particular beings that is important. It is in this vein that Mapara (2009) posits that Africans have their indigenous methods of respecting the environment as "being" worth reckoning. This respect has significantly assisted the Africans to cope with natural diseases and disasters.

## 7 A Comparative Analysis of the Manyika and the Western Concept of the Environment

A comparative analysis of the concept of environment among the Shona people and that of the West serves to shed light on the areas of divergence between the two worldviews. One's attitude to nature depends on and is shaped by the angle from which one views the world. The researchers are convinced that a clear picture on the differences in approach to the environment between the Manyika and the West is helpful in assessing the extent to which colonialism affected the traditional conservation strategies. While the West considers humanity as the overlord of nature, the Manyika people view themselves as an integral part of creation. This comparative analysis lays a foundation for the next section that evaluates how the traditional conservation practices have been degraded by colonialism from the West.

As noted by Kopnina et al. (2018), the western concept of the environment is anthropocentric, that is, it has a bias towards humanity. Such attitudes to nature see nothing wrong with the cruel treatment of non-human beings unless such treatment leads to bad consequences for humanity. Such a mentality proves that the westerners have a self-centred approach to life and the environment. They are concerned about their welfare even when it means plundering of resources. Non-human beings are thus regarded as secondary. They are "objects" while humans accord themselves a comfortable position of "subjects". All non-human beings are therefore presented as instruments for humanity's satisfaction. Exploitation of the environment is deemed justified as long as it serves to sustain the human race's interests (Kopnina et al. 2018). This shares resonance with the egoism and selfism ethical theories which focus on the individual's personal interests.

Singer (1995:79) submits that there is need for human species to be morally concerned with non-human animals especially those that do have the conscious feeling of pain and pleasure. Though Singer tried in according moral status to some non-human beings, his consideration is narrow given the fact that he based his argument on the ability to feel pain or pleasure. While his argument is plausible, he however leaves other beings outside the "enclosure" for moral consideration. The part of being that does not have the conscious feeling of pain and pleasure is thus left out in the equation for moral consideration. In this light, the Western understanding of the environment remains skewed. This position is supported by Mangena (2012:13) who notes that reason and sentience cannot satisfactorily settle the moral status puzzle in environmental ethics. The western mind takes humanity as the "overlord" of all creation which pushes humanity into thinking that they can exploit everything to their advantage. The "responsible stewards" emblem thus, disappears leaving the rogue face of humanity as a polluter, destroyer, desertifier and generally, the enemy of the environment.

Unlike the Western understanding of the environment that gives human beings unlimited control over nature, the traditional Manyika people used to be very considerate about the welfare of both human as well as non-human beings. The traditional Shona people understood the environment as three-tier, that is, the interplay of three major beings namely human beings, non-human beings, and spiritual beings. Mangena (2012)'s sentiments clearly present the all-inclusiveness of the African environment. From the foregoing, it can be observed that the Africans are aware of the fact that the universe is a composite unit calling for mutual respect from all its members. While human beings appear to be at the centre of the African environment, their existence finds expression in their association with human animals through totemism (Taringa 2008). Human beings and the broader environment are so conjoined and intertwined such that no force can disentangle that bond.

Although Western anthropocentric thinkers maintain that humanity has no obligation for future generations, a closer analysis shows that there is a strong obligation. The question that comes to mind is, if the past generation had been so exploitative and selfish, then what could these greedy and egoistic thinkers be depending on as they speak now? There is therefore need for sustainable utilization of available resources. The traditional Manyika society was very much aware of the interdependence between humanity and the environment. They were all aware of the fact that an affront to the environment today is an affront to humanity either in the present generation or in the generations to come. Armed with this understanding, they tried their best to preserve the environment through different ways like prescribing hunting laws, enforcing taboos, myths, promoting environmental education through proverbs, folklores, songs, branding endangered animals and trees as sacred species. The major reason for protecting the resources was "to promote harmony with the ancestors as well as concern for *kugadzira nhaka yevana* (preserving resources for the benefit of the future generations)" (Interviewee 3: 2019).

In the traditional African worldview, there is no dichotomy between plants, animals and inanimate things between the sacred and the profane, the communal and the individual (Eliade 1963). This approach to reality is manifest among the Shona people. Shoko (2013) noted that there is evidence on the ground for the interplay of the spiritual realm and humanity among the Shona people. Shoko illustrates this point by citing the 2007 diesel saga in Chinhoyi whereby a self-styled traditional diviner, Rotina Mavhunga duped the government into believing that she had discovered a diesel producing rock in Chinhoyi, Mashonaland West province in Zimbabwe. This helps to understand how the indigenous Africans perceive the environment. Government officials led by Chris Mushowe visited the place and followed the ritual procedures as directed by Rotina Mavhunga with the hope of bringing good news to the nation that the ancestors had intervened in arresting the multiple socio-economic woes that bedevilled the nation during the peak of the country's economic crisis during the years 2007 and 2008 (Shoko 2013).

Despite the Chinhoyi diesel saga being described as the government's desperate attempt to find a solution to the ailing economy and fuel shortages during the hyper-inflationary era in Zimbabwe, the belief that the ancestors are capable of intervening in human life is also foregrounded. Shoko (2013) makes it clear that Mavhunga's operations unravel the potency of spiritual forces that populate the spiritual realm and sacred places in Zimbabwe. It also clearly demonstrates that in Zimbabwe, sacred places are perceived as the abode of ancestors. It therefore follows that the concept of the environment among the Shona people of Zimbabwe is not human-centred as that of the West. Instead, it even includes all those entities like mountains, caves, forests, river bodies, plants and other natural phenomena make up the cosmos. Since the ancestors and the environment do interplay, therefore, humanity is motivated into respecting the environment (Bishau 1997). Hence, sacred places are symbolic in as far as they are the meeting point between the heavens, the sky and the Earth, of the visible and invisible worlds (Bishau 1997).

## 8 How the Traditional Manyika People Revered and Conserved the Environment

Non-human entities constitute part of the Shona cosmology, it is believed to be imbued with the spiritual dimension (Aschwanden 1985). It is the dynamic nature of spirits that pushes the Shona to invoke or talk to trees, rivers, mountains, etc. As noted by Cox (2006), there is no dichotomy between the sacred and the profane, this leads the Manyika to revere the environment. Similarly, Taringa and Sipeyiye (2013) postulated that there are rules applied to humanity's attitude towards nature. Hence, nature cannot be exploited willy-nilly among the Shona people as would obtain in a materialist society, instead, set rules must be adhered to. Observance of taboos, belief in totemism and sacred places are all efforts by the Shona people to maintain harmony with the environment.

An affront on the environment is in fact an affront against the ancestors since they are domiciled in the natural habitat. Gombe (1998) affirms that the ancestors are responsible for safeguarding the welfare of the living, they enforce harmony between humanity and the environment. There is a strong belief among the Shona that even resources like minerals are bequeathed by the ancestors. The land itself is a preserve of the ancestors. On this note, Interviewee 4, had this to say,

> *Isu sewaManyika tinodaira kuti vadzimu ndiwo vanopa hupfumi hwakaita sengoda negoridhe. Vadzimu ndiwozve varidzi venyika.* (We as the Manyika people believe that wealth such as diamonds and gold come from the ancestors. Ancestors are also the owners of the land (Interviewee 4: 2019).

One of the renowned musicians in Zimbabwe, Hosiah Chipanga composed a song when diamonds were discovered in Chiadzwa area of Manicaland. In the song, he remarked that "*Zamu raNehanda rasisa ngoda*" (the breasts of Nehanda, the spirit medium are oozing with diamonds). These lyrics bear testimony of the Manyika worldview igniting the belief that the ancestors are the guardians of all the resources. It confirms that there is a close relationship between the living and the ancestors with the latter facilitating even the discovery of minerals like diamonds. The indigenous Manyika people uphold the general belief that as people became greedy in extracting the Chiadzwa diamonds, the diamonds became scarce. Such a belief bolsters the point that there is a holistic approach to life among the Manyika. Ancestors among the Manyika people even hold their descendants responsible for the proper conduct of lineage affairs including care for the environment. The dead are thus respected more than the living. Upholding the belief that the "living dead" as Mbiti (1969) would like to describe the ancestors, are the guardians of nature, the Manyika people have developed various myths and values related to environmental conservation in an endeavour to promote and maintain harmony with the ancestors.

## 9 Totemism as an Environmental Conservation Ethic Among the Traditional Manyika People

The concept of totemism (*mutupo*) clearly demonstrates the Manyika people's respect for the environment. According to Nyajeka (1996:138),

> The *mutupo* (totemism) principle focuses on fostering the primary relationships between animals and humans, animals and the deity, humans and humans, deity and humans, nature and humans, the dead and the living. The *mutupo* principle attempts to enumerate or approximate the ideal mode of life which assures a sustainable future of all existence. An analysis of the fundamental elements of the *mutupo* principle reveals that it is a principle which seeks to create cosmology that takes the existence of non-human entities seriously.

Totemism is a system of thought and social practice which is based on a relationship posited between a clan and/or a person and an animal, an object or a plant. Humans, thus, appropriate the positive attributes of an animal or natural phenomena like bravery, generosity, hunting prowess, etc. so as to claim a higher social status over their fellows. Among the Shona people of Zimbabwe, there are those of the *Shumba* (lion), *Humba* (pig), *Moyo* (cow), *Beta* (termites), *Nzou* (elephant), *Nhewa* (leopard), *Soko* (monkey), *Chihwa* (wild cat), *inter alia.* Actually, almost every animal is someone else's totem. Totemism clearly demonstrates that the Manyika people value the non-human beings. This is the main reason why the Manyika value these animals.

Mangena (2016) explained the essence of totemism in environmental conservation. He noted that if one's totem is *Humba* (pig/*nguruve*), one cannot therefore eat pig meat. Mangena (2016) holds that this is meant not only to protect the pig species from extinction through arbitrary hunting for meat but also to show that pigs and humans are related. For a person of the pig totem, eating pig meat will be like eating one's self. It is even taboo to eat one's totem for it is believed that it will cause one's teeth to decay. Each clan therefore, will accord respect to their totemic animal. In this way, the animal species are preserved and protected from extinction.

Although totemism in African societies and the Manyika people has been praised as presented above, there are still concerns about environmental management through totemism. For instance, despite the attractive outlook of totemism for environmental conservation, there is an ongoing concern that environmental damage is rising in Manyika communities and Zimbabwe at large. As Daneel (2001:9) rightly observed, "If one visits most of Zimbabwe's rural areas, one may despair at the sight of a wounded Earth". Zimbabweans still respect each other using their totems. Among the Manyika, they usually address each other through totems (*mitupo*) and praise names (*zvidao*) in greetings for example, "*Muri wadi here Shumba* (How are you man of the lion totem?)". It is worrying that though totems are still used in "modern" Zimbabwe, they are not fostering the much-expected conservation. It is the contention of this chapter that the worsening environmental situation among the Manyika people and Zimbabwe in general does not nullify the essence of totems in promoting environmental conservation. Instead, it gives a clue to the effect that some discord infiltrated and polluted the purity and effectiveness of traditional environmental practices. As such, there is need to investigate how and why traditional environmental conservation methods lost their palatability and efficacy as far as environmental conservation is concerned.

## 10 Environmental Concept of *Chadzimira Musango* (Wandering in the Forest)

As a way of guarding against the violation of the environment, the concept of *chadzimira musango* (wandering in the forest) scares people from ruthless exploitation of the environment. It is common in the traditional Manyika society that if a person gets into a forest and makes nasty comments about what he/she sees there, for instance, commenting that fruits like *mazhanje* (wild loquards) in the forest are not tasty, pulling unripe fruits from a tree which is described by Mawere (2013) as "*kukwazha michero*", (pruning and hoarding wild fruits), this will automatically lead to blindness and disorientation such that one will not find his/her way home.

For example, one of the weekly newspapers in Zimbabwe, *The Manica Post* of the week 6–12 August 2004, published the story of 19 years old Loveness Bhunu who disappeared in the sacred Nzunza mountain in Manicaland. She had gone there to look for sweeping brooms. She was with her 8 years old sister who survived death after falling down a slope. The story surrounding her disappearance is that she angered the spirits of the mountains by despising the size of the sweeping brooms. The villagers in this area are convinced that the spirits of the mountains were angry and caused the girl's death (Manica Post, Mutare, 6–12 August 2004, "Missing Girl

Found Dead in Sacred Mountain" p. 1). Gelfand who conducted research among the Shona confirms this belief. He writes,

> So strong is the feeling among the Shona that one entering a strange area in the forest, a mountain or a beautiful spot is not allowed to comment on it lest he [sic] upsets the ancestral spirits (*vadzimu*) of the region (Gelfand 1981:54)

The idea of losing one's way back home because of violating the environmental stipulations of the ancestors is indicative of the well-knit rules and regulations about respect for the environment. The ideas presented above are part of the lengthy networks of rules and myths surrounding environmental conservation in traditional Manyika society. It is therefore evident that there is a sense in which the traditional Shona society was very much aware of the need to respect the natural environment as the habitat of the ancestral spirits. Simple and non-human beings of the universe like wild fruits and mushrooms were equally accorded respect. No one was expected to collect more than one could consume for it was a manifestation of greed. This is completely different from the Western mentality which disregards moral status to non-sentient beings of the universe, resulting in some individuals selfishly amassing wealth. Contrariwise, the Shona are aware that though non-sentient, such beings are an embodiment of ancestral spirits, hence, the need to be respected. Fear of nature's aggression through misfortunes, illnesses or simply fear of the unknown would constantly ring a bell in the mind of a traditional Manyika person about the need to respect the environment.

## 11 The Concept of Sacred Pools and Places as an Environmental Conservation Method

The traditional Shona people knew how to protect the purity of their water sources. In an interview with Interviewee 5, she articulated this as follows:

> Some sacred pools were no-go areas for the ordinary people. Some of the pools were known as *dziva renjuzu* (mermaid pools). The mermaid played a vital role of safe-guarding the purity of the water. It was discouraged to use soap in such pools, especially perfumed soaps. Pots or any containers that had been set on the fire or with soot, were not allowed to be used to fetch water in any well or else the well would dry up. Violators risked *kutorwa nenjuzu* (being drowned into the pool by the mermaid). The fear of disappearing into the pool was enough deterrent for potential polluters to stay away from the pools. It was also believed that violation of rules pertaining to the pool would result in the mermaid spirit relocating and the subsequent drying up of the pool (Interviewee 5: 2019).

Due to the fear of the consequences of their actions, pollution of the water sources especially by intentional human actions was minimised. The Shona people can therefore be applauded for making giant strides towards maintaining the environment, in this case, the water sources. Taringa and Sipeyiye (2013:57) aver that, "The spiritual attachment to the land inspired by indigenous religion and revered by the people ensured a very positive environmental ethic. In the past, the Shona knew how to deal with nature and the environment".

It can be concluded, therefore, that the Shona people knew how to protect forests and water sources with the use of belief systems and value systems attached to places. This section has presented the Shona as a people who strongly value their ancestors and the environment. The harmony that existed in the traditional Shona society between humanity and the environment has also been presented together with some of the ways in which humans tried to safeguard that harmony. The next section explores how the capitalist economy has caused discord in as far as the Shona people are related to their environment. It examines the extent to which the Western colonial system affected the traditional environmental conservation methods.

## 12 The Capitalist Economy and How It Disrupted the Shona People's Unity with Their Environment

The colonization of Zimbabwe in general and the Manyika in particular disturbed the whole system of environmental conservation methods. Granted, the traditional Manyika people could violate environmental purity through their use of bush toilets and other ecologically unfriendly behaviours. However, a closer look shows that the problems worsened as the Manyika got into contact with Western ideologies. Colonialism brought in a new economic system based on a profit-making model through the amassment of wealth by individuals. Daneel (1998) posits that the Western colonisers used racial superiority as a basis to subdue traditional practices including environmental conservation strategies. The "modern" capitalistic economy claims to be more adventurous and advanced such that it tries to invent and reinvent the order of the African society. This "modernity" has uprooted the Shona people from their firm traditional ground of environmental conservation. The cultural onslaught on the Shona worldview has unsettled the harmonious relationship that existed in the traditional Shona society between humans and the environment. An alien, individualistic and selfish economic mode has caught the generous and communal Shona philosophy unaware. The Shona people have thus been thrown into a mud of confusion. This section therefore, unravels ways in which colonialism negatively affected the Shona people's attitudes to the environment. It foregrounds how capitalism has triggered avarice, selfism, poverty and general neglect of the environment among the Shona people. More than forty years after attaining political independence in Zimbabwe, the imprints of colonial aggression on traditional Shona ways of life and environmental conservation systems are still glaringly manifest.

## 13 The Impact of Colonialism on the Manyika People's Socio-economic Life

Colonialism brought with it a new approach to life among the Manyika people. The concept of "*Hunhu*" and the general individual obligation to the maintenance of the society's communal good was threatened by the coming of colonial masters in Zimbabwe. *Hunhu* is the underlying ethical philosophy among the Shona (Bourdillon 1976). Mawere (2013) states that land policies like the Land Apportionment Act congested the indigenous people into impoverished areas. Pressure on resources ensued such that the communal responsibility in conserving the environment became difficult. The introduction of an economy based on profit and competition between individuals also impacted negatively on the traditional Manyika people's environmental conservation systems. Several novel approaches to socio-economic life were introduced to the Manyika community, for instance, the introduction of money as a medium of exchange, the individualistic approach to life, the idea of profiteering, *inter-alia*. How these impacted negatively to the environmental conservation methods is going to be discussed in the ensuing sections.

## 14 Profit Making and Profiteering as the New Approach to Economic Life in the Post-colonial Manyika Society

Unlike in the traditional Shona setup where there was no profit -making motive in the exchange of goods and services, the goal of business in the modern Manyika environment which was introduced by the colonialists is profit maximisation among other benefits. According to Brady (1999:434), business is a profit-oriented enterprise. It refers to a nexus of commercial activities aimed at gaining profit. For Brady (1999), profit is a mark-up or the rate of return on capital. Smith (1976) emphasises that profit is the motivating factor in a business transaction. Weber (1958:53) notes that humans are dominated by the making of money by acquisition as the ultimate purpose of life. From this understanding, business is not a way of life as the case with the traditional Shona people's sense of business, it is not a way of earning a living. There is limited to no room for generosity, compassion, courtesy or concern for the environment. The general thrust is to reduce expenditure as much as possible and to accrue as much profit as possible by exploitation and acquisition. In this sense, business revolves around the politics of the stomach, wealth and self-satisfaction as the primary goal and everything else is secondary.

Bossel (1998: xi) foregrounds how westernisation follows the bandwagon of profiteering coupled with looting. The situation is pathetic with individual goals or satisfaction promoted at the expense of majority goals. In a capitalist economy, the need to amass wealth avails a lush breeding ground for competition. It is true that corruption wracks havoc in a capitalistic economy since everyone will be thinking of capitalising on any slight opportunity so as to accrue wealth under his/her name.

Generally, leaders in a capitalistic economy have "no maps" that lead to the general good of the society. Their goals and objectives are "clauses" that lead to personalised destinations and personalised benefits. The leaders lack clear goals. The individualistic nature of capitalism thus, vividly manifests itself through solid concern for personal welfare at the expense of societal good (Bossel 1998: xi). It is interesting to note that the sale and transfer of land was unknown in the traditional Shona society. Interviewee 6 echoed the same sentiments when he said,

> *Makare-kare hataiziva kuti nyika inotengeswa. Zvaiera. Nyika yakange iri yemunhu wese munharaunda. Saka hapana akanga aine mvumo yekutengesa ivhu rinomuriritira.* (In the past, it was taboo for anyone to sell the land. The land belonged to the whole community and no one had the right to dispose the soil from which humans derive their sustenance (Interviewee 6, 2019).

The above observation affirms the fact that the traditional Shona society had no profit motives in its dealings. It is this emblem that sets the traditional Shona people apart and so different from the Western, capitalistic society. Bossel (1998: xi) laments such a status quo whereby individual satisfaction is promoted at the expense of majority goals. Capitalism makes use of the idea of the market which is nothing but a selfish exploitation of those who have no choice, those that have no voice. Value in this exploitative market is determined by neglecting "external costs" to society, the environment and the future. It is regrettable that capitalism supports a small population in luxury instead of providing a large population with the essentials of life. As the majority is buried, they will embark on anything that can help them to earn a living. In the process, natural resources are the easiest target. Such a scenario forces the traditional Manyika people to ignore some, if not all of the traditional environmental conservation practices. They are making frantic efforts to survive first, then ethical consideration of the environment latter.

Bossel (1998) further observed that the colonial government has also accorded transnational corporates space to harvest wealth, from the colonised nations. These corporates wield more power than most national governments, especially in developing nations. The end result is the prosperity of some regions through exploiting others. The sharp contrast between the traditional Shona society and that of the west lies on the aspect of profit. It is also important to note that whilst the Manyika people in a traditional society view forests as protected treasures, heeding the ecological laws of the ancestral guardians of the land, the western capitalist figures are the reverse. The imperialists, for instance, looked upon the wealth of trees in Africa as a kind of "Christian paradise" which evoked afresh God's primordial laws of human stewardship of all nature (Bossel 1998). Armed with this mentality, the foreign missionaries who accompanied the colonial entourage devised means and ways of exploiting the environment to their advantage. This lays bare the fact that profit making is the sole goal in a capitalist's mind.

Although the Western colonisers had their approach to environmental conservation, like enforcing legislation in favour of environmental conservation, the confusion and pressure they inflicted on locals is a cause for concern. Mawere (2013) has highlighted that colonialism forced the traditional African society to ignore their indigenous conservation methods. The imbalance in the distribution of resources like land worked against the implementation of the modern methods of environmental conservation like crop rotation and fallow farming. As such, pressure on the environment kept on piling especially with the rise in population.

## 15 Selfism and Egoism as a New System of Life Among the Manyika People

Capitalism is characterised by selfish and egoistic motives. Westernisation brought with it value for individual reasoning without any space for communal reasoning. *Hunhu* for the Shona people has been abandoned and thrown into the rubbish pit. The Westerners therefore, believe that it is through an individual's reasoning capacity, planning and acute entrepreneurial skills that he/she accrues wealth and property. The value given to the individual's reasoning at the expense of group thinking is the breeding ground for selfish motives in a capitalistic society. When employed within the Shona society, the concept of *Ubuntu/hunhu* was displaced. Communal responsibility in managing the environment waned away. Such developments had detrimental effects on the environment as each individual can now exploit the environment to satisfy personal needs. Worth noting is the fact that Westernisation is alien to the Shona people of Zimbabwe. It is in fact, an intruder causing discord in the smooth running of their indigenous environmental management systems. In the process, the harmony which existed between the Shona people, the ancestors and the environment in the traditional society is disturbed and broken. In short, the *Ubuntu/hunhuist* philosophy is shot down. Traditional methods of conserving the environment were demonised. The utility of myths, taboos, ancestors and sacred places to conserve the environment was regarded as backward, uncivilised and barbaric. The traditional Shona people ended up shunning the "backward" conservation methods for the "modern". Important to note is that the traditional methods of environmental conservation are nearer home for the Shona people than imported brands which value the "self" and not the "other" person. Capitalism waters its riches with the tears of the poor. Hence, the plight of the poor becomes a very lucrative fishing pond for the rich.

## 16 How Colonisation Discouraged Communal Responsibility in Resource Management

Economic liberalisation introduced to the African society by the West has the prospect of recolonization of the vast natural resources of Africa like land, water and minerals. Greed by the elite members of the society causes resources' capture whereby resource distribution is shifted to the favour of a small group. Before the coming of the capitalist economy, the Shona people had managed to maintain a delicate balance between cultivation and grazing. Their operations were guided by a rich philosophy of *Ubuntu/hunhu*. Signs of conflict between the capitalistic economy and the traditional Shona values began to emerge when new ideas and techniques from Europe began to dominate the Shona people. Truly, the adoption of imported perceptions on business and survival eroded the indigenous process of resource conservation. The main priority of the capitalistic economy was the generation of cash and everything else became secondary. Tevera and Moyo (2000) makes it clear that colonialism has further marginalised the indigenous people. The poor became poorer with their numbers growing exponentially. In the process, damage to the environment worsened.

In most African communities like that of the Shona, natural resource management and conservation are products of people's spirituality, culture, traditional customs, taboos and indigenous knowledge systems accumulated over centuries by millions of people and passed down from generation to generation. The knowledge is therefore, tried and tested. Availability of resources for the Shona people is, therefore, a testimony of the firmness of the bond between the dead and the living. In this vein, conserving the environment is conserving and protecting the habitat of the spiritual beings (Nyahunda and Tirivangasi 2021). However, fierce competition in a globalised economy destroyed the Shona people's communal ecological systems and economies. Social systems were stressed to the maximum, for instance, instead of community elders leading the society, it is now politicians who control people's lives.

Globalisation has been described by Bossel (1998: xi) as the "rape" of societies and the environment by transnational economic interests in the name of a fictitious "free market" and it's supposed benefit for all. This globalisation revolves around technology as the compass of development. Technology however, should be understood as the "mindless production and consumption" in the name of "progress", "export advantage" and "employment" of everything that can be made and be sold at a profit without minding the social and environmental cost of such" (Bossel 1998).

The African society had been known to be a communal society with the resources communally owned as well. This standpoint is supported by Gelfand (1973) who argues that resources in Africa are seen as a bundle rather than sectorally. In the capitalistic governments and other institutions, they perceive them in concurrence. Gombe (1998) posits that in Africa, people live in the same area or village and the village members are almost from the same family. Among the Manyika, this extended family is called *dzinza* (clan). As such, they can manage their resources together. Such an arrangement ascertains and confirms the concept of collective responsibility. The West however, is individualistic, it alienates an individual nuclear family from the extended family. Land, for instance, is divided into farms and plots which are no go areas to strangers. Warning signs like "**Trespassers will be prosecuted**" will be pinned on the fence or durawalls, an indication that the property is a preserve of that individual. This is normal in a capitalistic society, but for the Shona people, "*musha usingasviki vaenzi wakatukwa* (a homestead not frequented by visitors is considered to be cursed)" (Interviewee 7, 2019).

The Herald of 21 June 2012 published a story that accused the ministry of mines of handing mining permits to Chinese and Russian firms to explore gold and diamonds from forests in Zimbabwe. The Chief Executive officer of Allied Timbers, Dr. Joseph Kanye-Kanye was quoted complaining about such developments. The same concerns were also aired by the members of the Manyika community. Interviewee 8 succinctly put it across as follows:

> It seems as if the Zimbabwean government is driven by the profit motive in this case, than care for the environment. It has also embraced the colonial approach to life. The government's blind eye towards illegal settlers and miners will only leave a legacy of environmental destruction and degeneration to the future generation as the indigenous people are alienated from their resources. Important to note is the fact that the mining permits awarded do not serve the interests of the broader community but a small group of investors. Communal responsibility is thus no longer visible (Interviewee 8, 2019).

This section has discussed the nature of a capitalistic economy. It exposed how the incorporation of a selfish and greedy type of economy in a communally oriented and ancestral society creates discord that is extremely difficult if not impossible to redress. The section also unveiled the fact that a cancerous ailment of greed, individualism and profiteering has found its way amongst the Shona people after their interaction with a Westernised mentality. Each individual is now exploiting every available resource for personal benefits and alleviation of poverty. The next section shows how an affront on the environment harbours disaster for humanity and why "environmental retaliation" is a more appropriate phrase to use than "environmental crisis" in reference to the numerous environmental challenges faced by humanity.

## 17 The Concept of Environmental Retaliation as a Way of Promoting Concern for the Environment

Rolston (1989) argued that, "to harm nature is to harm ourselves and to defend the Earth is self-defence". Probably, it is from this understanding that the Shona people, for instance, were very cautious in interacting with the environment. They were quite aware that each of their actions was subject to scrutiny from God and the ancestors. This constant fear of the retaliating nature of the environment gave the Shona people a sense of duty in maintaining an intact balance between nature and the environment. The same sense of retaliation can be used even in the modern society to remind people of the need to maintain an ecological balance. Calamities like droughts, the spread of deadly diseases like cholera and other natural disasters can knock a sense of responsibility in the minds of the people in as far as environmental management is concerned.

## 18 *Ngozi* (Avenging Spirits) and Environmental Retaliation: A Comparison

The idea of *ngozi* (avenging spirits) presents multiple lessons in understanding the relationship between humanity and the environment. Since *ngozi* is ignited by the unjust killing or ill-treatment of a person as noted by Kileff (1970), similarly, humanity's unjust treatment of the environment also causes ecological problems. As human beings, "kill" or mistreat trees, wildlife, water courses and sources, the land and the atmosphere, inevitably, the delicate relationship with nature will be torn in the process. Nature as the abode of the ancestors cannot watch as it is being amputated, its skin scratched and its blood gushing out. The noble idea is for the environment to pose problems for humanity so that "compensation" is enhanced through care for the environment. Humanity has to pay for the *ngozi* committed to the environment through ecological mismanagement.

The concept of *mutumbu* (human body) for compensation can be literally used in the interpretation of environmental conservation. Just as humanity is afraid of *kupara ngozi* (to trigger the wrath of avenging spirits), the same fear should guide humanity into living in harmony with nature for fear of receiving the wrath of the environment as well as the fear of compensating the environment for the damage caused on it. Massive erosion, siltation of rivers, and the rising atmospheric temperature are all manifestations of the *ngozi* from the environment. Whenever such dangers strike, humanity has to pay for the damage caused through afforestation, gully reclamation and implementing conservation rules.

*Mwari* (God), together with the ancestors are pained when humanity ruthlessly attack forests, water bodies and the land. The Shona believe that God gave the world to humanity in all its abundance and splendour. The role of humanity was to serve as a steward. An honest steward should be responsible for maintaining the fragile balance of nature as intact as possible. In this regard, humanity was expected to act as ecological watchdogs, caretakers of nature or to serve as patrons for the mutual benefit of humanity and nature.

It is regrettable that despite the responsibility given to humanity to safeguard the ecological balance, human beings have proved to be irresponsible. Motivated by greed, the profit motive, ignorance, especially following the interception of a capitalistic mode of economy, human beings proved to be dishonest stewards. They indulge in over exploitation and plundering of resources. The *Ubuntu/hunhu* that once encouraged the maintenance of an ecological balance in nature in a traditional Shona society is no longer vibrant due to the intrusion of a profit oriented and individualistic mode of economy in the face of capitalism. All these are evils against the environment and the rise of a "vengeful environmental spirit" is sure to manifest itself through droughts and other similar problems. In other words, God and the ancestors withdraw from creation when offended thus exposing humanity to a myriad of problems.

The ecological crisis that is currently confronting humanity needs to be understood as just effects to the antecedents. It is humanity's interaction with the environment in the absence of *Ubuntu/hunhu* that triggers a negative response from the environment. The Shona proverb *tsvaru akadana tivu* (a light stroke invites a heavy blow) can be used to understand the harshness with which the environment will retaliate to the onslaught on it by humanity. It is humanity's negative manipulation of the forces of nature that invite tragedies in human life.

## 19 Conclusion

As has been articulated above, the traditional Manyika people undoubtedly lived in harmony with their environment. Although traits of environmental pollution could be witnessed, for instance, pollution of water sources through human waste due to the use of bush toilets, the fact remains that the Manyika people made concerted efforts to conserve the environment. It needs to be affirmed that torrents of environmental damage ballooned after the interference of the colonial, social, environmental and economic system. Western oriented approaches to environmental conservation and management displayed some deficiencies when applied to the Manyika communities. In response, the environment retaliated, resulting in what humans refer to as the environmental "crisis," however, in this chapter we prefer to refer to the same as "environmental retaliation." The fact that punishment befalls humanity for ecological mismanagement which is wounding the world, for instance, illegal mining, deforestation, pollution of water bodies and the atmosphere, *inter alia*, serves to reinforce the point that the spirit world retaliates when offended. Being aware of the fact helps humanity to reconcile with the environment and to avoid all activities that would wound the Earth as these would invite the wrath of the spiritual world or nature's retaliating processes.

## References

### *Secondary Sources*

Aschwanden, H. 1985. *Karanga Mythology*. Gweru: Mambo Press.

Bishau, T. 1997. *Religion and the natural environment: An investigation into the role of Jindwi traditional beliefs and practices in environmental protection*. BA dissertation, University of Zimbabwe, Department of Religious Studies.

Bossel, H. 1998. *Earth at the crossroads: Paths to a sustainable future*. Cambridge: Cambridge University Press.

Bourdillon, M.F.C. 1976. *The Shona peoples: An ethnography of the contemporary Shona with special reference to their religion*. Gweru: Mambo Press.

Brady, C.A. 1999. Environmental enrichment for captive animals. *Zoo Biology* 18: 239–241. https://doi.org/10.1002/(SICI)1098-2361(1999)18:3%3C239::AID-ZOO8%3E3.0.CO;2-R

Cox, J.L. 2006. *A guide to the phenomenology of religion: Key figures, formative influences and subsequent debates*. London/New York: T and T Clark International, A Continuum Imprint.

Daneel, M.L. 1998. African Earthkeepers. In *Interfaith mission in earthcare*, vol. 1. South Africa: University of South Africa Press.

———. 2001. *African Earthkeepers: Wholistic interfaith Mission*. New York: Orbis Books.

Eliade, M. 1963. *Patterns in comparative religion*. Cleveland: The World Publishing Company.

Etim, F. 2013. African metaphysics. *Journal of Asian Scientific Research* 3 (1): 11–17.

Gelfand, M. 1973. *The genuine Shona: Survival values of an African culture*. Gweru: Mambo Press.

———. 1981. *Ukama: Reflections on Shona and Western cultures in Zimbabwe*. Gweru: Mambo Press.

Gombe, J. 1998. *Tsika Dzavashona*. Gweru: Mambo Press.

Kileff, C. 1970. *Shona customs*. Gweru: Mambo Press.

Kopnina, H., H. Washington, B. Taylor, and J.J. Piccolo. 2018. Anthropocentrism: More than just a misunderstood problem. *Journal of Agriculture and Environmental Ethics* 31: 109–127. https://doi.org/10.1007/s10806-018-9711-1.

Mangena, F. 2012. *Moral status and the state of creation account: Critical prospects*. ZAMBEZIA: Journal of Humanities of the University of Zimbabwe.

———. 2016. African ethics through Ubuntu: A postmodern exposition. *Africology: The Journal of Pan African Studies* 9 (2): 66–80.

Mapara, J. 2009. Indigenous knowledge systems in Zimbabwe. *Juxtaposing post-colonial theory Journal of Pan African Studies* 3 (1): 139–155.

Masaka, D., and M. Chemhuru. 2010. Taboos and sources of Shona peoples environmental ethics. *Journal of Sustainable Development in Africa* 12 (7): 121–133.

Mawere, M. 2013. Traditional environmental conservation strategies in Precolonial Africa: lessons for Zimbabwe to forget or carry forward into the future. *Afro Asian Journal of Social Sciences* 4 (4.1) Quarter 1.

Mbiti, J.S. 1969. *African religions and philosophy*. London: Heinnemann.

Momoh, Campbell. S. 2000. Philosophy in African Proverbs. In *The substance of African philosophy*, 2nd ed., ed. Campbell Momoh, 359–376. Auchi: African Philosophy Project.

Muguti, T., and R.S. Maposa. 2012. Indigenous weather forecasting: A phenomenological study engaging the Shona of Zimbabwe. *The Journal of Pan African Studies* 4 (9): 102–112.

Muyambo, T. 2017. Indigenous knowledge systems: A haven for sustainable economic growth in Zimbabwe. *Africology: The Journal of Pan African Studies* 10 (3): 172–186.

Nyahunda, L., and H.M. Tirivangasi. 2021. Harnessing of social capital as a determinant for climate change adaptation in Mazungunye communal lands in Bikita, Zimbabwe. *Scientifica* 2021: 8416410. https://doi.org/10.1155/2021/8416410.

Nyajeka, T.M. 1996. Shona women and the Mutupo principle. In *Women healing earth: Third world women on ecology, feminism and religion*, ed. R.R. Ruether, 135–142. London: SCM Press.

Rolston (III), H. 1989. *Philosophy gone wild*. New York, NY: Prometheus Books.

Shoko, T. 2013. "Oozing from the rock": The diesel N'anga Saga in Chinhoyi, Zimbabwe. In *Prayers and players: Religion and politics in Zimbabwe*, ed. E. Chitando. Harare: SAPES Books.

Singer, P. 1995. Animal liberation or animal rights? In *People, penguins and plastic trees*, ed. C. Pierce and D. Van De Veer. Belmont: Wadsworth Publishing Company.

Smith, A. 1976. In *An inquiry into the nature and causes of the wealth of nations*, ed. R.H. Campbell, A.S. Skinner, and W.B. Todd. New York: Modern Library.

Tanyanyiwa, V. 2019. Indigenous knowledge systems and the teaching of climate change in Zimbabwean secondary schools. *SAGE Open*. https://doi.org/10.1177/2158244019885149.

Taringa, N. 2008. *A critical comparative analysis of Shona and Christian attitudes to nature: Phenomenological soundings*. Unpublished PhD Thesis. University of Zimbabwe.

Taringa, B. 2014. Implications of the portrayal of women in Shona proverbs for gender sensitive teaching and learning of Chishona. *ZJER* 26 (3): 395–409.

Taringa, N.T., and M. Sipeyiye. 2013. Zimbabwean indigenous religions and political Drama: The fast track land reform and the fast track change of attitude to nature 2000-2008. In *Prayers and players: Religion and politics in Zimbabwe*, ed. Chitando Ezra. Harare: SAPES Books.

Tatira, I. 2000. *The role of the zviera in socialization, indigenous knowledge and technology in Africa and diaspora communities*. Harare: University of Zimbabwe.
Tevera, D.S., and Sam, Moyo (Eds). 2000. *Environmental security in Southern Africa*. Harare: University of Zimbabwe.
The Manica Post. 2004. *Missing girl found dead in sacred mountain*, 6–12 August 2004, Mutare, Zimbabwe.
Weber, M. 1958. *The Protestant ethic and the Spirit of capitalism*. London: Allen and Unwin.

**Silindiwe Zvingowanisei** is a Lecturer at the Department of Peace Security and Society, University of Zimbabwe. She is currently a registered candidate with the same university. Her research interests include Religion and Gender & Religion and Society.

**Sophia Chirongoma** is a Senior Lecturer at the Religious Studies Department, Midlands State University, Zimbabwe. She is also an Academic Associate/Research Fellow at the Research Institute for Theology and Religion (RITR), College of Human Sciences, University of South Africa (UNISA). Her research interests and publications focus on the interface between culture, ecology, religion, health and gender justice.

# Part IV
# Gender, Ethics and Socio-economic Development in Africa

# A Blessing or a Curse: An Exploration of Zimbabwe's Plight in the Global Village

**Isaac Mhute**

**Abstract** International communication has promoted interaction and integration among various people, companies and governments of different continents, a process driven by economic, political and socio-cultural transformation. With the vast improvements in information technology, the entire world has become fully interconnected and compressed into a global village. The million-dollar question now is on the degree to which every nation is benefitting from this ethical idea now that the entire globe has been turned into a single unit. Inspired by globalization's theory of constructivism, the chapter explores the political, economic and socio-cultural fate of Zimbabwe in the globalized world. Purposively sampled Zimbabwean experiences are analyzed in light of the chosen theory to examine the extent to which the globalization exercise is either ethically or unethically impacting on the nation. The chapter establishes that the exercise has considerably come as a blessing as it is ensuring considerable progress towards ethical practices enjoyed by the nation such as abolition of inhumane practices like slavery, killing of twins and albinos as well as accommodation of impaired people in various walks of life. However, to a larger extent, the exercise proves to be a curse especially in light of the seemingly permanent aspect of economic, political and socio-cultural dependency that has since aborted any hopes for total emancipation from developed countries' clutches. As such, it concludes that most developing countries are going nowhere in as far as proper development is concerned and, as such, advocates for a closer look at how the limited developmental opportunities in the global village could be improved for the betterment of the entire global village.

**Keywords** International communication · Globalization · Theory of constructivism

---

I. Mhute (✉)
Department of Language, Literature and Culture Studies, Midlands State University's, Zvishavane, Zimbabwe
e-mail: mhutei@staff.msu.ac.zw



B. Okyere-Manu et al. (eds.), *Contemporary Development Ethics from an African Perspective*, Philosophy and Politics - Critical Explorations 27,
https://doi.org/10.1007/978-3-031-32898-5_9

# 1 Introduction

The concept of globalization has been accounted for from different angles though most of its proponents argue that its overall motive is to ethically allow political, economic and socio-cultural development of all countries to facilitate the emergence of a common conducive environment for proper human survival. Mittelman (1996) defines it as the compression of space and time. By this, emphasis is placed on the degree to which distance and time barriers have almost been nullified through technology thereby facilitating close connections between people in different corners of the world. Robertson (1992, p. 8) reiterates this perspective by describing globalization as "the compression of the world and the intensification of the consciousness of the world as a whole". The consciousness being alluded to points to the development of everyone's concern for humanity across the world. This properly relates to Giddens' (1990) definition of globalization as the intensification of worldwide relationships which link distant localities in such a way that local happenings are shaped by events occurring many miles away and vice versa. This sells the concept as an ethical development that the globe is blessed to have since a problem bedevilling a single nation would be of concern for the entire globe. This translates to true love and honest care for everyone within the entire global village. With such an approach to humanity, one would certainly expect nothing other than a perfect environment for human survival across the world. The position is confirmed by ethical global efforts towards the abolition of inhumane practices across the globe such as slavery, racism and discrimination against impairments, practices the entire world has joined hands to fight against.

As one would clearly deduce from the foregoing discussion, globalization has fully transformed a globe that used to be characterized by a collection of discrete communities interacting occasionally into an overlapping community that, in one way or the other, can no longer properly exist without interacting with each other. This chapter has been inspired by the debates orbiting around the ethicalness of the motive behind the entire concept. The debate has been properly captured by Osimiri (2015, p. 2) who notes that;

> To some, globalization is the "latest stage of imperialism" (Sivanandan 1999, p. 5); to others, globalization is the spread of western modernity" (Scholte 2005, p. 16).

In light of the atrocities typical of imperialism in its various waves, such debates raise concern over the degree to which the entire concept is bent on ethically transforming the entire globe for its betterment rather than for the achievement of the first world countries' selfish motives. The position gets its major boost from the fact that, in spite of the many years spent in the global village, where scholars believe positive relationships have been highly boosted, third world countries seem not getting nearer to positively benefiting, say by becoming developed or self-reliant in various ways. Rather, there seems to be a rise in unethical practices fuelling transnational harm (Osimiri 2015) which raises suspicion that the relationships are inspired by hidden unethical motives aimed solely at favoring the developed nations at the expense of the innocent developing ones. This is in line with critics such as Colado (2006) who have argued that the currently unfolding neoliberal globalization concentrates wealth in the hands of a few, while it leaves the majority in the condition of poverty. Ali also reiterates the position by noting that;

> ...globalization is seen as the aim of a new world order promoted by means of an identifiable geo-political, imperial strategy which corresponds to a global design to cement the position of dominant countries and to increase the affluence and promote the interests of the privileged minority of the world's population, relegating the rest to a structurally dependent and subordinate situation (2005, p. 13).

This is a major observation considering how developing countries appear not getting anywhere nearer crossing the bridge separating them from the developed ones. In fact, they seem unethically captured to cement their current status in relation to the first world countries. Osimiri (2015) notes that one way this order is being ensured is by the betrayal of third world states through the democratic deficit generated by the fact that, in the sphere of economic management, states are increasingly losing their sovereignty as the International Monetary Fund (IMF), World Bank, and World Trade Organization (WTO) take over their traditional functions. For instance, the World Bank and the IMF are often known for prescribing unpopular neoliberal policies such as currency devaluation, subsidy removal and the privatization of strategic public enterprise as conditionality for providing loans to financially distressed states. The unfortunate implication of this position is that elected indigenous leaders cede their prerogative over economic management to unelected officials of international organizations. Thus, in a way confirming the argument that globalization has come with unethical intentions of promoting captured economies for facilitating another wave of imperialism. In light of such submissions, the current chapter is set to explore the degree to which the concept of globalization has blessed or cursed the African continent in general and the Zimbabwean nation in particular.

## 2 Theoretical Framework

The current chapter was inspired by the theory of constructivism. The theory considers globalization as having arisen because of the way people have mentally constructed their social world with particular symbols, language, images and interpretation (Theys 2018). Constructivists concentrate on the ways through which social actors 'construct' their world both within their own minds and through intersubjective communication with others. They perceive all humans as equal inhabitants of a particular global world. As such, they say humans have an inbuilt belief in belonging to one global village as evident in religious and linguistic ties, among others. To them, globalization is, therefore, just an overdue effort towards realising the in-built perception of ourselves. They consider national class, religious and other identities to be responding to people's shared self-understanding for the betterment of the entire globe. Thus, the theory sees no room for structural inequalities and power hierarchies in social relations. It, therefore, perceives globalization as an ethical force with the focus of developing the entire globe into a village characterized by a common environment that is conducive for good human survival. The chapter considers this characteristic of the theory appropriate for examining the degree to which globalization has really emerged as a blessing or curse to the generation of the dream Zimbabwean nation that everyone would prefer to have for a perfect home.

## 3 Effects of Political Globalization

Political globalization deals mainly with ethical policies designed to ensure peace, health, enforcement of the rule of law, human rights protection, poverty alleviation, ensuring effective education as well as food and safety assurance. This is done through activities of global institutions such as the United Nations (UN), World Food Programme (WFP), World Health Organization (WHO), United Nations International Children's Fund (UNICEF), International Monetary Fund (IMF), World Bank and International Criminal Court (ICC).

Africa in general and Zimbabwe in particular has considerably benefited from this type of globalization. The nation used to be characterized by distinct warring kingdoms in both Mashonaland and Matabeleland segments, as they were identified by Clement Doke in 1931 (Guthrie 1948). The Kingdoms used to carry out bloody raids on each other for women, cattle and other forms of wealth. It would not be proper to ignore the ethical work done by globalization in putting an end to such an order through promoting a proper nation characterized by rule of law and democracy, though some still argue that the degree of their availability to date is still highly debatable, considering activities such as the 1987 Gukurahundi atrocities perpetrated in present day Matabeleland as well as the brutality that characterized the 2008, 2018 and preparations for the 2023 elections. Nevertheless, institutions such as proper law courts, health and education institutions inspired and informed by international standards have been introduced and developed. As indicated by the World Bank, this has seen the literacy rate in the country rising to 88.69% by 2014 (www.microtrends.net).

The efforts have also promoted the rise of a proper humane environment characterized by progress towards total eradication of unethical practices such as child marriages, child labor, slavery and gender-based violence (GBV). International organizations have readily demonstrated commitment towards ensuring progress towards the ethical goal. For instance, The World Bank (2019) confirms the idea by vowing its commitment towards addressing gender-based violence through investment, research and learning, as well as collaboration with stakeholders around the world. It indicates as well that since 2003, the World Bank has engaged with countries and partners to support projects and knowledge products aimed at preventing and addressing GBV. The bank dedicates $300 million in development projects aimed at addressing GBV in World Bank Group-financed operations, both through the integration of GBV components in sector-specific projects in areas such as education, social protection and forced displacement (The World Bank 2019). The international commitment is reiterated by Relief web's (2020b) report on the UN's continuous efforts to end GBV as well as provision of life-saving services for survivors of GBV during Zimbabwe's COVID-19-related lockdown thereby clearly demonstrating beyond doubt the ethical commitment that international institutions have towards members of the global village's well-being.

Just like other African nations (such as the Democratic Republic of Congo during her fight against the Ebola virus), Zimbabwe has immensely benefited from the global efforts against pandemics such as cyclones, droughts, HIV and Aids, as well as the current humanity threatening COVID-19 pandemic. Apart from Zimbabwean droughts of 1987, 1992 and 2007, all of which international food aid groups like WFP and others took upon themselves to fight, various cyclones have been experienced since year 2000. These include cyclone Eline of year 2000 and Idai of 2019, all of which have resulted in considerable damages to the Zimbabwean nation. In response, the international community swiftly responded with considerable aids of different forms coming from as far as Europe and Asia. For instance, describing cyclone Idai (which totally destroyed some areas in Manicaland province) as the worst natural disaster in Southern Africa in nearly two decades, Reliefweb (2020a) reports on the Chinese government's provision of USD two million in aid to Cyclone Idai-affected families in Zimbabwe, a contribution specifically made by the South - South Cooperation Assistance Fund (SSCAF). Similarly, the HIV and Aids as well as the COVID-19 pandemic have seen the international world swiftly coming to Zimbabwe's rescue, courtesy of globalization. The invaluable information and drugs for ensuring prevention and survival from attacks by such deadly diseases have been availed by the international community through the World Health Organization. For instance, to this date, Zimbabweans with the HIV virus are being bailed out by the antiretroviral drugs from the international world and the initiative has already given rise to an AIDS levy towards which every worker in the country contributes monthly. The same has been done by countries such as China, Japan and India who immensely supported the nation with donations in form of vaccinations and test kits to assist her fight against the deadly COVID-19 pandemic. Xinhua (2020), for instance, describes China as one of the few countries that have been on the forefront in helping Zimbabwe's fight against the COVID-19 pandemic adding that Chinese companies operating in the country were the first to offer over USD 500000 in March 2020 for the rehabilitation of Wilkins hospital in Harare, a move that went a long way in equipping the nation for handling the delicate COVID-19 patients. However, Xinhua is quick to point out that, as a country under western sanctions, Zimbabwe has failed to obtain significant financial bail-outs from major multilateral lenders in her fight against the deadly disease. This demonstrates how much members of the global world can unethically ignore even the deadliest pandemics threatening to extinguish humanity in order to uphold their sanctions on countries. Such a stance raises eyebrows on the genuineness of their apparent intentions towards assisting African countries as members of the global community.

It is key to note as well that, following attainment of her independence from Britain in 1980, Zimbabwe's first years saw the then President Robert Gabriel Mugabe trying to continue with Rhodesia's protectionist policies of the Unilateral Declaration of Independence (UDI) which, in his case, were characterized by economic sanctions following the refusal of Britain to recognize Zimbabwe's independence and the calling for the UN sanctions (MacLean 2002). This clearly demonstrates how, instead of supporting the emancipation of the African state from ninety long years of colonialism, the UN decided to side with the former mother power at the expense of the Zimbabweans' wellbeing. After it was proving to be unworkable, Mugabe then decided to shift to a market-friendly Economic Structural Adjustment Programme (ESAP) (1991–5). This involved the IMF and the World Bank's economic reforms which were applied to Zimbabwe in a five-year period. Unfortunately, as properly noted by Osimiri (2015), the expected dividends did not materialize as virtually a high number of jobs were lost without the creation of any replacement leading to a subsequent total economic breakdown that saw the country drowning in debt for many years. The debts have seen the nation struggling to break free for years only to do so at the end of 2016 though the impact is still being felt. This makes the unethical actions of the UN as well as the IMF considerably responsible for the blame that goes with the suffering of the Zimbabwean people for these as well as many other years to come.

The suffering of the Zimbabwean majority as a result of ESAP, the IMF and other debts that accumulated in the process saw the rise of more political players like the Movement for Democratic Change (MDC), a party whose ties with the west have always been considerably visible. The ties have invited Mugabe and ZANU PF's usual allegation that the MDC party is a western-funded project of the west meant to facilitate regime change to ensure the return of western control on the nation. The consequences were felt by every human within the nation. For instance, the MDC's celebration of a surprise victory against ZANU-PF in a constitutional referendum in 2000 made Mugabe feel faced with his first real political threat since independence and reacted with an iron fist (Melber 2003). He cracked down on dissent and orchestrated a series of violent elections which resulted in deaths and severe injuries of activists. The fact that many white landowners or commercial farmers had openly supported and bankrolled the MDC not only infuriated Mugabe and his party, but also made land a viable election and political issue for both parties. The resort to authoritarianism (Melber 2003) and the politics of the liberation struggle essentially dictated the need for the revival of ZANU PF's long forgotten comrades in arms, the war veterans of the pre-independence period. They were given the lead in violently expropriating land from white farmers without compensation, a sudden reversal of the previous Lancaster House arrangement to maintain white occupation of the land on a 99-year lease agreement. Apart from the hunger and economic meltdown that followed and being experienced to date, deaths and severe injuries were as well experienced during the land expropriation. In many cases, the relations between ordinary parents (supporting the revolutionary ZANU PF party) and children (supporting the maiden MDC party) soured beyond repair. The chapter links all this avoidable suffering, enmity, racist tendencies and the inhumane attacks to the unethical selfish practices of the aforementioned global nations and institutions who decided to ignore the humane effort towards putting an end to imperialism. This clearly demonstrates how much globalization efforts are also politically meant to fulfil some unethical neo-colonial motives. If not the case, one could probably argue that the commitment to the motives of the globalization agenda are not strong enough to defeat the imperialist aspirations that have been typical of the developed nations for years.

## 4 Effects of Economic Globalization

This type focuses on the unification and integration of international financial markets. It encourages each country to specialise in what it produces best using the least amount of resources, known as comparative advantage. The approach makes production more efficient, promotes economic growth, and lowers prices of goods and services, making them more affordable especially for lower-income households. In the process, the entire globe's major financial institutions would then be ready to ensure affordable loans while the entire global village ensures wider markets characterized by free trade and corporate use of foreign labor markets to maximize returns.

Zimbabwe has considerably benefited from this type of globalization with companies such as the Cold Storage Commission (CSC) producing and selling high quality meat to countries as far as the UK, though the suspension of the country from the Commonwealth group of nations, following controversial elections, later put an end to it (www.thenewhumanitarian.org). As per the arrangement, financial aids have been accessed from institutions such as the World Bank, IMF and African Bank, though in some cases failure to honor the debts as prescribed has often resulted in denials. Zimbabweans are also accessing international job markets, cheaper goods from countries like Dubai and China as well as cars (for example, from Japan, Singapore, and the United Kingdom (UK), among others. However, the amount of duty charged on imported goods has arguably been viewed as defeating the international efforts towards free trade as governments end up extorting money from common human beings instead to satisfy their own selfish motives. This minimizes the impact of the order in as far as facilitating transformation towards the best living environment for everyone is concerned.

Zimbabwean efforts to tap resources for national gain are also considerably boosted by international aid in the global village. For instance, the mining of some low lying minerals, which require advanced machinery, have seen the country making deals with companies from as far as China, the USA and the UK. This has seen the nation benefiting from her resources for the betterment of her economy. However, local analysts have established that in some cases the deals appear modelled solely in favor of the foreign companies, especially in cases where the Chinese are involved. The position is in line with Noyes' (2020) observation that most of the many tenders received by the Chinese never benefited the Zimbabwean nation.

Noyes further argues that mining in Chiadzwa, for instance, saw a lot of diamonds being externalised without the miners even honoring the agreement to resettle and develop the infrastructure for the local community as per the signed agreement. Such moves demonstrate how economic globalization is bent on advancing imperialism's unethical focus on the expropriation of third world countries' resources by developed nations, a move cementing thoughts of globalization as a new approach towards realizing the usual imperialist goals.

As highlighted earlier, the Zimbabwean fast-track land reform was followed by hunger as production from the farms almost came to a sudden halt. It was also followed by souring of relations with the British leading to economic sanctions from the European Union as well as USA's Zimbabwe Democracy and Economic Recovery Act (ZIDERA) of 2001. In response, Mugabe engaged in large-scale corruption, and printed money to pay off veterans of the liberation war ZWD50 000 each and distribute patronage to other key bases of support (Blair 2002). These actions precipitated a political and economic crisis and earned Zimbabwe pariah status on the international stage, with the United States and the European Union levying targeted sanctions on dozens of officials (Blair 2002). The effects are being felt on the land to this date with many people's lives already disturbed beyond recovery.

The colonial regime offered its language of imperialism, English, the highest status in Zimbabwe. Since it is the international language, its adoption as a language of instruction facilitated Zimbabweans' fluency in the language as it has been accorded the greatest value as a subject in school. However, though this had some advantages such as enabling Zimbabweans to fit perfectly into the global job market (Nhongo 2013), Zimbabwe's economy since the Mugabe era has always been threatened by brain drain. For instance, from 2021, an unprecedented exodus of doctors and nurses to Europe has hit the country hard with 2022 seeing a greenlight being extended to teachers by the UK. Hungwe (2007) observes that, while there are some push factors responsible for the brain drain, such as the economic meltdown and poor remuneration in the coutry, a major pull-factor is also responsible for the recruitment of labor from Zimbabwe in form of English language skills. Thus, the international arrangement meant to ensure connectivity within the global village is considerably weighing down on the Zimbabwean nation with some critical sectors, such as health, running with disastrously inadequate skilled labor.

## 5 Effects of Socio-cultural Globalization

This type focuses on the social factors that cause cultures to converge such as arrangements on language use, as well as increased ease of communication and transportation, brought about by technology. Zimbabwe has considerably benefited from this type which includes decisions made on language usage such as English as the international language and the UN's six official languages. The arrangement ensures international communication which has seen Zimbabweans interacting with all corners of the globe for activities including sourcing financial, political as well as socio-cultural support. The decisions also ensured effective education, for instance, through the UN's declaration on mother tongue usage which mandated that all children are accorded the opportunity to be instructed in their first language during their first three or so years of education to allow proper cognitive development. The socio-cultural resolutions also promoted the modernization of the Zimbabwean society by guarding against some barbaric religious and cultural practices in some areas like killing of twins and albinos. Zimbabwe is also realizing considerable success in efforts against churches and cultural groups promoting rape, forced marriages, child marriages and resistance to immunization, among others. This has been realized through efforts like the 2016 outlawing of marriage for girls under the age of 18 (www.theguardian.com) as well as section 78 of the national constitution which enshrines gender equality and justiciable rights (The Constitution of Zimbabwe 2013). This confirms Hemer and Tufte's (2005) observation that globalization has considerably ensured and strengthened proper values in societies.

However, it is quite critical to stress that the policies on language usage introduced by globalization to Zimbabwe consequently promoted the accordance of the most respect to foreign languages, in this case English. This has resulted in promotion of foreign cultures, religions and everything associated with them at the expense of local ones. This has culminated in the demotion even of the practices that are advantageous to the people's survival such as the indigenous knowledge systems. Local foods and herbs, for instance, have been tagged as medieval and evil forcing people to resort to those of the first world countries most of which are proving to have very deadly side effects. As such, unlike before, challenges like hypertension, sugar diabetes and cancer are the ones heavily weighing down on the national life expectancy. The effects are being experienced even in the fight against the Covid-19 pandemic as well where Zimbabweans solely look forward to implementing measures and injecting foreign vaccines, some of which have very little or no impact against local corona virus strains, instead of making medical researches geared towards coming up with solutions from local herbs. This attitude is so serious that no research effort was accorded to local herbs that assisted many in Zimbabwe like *zumbani* (Lippia javanica) and *murumanyama* (xeroderris stuhlmannii) which ended up being sold in top supermarkets in the country for COVID-19. Whilst many people indicate that the herbs bailed them out, many considered them useless and succumbed to the disease. Efforts to research and produce it for the world to use could have benefitted the country in the same way such herbs transformed China into a developed country. Thus, the move on language use has created a powerful dependence syndrome that has permanently accorded Zimbabweans and many others the role of followers in global activities. There is no room even for being innovative with the foreign education being acquired in school as its nature facilitates imitating and following what has been done (Mhute 2021). This is a disastrous effect that would not be eradicated so easily, hence the observation that the nature of the adopted language policy has effectively tagged Zimbabweans and many other Africans as 'developing for ever' (Mhute and Musingafi 2015). This is in line with the 1986 conclusion made during the 22nd session of Heads of State and Government of the Organization of African Unity (OAU) meeting in the Ethiopian capital, Addis Ababa, that language is at the heart of a people's culture and in accordance with the provisions of the Cultural Charter for Africa, the cultural advancement of the African peoples and the acceleration of their economic and social development will not be possible without harnessing in a particular manner indigenous African languages in that advancement and development (Mkuti 2021).

Some very negative tendencies also came to Zimbabwe with the concept of globalization. One such is corruption which emerged as another major setback for the Zimbabwean economy. The 2017 coup that ended the Mugabe era, for instance, targeted criminals that surrounded the president. This referred to high office perpetrators of corruption who abused their offices for personal benefits, among other crimes. The question one would then ask is; how did this become possible in Zimbabwe, a country built on the traditional 'unhu/ubuntu philosophy' that emphasized the fact that 'I am because we are'? By adopting a language policy designed by the westerners, the Zimbabwean government has been forced to sustain a philosophy carried by foreign languages and cultures that is individualistic (summed up in 'I am because I think' and solely concerned about self-enrichment). This explains activities like involvement of former president Robert Gabriel Mugabe himself in the DRC where he amassed personal wealth using the national military (Nutt et al. 2011). Had the Mugabe administration considered placing a local language at the center of the national language policy instead of upholding the former colonizer's legacy, it would have succeeded in ensuring total embracement of the unhu/umuntu philosophy carried by the local languages as recommended by the Commission of Inquiry (Nziramasanga 1999). This philosophy would have inspired the Zimbabweans to ensure selfless love and respect for others at all costs. Such would have made the entire administration corruption free and more concerned about the communal good ahead of everything else on the land.

## 6 Conclusion

The chapter argues that globalization is in actual fact an ethical idea that has the necessary capacity to transform the entire globe into the best possible living environment for every human being. If looked at from the perspective of the theory of constructivism, the idea has the potential to nullify all the inequalities and discriminations that are currently bedevilling the entire world. To illustrate on that, one could refer to how much the effort is proving to be a Zimbabwean and African blessing by putting an end to inhumane practices like slavery, gender-based violence, illiteracy and hunger, among others. Access to international jobs, goods, markets and other services has also been ensured for locals thereby raising opportunities for personal and community advancement. However, the chapter demonstrates as well that there are considerable unethical effects being experienced by the nation through political, economic and socio-cultural globalization. It demonstrates how some activities of the international institutions meant to assist the entire globe tent to be partial in their duties. There is demonstration of the prevalence of some nations being considered important and to be supported or pardoned even when their activities are against the ethical motive considered to be fuelling globalization. The chapter also demonstrates how some global arrangements have indirectly placed third world countries in the same clutches that were typical of the colonial period. As such, they seem to be drowning in orchestrated challenges making them go nowhere in as far as development or self-reliance is concerned.

## 7 Recommendation

The chapter has confirmed the view that globalization has come more as a curse than a blessing to the African continent and the Zimbabwean nation in particular. The continent seems to have been captured and, as such unable to realize real progress towards independence and development. Therefore, the chapter recommends:

(i) The adoption of a fairer version of globalization in which the international institutions demonstrate total commitment towards the well-being of everyone rather than favoring the first world countries at the expense of their third world counterparts.
(ii) The commitment by international bodies towards monitoring the fate of third world countries whenever they are involved in deals involving their first world counterparts, as in most cases their position is bound to facilitate unnecessary compromises.
(iii) The third world countries must remove blinkers from their eyes and properly analyse how far they have to go out of their way to align their cultural practices with those of the first world countries as there are possibilities of ceding some traditional knowledge systems that should form the backbones of their societies' well-being.
(iv) Zimbabwe and other developing countries must advance from focusing solely on short-term benefits of their activities to long-term ones if their fate must be fully transformed into the perfect homes everyone desire.

## References

Ali, H.A. 2005. Globalisation as a generator of cultural and economic hegemony. *Canada Social Science* 1 (3): 11–20.

Blair, D. 2002. *Degrees in violence: Robert Mugabe and the struggle for power in Zimbabwe*. London: Continuum.

Colado, E.I. 2006. The ethics of globalization. In *Management ethics: Contemporary context*, ed. S. Clegg and C. Rhodes, 32–54. New York: Routledge.

Constitution of Zimbabwe Amendment No.20 Chapter 1 Sec.78. 2013. https://www.constituteproject.org. Accessed 14 July 20.

Giddens, A. 1990. *The consequences of modernity*. London: Polity Press.

Guthrie, M. 1948. *The classification of the bantu languages*. London: Oxford University Press for the International African Institute.
Hemer, O., and T. Tufte, eds. 2005. *Media and global change: Rethinking communication for development*. Buenos Aires: Publicaciones Cooperativas.
Hungwe, K. 2007. Language policy in Zimbabwean education: Historical antecedents and contemporary issues. Compare 37 (2): 135–149. https://doi.org/10.1080/03057920601165363.
MacLean, S.J. 2002. Mugabe at war: The political economy of conflict in Zimbabwe. *Third World Quarterly* 23 (3): 513–528.
Melber, H., ed. 2003. *Limits to liberation in southern Africa: The unfinished business of democratic consolidation*. Cape Town: Human Sciences Research Council Press.
Mhute, I. 2021. Language and communication issues in the education of Africa. In *Education in Africa: Perspectives, opportunities and challenges*, ed. Gilbert Motsaathebe. New York: Nova Science Publishers.
Mhute, I., and M.C.C. Musingafi. 2015. Centrality of language in development: A case of Zimbabwe. *Journal of Economics and Sustainable Development* 6 (20): 181–190.
Mittelman, J.H. 1996. The dynamics of globalization. In *Globalization: Critical reflections*, ed. J.H. Mittelman, 1–19. Boulder. CO: Lynne Rienner.
Mkuti, L.D. 2021. *Language and education in Mozambique since 1940: Policy, implementation, and future perspectives*. New York: The University of Arizona.
Nhongo, R. 2013. A National Language Policy for Zimbabwe in the twenty-first century: Myth or reality? *Journal of Language Teaching and Research* 4 (6): 1208–1215.
Noyes, A.R. 2020. *A new Zimbabwe: Assessing continuity and change after Mugabe*. Santa Monica: RAND Corporation.
Nutt, C., et al. 2011. Muffling the sound of murder: Re-interpreting Zimbabwe's strategic choices in The Congo. *Strategic Comments* 5 (2): 232–258.
Nziramasanga, C.T. 1999. *Report of the presidential Commission of Inquiry into education and training*. Unpublished.
Osimiri, P. 2015. The ethical challenges of globalization. *Covenant University Journal of Politics and International Affairs (CUJPIA)* 3 (1): 1–14.
Reliefweb. 2020a. *Providing services to survivors of gender-based violence during COVID-19*. Harare: News and Press Release.
———. 2020b. *Government of China provides USD 2 million in aid to cyclone Idai-affected families in Zimbabwe*. Harare: News and Press Release.
Roberts, I. 1992. Industrial relations and the European Community. *Industrial Relations Journal* 23 (1): 3–13.
Scholte, J. A. 2005. *Globalization: A critical introduction*. Basingstoke: Palgrave Macmillan.
Sivanandan, A. 1999. Globalism and the left. *Race and Class* 40 (2/3): 5–19.
The World Bank. 2019. *Gender-based violence (Violence against women and girls)*. www.worldbank.org. Accessed on 13 July 2021.
Theys, S. 2018. Introducing constructivism in international relations theory. In *E-International Relations Theory*: 1–4.
Xinhua. 2020. *China stands in solidarity with Zimbabwe in battle against COVID-19*. Forum on China-Africa Cooperation. www.fmprc.gov.cn/zfh. Accessed on 13 July 2021.

**Isaac Mhute** is an Associate Professor with Midlands State University's Department of Language, Literature and Culture Studies. He is a chief examiner for language and literature with an international examining board, professional editor and translator/back translator (English and Shona). He graduated with a Doctor of Literature and Philosophy in African Languages from the University of South Africa whose focus was on the morphological, syntactic and semantic representation of grammatical relations. His research interests are in both theoretical and applied linguistic areas such as language policy and development, syntax and semantics, onomastics as well as language and strategic communication issues in education, among others.

# African Development and Disruptive Innovations: An Ethical Implication of the e-Hailing Services on the Metered Taxi Industry in South Africa

**Beatrice Okyere-Manu**

**Abstract** Disruptive innovations are generally described as current technologies that alter the incumbent global and local markets in terms of their impact on the production and consumption of goods and services. Examples of disruptive innovations include products and services such e-hailing also known as "ride-sourcing", "ride-hailing", "ride-sharing" Apps through Phones, Instagram, Google, Netflix, and many others. There is no doubt that these innovations with their higher quality products, aim to expand their market and reach mass clients thus, successfully addressing many social and economic challenges. The current study acknowledges the link and benefits of these disruptive innovations on the African development landscape but argues that a closer look at the ethics of these innovations raises some moral concerns for traditional businesses on the African continent. These innovations have ushered in a new era of economic disruption with uncertain socio-economic consequences for traditional businesses, presenting an ethical conundrum in Africa's development. Given the fact that these innovations are developed and owned by rich individuals and multi-million companies from different cultural settings, what implications do their products have on the traditional businesses in Africa? How should the local businesses respond to these innovations? Do we owe an ethical duty to keep and sustain the existing businesses and if so how and why? Which ethical framework will help to respond to these technologies to ensure that these new models of businesses do not completely displace the old ones? As a response to these questions, the chapter argues that (1) given the power behind the disrupters, the disrupter cannot be disrupted. (2) Using Kwasi Wiredu's political theory of consensus, I will argue or show that existing business have no choice but to change their strategy of operation to stay in business. This is because both industries aim to contribute to the development and 'common good' of the community they serve.

B. Okyere-Manu (✉)
Applied Ethics, University of KwaZulu-Natal, Pietermaritzburg, KwaZulu-Natal, South Africa
e-mail: Okyere-manv@ukzn.ac.za



B. Okyere-Manu et al. (eds.), *Contemporary Development Ethics from an African Perspective*, Philosophy and Politics - Critical Explorations 27,
https://doi.org/10.1007/978-3-031-32898-5_10

## 1 Introduction

It is a general knowledge that when it comes to development in Africa, the continent continues to face a plethora of challenges. These have been attributed to its colonial past, poor leadership, environmental challenges, exploitation of global powers, corruption, and many others. These challenges have negatively affected development on the continent, resulting in underdevelopment, poverty, famines, lack of services delivery, wars, diseases, etc. However, one of the hallmarks of development in recent times is the emergence and acceleration of innovative technologies. The advent of the internet in the 1990s and its accelerated development have ushered the continent into a new era of development, making technology the most powerful external force that is shaping the continent and the world today. The impact of technology has been felt in all aspects of life. As noted by the current South African President, Cyril Ramaphosa (2020): "the fourth industrial revolution represents the great tectonic shift of our time. It is creating new opportunities for improving people's lives. Disruptive Technologies like machine learning, artificial intelligence, and big data are changing the way we live, the way we work and do business, and the way we govern." The inference here is that these technological innovations have and continue to affect every aspect of development in terms of their impact on the production and consumption of goods. New products continue to appear on the market that either sustain or disrupt businesses. Being a consumer and not much of a producer, local businesses on the African continent have not been spared from the influence of these innovations.

Development in terms of technological innovations comes in two forms; while some sustain and improve businesses others disrupt them. The technologies that sustain existing businesses do not necessarily produce or introduce new products but sustain existing products to benefit both the producer and clients. On the other hand, disruptive technologies are the technologies that significantly alters the way that businesses operate (Gitura Mwaura 2016). Examples may include products and services such as Apple phones, Instagram, Google, Netflix, ride-sharing services, AIRBNB, and many others. Though these innovations are perceived as the marks of development in Africa, their unintended consequences have potentially presented an ethical challenge for local businesses. Particularly, their higher quality products to expand their markets, have infiltrated the social, communication, and tourism sectors just to mention a few. It is with this backdrop that this study explores the ethical implications of one of such disruptive innovative business models on the incumbent African business – in this case, e-hailing services within the transport industry in South Africa and the local incumbent metered taxi industry. It asks, what are the ethical implications of e-hailing services on the local metered taxi industry in the country? How should the incumbent metered industry respond to these innovations? what will it take to respond to these technologies in such a way that ensures that these new models of business do not displace the old ones?

As a response to these questions, this chapter will argue that (1) the disrupter cannot be disrupted given the global authority and the financial power behind the disrupters, something that the local industries do not have. (2) Using Kwasi Wiredu's moral theory of consensus, I will argue or show that existing business have no choice but to think of ways to change their strategy of operation to stay in business. This is technology is impacting on everything thing around us, the way we live and the way we do business.

It is the position of the paper that the moral underpinning of the moral theory of consensus can make for a strong community where the role players can have a mutual dialogue which may lead to working together to demonstrate communal co-existence in becoming a true community to enhance African development. I develop these arguments by assessing the relationship between e-hailing platforms services and the metered taxi industry in South Africa. The aim here is first to gain an understanding of how the incumbent traditional taxi industry operates. Second, how e-hailing services operate and the tension that has arisen in this sector since its advent. Third, it will explore how the metered taxi industry has and continue to respond to the competition that has been created on the market.

## 2 The Metered Taxi Industry in South Africa

In South Africa, the public transport system is one of the basic modes of transport, the metered taxi industry emerged during the apartheid government when it introduced the Native Land (No 27 of 1913), which dispossessed the natives of their land and forced them into the urban labor market (Baloyi 2013: 343). Since its advent on the market, it has and continues to play an important role in the economic development landscape. The industry has grown exponentially over the years. Gloria Sauti (2006: 13) quoted Bosman and Browning (1989: 8) that the industry has grown rapidly since the late 70 s and at the time of their study, there were 60–80,000 minibus taxis that carried approximately 500,000 passengers daily. It is worth noting that this number may have doubled by now. Being a private industry suggests that within this industry, there are individuals who own and drive their metered taxies, and there are rich individuals who employ drivers to work for them. Gloria Sauti (2006: 13) in her study, noted that people do not need any formal qualification to be involved in the business except a driver's license. Even though the majority of taxi drivers in her study had a secondary qualification and others a technical qualification. It must be noted that the taxi industry is regulated by its organization and the government through the department of transport.

According to Meshack M. Khosa (1990: 56), there are three forces that encourage the growth of the industry in the 80s and 90s. The first is the bargaining power of taxi associations, in mobilizing the involvement of big business in the industry; the second is the penetration of finance capital in the Black community; and the third is the shift in the apartheid state from previous ruthless policies on black trading in general to the accommodation of the taxi industry in particular, in the 1980s and 1990s. Apart from the fact that the industry contributes to the economic development of the country by employing a large number of people, it also provides private transportation services to commuters to and from work daily and thus circulating substantial large amounts of money in the system. The growth of the taxi industry has had a tremendous impact on buses and trains over the years. Adding on to the impact of the growth, Collen McCaul (1990: V) observed that the "total bus passenger loads nationally dropped from 100 passengers to 72 passengers per trip between 1980 and 1988, due to commuters". During the same period, the number of train commuters also dropped from 100 passengers to 81 passengers per trip (McCaul 1990: 35). This may be due to the accessibility and convenience of the metered taxi.

The metered taxi industry is a privately-owned industry that is regulated by the National Land Transport Act. It offers a faster, flexible, and easily accessible mode of transport compared to other modes of transportation in the country such as trains, busses, and minibuses. They are available to commuters through the following means: y telephone, or at a designated taxi rank. An important feature of the metered taxi is that it is equipped with a sealed meter that calculates the fare of commuters (Section 1 of the National Land Transport Transition (NLTA) 2009). Even though the sealed meter calculates the fare, in some cases, commuters can negotiate the fare with the driver. To operate in this industry, the NLTA has laid down requirement which needs to be followed. For example, one needs to apply for an area-based permit, suggesting that drivers or operators can only function in specific areas to avoid clashing and competition with other taxi operators. In addition, information such as the route or radius of operation, the specific taxi rank, and pick up and drop off points must be submitted before licenses can be obtained. Commuters may only be picked up outside the designated areas if it is pre-booked and if the commuter will be required to be dropped off at the same place (Section 66(1)(a)–(d) of NLTA).

Metered Taxis are guided by 3 regulatory compliances to maintain a high standard of service. They include the following; first, the regulation of quantity – this regulation has been put in place to inform the number of vehicles that can enter the market and to ensure that potential applicants meet the minimum requirement. The second is quality of service: this is particularly directed towards the driver and the vehicle. It is to ensure that the driver is fit and meets mandatory national standards to ensure the safety of both commuters and the driver. The third regulation concerns prizing to monitor and promote fix charges per kilometer depending on time and distance to avoid exploitation of commuters (OECD 2007). Further, the NLTA allows for the Minister of Transport or any executive member of the council to make regulations and special requirements for drivers and their vehicles.

## 3 Disruptive Innovations: e-Hailing Services

The emergence of e-hailing services has sparked debate across several countries, with policymakers implementing numerous approaches to regulating these services. As mentioned above, disruptive innovations with their aim of presenting unpredictable and radical changes in the market can affect some incumbent businesses negatively (OECD 2007). They create a highly competitive market that can destroy the local businesses with their new models, products, and manufacturing processes, which inevitably affects how incumbent firms compete. A major characteristic of these innovations is their ability to study a particular market and identify gaps and areas where costs can be perfected and in so doing take advantage of the provision of specific products or services to fill the gap. Examples of the e-hailing services in south Africa include Uber, Bolt, etc. Kemal Dervis explains that:

> Uber is just one example of disruptive innovation that brings a huge increase in efficiency, as well as real social and regulatory challenges, it is one of the less problematic innovations because it is a net job creator; the rise of the computers capable of replacing call-center workers is resulting in large net job losses (2015: 2).

As indicated above, Uber just like all the other e-hailing services, is an online-based door-to-door service provider that uses an application (App) that allows passengers to connect with drivers to request a trip to the desired destination. This industry has become one of the fastest-growing start-ups not only in South Africa but worldwide. With its headquarters in the United States of America, currently Uber operates in about 82 countries worldwide (Lana Pepić 2018: 127). Given the popularity and the presence of uber in most countries, current paper will focus on Uber. The mode of Uber's operation is that users or commuters must have cell phones and download their Apps. The user then selects a location from where they can be picked up, then a message will be sent to the driver in the vicinity via the App to notify him/her of where the commuter is located and the pick-up point. At this point, the driver has an option to either accept or even ignore the notification. Upon acceptance of the request from the commuter, the Uber app will display the name of the driver, the color and type of car as well as the registration number. More importantly, the app displays the estimated time of arrival of the vehicle. The journey up to where the customer is also displayed by the app. In this way, the customer can follow the vehicle and its location, be aware of the color and name of the driver, the registration number as well as the exact waiting time.

This industry has grown within a short period, now it has many options for commuters to choose from. Apart from the various class of vehicles such as Uber X, Uber Van, and Uber black offering luxury black cars, there is also UberBOAT for cities with maritime traffic. In addition, Uber has even extended its offering to a variety of services in the hospitality industry such as Uber Eats. This is a cooperation between Uber and local restaurants for food delivery. For a customer looking for a specific type of service, Uber offers many convenient options. In terms of pricing, Uber uses an Algorithm to calculate the pricing (Constine 2017).

A study conducted in South Africa in 2015 suggested that among all the local taxi businesses, Uber is the lowest charging taxi industry (Dube 2015; Barry 2015) and this is among one of the advantages it has even over the metered taxi whose premiums peak at 265% higher than Uber's services. The Uber app allows customers to pay their fare electronically, allowing credit and debit card facilities. This important feature has benefited some customers who do not want to carry physical cash on their trips. Uber uses a cashless payments system, however, according to

Bekezela Phakathi (2016), Uber in May 2015, indicated that it was going to experiment with cash payments to make it easy for those without credit cards to be able to access their services, suggesting that it was ready to expand its clientele, especially to the low-income earning commuters. Not only does uber charge lower than other taxis but another peculiar feature informing the quality of service that Uber offer is the rating system just like all other e-hailing platform services. This is where both customers and drivers can rate each other after each trip. The areas of evaluation may include the behavior of both the driver and customer and also the driving skills of the driver. Damien Geradin (2015) adds that this feature serves as checks and balances to help maintain quality of service as well as maintain the high reputation of drivers. Judd Cramer and Alan B Krueger (2016) believe that the following four factors have increased its application and growth: first, Uber's more efficient driver-passenger matching technologies, second, its larger scale, (which supports, faster matches its inefficient taxi regulations), third its flexibility labour supply model and lastly, its surge pricing, which matches supply with demand throughout the day. Christofer *Laurell* & Christian *Sandström* (2016) assert that the reasons why Uber is preferred over traditional taxis are because of its price, service, convenience, safety, punctuality, experience, and trustworthiness. In addition, factors such as speed of service, familiarity with the app, and the in-app payment system also make it a more competitive option than a metered taxi.

## 4 The Relationship Between Uber and the Metered Taxi in South Africa

The presence of e-hailing platform services, particularly Uber, has generated conflict and violence in most cities in the country. Interestingly enough, the conflict is not only peculiar to South Africa but it seems to be a worldwide problem. News of similar conflict or violence has been noted in many other countries on the continent and worldwide between Uber and the existing local taxi industry. Drazen Jorgic (2016) recalls that Uber's expansion into countries such as Uganda, Tanzania, and Kenya, has witnessed Uber drivers being attacked physically and, in some instances, having their cars torched. Sonwabile Henama Unathi and Portia Pearl Siyanda Sifolo affirm such instances in South Africa. They maintain that "the emergence of Uber as a competitor has been met by violence in two fronts violence towards the Uber taxi operator and towards the Uber customers." Uber drivers have been victims of crime around the world. There are frequent rumours of uber drivers being ambushed and attacked. A personal experience in 2019 with uber confirmed the conflict. I traveled to one of the bigger cities, at the train station, I called for a ride. The driver called to say he could not come to the train station because he will be attacked by the metered taxi drivers, so I should walk about a kilometer away to where he was waiting for me. He further warned that when asked by the taxi drivers at the station, I should not mention that I was going to catch an Uber, because the train station is not their jurisdiction, therefore he could not pick up anyone from the train. Eventually, I was able to locate the driver, a conversation that ensued with the driver and I as we drove to my destination, revealed that indeed Uber has disrupted the traditional taxi business and that accounts for the series of violence between its drivers and taxi operators. The uber driver narrated his personal story of how he was nearly beaten at one time by a mob of taxi drivers. Similar forms of violence have been confirmed by Toby Melvile (2017) who recounts instances where uber vehicles were burnt with drivers sustaining serious burn injuries and hospitalized. In some cases, drivers' lives have been threatened.

To the uber driver I called, what accounts for the escalation of the violence is not only the competition that uber has created in terms of its low pricing but also Uber's larger supply of drivers on the market. He confirmed that there are a lot of Uber drivers in the city. He further mentioned that Uber has become an extra income for most people in the city where some fully employed individuals render such service after work. He affirms that some people who have lost their job like himself, have found this an option to earn some income to enable them to look after their families. In addition, the fact that Uber drivers are viewed as partners instead of employees of the company has also attracted several people into the industry. Suggesting that anybody at all who owns a car can become an Uber driver. In terms of taxes, he mentioned that because they are privately owned individuals, they can escape the payment of taxes to the state or any other value-added tax for the services that they render. This has been confirmed by Lisa Rayle et al. (2016: 168) that "ride-sourcing has attracted significant criticism from its most direct competitor, the taxi industry, which views ride-sourcing as an illegal service that flouts laws and competes unfairly".

So far, it is clear that the relationship between the metered taxi industry and the e-hailing platform services have been marked with serious tension that has impacted negatively on the industry as well as the economy of the country. As noted, the taxi industry sees the e-hailing services as a threat to their livelihoods, therefore, to protect their businesses, they have taken the law into their own hands with the view of disrupting the disrupter. Moat commuters are often anxious yet preferred uber to the local taxi. But can the disrupter be disrupted? In other words, can the taxi industry disrupt and eventually stop the uber industry? The next section will unpack these questions.

## 5 Can the Disrupter Be Disrupted?

Thus far, it is evident that the presence of e-hailing services is disrupting the existing local taxi business, and as a response, the taxi owners and drivers have taken the law into their own hands to disrupt the activities of the e-hailing services. However, the question that stands to be answered is that: can the disrupter be disrupted? To answer this question, I will argue for the reasons why the disrupter, and in this case, e-hailing, cannot be disrupted. First, as noted above, the e-hailing platform services, and for that matter, Uber, is a foreign-owned company with its headquarters in the

US. This company has networks all around the globe and is therefore here to stay. Second, the competition it brings on the market is progressive: its business model is efficient and reliable, among other things, it has an advantage of reducing the need for a second family car, which can reduce traffic congestion. There is no doubt that its presence in the industry has improved both inter and intra-city mobility by providing a cheaper transportation option.

Adding onto the efficiency of these services, Unathi et al. (2017: 7) noted that, Uber encourages its drivers to go beyond the call of duty by offering extra services such as opening and closing doors for customers, offering a bottle of water, asking the customer about music station preference, and offering mobile phone charging points in the Uber taxis. These extra services have ensured that Uber driver ratings keep high, ensuring that customer satisfying service delivery is incomparable. There is no doubt that uber has been able to create more jobs than it has destroyed and will continue to create backward and forward linkages in the economy with local partner drivers, where it sees the drivers as partners and not workers. For instance, "Since launching in South Africa in August 2013, Uber has created 2000 jobs for drivers, mainly in disadvantaged communities, and it could easily create 15,000 over the next two years" (Eye for Travel 2015). This report was compiled in 2015 and the numbers may have increased tremendously by now.

Uber has been accused of functioning unethically such as not complying with licensing regulations as well as destroying the market by cost charging below costand even up until now Uber has not yet been regulated by any local commission. Zenzile Khoisan (2016) acknowledges that in June 2015, 15 metered taxi operators were charged with the public disorder after violence broke out when they protested the presence of Uber in Cape Town.

E-hailing services have rapidly become part of everyday life and a regular part of the public lexicon. They have an important role to play not only in the transport industry but the growth of the economy and as such to disrupt to the extent of eventually banning them from the market would be a grave disadvantage to innovation, competition growth, and development in the economy. Therefore, I argue that as a disrupter, the e-hailing industry cannot be disrupted.

## 6 Wiredu's Theory of Consensus as a Way Forward?

The violence against e-hailing services by the metered taxi industry in the country has brought to the public realm two important characteristics of organizational and individual life that have until recently remained in the private sphere, namely the fear of competition and resistance to change. As individuals taxi owners as well as the industry, it is clear that they are very comfortable with routine and have been ill-equipped to deal with and respond to the moral complexities of competition and change. For example, in the attempt to deal with the competition that e-hailing platform services have brought to the transportation industry, the inadequacies of the industry have surfaced through the violent responses and death of some Uber drivers and in some cases even commuters. This is because stakeholders have failed to provide normative clarification and guidance in the form of insider ethics or organizational restructuring ethics. I believe that it is not because the taxi industry wants to eliminate the uber drivers but they do so because of fear based on some social realities which raises further issues of lack of justice and effective decision-making processes, so that the operations of the industry are more geared towards ethical principles. For example, some of the taxi owners and drivers are the breadwinners of large families, with the industry as their only source of income. Some of them have children in schools, so the sudden boost of the e-hailing platform services has kept them out of business.

A critical look at what is happening reveals a gap in a whole range of ethics-based in the organizational instruments and tools in the industry, ranging from codes of conduct and ethical assessments to all embracing methods, for running the organization the ethical way.

The fact of the matter is that the e-hailing industry is here to stay, particularly because we are in a globalized world that is characterized by powerful global and big technological companies. Also, it has opened employment doors for the many retrenched unemployed individuals as well as those who want to supplement their income.

These and the many unresolved moral issues around the presence of e-hailing platform services call for an ethical approach in dealing with the issue. It is with this backdrop that tools from Kwasi Wiredu's political theory of consensus (2001) is used to inform our ethical approach in dealing with the tension between the two industries. For Wiredu, a consensus is needed when there are two different opinions, ideas, or interests that have to be coordinated to allow for common action. His idea of consensus suggests compromise where "compromise is a certain adjustment of the interests of individuals (in the form of disparate convictions as to what is to be done) to the common necessity for something to be done" (2011: 1058). The inference here is that consensus is seen as some form of agreement of opposing interests based on taking into consideration the viewpoints of all the opposing parties to develop peaceful coexistence. Kwasi Wiredu believes that to attain this consensus, discussions and negotiation leading to persuasion need to be made to achieve a consensual agreement on the right action. It is his position that mutual dialogue and persuasion enable people to overcome their disagreements and attain agreed positions. Relating this moral approach to the relationship between the metered taxi industry and uber suggests that since both industries are serving the common good of the citizens of the nation, there has to be forums where the stakeholders of these industries engage in mutual discussions on what ought to be the best ethical practices to respond to the issue of justice and accountability. However, the question that remains to be asked is who are the stakeholders of Uber who needs to come to the discussion table? Who takes the responsibility when things go wrong with these disruptive technologies? Not until the developers of these disruptive technologies come to the discussion table, the hope of this consensus will only be a dream.

So practically, what does it mean for the two industries to work together? To the local taxi industry. There is an African proverb that says, *If the rhythm of the drumbeat changes, the dance step must adapt*. The quote above is one of the many African proverbs[1] that speaks to the idea of consensus. The literal meaning of the proverb suggests that change is inevitable and when conditions change, role players have no choice but to embrace the change. Any resistance will render the role players vulnerable. This seems to be the challenge that confronts the metered taxi industry in South Africa. There is no doubt that the landscape of the transport industry has changed and the change is here to stay, given that we have entered the Fourth Revolution, which has and continues to alter our way of life. It seems for a long time the taxi industry has become complacent and therefore, the innovation of Uber took the industry by surprise. However, it must be noted that innovation is a catalyst for development, the continent cannot develop without innovations whichever form it may take. Therefore, the presence of these services must be seen as a catalyst to push the taxi industry to innovate. Arguably, the regulations that have protected the taxi industry since its inception has not changed yet vehicles have become more efficient and technology has brought massive change as we have noted in the discussion above, but up till now, the industry has stayed the same. What I see here is that the taxi industry is being challenged to take advantage of the opportunity presented by the current situation to provide a more efficient system for the general public. They have been around for a long time and therefore can beat back the entrant by offering even better services or products at a comparable level. It may need to do so by reforming some of the outdated regulations with taxis and addressing some of the regulation concerns of e-hailing services. In the end, the proposal would allow both entities to coexist and their combined benefits would provide a more efficient transportation market.

For the e-hailing platform, there is the need for an active participation of its stakeholders. It is becoming necessary for stakeholders to take a responsibility-driven attitude thus they must be visible and prepared to be held answerable and accountable when the need arises.

## 7 Conclusion

The chapter has argued that e-hailing platforms such as the Uber industry is here to stay, as such there is the need for stakeholders of e-hailing and the local taxi industry to engage in a consensus with the aim of working together in a peaceful manner for the common good of the African people. This will in turn enhance the economic development of South Africa and Africa as a whole. It has warned that not until developers of these e-hailing platforms come to the discussion table with the local stakeholders, the hope of peaceful coexistence will only be a dream.

[1] See: https://www.inspirationalstories.com/proverbs/african-if-the-rhythm-of-the-drum-beat-changes/

This is because of the violence, killings, and destruction of life and e-hailing vehicles that is currently taking place in some African countries.

There has to be a stricter regulation to govern both industries rather than a complete ban on these services. This is because even though e-hailing services have and continue to disrupt the local industry affecting individuals and their families, they are filling in a gap on the market: the general public needs an effective transportation system and the e-hailing services are available to provide the needed services.

## References


Baloyi, M.M. 2013. The taxi recapitalization policy: Is it a hollow dream? *Journal of Public Administration* 48 (3): 342–352.

Barry, H. 2015. *Does it pay to own an Uber? Moneyweb*. Retrieved from: http://www.moneyweb.co.za/moneyweb-radio/safm-market-update/. Accessed 11 Oct 9, 2021.

Constine, J. 2017. Uber "Express POOL" offers the cheapest fare if you walk a little. *Tech Crunch*. Retrieved from https://techcrunch.com/2017/11/10/uber-express-pool/. Office. https://www.ilo.org/wcmsp5/groups/public/%2D%2D-ed_emp/%2D%2D-emp_ent/%2D%2D-ifp_seed/documents/publication/wcms_117698.pdf. Accessed 4 Oct 2021.

Cramer, J. and Krueger, A.B. 2016. *Disruptive change in the taxi business: The case of Uber*. NBER Working Paper No. 22083.

Bosman, J., and P. Browning. 1989. *The shared-taxi as a means to promoting economic upward mobility*. Annual Transformation Convention, August Pretoria.

Dervis, K. 2015. *The regulatory challenges of disruptive companies. World economic forum*. Retrieved from: http://www.weforum.org/agenda/. Accessed 11 Oct 2021.

Dube, S.C. 2015. *Uber: A game-changer in passenger transport in South Africa?* CCRED. Available at, http://www.competition.org.za/review/2015/11/22/uber-a-game-changer-in-passenger-transport-in-south-africa. Accessed 25 Marc 2021.

Geradin, D. 2015. Should Uber be allowed to compete in Europe? And if so how? *Competition Policy International*. At 4, available at https://www.competitionpolicyinternational.com/assets/Europe-Column-New-Format.pdf. Accessed 1 Mar 2021.

Jorgic, D. 2016. *Uber seeks to lure cabbies in Africa's expansion plan*. Moneyweb. http://www.moneyweb.co.za/news/tech/uber/. Accessed 11 Aug 2021.

Khoisan, Z. 2016. *Well'burn Uber down, say metered taxi drivers*. Retrieved from: http://www.iol.co.za/news/south-africa/western-cape/. Accessed 11 Aug 2021.

Khosa, M.M. 1990. Changing patterns of 'Black' bus subsidies in the apartheid city, 1944–1986. *GeoJournal* 22: 251–259. https://doi.org/10.1007/BF00192823

Laurell, C., and C. Sandstrom. 2016. Analysing Uber in social media-disruptive technology or institutional disruption? *International Journal of Innovation Management* 20 (5): 1–19.

McCaul, C. 1990. *No easy ride*. Johannesburg: SAIRR Press.

Melville, T. 2017. Uber driver suffers burns when a car is set alight, now fighting for his life in hospital. *Timeslive*. Available at https://www.timeslive.co.za/news/south-africa/2017-06-13-uber-driver-suffers-burns-when-car-is-set-alight-now-fighting-for-his-life-in-hospital/. Accessed 28 Aug 2021.

Mwaura, G. 2016. *Uber: The beauty and wrath of disruptive technologies in Africa*. Retrieved from: http://www.newtimes.co.rw/section/article. Accessed 26 July 2021.

National Land Transport Transition Act 22 of 2000. 2009.

OECD. 2007. *'Taxi services: Competition and regulation' roundtable*. Available at http://www.oecd.org/regreform/sectors/41472612.pdf. Accessed 20 Aug 2021.

Pepić, Lana. 2018, June. The sharing economy: Uber and its effect on taxi companies. *ACTA Economica* XVI (28): 123–136.
Phakathi, B. 2016. Uber to experiment with cash payments. In *Business Day*. Retrieved from: http://www.bdlive.co.za/national/transport/. Accessed 11 Oct 2021.
Ramaphosa, Cyril. 2020. A national strategy for harnessing the fourth industrial revolution: The case of South Africa. In *Africa in focus*. Friday, January 10, 2020. https://www.brookings.edu/blog/africa-in-focus/2020/01/10/a-national-strategy-for-harnessing-the-fourth-industrial-revolution-the-case-of-south-africa/. Accessed 12 Oct.
Rayle, L., D. Dai, N. Chan, R. Cervero, and S. Shabeen. 2016. Just a better taxi? A surveybased comparison of taxis, transit and ridesourcing services in San Francisco. *Transport Policy* 45: 168–178.
Sauti G. 2006. *Minibus taxi drivers are they all 'Children born from the same mother?'*. School of Social Sciences University of The Witwatersrand Masters Dissertation.
Unathi Sonwabile Henama and Portia Pearl Siyanda Sifolo. 2017. Uber: The South Africa experience. *African Journal of Hospitality, Tourism and Leisure* 6 (2): 1–10.
Wiredu, K. 2011. State, civil society and democracy in Africa. In *Reclaiming the human Sciences and humanities through African perspectives, Volume II*, ed. H. Lauer and K. Anyidoho, 1055–1066. Legon: Sub-Saharan Publishers.

**Beatrice Okyere-Manu** is a Professor in the Applied Ethics department at the University of KwaZulu-Natal in Pietermaritzburg. Her research interests cover the following areas: HIV and AIDS, Ethical issues Affecting African Women, AIKS, Ethics of Technology, and Environmental Ethics. She has written a number of journal articles and book chapters in these areas. She recently edited a book on "African Values, Ethics, and Technology: Questions, Issues, and Approaches" which provides critical and ethical reflections on technology from an African perspective. She co-edited a book on "Intersecting African Indigenous Knowledge Systems and Western Knowledge Systems: Moral convergence and divergence".

# Women's Rights: A Precursor for African Development

**Faith Matumbu**

**Abstract** In postcolonial Africa, development has, generally, been premised on the philosophy that; it is a product of collective or collaborative approach. This implies that men, women and all other groups are part and parcel of this development process. Demographic data for most African countries show that the highest population percentage is attributed to women and children. It can therefore, be expected that development on the continent is by and large driven by the collective or collaborative effort of both sexes. However, it is an established fact that women in Africa have had to endure enormous challenges in making their mark on development. For quite some time women in Africa have had to contend with being treated as minors who needed an adult male to represent them legally in making business transactions. Instances are abound to support this assertion. A gap, therefore, exists in the area of women's rights in their quest to make a claim in the development of the continent. For the continent to tap into women's potential to the fullest, an enabling environment has to be created. This actually brings the discussion to interrogate the question of how Africa can achieve its development when women are not given sufficient space to meaningfully participate. Yet it is well accepted that, women's rights as human rights are a precursor for catalyzing and achieving development in all spheres of human endeavor (social, cultural, economic, and political spheres). This chapter will therefore explore what the term development means from women's perspective. For instance, the term development for women in Africa may mean increased access to economic opportunities, resources and greater participation in decision making at all levels of society. This line of thinking actually comes with positive and negative effects to development in Africa which will be discussed as the chapter unfolds. Thereafter, the chapter interrogates whether women's rights are recognized in practical terms (that is their rights towards development in Africa). To this extent it will be demonstrated that women in Africa have been and are engaged in the formal and informal sectors of the economy as entrepreneurs. Outstanding issues relating to women's rights will be highlighted and used to discuss development or lack of it in

F. Matumbu (✉)
University of Zimbabwe, Harare, Zimbabwe



B. Okyere-Manu et al. (eds.), *Contemporary Development Ethics from an African Perspective*, Philosophy and Politics - Critical Explorations 27,
https://doi.org/10.1007/978-3-031-32898-5_11

Africa, maybe that's why Africa is still underdeveloped. Thus, in this chapter it is argued that human rights including women's rights are a vehicle towards development in Africa. The discussion on women's rights and development will be linked to development ethics grounding it on one of the applied ethics theories referred to as consequentalism (mainly utilitarianism). Thus, in this chapter the research is constructed using a phenomenological qualitative research design.

**Keywords** Development · Human rights · Precursor · Women's rights · Consequentialism · Utilitarianism · Africa

## 1 Introduction

Human rights are a precursor for development in Africa and the World at large. There is undisputed and critical link between human rights (including women's rights) and the concept of development in Africa. The word development carries different meanings to different people. Walter Rodney (1973) posits that development presupposes increased skills and capacity, greater freedom, creativity, self-discipline, responsibility and material well-being. According to Ndlovu-Gatsheni (2018:19), "African development can be defined from Marcus Garvey's perspective as constant and consistent African search for self-improvement." Thus, development aims at the constant improvement of the wellbeing of the entire population and of all individuals on the basis of their free, meaningful participation in development and in the fair distribution of benefits resulting there from (Muyoyeta 2004). The well-being of the entire population therefore includes all groups of people within a society, nation, continent etc. Kuhumba (2018), notes that Amartya Sen's understanding of human development focuses on enhancement of the lives we lead and the freedoms we enjoy, thus, human development is defined as the removal of major hindrances to our freedom. Some of these hindrances are poverty, tyranny, poor economic opportunities among others. In this context, the expansion of freedom is viewed both as a primary end and the principal means for development. For Sen (2000) human development is achieved when people have greater freedoms (capabilities). For the purpose of this analysis the concept of development is linked to human freedom (as a human right), it could be political, social or economic freedom. Thus, human development would really mean making the person more capable through investing in social sectors and public infrastructures. In the long term this will improve the political, socio- economic capabilities of people (Alexander 2004).

Development, from an African perspective, is attained through collective or collaborative approach (Soumana 2002). This implies that men, women, boys and girls are part and parcel of this development process. Demographic data for most African countries shows that the highest population percentage is attributed to women and children. African Development Bank (2015) notes that women comprise a little over half of Africa's growing population. According to Cherifa (2020:1), "The percentage of women in Africa is more than half the population of the African continent".

It can therefore, be concluded and expected that development on the continent is by and large driven by the collective or collaborative effort of women. However, if women are sidelined in the development process it implies a privation of women's freedom or rights. For Jeremy Bentham's utilitarianism, the right act or policy is the one that causes the greatest happiness of the greatest number, that is, maximize the total utility or welfare of the majority of all the affected parties. Therefore, women are supposed to be part and parcel or drivers of the development process. Their rights to development ought to be fully recognized in practical terms. Hence, an understanding of development from African and women's perspective ought to be discussed and establish the link between the two.

## 2 The Concept of Development from an African Women's Perspective

Kuhumba (2018) suggests that the community should be taken into account in the discourse of human development. By doing so, social freedom, economic freedom and political freedom can aim at fostering the wellbeing of the entire community (Kuhumba 2018). Africa's development priorities are grouped into six pillars namely; structural economic transformation and inclusive growth; science, technology and innovation; people-centered development; environmental sustainability natural resources management, and disaster risk management; peace and security; and finance and partnerships (Common Africa Position 2014). Of these six pillars, this discussion is interested more in people-centered development and inclusive growth. African Union's Commission (2019) points out that Africa's development is the product of a collaborative approach. The philosophy that underlies African development is that which focuses on working together for the common good. It therefore stands to reason that human society can only be effectively developed through the combined efforts of all its members. Hence, the urgent need for African women to maximize the realization of their potential in the interest of development at the individual, family, communal, national and regional levels. Hodgson (2002) notes that development for women in Africa means increased access to economic opportunities, resources and greater participation in decision making at all levels of society. This shows the need for the realization, recognition of women's potential and roles for a nation or continent to develop.

The idea that women have always played a central role in African societies cannot be doubted. From the colonial epoch to the present day, accounts of women's contributions to the development of a united Africa are aptly amplified (Iyadunni 2015). Politically, women participated actively in different colonial African states to liberate their countries from foreign domination. Economically they have contributed significantly to Africa's economic growth, particularly in areas such as agriculture, trade and commerce (Iyadunni 2015). Socially, they constitute the building blocks of family cohesion on the continent. They have consistently remained the driving force behind effective African family value system which is reflected in communal living and peaceful co-existence. For development to be meaningful to women all these roles have to be acknowledged (Muyoyeta 2004). There are significant development gains to be made in ensuring women's equitable access to and control over economic and financial resources, including in relation to economic growth, poverty eradication and the well-being of families and communities.

## 3 Women's Right and Development

The African Charter on Human and Peoples' Rights, presents development as a human right (thus including all sexes- males, females and the intersexed). Kamga (2020) argues that the first Article of the 1986 Declaration on the Right to Development (RTD) clarifies the nature of the RTD which portrays that the right to development is an inalienable human right by virtue of which every human person and all peoples are entitled to participate in, contribute to, and enjoy economic, social, cultural and political development, in which all human rights and fundamental freedoms can be fully realized. Thus the African Charter on Human and Peoples' Rights, unlike other Charters, has had a focus on development from its very inception. Article 22 (1) states boldly that "All peoples shall have the right to their economic, social and cultural development with due regard to their freedom and identity and in the equal enjoyment of the common heritage of mankind," (Atuguba 2018). In this regard it can be deduced that human rights are women's rights and vice-versa because women are also the people referred to.

From the African Charter on Human and People's Rights it can be deduced that the right to development is an inalienable human right by virtue of which every human person and all peoples are entitled to participate in, contribute to, and enjoy economic, social, cultural and political development. It is in this regard that all fundamental freedoms can be fully realized since the right to development entitles all people (including women) to free, active and meaningful participation in the development decisions that affect them. For Kamga (2020) this right to development may also mean fair distribution of the benefits of development, with the ultimate objective of fulfilling all human rights for all (rather than aiming for economic growth alone). It is in this context that there is a growing acceptance and recognition of the important role women play in the development process. Women are crucial to the success of family planning programs; bear much of the responsibility for food production and account for an increasing share of wage labour in Africa. Women's participation in the formal economy constitutes a viable strategy for promoting national development (Njoh and Rigos 2003). Women are considered as economically active for they function as both producers andconsumers of goods and services. Their capacity to actively serve in these areas can be enhanced if they are provided with a conducive environment. Therefore, their contribution to development ought to be supported. Barret (1995) argues that the pivotal role of women in society and in the process of development should be recognized in practical terms and given its true value. If their efforts are well recognized and appreciated, then one can conclude that the concept of development in Africa can be achieved through efforts of women.

It is worth to note the contribution of women in poverty eradication and food production in both rural and urban development. They play a catalytic role towards the achievement of transformational economic, environmental and social changes required for a nation to develop. They have been and are engaged in the formal and informal sectors of the economies of African countries as entrepreneurs to eradicate poverty and develop. However, without a holistic approach to looking at intersections of women's rights, it is impossible to attain the goals of women's empowerment and development in 2015 as well as agenda 2063 (Kwangwari 2015). In this context feminism advocates for the social, political and other rights for women as equal to those of men, women and men alike should be entitled to economic empowerment and equal political representation (Alobwede 2015). Women who possess economic and political power contribute to the wellbeing of their households, community, nation, region etc. For instance in Cameroon women constitute 52 percent of the entire population. They are actively involved in fighting poverty in households through farming, vending, trading etc. and thus make a crucial contribution to development of the society (Alobwede 2015).

Iyadunni (2015) says that through research, he has documented the concrete contributions of women to Africa's development; their input into the socio-political and economic transformation of the continent has been globally appreciated and acknowledged. It is in this context that, women's rights as human rights are considered a precursor for catalyzing and achieving development in all spheres of human endeavor (social, cultural, economic, and political spheres). Beyond their immediate continent, African women also occupy strategic positions in international development institutions such as the World Bank (WB), the United Nations (UN), the International Monetary Fund (IMF) and other similar global institutions worldwide making impacts on global development.

According to Kevane (2004:2), "Greater women's rights and more equal participation in public life by women and men are associated with cleaner business and government and better governance. Where the influence of women in public life is greater, the level of corruption is lower". Women can be an effective force for rule of law, good governance, hence, women can be regarded as drivers of development in any given continent. It has been recognized that gender equality, the empowerment of women, women's full enjoyment of all human rights and the eradication of poverty are essential to economic and social development, including the achievement of all the Millennium Development Goals (DAC Network on Gender Equality 2011). However, women's rights are not fully realized given that there are some challenges that women are encountering. The United Nations Human Rights Commission (2014) notes that women around the world nevertheless regularly suffer violations of their human rights throughout their lives, and realizing of their rights has not always been a priority, some face discrimination based on their age, ethnicity, nationality, religion, health status, marital status, education, disability and socioeconomic status, among other grounds. The realization of their right to development is beset by challenges rooted in these inequalities that pervade their lives. For women, the right to development does not simply require consideration of how income poverty, poverty, in the sense of women's lack of voice and participation in decision-making within their families and societies, also impacts upon their lives and further reinforces their powerlessness (Banda 2004).

## 4 Challenges Faced by Women in Africa Towards the Development of Their Continent

A gap exists in the area of women's rights in their quest to make a claim in the development of the continent. For instance, women face systematic prejudice and discrimination in access to land, water and other productive resources as well as participation in social and political movements that have a bearing on their farming activities (Kwangwari 2015). Despite the significant contributions women make to agriculture in Africa, they have limited and inequitable access and control of proper productive capabilities and productive resources. This negatively impacts on their abilities to feed themselves, their families and to contribute to the national economy (Edeme 2015). The challenges include; land, labor, livestock and livestock products, agricultural equipment, and productivity-enhancing inputs, technologies/innovations, education, training, extension services, and market information; and credit, farm income and off-farm income, insurance and risk financing capabilities (Edeme 2015). This gender gap hinders the productivity of rural women and reduces their contribution to the agricultural sector yet agriculture is one of the pillars of economic development.

Kwangwari (2015) argues that if men and women had equal access to productive resources in agriculture, food output in developing countries would increase by between 2.5 and 4 percent enough to pull 100–150 million people out of hunger. Yet women continue to be discriminated against in accessing these resources. In support of that, Edeme (2015) points out that women are the backbone of smallholder farming in Africa. Despite the fact that women comprise 70 percent of the labor used in the production of food, they continue being marginalized in the agricultural sector. As a result of this, women's productivity is lower than that of male farmers. The yield gap between men and women averages around 20–30 percent, yet evidence shows that if women farmers used the same level of resources as men on the land they farm, they would achieve the same yield level, which would result in the decrease of malnourished people in the world from 925 million to as low as 100–150 million (Southern African Trust 2018). Therefore, women's access to land is another area which needs urgent attention, governments in Africamust ensure that women's access, control and ownership of land is guaranteed. They must put in place measures for secure tenure to land for women smallholder farmers (Muyoyeta 2004).

Despite the great wealth enjoyed by the African continent, 59% of Africans live below the poverty line. Twenty-one African countries are classified under the food-insecure countries of 37 countries in the world, in this case, women account for half the population of Africa and are largely affected (Cherifa 2020). This implies that more than half of the continent's women are poor, yet, the right to development from an African perspective is considered to be a common good and universal. According to Cherifa (2020:6), "…it is estimated that women own less than 2% of land in Africa. It is clear that the lack of a commercial building or farm is a major impediment to women's economic progress. In many areas, women are robbed of land as a result of custom". This brings the discussion to the question of distribution of resources (land). For example, in Uganda, while women are allowed to own land that grows and receive their wages directly, the reality is quite different. When their husbands die or after divorce, most lose their property to her husband's relatives, as custom takes precedence over the law and many women are robbed of the right to own land. Although 80% of Ugandan women are agricultural workers, only 7% own their land (Cherifa 2020). Which is considered an unfair challenge to women in Africa. The question here is: How can Africa achieve its own development when women are not given sufficient space and resources to meaningfully participate?

Some people in Africa live in communal or tribal lands as peasants or smallholder farmers where customary law governs this land. The practice in customary law is for traditional authorities to give rights of use of land to adult males. Women's rights to land are often indirect, that is, through their male relatives (Muyoyeta 2004). They obtain their land rights through their roles as daughters, sisters or wives. This does not give women much control over land as is given to men, which works to the advantage of men and disadvantage of women. This limits women from realizing their full potential in the utilization of the land and contribution to development in all its manifestations. For Muyoyeta (2004) legal discrimination also limits women's access, control and use of productive resources. This includes marriage systems in countries such as Botswana, Swaziland and Lesotho that deprive wives of their right to enter into contracts in their own names. In other African countries inheritance laws and practices dispossess widows of their marital property. Long-standing inequalities in the gender distribution of resources have placed women at a disadvantage relative to men in their capability to participate in and benefit from broader processes of development; this has often left them dependent on male provision to meet some or all of the needs of their households.

Cherifa (2020) argues that although there is notable progress that has been made in an attempt to address women concerns in Africa and their role in social and economic life, African women continue to face gender barriers to their successful participation in the workplace, particularly employment policies and discriminatory employment practices. African women suffer from discrimination at work, unequal sharing of family and family responsibilities, lack of supervision of productive resources such as property, their lack of low-paid jobs, and the operation of micro-enterprises and scale. There is still a limit to the contribution of African women to social and economic life through their limited empowerment on the development side. Despite that women are considered internationally as one of the main pillars of economic development, they have suffered from an unjust social heritage in addition to discriminatory practices both in terms of gender equality and in the market.

In as much as women in Africa are contributing towards development of their nations, women in the vending business and manufacturing sector highlighted that there were inadequate infrastructure and services (International Labour Organization 2017). For example, women in Zimbabwe, cited poorly designed work spaces, hardly maintained public toilets and very limited access to water as their major concerns which made it particularly difficult for their operations. This has seen them allocating themselves working space (especially on the streets in the central business districts of cities and towns) which has increased confrontations with the police or municipal police. They also noted that the areas that they are sometimes allocated by the local authorities are far from the customers, which affect their daily earnings (International Labour Organization 2017). Harassment is another challenge faced by women in the informal economy. Women are, in most cases, subjected to verbal, physical and sexual harassment by municipal police, clients, service providers and fellow male informal workers. For instance, in Zimbabwe, there were alleged reports of women who have been asked to perform sexual acts by officials so as to ensure that they do not lose their wares to the local authority, Revenue collecting authorities and police. Within the locality they work in, some women noted that they had to move, as their male counterparts were taking over their working space and harassing them. Victims of harassment find it difficult to report cases or seek recourse as they are already regarded as "illegal operators" by both the local authorities and police. What this implies is that a conducive environment ought to be created such that women may exercise their right to fully participate in development.

Furthermore, the African Development Bank (2015) notes that there are indeed African women already working in the formal economy, whether in the public or private sectors, many of whom are educated but are relegated to the lower levels of employment. They tend to be underemployed and consequently undervalued, but they form the base of institutions that make them function and develop. Despite the legal recognition and protection of women's right to development in Africa, standards of their living remain unacceptably low (Ngang 2020). Gender exclusion still exists and this constraints women's enjoyment of the right to development, maybe this justifies why Africa is still under developed. Despite their efforts, women constitute the poorest and the least powerful segment of the population throughout the world, gender bias or gender discrimination is thus a fundamental cause for poverty, because in its various forms it prevents hundreds of millions of women exercising their right to development (Anunobi 2002). Kongolo (2009) suggest that the lack of government assistance and lack of resources, cultural values and discrimination against women are the most important factors contributing to their passive involvement in development. Moyo (2020) recommends adoption of a more holistic and transformative approach which attempts to change radically, the ideological, philosophical, psychological and cultural foundations that construct, reproduce and sustain the unequal, unjust, oppressive and exploitative gender power relations that still exist.

## 5 Conclusion

The concept of development in Africa is premised on a collaborative approach. African charter on People's Rights stresses on the right to development to all human beings in Africa. Thus it is linked to human freedoms too. Human rights, in this context, women's rights, are a precursor for development in Africa. Women's participation in community development services and programs greatly increases economic growth, reduces poverty and gender discrimination, enhances societal well-being and helps ensure sustainable development in Africa. Despite their contribution or roles towards development, women are still facing challenges which are initiated by patriarchal thinking and narrative. This narrative of development can also undermine the role, status and position of women in society. The current development approach has failed women by not being able to enhance their welfare. However, for the continent to tap into women's potential to the fullest, an enabling environment has to be created.

## References


African Development Bank. 2015. *Where are the women: Inclusive Boardrooms in Africa' stop listed companies?* Viewed 20 May 2021. www.afdb.org

African Union's Commission. 2019. *Africa's development dynamics 2019: Achieving productive transformation*. Paris: AUC, Addis Ababa/OECD Publishing. Viewed 15 May 2021. https://doi.org/10.1787/c1cd7de0-en.

Alexander, M.J. 2004. Capabilities, human rights and moral pluralism. *The International Journal of Human Rights* 8 (4): 451–469.

Alobwede, J. 2015. Breaking gender barriers: political representation and the economic self-empowerment of the Cameroonian woman In: *Year of Women's Empowerment and Development towards Africa's Agenda* 2063.

Anunobi, F. 2002. Women and development in Africa: From marginalization to gender inequality. *African Social Science Review* 2 (2): Article 3. Viewed 26 May 2021, https://digitalcommons.kennesaw.edu/assr/vol2/iss2/3.

Atuguba, R.A. 2018. *A presentation to conference experts invited by the United Nations special rapporteur on the right to Development. Under the theme: Regional consultation on the practical Implementation of the right to development: Identifying and promoting good practices*. Addis-Ababa 27, (27–29) March 2018.

Banda, F. 2004. *Women, human rights and development*. Viewed 15 May 2021, www.womenrightsanddevelopment.com.

Barrett, H. 1995, July. Women in Africa: The neglected dimension in development. *Journal of Geography* 80 (3): 215–224.

Cherifa, K. 2020. Role of African Women in Development and Economic Life: Reality and Challenges. *International Journal of Inspiration & Resilience Economy* 4 (1): 1–9. https://doi.org/10.5923/j.ijire.20200401.01. https://www.researchgate.net/publication/340935182.

Common Africa Position (CAP). 2014. *On the post 2015 development agenda African union*. Addis Ababa, Ethopia. Viewed 15 May 2021. www.africa-union.org

DAC Network on Gender Equality. 2011. *Women's economic empowerment*. www.oecd.org/dac/gender.

Edeme, J. 2015. Women in agriculture: Addressing the gender gap through relevant agricultural frameworks. In *Year of Women's Empowerment and Development towards Africa's Agenda* 2063.

Hodgson, D.L. 2002. *Women's rights as human rights: Women in law and development in Africa (WiLDAF) Africa Today, Summer* 49(2): 3–26. Women, language, and law in Africa 2 (Summer, 2002). Indiana University Press. Viewed 20 May 2021. https://www.jstor.org/stable/4187496.
International Labour Organization. 2017. *Situational analysis of women in the informal economy in Zimbabwe*. Viewed 30 May 2021, www.challemgesfacedbywomenintheinformaleconomy-inZimbabwe.com.
Iyadunni, I. 2015. Women's empowerment and development in Africa: strides and tides. *Year of women's empowerment and development towards Africa's agenda* 2063.
Kamga, S.D. 2020. *The right to development in Africa: Issues, constraints and prospects*. Ibadan, Nigeria: Pan-African University Press.
Kevane, M. 2004. *Women and development in Africa: How gender works*. Boulder, CO USA: Lynne Rienner.
Kongolo, M. 2009. Factors limiting women's involvement in development. *An International Multi-Disciplinary Journal, Ethiopia 3(4), July, 2009* ISSN 1994-9057 (Print) ISSN 2070-0083Lesson from Ithuseng, South Africa (pp. 13–30) Human Sciences Research Council (HSRC), Pretoria, South Africa.
Kuhumba, S.K. 2018. Amartya Sen's capability approach as theoretical foundation of human development published. *Journal of Sociology and Development*. Viewed 15 May 2021. https://www.researchgate.net/publication/324125531
Kwangwari, C. 2015. '2015: Year of women's empowerment and development' what is in it for women smallholder farmerS? *Year of Women's Empowerment and Development towards Africa's Agenda* 2063.
Moyo, T. 2020. Addressing gender exclusion for the realization of the right to development in Africa: The south African experience. In *The right to development in Africa: Issues, Constraints and Prospects*. Ibadan, Nigeria: Pan-African University Press.
Muyoyeta, L. 2004. *Women, gender and development*. Viewed 15 May 2021. www.women-genderanddevelopment.org.
Ndlovu-Gatsheni, S.J. 2018. *The African idea of development from: The Routledge handbook of African development Routledge*. https://www.routledgehandbooks.com/. https://doi.org/10.4324/9781315712482-3. Accessed 10 Nov 2021.
Ngang, C. 2020. The right to development in Africa: Implications of its ineffective implementation to prospects for development on the continent. In *The right to development in Africa: Issues, constraints and prospects*. Ibadan, Nigeria: Pan-African University Press.
Njoh, A.J., and Rigos, P.N. 2003. Female participation in the formal sector and development in Sub-Saharan Africa. *Journal of Third World Studies* FALL, 20(2). University Press of Florida.
Sen, A. 2000. *Development as freedom*. New Delhi: Oxford University Press.
Soumana, S. 2002. *Africa: Major development challenges & their capacity building dimensions*. Harare: Zimbabwe.
Southern African Trust. 2018. *The experiences and challenges of women in the SADC region, the case of trade and agriculture sector*. Viewed 12 May 2021. www.challengesfacedbywomenin-africatowardsdevelopment.com.
United Nations. 2014. *Women's rights are human rights*. United Nations Publication. ISBN 978-92-1-154206-6, E-ISBN 978-92-1-056789-3. http://www.womensrightsarehumanrights.com. Retrieved on 10/11/21.
Walter Rodney, W. 1973. *How Europe underdeveloped Africa*. http://www.marxists.org/subject/africa/rodney-walter/how-europe/preface.htm at 1. Accessed 20 May 2021.

**Faith Matumbu** is a doctorate student at the University of Zimbabwe. She holds a Master of Arts Degree in Philosophy from Great Zimbabwe University. She is a part-time tutor in the Department of Philosophy and Religious Studies. Her research interests are based on issues to do with ethics, gender, and human rights (with a focus on women's rights). As of now, she has co-authored two book chapters.

# The Economic Foundation of Racism

**Emmanuel Ifeanyi Ani**

**Abstract** This research exposes the connection between economic inequality and racism. The central argument is that racism is predicated on the economic superiority of the racist. The corollary argument is that conceptions of skin colour are consequences rather than causes of racism: racism does not arise because of skin colour, but because different skin colours have become associated with certain economic conditions for a very long period of time in history. The argument is in fact extended to posit that the topography of the racist relationship would be reversed if the economic tables were also reversed. The conclusion is that the relationship between racism and economic inequality is, therefore, more significant than the relationship between racism and skin colour. This conclusion has consequences regarding how races at the receiving end of racism should respond to racism.

**Keywords** Racism · Economic inequality · Migration · Philosophy · Color psychology

## 1 Introduction

Prevailing conceptions of racism assume that Caucasians (being white in skin colour) look down on people of darker colour simply because of the darker shades in skin colour. In this paper I contest this assumption by arguing that racism is predicated on the economic superiority of the Caucasian race (the Whites) over the Asian and Black African races. I defend my position by presenting data showing the economic topography of the different races. If my argument is correct, then it means that the manifestations of economic underdevelopment (which include extremely high levels of migration to White-controlled economies) exacerbate anti-Asian and

E. I. Ani (✉)
Department of Philosophy and Classics, University of Ghana, Accra, Ghana
e-mail: eiani@ug.edu.gh



B. Okyere-Manu et al. (eds.), *Contemporary Development Ethics from an African Perspective*, Philosophy and Politics - Critical Explorations 27,
https://doi.org/10.1007/978-3-031-32898-5_12

anti-Black African racism. The only effective way to minimize the feelings of White supremacy is for Asians and Africans to build their economies to the point where their youth lose the desire to migrate *en masse* to White-controlled economies.

The central argument of this paper arises from two factors: (1) the collective GDP per capita of countries in categories of race; (2) the economic income of the average member of each race in a comprehensively diverse sample country (such as the USA); and (3) data showing the degrees in the intensity of racism directed by Caucasians against members of other races (such as Latinos, Asians and Black Africans).

In Sect. 1, I suggest that in view of the sensitive nature of racism, it is best to find out what motivates anti-Black racism by looking at evidence in the external world. In Sects. 2 and 3, I show that the biggest evidence out there is economic inequality. In Sect. 4, I present data showing that the Black African is the most discriminated against. In Sect. 5, I argue that the correlation between economy and racism is so strong that the racism table would be reversed if the economic table were also reversed. In Sect. 6, I show that Caucasians do not hate the colour black, but rather love it in a number of instances and for many reasons; and in Sect. 7, I argue that this suggests that discrimination against the Black African cannot be simply based on colour alone.

## 2 How to Know What Causes Racism

Racism is a very sensitive topic. It is so sensitive that I do not believe that members of the Caucasian race will be frank enough regarding what motivates their feelings of superiority, whether it is their skin colour or some other factor(s). Fortunately, there is a far better way to find out what motivates feelings of racial superiority, which makes interviewing Caucasians unnecessary. That better way is not just better but (in my opinion) the best. It is to *study facts in the external world*; and it reveals that the correlation between racism and economic factors is far stronger than that between racism and skin colour. To be sure, other factors could crop up at specific periods, such as the corona virus pandemic causing a spike in anti-Asian racism over the last 2 years. But the economic factor is by far the most resilient and enduring, in a more long lasting category. In this essay I will lay out multidimensional evidence.

There have been some investigations of the correlation between skin colour and discrimination, and the correlation is found to be very high. Klonoff and Landrine (2000) found that darker-skinned people are far more likely to be discriminated against, compared to lighter-skinned people. Nancy Boyd-Franklin (2003) found that skin colour causes a lot of anxiety among African Americans. Joung and Megan (2020) found that more than 46% of hate crimes in the USA are based on conceptions of skin colour. Li et al. (2008) did a comprehensive study in Asian countries and found that Asians regard light skin as superior. In fact, skin-based discrimination is called colourism (Bagalini 2020) and "sales of skin-lightening products are projected to reach $8.9 billion by 2024" (Bagalini 2020: par 1). Also, "A recent study by the University of Cape Town suggests that one woman in three in South Africa bleaches her skin" (Fihlani 2013). All of these attitudes are predicated on the notion that darker skin colours are not as good as lighter ones. I will show in this article that these views are misleading, and understanding the true picture actually offers us vital motivation about developing the economies of Black African societies. My investigations show that it is not about skin colour *alone,* but *consistent economic perceptions* of skin colour.

The first scholars to be particularly interested in economic conditions and their influence on social conditions are Karl Marx (1998, 2013) and Frederick Engels (2008). They interpreted history in materialist terms (historical materialism), an economic conception of history. Although they were focused on the transition from feudalism to capitalism and from capitalism to socialism, the idea that comes out clearly is that economic conditions determine social conditions. The history of human relations *always* and consistently vindicates this idea. In interpersonal relationships, the richer partner tends to wield more social power in relation to the poorer partner (whether in marital, business, or political relationships). Similarly, in the relationships between countries (or societies), the richer countries wield more political power in relation to the poorer countries. I can, therefore, take it that the principle of economic relations is true and applies across the board in human interactions. My basic assumption for this paper is, therefore, that economic condition is the greatest influence on social relationships and transactions.

Having adopted this assumption, my task in this paper is to show that the economic conditions or positions of different races are related to the amount or level of respect generally accorded to them. I will show this by presenting what I call 'economic contributors' (showing that economic condition is the major cause of racism).

## 3 Economic Contributors

Here I present computation (in the form of tables) showing that economic capacity correlates with the global topography of racial discrimination. My computation of racial economic capacity follows a grouping of countries (or economies) controlled by members of different races. This comprises Caucasian-controlled economies, Latino-controlled economies, Asian-controlled economies, and Black African-controlled economies.

I classified the USA and Canada as the Caucasian-controlled economies in North America. The rest of the North American countries and the Central American ones have witnessed long-standing mixing of races, but Caucasians have been politically and economically in charge of the USA and Canada. The South American countries have the same feature of deep racial mixing.

Caucasian-controlled economies include Western and Eastern Europe, USA and Canada in North America, and Australia and New Zealand in Australasia.

Asian economies include Japan, China, Thailand, Korea, India, Singapore, Malaysia, Indonesia, Philippines, Vietnam and Pakistan, as well as all the Arab and other neighbouring economies that are neither Caucasian- nor African-controlled. Sub-Saharan African economies exclude North Africa. There is the question about whether North Africans (Egyptians, Algerians, Tunisians, Libyans, Moroccans, and citizens of Western Sahara Republic) are Caucasian or Asian. The US Census Bureau categorizes North Africans as White, but North Africans (and other Arabs) protest that Caucasians discriminate against them as being different, and categorizing them as Caucasians denies them the attention due to them as a community of their own. They argue that it is an attempt to erase them. In sum, they do not agree they are Caucasians (Parvini and Simani 2019; Eitohamy 2019). In any case, the per capita of North African countries(3950 USD) is roughly half way between that of Sub Saharan Africa (I, 585.4 USD) and that of Asia (7, 351 USD).

I would have included South Africa among Caucasian controlled economies, because the Black African political leaders of South Africa are largely ceremonial heads, and in any case are not responsible for the stature of the South African economy, having only recently won political control of the country in 1994. For fairness and political correctness, I will include South Africa among Black-African-controlled economies. But this inclusion does not affect the broader racial economic table.

I believe that in my tables below I have represented different sections of peoples around the world in various racial groups. If there were any other pockets of peoples left out, their GDPs would not affect my main argument.

The compilations have been based on the computation of economies in 2019, mainly because the 2020 computations were not yet as comprehensive or all encompassing. Preliminary computation of economies in 2020 shows that that year (dominated by the corona virus pandemic) had not seen economic change significant enough to change my central argument. Indeed, economic changes of probably up to 50 years from now (the most conservative estimate) may not make any difference.

One can see from Table 1 that the combined economic strength of all 22 Latino controlled economies in North and Central America is only 7.6% of the economic strength of only two White-controlled economies (USA and Canada). When we add 12 South American economies, the total Latin American economies are 40, and their combined economic strength is 8.6 trillion US dollars, which is just 37% of USA and Canada's combined 23.2 trillion (Table 2).

Strictly speaking, Latin-American countries are also White-controlled economies, except that their racial mix-up makes it more difficult to get a Latin American of pure White blood, and therefore makes it difficult to categorize them as White-controlled economies. There is, however, no consensus that Latinos are a race of their own, and White Latinos generally see themselves as Caucasians. To avoid unnecessary debate, I will exclude Latino economic power from White economic power. But this exclusion does not even slightly dent the economic superiority of the

**Table 1** North American economies 2019

| Economy | Gross domestic product (US$) | GDP per capita (PPP) (US$) | Population |
|---|---|---|---|
| USA (Caucasian controlled) | 21.4 trillion | 65,111.6 | 332 million |
| Canada (Caucasian controlled) | 1.7 trillion | 50,757.4 | 38 million |
| Latino controlled North and Central American economies (Mexico, Puerto Rico, Dominican Republic, Guatemala, Panama, Costa Rica, El Salvador, Honduras, Trinidad and Tobago, Jamaica, The Bahamas, Nicaragua, Haiti, Barbados, Aruba, Belize, St Lucia, Antigua and Barbuda, Grenada, St. Kitts and Nevis, St Vincent and the Grenadines, Dominica | 1.76 trillion | 18,811.6 | 212 million |

Source: Author's compilation from Worldometer (2020a–i, k–y) and Statistica (2020b)

**Table 2** South American economies 2019

| Economy | Gross domestic product (US$) | GDP per capita (PPP) (US$) | Population |
|---|---|---|---|
| Latino controlled economies (Brazil, Argentina, Colombia, Chile, Peru, Ecuador, Venezuela, Uruguay, Bolivia, Paraguay, Guyana, Suriname | 6.8 trillion | 16,041.1 | 433 million |

Source: Author's compilation from Statistica (2020c)

**Table 3** European economic power (all Caucasian controlled)

| Economy | Gross domestic product (US$) | GDP per capita (PPP) (US$) | Population |
|---|---|---|---|
| Europe (Germany, United Kingdom, France, Italy, Spain, Netherlands, Turkey, Switzerland, Poland, Sweden, Belgium, Austria, Norway, Ireland, Denmark, Finland, Czechia, Romania, Portugal, Greece, Hungary, Slovakia, Luxemburg, Bulgaria, Croatia, Lithuania, Slovenia, Latvia, Serbia, Estonia, Cyprus, Iceland, Bosnia and Herzegovina, Albania, Malta, North Macedonia, Liechtenstein, Montenegro, Russia, Ukraine, Belarus, Kosovo) | 20.4 trillion | 46,467.5 | 748 million |

Source: Author's compilation from Statistica (2020d, e); Worldometer (2020j); and World Bank (2020a, b), Eurostat (2020)

Caucasian race. Let me now turn to the mainstay of Caucasian economic power, Europe and Australasia (Tables 3 and 4).

Table 5 shows that Asian economies have a combined strength of 36 trillion US$, but with over 60% of the world's population, Asia has a per capita GDP of 7 thousand dollars per annum, compared to 55 thousand dollars for combined Caucasian economies (Table 6).

**Table 4** Caucasian economies in Australasia 2019

| Economy | Gross domestic product (US$) | GDP per capita (PPP) (US$) | Population |
|---|---|---|---|
| Australia, New Zealand | 1.8 trillion | 56,431 | 31.53 million |

Source: Author's compilation from Statistica (2020f), Macrotrends (2023a)

**Table 5** Asian-controlled economies

| Economy | Gross domestic product (US$) | GDP per capita (PPP) (US$) | Population |
|---|---|---|---|
| Asia (Afghanistan, Armenia, Azerbaijan, Bahrain, Bangladesh, Bhutan, Brunei, Cyprus, Myanmar, Cambodia, China, Hong Kong (PRC), Georgia, India, Indonesia, Iran, Iraq, Israel, Japan, Jordan, Kazakhstan, North Korea, South Korea, Kuwait, Kyrgyzstan, Laos, Lebanon, Macau, Malaysia, Maldives, Mongolia, Nepal, Oman, Pakistan, Philippines, Qatar, Saudi Arabia, Singapore, Sri Lanka, Syria, Taiwan [ROC], Tajikistan, Thailand, Timor-Leste, Turkmenistan, United Arab Emirates, Uzbekistan, Vietnam, Yemen) | 36.27 trillion | 7.885 | 4.6 billion |

Source: Author's compilation from Trade Economics (2023), Bank of Korea (2023), Macrotrends (2023b), World Bank (2023a, b)

**Table 6** Black-African controlled economies

| Economy | Gross domestic product | GDP per capita (PPP) (US$) | Population |
|---|---|---|---|
| Black-Africa (Angola, Benin, Botswana, Burkina Faso, Burundi, Cameroon, Central African Republic, Chad, Congo (Brazzaville) Congo (Democratic Republic), Cote d'Ivoire, Eritrea, Ethiopia, Gabon, Gambia, Ghana, Guinea, Guinea-Bissau, Kenya, Lesotho, Liberia, Madagascar, Mali, Mauritania, Mauritius, Mozambique, Namibia, Niger, Nigeria, Rwanda, Senegal, Sierra Leone, Somalia, South Africa, Tanzania, Togo, Uganda, Zaire, Zambia, Zimbabwe) | 1.76 trillion | 1585.4 | 1.12 billion |

Source: Author's compilation from World Bank (2020c), Statistica (2020a)

From all these tables, it is evident that the average per capita income of anyone living in all the Caucasian economies scattered around the globe (USA, Canada, Western and Eastern Europe, Australia, New Zealand) is approximately 55 thousand dollars per annum. We already have that of Asian economies as approximately 8 thousand dollars and Sub-Saharan Africa as 1.6 thousand dollars. It means the average person in a Caucasian economy is 34 times as rich as the average person in an African economy, and an average person in an Asian economy is five times as rich as an average person in an African economy. The economic value chain has the Caucasians at the top, the Asians at the middle, and the Africans at the bottom.

Let me at this point respond to a potential objection. It may be argued that the above statistics are not good estimates of European, Asian and African economic power, because there are Africans working in European and Asian economies, Europeans working in Asian and African economies, and Asians working in European and African economies. My response to this objection is that what really matters is who *designs* an economy and *decides* how such an economy should be built, not whose sweat was used to build it. African slave labour was used to build America into economic prominence in the eighteenth century, but Caucasians designed it to be so. There is abundant labour in Africa, but designing and other decision-making are problematic at the political level.

## 4 Intra-national Economic Disparities by Race

We not only see superior Caucasian economic power by comparing groups of countries, but by looking at the economic data from different races living and working within a single sample country. The most ideal case study is USA, where there is already a comprehensive study of this, and probably the most diversity in terms of spread or number of cultures (updated regularly with a very diverse pattern of immigration). According to research on racial economic inequality in the USA, "the median White family has 41 times more wealth than the median Black family and 22 times more wealth than the median Latino family" (Inequality.Org 2020; par 8).

## 5 Research Findings on Racial Discrimination

In 2001, the American National Research Council put together what it called a "Panel on Methods for Assessing Discrimination". The work of this panel has been published as a book titled *Measuring Racial Discrimination* (2004). According to the research, the Black African race is the most discriminated against. I have already cited literature showing that much of discrimination around the world is colour-related (even though I have argued that it is about financial perceptions of skin colour).

## 6 Analysing All the Data

When we examine the topography of racial discrimination in existing research, and consider this in the light of the topography of economic positions revealed in the international and intra-national data on racial economic inequality, we find ourselves with at least two conclusions:

1. The racial respect value chain is identical to the economic value chain.
2. The richest race is the most respected globally and the poorest most disrespected.

Respect value chain is a *human reality.* It is evident in the relationship between the business tycoon and his driver, a Professor and her student, even between former schoolmates who have become economically unequal, and between economically unequal spouses. The most respected international passports are those from economically well performing economies, and vice versa for the least powerful passports. Another example of economic power is that the US government has not paid any reparations to African-Americans for slavery (Davis 2014), but paid reparations to Japanese-Americans for their incarceration during World War II (Yamamoto et al. 2013). What is the difference between the Japanese and African societies? It is that the economic stature (or relevance) of the Japanese society is a source of deterrence and caution to Americans.

## 7 Behavioural Contributors

If we are to accept my thesis about the relationship between GDPs and racism, it follows that there are secondary economic contributors to racism. These contributors arise from the primary contributors (the GDPs themselves) but the secondary contributors are *behaviours* that amplify (and sometimes exaggerate) the image of been seen as poor. The secondary contributors are things that governments and members of developing countries do to intensify racism, such as borrowing money from Caucasian countries, preferring to save their money in Caucasian banks, employing Caucasian engineers for the most important projects, preferring Caucasian schools, travelling across the seas to Caucasian hospitals for trite medical problems, doing all the other things that show a complete lack of faith in non-Caucasian facilities/institutions, and of course, the mass migration of their unemployed youth towards Caucasian-controlled economies. I would describe these as racism-exacerbating behaviours. Their emergence from the primary contributors is not automatic, and they could be curbed or moderated.

I will briefly illustrate just one of these behaviours (massed migration) and show that it correlates with increased levels of discrimination, and I will provide examples that are outside racism. Extraordinary levels of migration lead to "go back home" reactions from destination indigenes, *whether across or within races.* Examples abound. When the migration of Nigerians to Ghana spiked up in the 1960s, it led to "Go back home" protests by Ghanaians, and the Kofi Busia government put this demand into action by deporting a large number of Nigerians (Aremu and Ajayi 2014). The reverse happened when Nigeria experienced the oil boom of the 1970s, and Ghanaians fleeing from high-level corruption and economic crisis in Ghana came to Nigeria in large numbers, leading to the "Ghana must go" mantra, and the exit of many Ghanaians from Nigeria (Lawal 2020). This drama replayed itself when Nigerian migration to South Africa spiked, leading to xenophobic and hostile reactions from South African indigenes (DW 2020). During President Trump's campaign in 2015, one of the placards of his supporters read "Go back to Africa". Indeed, excessive migration leads to the emergence (and higher chances of take-over) of nationalist and racist leaders and political parties in destination countries (see Davis and Deole 2017).There could be no stronger evidence of the correlation between massed migration and discrimination. Unfortunately, by 2015 alone, 1.8 million migrants tried crossing the Mediterranean Sea in an attempt to get into Europe (although this number has been declining due to stricter border laws in Europe), and "50% of missing/dead migrants recorded on the Mediterranean Sea are of African origin" (Idemudia and Boehnke 2020: 15). The effect of this phenomenon alone on Caucasian racist tendency can at least be imagined. The same scenario is playing out elsewhere. According to the World Migration Report 2020, India (followed by Mexico and China) has the world's largest number of migrants abroad (with an estimated 17.5 million), the top country of destination is the USA, and there is notable anti-Asian racism there, which has surged by 169% across 15 US cities in 2020–2021 (World Economic Forum 2021). The corona virus scourge in 2020 and its originating from Asia could also be a contributing factor, but it does not seem to me that it displaces the bigger economic one.

## 8 Is Skin Colour the Cause of Racism?

There are indications that skin colour is by itself not the major cause of racism. History does not show that black is an inferior colour. In Japanese culture, black stands for seniority and experience. In fashion designing, black denotes depth, and many fashion designers have dedicated their careers to unpacking this depth (Bateman 2020; par 3). A well-known French artist, Pierre-Auguste Renoir, had this to say, "I've spent 40 years discovering that the queen of all colours is Black" (Ibid, par 14). In the words of Louise Nevelson, "I feel in love with black; it contained all color. It wasn't a negation of color…Black is the most aristocratic color of all…You can be quiet, and it contains the whole thing" (Uddin 2020; par 20). Ricardo Tisci had this to say, "Black is always elegant. It is the most complete color in the whole world, made of all the colors in the palette" (Uddin 2020; par 15). And according to Ann Demeulemeester, "Black is not sad. Bright colours are what depresses me. They're so…empty…" (Bateman 2020: par 15). "According to CarMax, the largest used car retailer in the US, black was the best-selling car color last year, accounting for 22.25 percent of sales, followed closely by white at 19.34 percent of sales, gray (17.63 percent), and silver (14.64 percent)" (Tahaney 2020: par 1). Black is also the official colour for the entourage of most of the world's Heads of State; evidence that it is regarded as the most *mature* of all colours. Black is the official colour of the high society (priests, judges, tuxedos, and credit cards) (Cherry 2020). It "… represents strength, seriousness, power and authority" (Bourn 2010). Most of all, Caucasians have a penchant for black colour (black suits, black cars, black shoes, black TVs and home theatres, black computers [both desk tops and lap tops]. Indeed, the stereotypical Caucasian conception of a handsome man irrespective of race is a 'tall, dark and handsome' man, a phrase that originated with upper class Europeans in the seventeenth century, and became synonymous with Hollywood leading men, along with "the thrilling dark hero" (Smith 2020).

## 9 Analysis of Findings

In the face of this overwhelming evidence, could colour solely explain the disrespect for Black Africans? The other pieces of evidence I have canvassed show that Black Africans are disrespected because their societies have been too strongly associated with underdevelopment. Colour alone is not a source of racism; it is what the colour is associated with. For Black Africans, the association of colour with societal underdevelopment continues to wreak psychological havoc, which does not change in the face of the wealth of a few individual Black Africans.

Anti-African racism is, therefore, predicated on the economic superiority of the racist. The corollary argument is that conceptions of skin colour are consequences rather than causes of anti-African racism: racism does not arise because the African is black-skinned, but because the black skin has been associated with society-level underdevelopment for a very long period of time in history. Indeed, the evidence suggests that the topography of the racist relationship would be reversed if the economic tables were also reversed. From the perceptions of the Black colour seen above, Black Africans would easily be the most respected if they were the wealthiest race. The most ideal distribution of respect would have been a world where cross-racial economic levels were a bit more equal. The conclusion is that the relationship between racism and economic inequality is, therefore, more significant than the relationship between racism and skin colour.

If we accept this argument, then we need to face up to some serious implications. Skin colour is from Mother Nature, but economic inequality is man-made. Because we previously assumed that skin colour (and just skin colour) was the cause of racism, our response was to simply protest and say "Stop discriminating based on skin colour." But accepting that racism has more to do with economic condition means that such a moral protest is so simplistic that it misses the problem. Instead of looking at racism as simply a moral evil, races at the receiving end of racism would need to also look at racism as an offshoot of a political struggle in which they must gain some advantage. Those who are at the worst end of racial discrimination need to also ask themselves *what to do* in order to reduce racial discrimination. A racist is an economic bully. We know how we overcame our bullies in elementary school. You do not stop a bully by saying, "Please stop bullying me!" We stopped being bullied by *outgrowing* our bullies (we grew taller, bigger, stronger, and so on). It means that growing out of underdevelopment is the most powerful factor in reducing anti-Black racism. The difference between biological and economic growth is that the former is automatic but the latter needs to be *decided* and executed with commitment.

## 10 Development as a Response to Racism

We normally see development as a means to make life better. But development has likely never been seen as a way to combat racism. In this essay, I canvass this latter view. Evidence generated in this research shows that the best response to racism is to *develop* in the long term and for developing countries to promulgate policies moderating the racism-exacerbating behaviours (the secondary economic contributors to racism) in the short term.

Regarding the long term project, this research debunks pessimism regarding the possibility of African development by citing Kwame Nkrumah's reference to Africa's resources. According to Nkrumah, Africa had (at Nkrumah's time) 66% of the world's cocoa, 65% of the world's palm oil, 58% of global sisal, 14% of global coffee, 26% of global groundnut, and 11% of global olive oil. Africa has an even bigger share of the world's minerals, with 96% of the world's diamond, 69% of the world's cobalt, 63% of the world's gold, 48% in antimony, 37% in manganese, 34% in chromite, 32% of the world's phosphate, 24% in copper, 19% of the world's asbestos, 15% of the world's tin, 4% of the world's iron, and 4% of the world's bauxite (Nkrumah 1998: 150–151). In terms of human resources, Africa has among the best technocrats in the world. What is needed is good leadership; and what is needed for good leadership is to protest bad leadership. So protesting bad local leadership in Africa is *by far* the most effective way to begin to tackle the problem of external racism. In the long term, it is even more effective compared to protesting racism itself, but this is not to say that protesting racism should be discouraged. Although less effective than growing up, it was still good if we told our elementary school bullies to please stop bullying us.

Regarding the short term, developing countries could take steps to ensure that they depend less on Caucasian societies for virtually all their needs. In sum, they need to show less of *dependency*. To begin, they could take steps to ensure that their educational systems are improved to be robust enough to encourage patronage by their own youth. But more importantly, they could promulgate policies that make it mandatory for employers (at least government-owned institutions) to stop discriminating against candidates with local or non-Caucasian educational qualifications in recruitment, promotion, and appointments to important responsibilities. It is common practice, when writing the names of members of organizations, to append their highest qualifications. But this by itself is not the problem. The major problem for developing countries is that qualifications are indicated together with the name of the school that provided the qualifications (such as Michael Roberts [PhD, Manchester], Theresa Mannaseh [MA, Michigan], George Abu [PhD Harvard]). In developing countries, this practice generates a discriminatory attitude to educational qualifications acquired outside Caucasian societies. It is among many other practices that directly fuel the preference for Caucasian formal education. It is not possible for me to track down all of such practices in this essay. But I must remark that these practices have not exactly translated into development, since the moral profiles of administrators are much more crucial to development than the prestigious nature of their certifications. Such are the kinds of practices that developing countries should be curbing.

We can still find practices with similar effects outside employment and labour productivity. One of them is flying to Caucasian hospitals for medical treatments that could be provided back home in developing countries, especially when such countries have sufficiently qualified medical experts. Again, I cannot track and document all these practices, but it should be an imperative for developing countries to take a comprehensive inventory of them and take measures to curb or moderate them.

## 11 Conclusion

This research explores the correlation between racism and economic conditions and finds the correlation to be very strong. Suggestions are then made about how those at the receiving end of racism could respond to racism in the light of this strong correlation.

## References

Aremu, Johnson, and Adeyinka Ajayi. 2014. Expulsion of Nigerian Immigrant Community from Ghana in 1969: Causes and Impact. *Developing Country Studies* 4 (10): 176–186.

Bagalini, Adwoa. 2020. Colourism: How skin-tone Bias affects racial equality at work. *World Economic Forum* (26 August). Available at: https://www.weforum.org/agenda/2020/08/racial-equality-skin-tone-bias-colourism/. Accessed 1st Dec 2020.

Bank of Korea. 2023. Gross domestic product estimates for North Korea in 2019. Available at: https://www.bok.or.kr/eng/bbs/E0000634/view.do?nttId=10059560&menuNo=400069.

Bateman, Kristen. 2020. *15 Quotes that prove black is the most powerful colour in fashion*. Available at: https://stylecaster.com/feature/fashion-quotes-color-black-589324/. Accessed 1 Dec 2020.

Bourn, Jennifer. 2010. Color meaning: Meaning of the color black. In *BourneCreative*. Available at: https://www.bourncreative.com/meaning-of-the-color-black/.

Boyd-Franklin, Nancy. 2003. Racism, racial identity, and skin colour issues. Chapter in Nancy Boyd-Franklin (Author). In *Black families in therapy*, 2nd ed. New York: Guilford Press.

Cherry, Kendra. 2020. The Color Psychology of Black. *VeryWellMind* (Theories: Cognitive Psychology). Available at: https://www.verywellmind.com/the-color-psychology-of-black-2795814

Davis, Angelique M. 2014. Apologies, reparations, and the continued legacy of the European slave trade in the United States. *Journal of Black Studies* 45 (4): 271–286.

Davis, Lewis, and Sumit Deole. 2017. Immigration and the Rise of Far-Right Parties in Europe. *Ifo DICE Report* 15: 1–4.

DW (Made for Minds). 2020. *South Africa: Hatred of migrants reaches new heights*. Available at: https://www.dw.com/en/south-africa-hatred-of-migrants-reaches-new-heights/a-55093941. Accessed 1 Dec 2020.

Eitohamy, Farah. 2019. 2020 Census: Middle Easterners and North Africans don't fit the box. *Ceonkite News* (17 December). Available at: https://cronkitenews.azpbs.org/2019/12/17/2020-census-mena-category/

Engels, Frederick. 2008. *Socialism: Utopian and Scientific*. London, Sydney, Montreal, Atlanta: Pathfinder Press.

Eurostat. 2020. *EU Population in 2020: Almost 448 Million*. Available at: https://ec.europa.eu/eurostat/documents/2995521/11081093/3-10072020-AP-EN.pdf/d2f799bf-4412-05cc-a357-7b49b93615f1. Accessed 26 Nov 2020.

Fihlani, Pumza. 2013. Africa, where black is not really beautiful. *BBC News* (1 January). Available at: https://www.bbc.com/news/world-africa-20444798. Accessed 1 Dec 2020.

Idemudia, Erhabor, and Klaus Boenhke. 2020. *Psychological experiences of African Migrantsin six European Countries*. Springer.

Inequality.Org. 2020. *Racial economic inequality*. Available at: https://inequality.org/facts/racial-inequality/. Accessed 2 Dec 2020.

IOM UN Migration. 2020. *World migration report 2020*. Available at: https://publications.iom.int/system/files/pdf/wmr_2020.pdf

Joung, Madalein, and Hatch Megan. 2020. Bias against skin colour seen globally. *Voice of America* (24 June). Available at: https://www.voanews.com/student-union/bias-against-skin-color-seen-globally. Accessed 1 Dec 2020.

Klonoff, E.A., and H. Landrine. 2000. Is skin colour a marker for racial discrimination? Explaining the skin colour hypertension relationship. *Journal of Behavioural Medicine* 23 (4): 329–338.

Lawal, Shola. 2020. Ghana must go: The ugly history of Africa's most famous bag. *Mail Guardian*. Available at: http://atavist.mg.co.za/ghana-must-go-the-ugly-history-of-africas-most-famous-bag. Accessed 1 Dec 2020.

Li, Eric P.H., Hiun Jeong Min, Russell Belk, Junko Kimura, and Shalini Bahl. 2008. Skin lightening and beauty in four Asian cultures. In *Advances in Consumer Research*, ed. Angela Lee, Dilip Soman, and M.N. Duluth, vol. 35, 444–449. Association of Consumer Research. Available at: https://web.archive.org/web/20190618001443. http://www.acrwebsite.org/volumes/13415/volumes/v35/NA-35. Accessed 1 Dec 2020.

Macrotrends. 2023a. New Zealand GDP 1960 to 2023. Available at: https://www.macrotrends.net/countries/NZL/new-zealand/gdp-gross-domestic-product.

Macrotrends. 2023b. Cyprus GDP 2019. Available at: https://www.macrotrends.net/countries/CYP/cyprus/gdp-grossdomestic-product.

Marx, Karl. 1998. *The German Ideology*. New York: Prometheus.

———. 2013. *Capital*. Cody, Wyoming: Woodsworth.

National Research Council. 2004. *Measuring racial discrimination*. Washington, DC: The National Academies Press. Available at: https://doi.org/10.17226/10887. Accessed 1 Dec 2020.

Nkrumah, Kwame. 1963/1998. *Africa Must Unite*. London: Panaf.

Parvini, Sarah, and Ellis Simani. 2019. Are Arabs and Iranians white? Census says yes but many disagree. *Los Angeles Times* (28 March). Available at: https://www.latimes.com/projects/la-me-census-middle-east-north-africa-race/.

Smith, Brian. 2020. The not-so-attractive origins of 'Tall dark and handsome'. *Mel Magazine*. Available at: https://melmagazine.com/en-us/story/the-not-so-attractive-origins-of-tall-dark-and-handsome. Accessed 1st Dec 2020.

Statistica. 2020a. *Sub Saharan Africa: Total population from 2009 to 2019*. Available at: https://www.statista.com/statistics/805605/total-population-sub-saharan-africa/. Accessed 26 Nov 2020.

———. 2020b. *List of North American countries by GDP 2019*. Available at: http://statisticstimes.com/economy/north-american-countries-by-gdp.php. Accessed 1 Dec 2020.

———. 2020c. *List of South American countries by GDP 2019*. Available at: http://statisticstimes.com/economy/south-american-countries-by-gdp.php. Accessed 1 Dec 2020.

———. 2020d. *Ukraine gross domestic product from 1994 to 2021*. Available at: https://www.statista.com/statistics/296140/ukraine-gross-domestic-product/. Accessed 1 Dec 2020.

———. 2020e. *Gross domestic product (GDP) at current market prices of selected European countries in 2019*. Available at: https://www.statista.com/statistics/685925/gdp-of-european-countries/. Accessed 1 Dec 2020.

———. 2020f. *Gross domestic product (GDP) in current prices from 1987 to 2028*. Available at: https://www.statista.com/statistics/263573/gross-domestic-product-gdp-of-australia/

Tahaney, Ed. 2020. Black, white and gray are the most popular colours in the US. *Motortrend*. Available at: https://www.automobilemag.com/news/most-popular-car-colors/. Accessed 1 Dec 2020.

Trading Ecomomics. 2023. GDP Asia. Available at: https://tradingeconomics.com/country-list/gdp?continent=asia

Uddin, Minhaz. 2020. *Black color quotes/wearing black quotes/black dress quotes*. Available at: https://www.cutequotesmessages.com/2020/04/wearing-black-color-quotes.html. Accessed 1 Dec 2020.

World Bank. 2020a. *GDP (Current US$) European union*. Available at: https://data.worldbank.org/indicator/NY.GDP.MKTP.CD?locations=EU. Accessed 26 Nov 2020.

———. 2020b. *GDP (Current US$) Russian federation*. Available at: https://data.worldbank.org/indicator/NY.GDP.MKTP.CD?locations=RU. Accessed 1 Dec 2020.

———. 2020c. *GDP (Current US$) Sub-Saharan Africa*. Available at: https://data.worldbank.org/indicator/NY.GDP.MKTP.CD?locations=ZG. Accessed 26 Nov 2020.

World Bank. 2023a. GDP (Current USD) *Syrian Arab Republic*. Available at: https://data.worldbank.org/indicator/NY.GDP.MKTP.CD?locations=SY.

World Bank. 2023b. GDP (Current USD) *Timor Leste*. Available at: https://data.worldbank.org/indicator/NY.GDP.MKTP.CD?locations=TL.

World Economic Forum. 2021. *Anti-Asian Racism is on the rise: Here is what we can do about it*. Available at: https://www.weforum.org/agenda/2021/06/anti-asian-racism-what-we-can-do-to-combat-it/.

Worldometer. 2020a. *Antigua and Barbuda population*. Available at: https://www.worldometers.info/world-population/antigua-and-barbuda-population/. Accessed 1 Dec 2020.

———. 2020b. *Aruba population*. Available at: https://www.worldometers.info/world-population/aruba-population/. Accessed 1 Dec 2020.

———. 2020c. *Bahamas population*. Available at: https://www.worldometers.info/world-population/bahamas-population/. Accessed 1 Dec 2020.

———. 2020d. *Barbados population*. Available at: https://www.worldometers.info/world-population/barbados-population/. Accessed 1 Dec 2020.

———. 2020e. *Belize population*. Available at: https://www.worldometers.info/world-population/belize-population/. Accessed 1 Dec 2020.

———. 2020f. *Canada population*. Available at: https://www.worldometers.info/world-population/canada-population/. Accessed 1 Dec 2020.

———. 2020g. *Costa Rica population*. Available at: https://www.worldometers.info/world-population/costa-rica-population/. Accessed 1 Dec 2020.

———. 2020h. *Dominica population*. Available at: https://www.worldometers.info/world-population/dominica-population/. Accessed 1 Dec 2020.

———. 2020i. *El Salvador population*. Available at: https://www.worldometers.info/world-population/el-salvador-population/. Accessed 1 Dec 2020.

———. 2020j. *Europe population*. Available at: https://www.worldometers.info/world-population/europe-population/. Accessed 1 Dec 2020.

———. 2020k. *Grenada population*. Available at: https://www.worldometers.info/world-population/grenada-population/. Accessed 1 Dec 2020.

———. 2020l. *Guatamela population*. Available at: https://www.worldometers.info/world-population/guatamela-population/. Accessed 1 Dec 2020.

———. 2020m. *Haiti population*. Available at: https://www.worldometers.info/world-population/haiti-population/. Accessed 1 Dec 2020.

———. 2020n. *Honduras population*. Available at: https://www.worldometers.info/world-population/honduras-population/. Accessed 1 Dec 2020.
———. 2020o. *Jamaica population*. Available at: https://www.worldometers.info/world-population/jamaica-population/. Accessed 1 Dec 2020.
———. 2020p. *Mexico population*. Available at: https://www.worldometers.info/world-population/mexico-population/. Accessed 1 Dec 2020.
———. 2020q. *Nicaragua population*. Available at: https://www.worldometers.info/world-population/nicaragua-population/. Accessed 1 Dec 2020.
———. 2020r. *Panama population*. Available at: https://www.worldometers.info/world-population/panama-population/. Accessed 1 Dec 2020.
———. 2020s. *Puerto Rico population*. Available at: https://www.worldometers.info/world-population/puerto-rico-population/. Accessed 1 Dec 2020.
———. 2020t. *Saint Kitts and Nevis population*. Available at: https://www.worldometers.info/world-population/saint-kitts-and-nevis-population/. Accessed 1 Dec 2020.
———. 2020u. *Saint Lucia population*. Available at: https://www.worldometers.info/world-population/saint-lucia-population/. Accessed 1 Dec 2020.
———. 2020v. *South America population*. Available at: https://www.worldometers.info/world-population/south-america-population/. Accessed 1 Dec 2020.
———. 2020w. *St. Vincent and Grenadines population*. Available at: https://www.worldometers.info/world-population/saint-vincent-and-the-grenadines-population/. Accessed 1 Dec 2020.
———. 2020x. *Trinida and Tobago population*. Available at: https://www.worldometers.info/world-population/trinidad-and-tobago-population/. Accessed 1 Dec 2020.
———. 2020y. *United States population*. Available at: https://www.worldometers.info/world-population/us-population/. Accessed 1 Dec 2020.
Yamamoto, E.K., M. Chon, C.L. Izumi, J., Kang, and F.H. Wu. 2013. *Race, rights, and reparation: Law and the Japanese internment*. Second Edition. Alphen aan den Rijn (Netherlands): Wolters Kluwer.

**Emmanuel Ifeanyi Ani** is a Senior Lecturer at the University of Ghana, Accra, and was a Visiting Scholar at the Centre for Deliberative Democracy, Institute for Governance and Policy Analysis, University of Canberra. He is an Associate Editor of the *Journal of Deliberative Democracy* as well as *Thought and Practice*.

# Part V
# Migration and African Development

# Medical Brain Drain and Healthcare Delivery in Africa: Beyond Restrictive Migration Policies

**Damilola Victoria Oduola**

**Abstract** The health of a particular population cannot be maintained or enhanced without the active participation of health care workers. This is because health care workers (doctors, nurses, midwives, pharmacists, etc.) are critical individuals in ensuring health, as they determine the quality, equity and sustainability of health care services that can be available to a population. In this paper, I argue that Africa, in recent times, has continued to witness enormous shortages of health-care workers as a result of "medical braindrain". I draw from Michael Blake's liberal orthodoxy doctrine to argue that although some African countries have adopted restrictive migration policies to combat medical brain drain, yet, restrictive migration is not an effective approach because it not only limits individual's liberty but also places the totality of health burdens onhealth workers at the neglect of other determinants of health. Hence, I argue that to successfully combat medical brain drain, African countries need to address the underlying factors that are responsible for bad health outcomes in Africa and also adopt viable health and public policy approaches that are considerate of individual liberty and at the same time sympathetic to the "plight" of developing African countries.

**Keywords** Africa · Health · Development · Medical brain drain · Restrictive migration policies

## 1 Introduction

The United Nations Sustainable Development Goals (UN SDGs) places health at the centre of development as expressed in the Article 3 of UN SDGs which aims at "ensuring healthy lives and promoting well-being for all at all ages". Also, almost all of the other 16 SDG goals are directly related to health or their achievement will

---

D. V. Oduola (✉)
Damilola Victoria Oduola Department of Philosophy, University of Ibadan, Ibadan, Nigeria



B. Okyere-Manu et al. (eds.), *Contemporary Development Ethics from an African Perspective*, Philosophy and Politics - Critical Explorations 27,
https://doi.org/10.1007/978-3-031-32898-5_13

indirectly contribute to health (WHO 2021a). This suggests an intricate relationship between the notion of health and the concept of development. To buttress this, Amartya Sen (1999a: 11) comments that development is concerned with the achievement and enhancement of a quality life. But among the most important freedoms, which could constitute a quality life is the freedom from avoidable ill-health andescapable mortality. Therefore, health constitutes an integral part of development, for without it; individuals cannot easily earn an income, have good nutrition, and more importantly have the freedom to lead quality lives. The health of a particular population, which influences their freedom to lead quality lives, however, cannot be maintained or enhanced without the active participation of health care workers. That is, health care workers (doctors, nurses, midwives, pharmacists, etc.) are critical individuals in ensuring health, because they determine quality, equity and sustainability of health care services that can be available to the population.

This paper, divided into four sections, however, examines the mass migration of health care workers from Africa to high-income settings and the challenges it poses to health and development in Africa. The first section attempts to establish the relationship between health, health workers and development. The second section explains that Africa, in recent times, has continued to witness enormous shortages of health-care workers as a result of medical brain drain and this has not only incurred huge human and financial costs and losses for Africa but has also contributed to a weak health-care system, a decline in the population's health status, an increase in health inequalities and more importantly, an underachievement of the health-related Sustainable Development Goals. The third section discusses the arguments for the justification of restrictive migration policy as a viable response to medical brain drain. Drawing from Michael Blake's liberal orthodoxy doctrine, this section submits that although some African countries have adopted restrictive migration policies to combat medical brain, restrictive migration policy is not an effective approach because it does not only limit individual liberty but also places the wholeburden of health outcomes on health workers.

The study, therefore, seeks to show that the overall health and quality of life of a population is not only determined by the availability of health workers but also by a complex interaction of cultural, social, political, environmental, biological and genetic factors of which their absence also contribute to bad health outcomes. In the final section, the study submits that medical brain drain can only be successfully addressed if underlying factors such as inefficient management and maintenance of the health sector, low resources allocation and corruption which are responsible for bad health outcomes in Africa are addressed and if viable policies, such as skill transfer programs, cyclical migration and Diaspora engagement programs, which are quite considerate of health workers' liberty and at the same time sympathetic to the "plight" of developing African countries, are adopted.

## 2 Health, Health Workers and Development

In the 1980s, the Nobel Prize-winning economist, Amartya Sen with his "capabilities approach", revolutionized the general understanding of the concept of development. Also, in the late 1990s, he furthered the argument that conceives development as freedom (Sen 1999a). This view has now been widely accepted by the UN Human Development Index and the Multidimensional Poverty Index (Barder 2012). Before Sen, traditional welfare economics generally conceived development to mean economic growth with visible increase in gross national product and personal income (Edeme 2018). But with Sen's capability approach, development cannot be measured simply by changes in income or economic growth, but by its impacts on people's lifestyles, choices, capabilities and freedom.

In his influential book, *Development as Freedom*, Sen conceives development as "a process of expanding the real freedoms that people enjoy" (Sen 1999a: 3). He argues that narrower views of development have identified development with the growth of indices like gross national product; a rise in personal incomes; the presence of or rise in industrialization, and technological advancement and social modernization. He goes on to note that while these determinants of development are important means to expanding the freedom people can enjoy, freedom is also dependent on other influences, such as socio-economic facilities and socio-political rights (Sen 1999a: 4).

Sen, comments that the most basic primary freedom that development aims to achieve is the freedom from avoidable ill-health and escapable mortality. Heopines that the qualified and contingent nature of the relationship between economic prosperity and good health is such that an increase in per capita income does not necessarily contribute to health and longevity of life. This is because the ability to live long and maintain good health is dependent on other social arrangements such as availability of healthcare, medical coverage and basic education. Hence, given other factors, increase in income does not necessarily make an individual or a community more able to avoid premature mortality. Rather, variables such as availability of medical and healthcare facilities influence and contributeto individual's quality of life (Sen 1999b: 619–620). Hence, for Sen, the enhancement of health, through the provision of accessible healthcare and medical facilities, is a constitutive part of development as the availability and accessibility of healthcare facilitates economic development. It also creates favourable circumstances for the expansion of life expectancy and reduction of mortality rate (Sen 1999b: 622).

Ruger (2003) also attempts to demonstrate a strong link between health and development. She (2003: 678–679) argues that the opportunities for health and health care can be seen as constituent components of development because good health enables individuals to be active agents of change in the development process. Good healthcontributes to human well-being, for without health, no other human functioning such as individual's opportunities to exercise their agency and participate in political and social decision making can be possible. This means that good health is a means to further economic and political development. It also avails individuals the opportunity to participate in political and social deliberations about public policies that affect them.

This simply suggests that good health is an intrinsic and instrumental constituent of development. Also, the availability and accessibility of healthcare isone of the primary freedoms that contribute to individual's quality of life. Hence, health workers who are the personnel who work to promote health with the ultimate goal of meeting the health needs and expectations of individuals and populations are key players in the development process (WHO 2013: 57). Health workers are people who engage in actions intended to enhance health. They (e.g. doctors, nurses, midwives, pharmacists, laboratory scientists etc.) are personnel who diagnose, treat and comfort people who are in ill-health (Action 2021). Also, they are professionals who promote daily overarching practices and policies that connect the daily conditions of people's lives to their chances of recovery from ill-health, and draw public attention to needed prevention efforts and health systems coverage issues, which address the problems faced by the sick population (Action 2021). In addition, health workers play a central role in addressing actions on the social determinants of health to promote health equity and make important contributions to the functioning of health systems (Action 2021). They also play critical roles in the promotion of equitable expansion of health coverage for a particular population. Hence, given their critical role in ensuring health, health workers remain relevant in the achievement of development and also ensure the advancement of the freedom from ill-health and escapable mortality (Sen 1999b: 620).

## 3 Health Workers' Migration and Its Challenges to Health and Development in Africa

In one of its published studies, the World Health Organization (WHO 2006) estimates that 57 countries, mostly in Africa and Asia, face a severe health workforce crisis and at least a total of 4.2 million health workers are needed to avert the crisis. Without prompt action, the shortage will worsen (WHO 2006). Another available WHO (2021a, b, c) study estimates that the world is going to face a shortage of 18 million health workers by 2030, with countries in Africa and other low-middle income countries in Asia and South America being hit hardest by thehealth workforce crisis (WHO 2021b). The WHO, also, reveals that Sub-Saharan Africa faces the greatest health workforce crisis, because while it has 11% of the world's population and 24% of the world's diseases burden, it has only 3% of health workers (WHO 2006). It is imperative to note that while all countries at all levels of socioeconomic development face, to varying degrees, difficulties in the retention and performance of their health workforce, the health workforce shortfalls, particularly in Africa, is exacerbated by the increasing international migration of health workers from developing countries in Africa to Organisation for Economic Co-operation and Development (OECD) countries such as USA, UK, Germany, France, Australia etc.

Most countries in Africa, in the past few decades have witnessed the loss of large numbers of health workers to more developed countries in the form of "medical brain-drain". Recent studies have shown that medical brain drain has had both short- and long-term consequences on the sustenance of health systems in Africa (Misau et al. 2010: 20). Medical brain drain refers to the mass movement of health personnel in search of a better standard of living and life quality, higher salaries, access to advanced technology and more stable political conditions in different places worldwide (Misau et al. 2010: 20). For instance, a research study carried out bythe African Capacity Building Foundation (2018: ix) showsthat Malawi trains 60 nurses a year, but loses around 100 to emigration. Malawi has 1.1 doctors and 25.5 nurses for every 100,000 people which means that the entire country has only about 250 doctors (AFCB 2018: x).

In comparison, neighbouring Tanzania has 2.3 doctors and 36.6 nurses per 100,000 population, while the regional density in Africa is 22 doctors and 90 nurses per 100,000 populations (AFCB 2018: x). In Nigeria, the density of physician ratio is 4 per 10,000 and for nurses and midwives 16.1 per 10,000 (Imafidon 2018:12). In Zimbabwe, the density ratio for physicians is 1.6 per 10,000 and 7.2 per 10,000 for nurses and for midwives (WHO 2021a). Another research study conducted by Joses Kirigia et al. (2006: 3) reveals that about 18, 349 nurses from the African region were registered with the NMC between 1989/90 and 2004/2005 in the United Kingdom. Approximately, 50.4% were from South Africa; 14.5% from Nigeria; 12.6% from Zimbabwe; 7.2% from Ghana; 4.3% from Zambia; 3.5% from Kenya; and 7.4% from six other countries (Kirigia et al. 2006: 3–4). These data not only reveal the failure of African countries to meet the United Nations' recommended minimum level of health workforce density at 2.5 health workers per 1000 population but also they reveal the extent and effect of medical brain drain on the health workforce in Africa (Imafidon 2018:13; Kirigia et al. 2006).

"Push" factors which prompt health workers to leave low income countries in Africa to higher income countries include insufficient suitable employment, low remunerations, unsatisfactory working conditions, poor infrastructure and technology and repressive government. On the other hand, "pull" factors, which attracts health workers to migrate to wealthier countries include training opportunities, financial security, better work environment, and higher living standards (Hagopian et al. 2004: 4). Medical brain drain constitutes a huge net loss for African countries, both in terms of public finances and the potential for development. Reacting to the effects of medical brain drain on health and development in Africa, Moullan and Bourgueil (2014) comment that developing countries which suffer medical brain drain are oftenthemselves confronted with public health issues. Also, although these countries intend to participate in the Millennium Development Goals (MDG), medical brain drain tends to reduce the sufficient number of health workers that is required in order to meet these goals (Moullan and Bourgueil 2014: 2). They further comment that the emigration of doctors plays a significant role in the deterioration of medical and sanitary conditions of developing countries, which could in turn incite other doctors to emigrate (Moullan and Bourgueil 2014: 3).

In the same vein, using the HIV/AIDS prevalent rate in Sub-Saharan Africa as an illustration, Bhargava and Docquier (2008: 346) argue that the risks associated with caring for HIV/AIDs patients exacerbate medical brain drain which in turn increase deaths from AIDS and the number of orphaned children. Also, commenting on the estimated social cost of emigration of doctors and nurses from the African Region to developed countries, Kirigia et al. (2006: 3–5) argue thatthe total education cost of a single doctor in Kenya, for instance, is approximately US$65,997 while that of a nurse is US$43,180. Hence, for every doctor that emigrates, a country loses about US$ 1,854,677 and for every nurse that emigrates, a country loses about US$1,213,463. From the foregoing, this study avers that when health workers emigrate, African countries lose far much more than the cost incurred by the society to educate them.

To conclude this section, this study holds that medical brain drain presents developing African countries with serious health and development challenges in the sense that itexacerbates the human resource shortage within national and district health systems; reduces health workers' capability toperform their functions optimally; incurs huge human and financial costs and losses; increases health inequalities and more importantly, reduces the chances of achieving the MDGS and SDG goals in Africa.

## 4 Medical Brain Drain, Restrictive Migration Policies and the Quest for Justification in Africa

As shown in the previous section, medical brain drain presents developing African countries with a serious challenge. However, in an effort tooffsetthe effects of medical brain drain, some African countries have adopted restrictive migration policies to limit health workers' migration. These restrictive migration policies often set restrictions on the conditions for issuing work visas and the conditions under which exit visas can be obtained. For instance, South Africa had implemented a compulsory community service requirement scheme in which new medical graduates are required to carry out 2 years community service mostly in remote locations. (Mortensen 2008: 19). Also, in 2011, Zambia, Ghana, Malawi and Zimbabwe implemented restrictive migration policies to lower their emigration level in an effort to mitigate medical brain drain (UN 2013: 69).

Restrictive migration policies, in recent times, have become a subject of heated debate among philosophers, social scientists, economists and policy makers. A number of philosophers havequestioned the assumption that states have the justification to restrict the movement of health workers on the basis of medical brain drain. In their view, restrictive migration policies are restrictions on individual's liberty or freedom to emigrate because since individuals require freedom of movementto fulfil their basic life projects and since freedom of movement is internationally recognised as a fundamental human right, then the freedom to migrate whether domestically or internationally is a fundamental human right that should not be restricted. (Oberman 2013: 427–428). This debate has generated some of the hardest questions about medical brain drainand two major perspectives have developed in response to the debate. On the one hand, scholars like Brock (2015a), Oberman (2013) and Dwyer (2012) have argued that medical brain drain provides legitimate ground for restrictive migration policies while scholars such as Blake (2015), Clemens (2013) and Hildago (2013), on the other hand, have argued that medical brain drain does not justify restrictive migration policies because the unavailability of health workers does not significantly affect the health of a particular population.

In the book *Debating Brain Drain*, Gillian Brock and Michael Blake extensively discuss their positions on the medical brain drain debate. Brock (2015a: 12) comments that medical brain drain poses serious challenge to the health systems of developing countries and given that health workers do have responsibilities to their fellow citizens and to their countries of origin, then developing countries may be justified in managing the migration flow of health workers in order to ensure that the burden of migration does not disproportionately impose impermissible severe losses or affect other citizens who may be at a disadvantage because of the migration. Brock (2015b: 46–52), therefore, opines that developing countries may permissibly manage medical brain drain by demanding compensation from recruiting countries, creating incentives and opportunities for health workers to remain in their source countries, introducing compulsory service programs and introducing taxation programs.

Blake, in response to Brock, however argues that medical brain drain does not justify restrictive migration of health workers. Blake (2015: 111) opines that individuals have the fundamental right to leave any country, including their country of origin provided the country is a liberal state and any attempt by originating countries to forcibly prevent individuals from emigrating is fundamentally unjust and also a violation of human rights. Blake (2015: 112) comments further that in a liberal state, the human rights are contained in the Universal Declaration of Human Rights (UDHR) of which freedom of movement is one, and does not allow for limitations. Hence, limitations to freedom of movement are "unavailable for use by a liberal state". Blake (2015: 112) therefore submits that human rights of persons prevent societies from interfering with their freedom of movement; hence, it would be unjust for liberal states to restrict the movement of health workers.

Contributing to the argument, Oberman (2013: 430) is of the opinion that migration restrictions on the movement of health workers can be justified if some demanding conditions are met. According to him, restrictive migration policies on the basis of medical brain drain can only be justified if

> the health worker has a compelling duty to assist her fellow citizens; if this duty to assist requires that the health worker stays in her country of origin than her state of destination and if staying will not be unreasonably costly; if the health worker has no alternative means of assisting her fellow citizens; and if the rich state has the legitimacy to impose counter-brain-drain immigration policies (Oberman 2013: 453).

In contrast to this, Clemens argues that restrictive migration policy is not an effective approach because medical brain drain does not significantly affect population health in developing countries. Clemens (2013) argues that the presence of highly trained health workers do not necessarily affect or influence health outcomes. For instance, in rural Mozambique, he opines,

> Children do not die due to a lack of cardiologists and nurse practitioners; they die principally from lack of oral rehydration during diarrhoea and lack of basic primary treatment for acute respiratory infections none of which require highly trained personnel to deliver (Clemens 2013: 38).

Hence, for him, the emigration of health workers does not necessarily have significant effects on the availability of healthcare and on health outcomes. This simply suggests that bad health outcomes are determined by a myriad of factors which may not be dependent on the availability of health workers.In a similar vein, Hidalgo (Hildago 2013: 606) argues that restrictive migration policy is not an effective approach to address medical brain drain because bad health outcomes are as a result of factors such as poor infrastructures, poor sanitation system, lack of access to medical and pharmaceutical supplies and low level of literacy and education which are unrelated to the emigration of health workers. He goes on to note that if at all there is any negative impact of medical brain drain on health outcomes, the negative impact is not statistically significant. Hence, for Clemens and Hidalgo, since bad health outcomes in Africa are as a result of myriad of socio-economic, political and health factors that may be unrelated to medical brain drain, then, it would be consequentially unjust to restrict the movement of health workers on the basis of medical brain drain (Hildago 2013: 609).

From our discussion, what becomes glaring is the fact that justifying restrictive migration policies on the basis of medical brain drain is more problematic than imagined. It is the case that although African countries that adopt and enforce restrictive migration policies do so with the best of intention which is to improve the health status of the overall population, yet, population health outcomes are not only determined by the availability of health workers but also by other important factors such as quality health infrastructures, access to medical services and supplies and availability of health insurance,some of which are not being given considerable attention in most African states (Hildago 2013: 606).

Anaemene (2018: 208) explains that the WHO (1948: 1) defines health as "a state of complete physical, mental and social well-being and not merely the absence of disease or infirmity" which suggests that health is a comprehensive concept which emphasizes the significance of the physical, mental and socio-economic welfare of a population. This means that the health and well-being of a particular population is not only determined by the presence of quality medical care provided by health workers but also by the complex interaction of cultural, social, political, environmental, biological and genetic factors such as peace, freedom from violence, low rate of illness, balanced nutrition, qualitative and quantitative housing, good water supply, good working and living conditions, quality education, social justice etc. However, most countries in Africa are battling with serious state of affairs such as natural disasters, economic meltdown, military and ethnic conflicts, corruption, and terrorism, which makes the achievement of health related goals almost impossible.

Anaemene (2018: 219–221) further observes that in addition to the myriad of socio-political problems confronting Africa, corruption being chief of them, Africa is also confronted with a number of unpalatable health situations such as ill equipped health systems, lack of access to health facilities, inequalities in the distribution of health resources, and low allocation of resources to the health sector some of which are responsible for the precarious health situation in Africa (Anaemene 2018: 222). This simply reveals to us that the health challenges in Africa may not only be attributed to the emigration of health workers in the form of medical brain drain but also to the absence of some factors such as inclusive government policies, adequate resources allocation, adequate nutrition, and quality education among others. The sad reality is that most African states are constrained by resource scarcity, corruption and mismanagement such that the average expenditure in the health sector in Africa rarely exceeds 5%. Most African states have failed to allocate as little as 15% of their national budget to the health sector, and so, it is not a surprise to see most African states struggle with weak health systems and bad health outcomes (Anaemene 2018: 218–219).

It therefore becomes obvious that when African states adopt restrictive migration policies to restrict the emigration of health workers, they simply place theburden of population health on the availability ofhealth workers. Blake expresses this view with his liberal orthodoxy doctrine. Blake argues that although individuals owe one another the obligations to ensure a social world that is minimally just andto build and sustain just institutions,yet, these obligations are to be equally distributed in such a way that no individual is made to bear a disproportionate share of the burden (2015: 129). According to him, the principle of fairness demands that social responsibilities must be distributed in a way that it is compatible with the fundamental interest of the individual in developing a plan of life for him/herself. However, restrictive migration violates this principle of fairness because it forces health workers to bear a disproportionate share of the social burden so much so that they are made to give up a central interest in their lives while others are not asked to do the same (2015: 132). Hence, Blake argues that even ifsocial obligations require that individuals sacrifice their freedom in the name of the common good, a targeted group of persons (in this case, the health workers) cannot be forced to do so when others are not being asked to do the same or when others fail to live up to the same obligation (2015: 135).

This simply suggests that the principle of justice entails that the burdens and benefits of a society should be shared appropriately among members of the society. Hence, the burden of ensuring population health should rest not only on the availability of healthcare workers and services but also on the provision of other determinants of health. Be it as it may, restrictive migration policies places the totality of health burdens on health workers, at the neglect of other important determinants of health whichshould be addressed by African governments. This is premised on the assumption that the availability of health workers wholly determines population health outcomes. While it may be true, as some studies have shown, that the emigration of health workers affectspopulation health outcomes in Africa yet, health outcomes are not solely determined by the availability of health workers but also by a myriad of other socio-economic and environmental factors which are not given sufficient attention in African states.Hence, the apparent neglect of thesefactors of healthby African governments at the expense of health workers' freedom to emigrate,makesrestrictive migration policies a problematic approach in addressing medical brain drain.

## 5 Conclusion and Recommendation

The gist of our discussion is to show that although medical brain drain constitutes a challenge to health and development in Africa, yet, health and developmental challengesin Africa are as a result of a myriad of factors —of which medical brain drain is only one of them. This suggests that there is the need for developing African countries to move beyond restrictive migration policies to inclusive policies that would not only address medical brain drain but also respond to other factors that are responsible for health and developmental challenges in Africa. For instance, one of the major factors responsible for weak health systems and bad health outcomes in Africa is inefficient management and maintenance of the health sector as a result of low resources allocation and corruption. Without adequate resource allocation, health systems cannot function optimally. And, with corruption, there will be lack of access to essential medicines and healthcare services.

Hence, to address these issues, major stakeholders of health such as African political leaders, health ministers, policy makers, academics, researchers and health workers must collaborate to achieve their health and developmental target. For instance, African leaders must be committed to investing a substantial percentage of resources in maintaining the health sector and providing better working conditions for health workers. Development partners and health leaders must be ready to provide competent leadership, improved monitoring and evaluation of healthcare services and maintenance, management and upgrading of health services and infrastructures (Oleribe 2019: 400). Policy makers must also be committed to adopting, strengthening and enforcing strategic planning and public health laws that will ensure transparency and accountability in healthcare.

To successfully combat medical brain drain, there is the need for developing African countries to address push factors that are responsible for health workers' migration. This can be done by offering benefits, attractive salaries, better career opportunities and better working conditions to health workers. Similarly, migration-friendly policies such as cyclical migration, skill transfer programs and diaspora engagement programs that would engage the skills of health workers in the diaspora must be adopted.African countries can tap into the pool of diaspora resources by strengthening ties with health workers in the diaspora, formulating initiatives that will encourage health workers in the diaspora to transfer skills physically, virtually or through mentoring and by encouraging temporary return of health workers for short-term capacity building assignment.The adoption of these programs willallow for the full exercise of individual liberty and as well encourage citizens in the diaspora to participate in the development of their countries.With the reality of medical brain drain and the quest for development, African countries must expand their health and public polices to accommodate initiatives capable of maximizing the benefits of migration for the realization ofhealth and development goals through various engagement with their nationals in the diaspora.

## References

Action, S.D.G. 2021. *Health workers and services*. Available at: https://actionsdg.ctb.ku.edu/health-workers-services/. Accessed 1 July 2021.

African Capacity Building Foundation (AFCB). 2018. *Brain Drain in Africa: the case of tackling capacity issues in Malawi's medical migration*. Harare: The African Capacity Building Foundation. Available at: https://www.africaportal.org/publications/brain-drain-africa-case-tackling-capacity-issues-malawis-medical-migration/. Accessed 6 July 2021.

Anaemene, B. 2018. Health and diseases in Africa. In *The development of Africa: Social indicators research series*, ed. O. Akanle and J. Adesina, vol. 71, 207–226. New York: Springer.

Aregbesola, B. 2019. *Healthcare in Nigeria: challenges and recommendation*. Available at: https://socialprotection.org/discover/blog/health-care-Nigeria-challenges-and-recommendations#. Accessed 27 July 2021.

Barder, O. 2012. *What is development?* Available at: https://www.cgdev.org/blog/what-development. Accessed 26 June 2021.

Bhargava, A., and F. Docquier. 2008. HIV pandemic, medical brain drain, and economic development in sub- Saharan Africa. *World Bank Economic Review* 22: 345–366.

Bhargava, A., et al. 2011. Modelling the effects of physician migration on human development. *Economics and Human Biology* 9: 172–183.

Blake, M. 2015. The right to leave: looking back. In *Debating brain drain: may governments restrict emigration?* ed. G. Brock and M. Blake, 111–154. New York: Oxford University Press.

Brock, G. 2015a. Introduction to Part I. In *Debating brain drain: may governments restrict emigration?* ed. G. Brock and M. Blake, 11–23. New York: Oxford University Press.

———. 2015b. Prosperity in developing countries, the effects departing individuals have on those behind and some policy options. In *Debating brain drain: may governments restrict emigration?* ed. G. Brock and M. Blake, 36–59. New York: Oxford University Press.

Clemens, M. 2013. Do Visas kill? Health effects of African health professional emigration. *Center for Global Development,* 114: 1–56. Available at: https://www.cgdev.org/content/publications/detail/. Accessed 25 July 2021.

Dwyer, J. 2012. What's wrong with the global migration of health care professionals? *Hastings Center Report* 37 (5): 36–43.

Edeme, R.K. 2018. Revisiting the economic growth-welfare linkages: empirical evidence from Nigeria. *Asian Themes in Social Sciences Research* 1 (1): 28–33.

Hagopian, A., et al. 2004. The migration of physicians from sub-Saharan Africa to the United States of America: measures of the African brain drain. *Human Resources for Health* 2 (17): 1–10.

Hildago, J. 2013. The active recruitment of health workers: a defence. *Journal of Medical Ethics* 39 (10): 603–609.

Imafidon, J. 2018. *One way traffic: Nigeria's medical brain drain. A challenge for maternal health and public health system in Nigeria?*. MA Dissertation. Los Angeles: University of California.

Kirigia, J.M., et al. 2006. The cost of health-related brain drain to the WHO African Region. *African Journal of Health Sciences* 13 (3–4): 1–12.

Misau, Y., et al. 2010. Brain-drain and health care delivery in developing countries. *Journal of Public Health in Africa* 1 (e6): 20–21.
Mortensen, J. 2008. *South Africa's medical brain drain: Myths, facts and what (not) to do.* Copenhagen: Danish Institute for International Studies.
Moullan, Y., and Y. Bourgueil. 2014. The international migration of doctors: impacts and political implications. *Issues in health economics (Questions d'économie de la santé) n°203.* Available at https://papers.ssrn.com/sol3/papers.cfm?abstract_1d=2589070. Accessed 6 July 2021.
Oberman, K. 2013. Can brain drain justify immigration restrictions? *Ethics* 123 (3): 427–455.
Oleribe, O.O. 2019. Identifying key challenges facing healthcare systems in Africa and potential solutions. *International Journal of General Medicine* 12: 395–403.
Ruger, J.P. 2003. Health and development. *The Lancet* 362: 678–679.
Sen, A.K. 1999a. *Development as freedom.* New York: Alfred A. Knopf, Inc.
———. 1999b. Health in Development. *Bulletin of the World Health Organisation: The International Journal of Public Health* 77 (8): 619–623.
United Nations. 2013. *International migration policies: government views and priorities.* New York: Department of Economic and Social Affairs, United Nations.
World Health Organisation. 2006. *Global shortage of health workers and its impact.* Available at: https://www.who.int/mediacentre/factsheets/fs302/en/index.html. Accessed 6 July 2021.
World Health Organization. 1948. *Constitution of the World Health Organisation.* Geneva: WHO.
———. 2013. Transforming and scaling up health professionals' education and training: World Health Organization Guidelines 2013. Geneva: World Health Organization. Available at: https://www.ncbi.nlm.nih.gov/books/NBK298950/. Accessed 30 June 2021.
———. 2021a *Sustainable Development Goals (SDGs).* Geneva: World Health Organization. Available at: https://www.who.int/health-topics/sustainable-development-goals#tab=tab_1. Accessed 1 July 2021.
———. 2021b. *Health workforce.* Available at https://www.who.int/health-topics/health-workforce#tab=tab_1. Accessed 6 July 2021.
———. 2021c *The global health observatory: Zimbabwe.* Available at: https://www.int/data/gho/data/countries/country-details/GHO/zimbabwe?countryProfile. Accessed 6 July 2021.

**Damilola Victoria Oduola** holds a Bachelor of Arts and Master of Arts degrees in Philosophy from the University of Ibadan, Ibadan, Nigeria. Her areas of research include social and political philosophy, African philosophy and migration studies. She occasionally publishes some of her articles in the Nigerian Tribune – a leading Nigerian newspaper.

# Part VI
# Education and African Development

# Epistemic Decolonisation in African Higher Education: Beyond Current Curricular and Pedagogical Reformation

**Husein Inusah**

**Abstract** In recent years, the struggle to decolonize knowledge in academia has largely focused on addressing cognitive concerns such as curricular development matters (materials to be taught) and pedagogical strategies (how it is taught) to transform education in Africa. Hardly does the issue of non-cognitive concerns such as the right attitude required to guide the development of this reformed curricular and pedagogical strategies get explored. Indeed, what is lacking in our struggle to decolonise the curricular and pedagogical strategies is an interdisciplinary perspective because the extant approaches rely largely on curriculum theories and practices that leave the role of allied disciplines such as social epistemology (specifically virtue epistemology), educational psychology and paremiology that deal largely with non-cognitive concerns utterly unexplored. However, it is widely argued that curriculum and pedagogy (material to be taught and students' processing of the material) is insufficient to make any meaningful impact on educating the mind without the help of allied disciplines that will teach the right attitude. This chapter, therefore, underscores the importance of the study of non-cognitive factors in the curriculum development and transformation effort by connecting it with the resources in virtue epistemology, educational psychology and paremiology to emphasize the teaching of epistemic virtues in Akan proverbs to provide a comprehensive approach to the concerns of decolonising knowledge in Africa.

## 1 Introduction

In recent years, the struggle to decolonise knowledge in academia has largely focused on addressing cognitive concerns such as curricular issues (involving materials to be taught) and pedagogical strategies (how it is taught) to transform

H. Inusah (✉)
Department of Classics and Philosophy, University of Cape Coast, Cape Coast, Ghana
e-mail: hinusah@ucc.edu.gh



B. Okyere-Manu et al. (eds.), *Contemporary Development Ethics from an African Perspective*, Philosophy and Politics - Critical Explorations 27,
https://doi.org/10.1007/978-3-031-32898-5_14

education in Africa. Hardly does the issue of non-cognitive concerns such as the right attitude required to guide the development of this reformed curricular and pedagogical strategies get explored. It is widely argued that curriculum and pedagogy (material to be taught and students' processing of the material) is insufficient to make any meaningful impact on educating the mind without the help of allied disciplines that will teach the right attitude. This chapter, therefore, underscores the importance of the study of non-cognitive factors in the curriculum development and transformation effort while emphasising the teaching of epistemic virtues to provide a comprehensive approach to the concerns of decolonising knowledge in Africa. The chapter comprises four main sections. The first section explores epistemic decolonisation as a moral problem. The second section analyses the problem of curriculum and pedagogical solutions as insufficient for epistemic decolonisation in African higher education. The third section suggests moral restitution in the form of teaching epistemic virtues as a solution to the epistemic decolonisation agenda in higher education and the final section draws implications for development in Africa.

## 2 Epistemic Decolonisation as a Moral Problem

To appreciate the point that epistemic decolonization is indeed a moral problem invites us to consider the definitions of a few terminologies such as colonialism, de-colonialism, and anti-colonialism on the one hand and coloniality and decoloniality on the other. Colonialism denotes a "process by which a people exploit and/or annex the lands and resources of another without their consent and unilaterally expand political power over them" (Porter 2005, 108). Here, the sovereignty of the people whose lands and resources have been annexed and appropriated will rest on the power of the exploiter. From this, I take de-colonialism to mean the removal of the sovereignty of powerful nations from exploited nations so that at least at the macro-level the exploited nations or people are seen to be managing their affairs. Anti-colonialism, according to Sabelo J. Ndlovu-Gatsheni, "is largely an elite-driven project in which elites mobilized peasants and workers as foot soldiers in a struggle to replace direct colonial administrators" (Ndlovu-Gatsheni 2015, p. 488).

Colonialism is different from coloniality in terms of scope because the latter goes beyond the mere acquisition and political control of another nation to the silent domination and hierarchical inequalities that transpire in different facets of the lives of the exploited nations (Tamale 2020). According to Ndlovu-Gastheni, coloniality is an "invisible power structures that sustain colonial relations of exploitation and domination long after the end of direct colonialism" (Ndlovu-Gatsheni 2012). In contrast, decoloniality as Nelson Maldonado-Torres describes it, is "the dismantling of relations of power and conceptions of knowledge that foment the reproduction of racial, gender, and geopolitical hierarchies that came into being or found new and more powerful forms of expression in the modern/colonial world" (Maldonado-Torres 2011, 117).

From the definitions provided in the foregoing, one notes that colonialism, anti-colonialism, and de-colonialism have been tackled at one point in the history of the colonized nations by the attainment of political independence that offered direct political and economic sovereignty to colonized people. Hence, colonialism anti-colonialism, and de-colonialism can be considered events that have received some considerable amount of treatment in the past. But unlike colonialism and its associated terms, coloniality extends beyond the event of colonialism, it is the remnant of cultural, political, economic, social, and epistemic impositions that continue to hold sway the unequal power relations between the colonized nations and the colonizer which continue to have a tremendous impact on the orientation of the colonized people not by their own making but by historical circumstances (Wiredu 1998, 17). Coloniality is a form of injustice where epistemic and ontological discursive forms are shaped by Ango-American and European paradigms (Ndlovu-Gatsheni 2018). From an epistemic perspective, coloniality relates to the injustices that occur in existing power asymmetries in knowledge production and dissemination where western perspectives, concepts, and terminologies dominate (Mignolo 2009). It also denotes a point where knowledge of colonized nations is offered credibility deficit or ignored, neglected, or even destroyed (Santos 2016). This accounts for the reason why Ndlovu-Gatsheni defines coloniality as "an invisible power structure, an epochal condition, and epistemological design, which lies at the center of the present Euro-North American-centric modern world...[and] sustains asymmetrical global power relations and a singular Euro-North American-centric epistemology that claims to be universal, disembodied, truthful, secular, and scientific (Ndlovu-Gatsheni 2015, 489). Coloniality unlike colonialism thus started right at the inception of slavery and imperialism and lingered on after the collapse of colonialism.

The foregoing provides a space to sketch the main difference between de-colonialism and decoloniality namely, the former is a struggle for sovereignty but not *necessarily* for the sociological, psychological, and epistemological effects of colonialism on the colonized nations. Decolonialism is a struggle for a visible control and autonomy of colonized nations by colonized people in most cases without a recourse to the mental, sociological, and conceptual influences of colonialism on the colonized people whereasdecoloniality is an exercise to disentangle the ex-colonized part of the world from coloniality – the effects of colonialism that sustains asymmetrical power relations between western and marginalised societies. Decoloniality is a project to liberate the epistemologies of the South and re-position Africa or the epistemologically marginalised nations and people at the centre of intellectual discursive forms. It is a project that repudiates eurocentrism couched as epistemic universalism that seeks to "de-link from the tyranny of abstract universals" (Mignolo 2011, pp. 93) and reinvigorate the epistemic agency of the African as the focus of discourses relating to Africa and epistemologically marginalized nations. Decoloniality started as a struggle for resistance and later assumed many forms such as Ethiopianism, Garveyism, Negritude, Pan-Africanism, African Socialism, African Humanism, Black Consciousness Movement, and African Renaissance (Ndlovu-Gatsheni 2015, 488).

Over the years, however, some of these efforts at decolonising knowledge have tried to revamp the idea that has become known as Afrocentricity, the view that Africa should be the center of all discourses and practices including history, politics, knowledge, and so on: a paradigm that emphasises location and center as a way of redirecting attention towards Africa and shunning away from the Eurocentric constructs of universalism that regards knowledge as culturally neutral (See Asante 1988). The Afrocentric agenda of epistemic decolonization is to retain and preserve Africa's indigenous knowledge systems against the dominant powers, the so-called Western Educated Industrialized Rich Democracies (WEIRD) nations from completely assimilating and subsuming African indigenous ways of knowledge especially in this globalised world where epistemic multiculturalism appears more attractive. To achieve this objective requires that African education systems contest dominant Eurocentric epistemic standpoints as a method of affirming Africa's epistemic superiority and dominance in the production and dissemination of knowledge within the global arena (Asante 1988).

But some of these clamours of epistemic decolonization havefor some time now become acrimonious and combative promoting a crusade for monolithic constructs of African epistemologies. Strictly speaking, they have become a crusade for an epistemic monoculture advancing a conflict-driven agenda for epistemic decolonization. Molefe Kete Asante, one of Afrocentric popular advocates, made the declaration that "We [Afrocentrists] must open the floodgates of protest against any non-Afrocentric stances taken by writers, authors, and other intellectuals or artists… who use symbols and objects which do not contribute meaningfully to our victory" (Asante 1988,30). For Asante, to decolonize knowledge either in terms of epistemology, curriculum, or pedagogy, the black person or African must be located and centered within African culture and this is the only way knowledge production, content, and dissemination could be validated (Asante 1993).

Several scholars especially Tunde Adeleke has argued that this construct of Afrocentricity has the potential to "stifle opposing views and nurture a monolithic intellectual cult" and calls for "reconceptualizing constructs and paradigms that have traditionally been the underpinning of a unifying essentialist world view" (Adeleke 2009, p. Xi). AtoSekyi-Otu has described this conflict-driven paradigm of Afrocentricity as a "counter-hegemonic discourse" and bemoaned its potential for genuine decolonial thinking (Sekyi-Otu 2019, pp. 134). Ramon Grosfoguel sees such monolithic and essentialist paradigm as being far off track from the idea of decoloniality. He argues that decoloniality"is not an essentialist, fundamentalist, anti-European critique. It is a perspective that is critical of both Eurocentric and Third World fundamentalisms, colonialism, and nationalism. What all fundamentalisms share (including the Eurocentric one) is the premise that there is only one sole epistemic tradition from which to achieve Truth and Universality (Grosfoguel 2007, 212).

To mitigate this conflict-driven idea of decoloniality, C. Tsehloane Keto has argued for an epistemic diversity paradigm that regards decolonialityas "a constituent aspect of a global intellectual movement of liberation and a step towards the creation of a 'multi-centered' and diversity affirming perspectives for all the peoples of the world of the future" without privileging any (Keto 1995, 64). This non-conflict-driven perspective promotes epistemic inclusion and recognizes cultural differences while encouraging a sense of belonging. It fosters diversity from studying the *essence* of African and marginalised epistemologies without *essentialising* them as a way of decolonizing knowledge and liberating subjugated epistemologies. It is an approach that recognizes and highlights negative historical experiences such as slavery, racism, and colonialism not as a weapon for championing confrontational and combative paradigms, but as strategies for acknowledging experiential variations and complexities within the human propensity to promote epistemic multiculturalism that could lead to epistemic decolonization in the long run.

This is the whole point epistemic decolonization lapses into morality. The idea of showing clemency to others who have wronged us, the recognition of the universality ofhuman epistemic flourishing, the rejection of unbridled nationalism and epistemic superiority, the embrace of cross-cultural dialogue, and the repudiation of epistemic monoculture are indicative of the fact that the clamour for epistemic decolonisation has metamorphosed from a conflict-driven and monolithic agenda into a kind of morality that places humanity at its centre. The ethical dimension of decoloniality abhors what Ndlovu-Gatsheni (2015, 492) describes as "romanticism, nativism, and fundamentalism". It is a decolonial constructthat seeks epistemic liberation as a collective and encourages epistemic pluralism asa means to enrich our moral depth in what Joseph P. Hester and Don R. Killian call "ethical sensitivity" to the human plight (Hester and Killian 2019, 2). Epistemic decolonization as a moral problem calls for epistemic collaboration instead of epistemic independence, epistemic multicultural instead of epistemic monoculture, and the liberation of marginalised epistemologies instead of epistemic arrogance, subjugation, and oppression. It poses the problem IntaAllegritti describes as "the ethical challenge of living with others" (Allegritti 2002).

How then do we engage this challenge of living with others as a way of decolonizing knowledge in Africa? The answer lies in what Ngugi wa Thiong'o's describes as the philosophy of decolonizing the mind (Ngugi wa Thiong'o 1986). How then to we engage this project of decolonizing the mind in higher education in Africa? What are the operational modalities? These are the questions this essay seeks to answer. It is argued in what follows that the answers to these questionsconsist in cultivating epistemic virtues to augment the recent clamour for curricula and pedagogical transformation towards epistemic decolonization in African high education.

## 3 Curriculum and Pedagogical Strategies of Decolonisation

The clamour for epistemic decolonization from the tutelage of Eurocentric epistemic standpointshas agitated several strategies in recent times. It started in 2015 with the removal from university campuses the remnants of racism and colonial heritage. While in South Africa the statue of Cecil John Rhodes was removed, at Oriel College, Oxford, there waswidespread agitation for its removal (See Maylam 2016). In Ghana, for example, the statue of Mahatma Gandhi was removed amidst overwhelming agitations from the University of Ghana faculty members (Aryeetey 2019).

These pockets of agitations consequently fueled and resuscitated the interest in the epistemic decolonisation debate as African scholars devised strategies to eradicate epistemic decolonisation and restore knowledge systems that eliminate Eurocentric perspectives thatthey consider perilous to the African mind. While some clamour for change in the form of lessons to be learned from the African experience outside the classroom to drive home the epistemic decolonisationeffort (See Nyamnjoh 2019, 2020), for others epistemic decolonisation involves a fundamental rethinking and reframing of the curricular and pedagogical tools to make Africa the center of teaching, research, and learning (See Ezeanya-Esiobu 2019).

Nyamnjoh's strategyfor epistemic decolonisation, for instance, draws inspiration from Amos Tutuola's creative workand Chinua Achebe's proverbs to underscore the importance of decolonising knowledge in a convivial atmosphere in Africa and other parts of the world. Nyamnjoh canvasses the idea that Africans must begin to look beyond the academy for the remedy to the epistemic decolonisation effort and to pursue cross-fertilization of ideas to foster an atmosphere for congenial scholarship (Nyamnjoh 2020, 17). He dubbed this as the theory of incompleteness of being and convivial scholarship against the background that it promotes epistemic inclusivity and the recognition of intellectual debt (arising from one's incompleteness of being) to the institutional memories that have shaped one's ideas and academic trajectories.

Nyamnjoh's conceptionof decolonisation is compelling but its frontiers and theoretical assumptions require detailed further analysis to capture concrete virtue concepts that are required to foster the kind of epistemic decolonisation agenda he envisages. However, to embark on such objectives is beyond the scope of this essay.

On the matter of those scholars who canvas the idea of reforming the curricula and pedagogy in African higher education, Ezeanya-Esiobu makes significant strides in this regard. His strategy for epistemic decolonisation is underpinned by the assumption that mainstreaming indigenous knowledge systems in curricular and pedagogical reformation is crucial for setting the trajectories for Africa's advancement in all fields and sectors (Ezeanya-Esiobu 2019, 107). For example, there are several systems of indigenous knowledge ranging from agriculture, trade, economics, land, capital, political systems, judicial systems and so on that have not been tapped as a framework for formulating science and technology-based curricula for sustainable development in Africa (Ezeanya-Esiobu 2019). These rich indigenous resources, strictly speaking, ought to motivate those in charge of designing an educational structure to embed them in the curricular and pedagogicalreformation agenda.

As much as the foregoing agenda of making African indigenous knowledge the focus of curricula and pedagogical reformation a welcome enterprise, it seems to throw into oblivion the widely argued idea that curriculum and pedagogy (material to be taught and students' processing of the material) is insufficient to make a meaningful impact on educating the mind without the help of allied disciplines that will teach the right attitude.

Aside from the reason sketched above, there are other equally significant concerns why this strategy appears insufficient for epistemic decolonisation in African higher education. Chief among this is thetendencyto absolve the African of his role in the orchestration of the epistemic evils of the colonizers and rather crafts his role as the correctional agent who had no role in the perpetuation of epistemic colonization. Frank Fanon, for example, has detailed some thought-provoking remarks on the caliber of post-colonial African leadership that partly speaks to the predicament of our epistemic denigrating situation. According to Fanon, the leaders who took over the reins of power in Africa quickly inherited the greed of the colonizers (just as their colonial metropolitan counterparts) and subsequently failed to develop a heroic, positive, fruitful and just path that will reshape the thinking and the intellect of the African (Fanon 1963). This accounts for the reason why, as Eseanya-Esiobu rightly remarks, "those in charge of designing education structure continue to advance the colonially bequeathed foundations of education across the region" (Ezeanya-Esiobu 2019, 107).

It is instructive to note from the foregoing that the whole clamour of epistemic decolonization is beyond the idea of mainstreaming indigenous knowledge systems into the curricula of African higher education: it requires the training of attitudes, consciousness and values that undergird our curricular and pedagogical reforms. It is only the acquisition of values and the proper training of the mind that could sufficiently cure the problem of injustice, greed, and epistemic arrogance on the part of those holding brief for Eurocentric epistemic standpoints on the one hand and remedy the problems of avarice, epistemic timidity, and dependency on the part of those seeking epistemic liberation from epistemic coloniality, on the other.

But where does this lead us? If epistemic decolonisation is about avoiding greed, encouraging fairmindedness, promoting humility, and placing the human as the center of epistemic decolonization struggle and so on, then there is no gainsaying that it lies within the parameters of morality. On this account, it could be argued that if epistemic colonization is a moral problem, then its diagnosis should require moral restitution. However, any moral remedy to epistemic colonization must treat both the colonizer and the colonized as partners in the resolution process rather than as adversaries on the account that no race, no matter its extent of sophistication, is thesole repository of knowledge. Thus, Africans and marginalised people must epistemically decolonise but as Kuan-Hsing Chen puts it, the colonizer nations must also undertake 'a deimperialisation movement by reexamining their own imperialist histories and the harmful impacts those histories have had on the world" (Chen 2000, vii). This collaborative approach to epistemic decolonisation bacons to the ethical idea that knowledge is a social product that requires social collaboration to generate cross-fertilization of ideas that will inure to the prospects of the development of humanity.

The way forward is thus to look towards ethics of inclusiveness that allows for intellectual collaboration and coordination designed to foster a cross-cultural outlook that will birth different epistemic perspectives that over time will become universally applicable not because it is hatched from the West, but because it is knowledge that is self-directed and leans towards the ethical principles of fairness, justice, autonomy, humility, and empathy, to mention but a few.

## 4 Educating for Intellectual Virtues

The study of virtue in the form of moral and civic dimensions or it's mainstreaming into the curricula is not a new phenomenon. Most schools in Africa, especially Ghana, have over the years focused on the study of moral and civic virtues as subjects of study at the basic or tertiary levels as a way of developing character and reforming human development (See Danso 2018).

However, it is worthwhile to note that character development studies conceived as moral or civic virtues are not exhaustive of all aspects of virtue studies, and neither is it reducible to it (Baehr 2016a). The argument is simply that one can be morally virtuous but intellectually non-virtuous. Consider a person who practices moral virtues such as generosity and benevolence or civic virtues such as respect and tolerance butlacks epistemic virtues of empathy and humility because he does not consider the scholarly opinions of his colleagues. Such a person will be morally virtuous but epistemically non-virtuous. In the same vein, a person who deploys epistemic virtues such as empathy, humility and curiosity but lacks moral virtues of respect and tolerance because he is an abusive husband and discriminates against others based on sex and gender cannot be regarded as morally virtuous although he could be said to be epistemically so.

Given that moral, civic, and epistemic virtues are different areas of study, one wonders why educational institutions in Africa have paid less attention to the study of epistemic virtues let alone study their implicationsforeducation in Africa. Some Western scholars have made important incursions in the study of epistemic virtues and their application in a wide array of areas including historical scholarship (Paul 2011), business (de Bruin 2013), medicine (Marcum 2009) and education (Baehr 2016b). But one wonders why a crucial area like epistemic virtues has not gained any serious attention despite its close affinity to the issue and prospect of decolonising knowledge. If epistemic decolonisation attempts are moral concerns, as observed in the foregoing analysis, then the study of epistemic virtues must find its way into the educationaltransformation agenda as a drive towards decolonising knowledge in Africa and other epistemologically marginalised societies.

As much as it is crucial to unearth the potential of the study of epistemic virtues to the clamour of decolonising knowledge in African higher education, it is worthy of note that epistemic virtues cannot be taught as it is presently done within the Eurocentric circles where only European figures and stories are presented as exemplars to inculcating certain virtues in students. That is to say, epistemic virtues cannot be taught within a Eurocentric framework where only European examples are cited to aid students' understanding of epistemic virtues that are relevant to education and the decolonisation of knowledge.

Several extant epistemic decolonisation agendas have become anti-decolonialitysentiments that find expression in the destruction of colonialist vestiges and monuments or a complete abandonment of Eurocentric standpoints. The former strategy is reminiscent of the recent decommissioning of statues and the latter resonates with the call to substitute wholesale Eurocentric epistemic perspectives with African indigenous knowledge systems. But it needs to be pointed out that some of these conflict-driven or radical ideas that aim at physical confrontations with colonial vestiges and structures have since outlived their usefulness. Achille Mbembe has called these strategies "false philosophies" "nativism" and "Afro-radicalism" because they are particularly an expression of sentiments built from the reality of slave trade, colonialism, imperialism, racism and are constantly locked up in the display of victimhood and narcissism of difference that bears the potential to promote "territorialisation of the production of knowledge" (Mbembe 1999, 1–5). The above sentiments are an indication that the world is nowbecoming conscious of human value in a more momentous proportion.

For example, the history of Western intellectual thoughts is replete with mischaracterization and devaluation of women. Scholars such as Plato, Aristotle, Kant, Hegel and so on have made explicit statements of racism and misogyny meant to denigrate black people and women and exclude them from serious intellectual conversations (See Witt and Shapiro 2021). But these have changed considerably as black people's and women's rights are being recognised across the globe (although there is more room for improvement). Even in the intellectual sphere, the past 40 years have witnessed an explosion of literature on racial studies and feminism and other related gender discrimination issues in many areas of scholarly endeavours. Even more important is the fact that lower animals are being granted moral agency as deserving of respect (Horsthemke 2018).

Broadly speaking then, human beings across various demographic, religious and cultural divides are increasingly becoming conscious of human dignity, respect, and tolerance as a way of fostering all-inclusive humanity. It is the same with the decolonisation clamour in Africa where we see some scholars promoting epistemic inclusion and convivial scholarship as part of the agenda to decolonise knowledge in Africa. This attempt is reminiscent of the sentiment held by Mbembe who canvases the idea that:

> In order to set our institutions firmly on the path of future knowledges, we need to reinvent *a classroom without walls* in which we are all *colearners*; a university that is capable of convening *various publics innew forms of assemblies that become points of convergence of andplatforms for the redistribution of different kinds of knowledges* (Mbembe 2015, 6).

It equally resonates with Arturo Escobar's idea of "pluriversal' according to which knowledge production and the process of dissemination are open to epistemic diversity and inclusion: a process that accommodates via a horizontal strategy of openness to dialogue among different epistemic traditions (Escobar 2017). If these are plausible accounts of how to decolonise knowledge in African higher education, then our reflection should focus on how this epistemic diversity and inclusion are fostered as a way of decolonising knowledge without losing our autonomy in the process. This is because recognising epistemic diversity, inclusivity, collaboration, and coordination demand a profound consciousness of our beliefs and psychological states. It involves, specifically speaking, becoming aware of virtuous living as regards the production and dissemination of knowledge. This goes to buttress my initial claim that epistemic decolonisation has a moral undertone. Indeed, I deploy morality in a loose sense here. It is not supposed to indicate a kind of morality that focuses on moral actions but an approach that focuses on moral training. It is about the kind of morality that helps us develop the traits for internalising the strategies for decolonising without becoming the architect of the same style of epistemic coloniality we hope to dismantle.

So then what kind of epistemic virtue is required for decolonising knowledge and how do we teach them? To answer these questions, I provide a brief sketch of an analysis ofwhat is involved in this exercise. Epistemic virtues are also called intellectual virtues and they are attributes of a critical and conscientious thinker. Epistemic virtues are acquired character traits that involve epistemic responsibility, humility, autonomy, courage and so on. An epistemic intellectual education or culture often fosters an authentic motivation for knowledge that is buttressed by norms that uphold epistemic virtues such as open-mindedness, intellectual courage, intellectual integrity, and epistemic responsibility.

We could propose epistemic virtues based on the following broad categorisation as a conduit for teaching intellectual virtues in higher education. These are the kind of intellectual virtues that teach us (1) how to own our knowledge systems for epistemic decolonisation, (2) respect or recognise other knowledge systems and (3) stay in the right epistemic direction. Under the first categorisation, we could think of epistemic courage, curiosity and autonomy. The second group of epistemic virtues include epistemic humility and empathy and the third involves epistemic tenacity, thoroughness and attentiveness.

Let us take a look at the kind of epistemic virtues that teach us how to own our knowledge systems. Intellectual courage is the virtue that disposes us to respond appropriately to perceived threats in our intellectual lives. It is a virtue that disposes us to not be unduly intimidated so that we can take the appropriate risk to seek the truth (Elder and Paul 2012, 31). Acting courageously within the academic domain manifests an admirable commitment to epistemic goods in the face of anticipated or actual objection or harm. Epistemic harm or objections are a frequent occurrence in our scholarly pursuit especially when it comes to the issue of epistemic decolonization in Africa. Hence, there is a crucial need for epistemic agents whether individual or collective to be armed with the virtue of epistemic courage to maintain indigenous and endogenous perspectives without fear of objection and harm.

Epistemic curiosity is the disposition to have a deep and persistent desire to have cognitive contact with reality (Berlyne 1954). It is the ability to ask probing questions and seek answers. It involves asking penetrating questions to get to the foundational ideas bordering with issues that are relevant and significant for human inclusion and flourishing. Epistemic curiosity is required for decolonising knowledge because it provides the avenue for us to love seeking knowledge and unravelling the most mysterious aspect of nature. It allows us to quickly master information to see whycertain aspects of our lives work positively and others work negatively so that we can quickly adjust and make the necessary balances. It allows us to probe deeper into ourselves and provides us with a limitless quest to seek knowledge to be epistemically better and contribute our epistemic standpoint to the progress of the world.

Epistemic autonomy is the disposition to think for oneself and not be overly dependent on others when it comes to forming and defending one's beliefs (Zagzebski 2013). An intellectually autonomous person is not a mere receptacle for information and ideas deposited by others. Rather, an intellectually autonomous person is capable of forming her beliefs, initiating her reflection and asking probing questions that will unravel the hidden mysteries of reality. To decolonise knowledge, epistemic autonomy is crucial. It allows us to focus on our indigenous and endogenous knowledge systems and avoid complete reliance on other epistemic standpoints that appears to diminish ours. It helps us to develop authentic epistemic standpoints that emanate from our experiences of reality and provides us with the authorial voices to articulate these perspectives without fear amid other domineering epistemic perspectives.

The three virtues sketched above are crucial to grooming students to be epistemically virtuous and to prepare their minds and psychological states towards developing their epistemic perspectives and owning them despite the pressure of conformity. If we develop epistemic courage, curiosity and autonomy to ensure we own our knowledge systems, how do we foster intellectual collaborations, corporations and conviviality which are also crucial to decolonising knowledge (since knowledge is a social product, and no person or culture is a complete embodiment of it)? This calls for the kind of epistemic virtues that will promote respect and recognition of other epistemic standpoints to ensure intellectual collaborations and cross-fertilization of ideas in our bid to decolonise knowledge in higher education.

The first of the epistemic virtues to be discussed under this category is epistemic humility. It is the disposition to be aware of or recognise our intellectual limits or deficits. It also involved recognising and offering respect to genuine intellectual dimensions that offer a more human-centered perspective on existence (Elder and Paul 2012). In a more mundane sense, it refers to the disposition not to be bothered by intellectual accolades. The second is epistemic empathy which is the disposition to reason together with people of diverse cultures, statuses and geographies who share a different epistemic standpoint from ours. It is a way of reasoning fairly with different people from different epistemic backgrounds without prejudice or biases (Elder and Paul 2012). Epistemic decolonisation requires epistemic humility and empathy as a two-tie therapy: it requires that the structural forces that produce epistemic inequalities appreciate the symbiotic relationship in knowledge production and dissemination, and those at the receiving end of epistemic recognition become aware that being epistemic autonomous does not mean a complete rejection of other epistemic standpoints. In the first instance, it inspires the disposition to promote epistemic justice across cultures where groups that regardtheir epistemic standpoints as superior need to realize their epistemic deficit, if any, to avoid epistemic arrogance that could mar the potential for cross-fertilization of ideas. In the second case, it is a call for the enthusiasts of epistemic decolonization to adopt a more inclusive therapy towards epistemic colonization. In other words, it is a call to deflate our epistemic ego, *de-superiorize*andprevent the tendency to close doors to opportunities that will promote intellectual congeniality that is necessary for broadening our epistemic perspectives.

If we canachieve all the above, i.e., own our knowledge systems and recognise other perspectives, how do we sustain this momentum without sliding away from it? How do we stay on this epistemic track and head in the right direction? The callfor epistemic tenacity, thoroughness, and attentiveness. Epistemic tenacity is the willingness to accept epistemic struggles and focus on the challenge ahead to seek epistemic goods. Our daily routines are replete with obstacles and challenges, and so is our journey towards our intellectual goals. However, an epistemically tenacious person is willing to engage, confront and seek to overcome such challenges instead of throwing her hands in despair. Indeed, epistemic decolonisation is an obstacle and a challenge towards becoming epistemically autonomous while being intellectually congenial at the same time. This balance between epistemic autonomy and congeniality is what makes the effort of decolonising knowledge much more challenging. It, therefore, requires an epistemically tenacious mind to face these challenges and help us achieve the balance that will sustain us on the right path so that we do not go off-track. An intellectually tenacious mindset informs us aforehand about the meandering intellectual journey that lies ahead of us – a journey littered with scars ofintellectual bullying of indigenous and endogenous thinking driven by Eurocentric intellectual traditions – so that we may embrace this risk and forge ahead for epistemic emancipation.

Epistemic thoroughness also helps us to stay on track on the journey to decolonise knowledge. It is the disposition to probe deeper, consider all available evidence (not what is conveniently available) and consider multiple perspectives before passing judgment (Zagzebski 1996). Being intellectually thorough helps us to transcend superficial perspectives and explain why things are the way they are and if we need to make a judgment, we do. An epistemically thorough person is not likely to be dissuaded by flimsy scholarly persuasions that seem to promote intellectual segregation and inequality despite its ambience. Rather, it engenders a positive attitude towards knowledge and emphasises epistemic due diligence so that in our quest to decolonise knowledge, we could offer a detailed and probing perspective on the global intellectual platter. Intellectual attentiveness is the disposition to listen more to understand subtle but significant details of one's experiences and that of others. Epistemically attentive persons can exercise great restraint and observe more than they speak. They are often less prone to indulge in debates they have no clarity over. This disposition is quite significant for epistemic decolonisation projects which among other things require that we become autonomous at the same time maintain congenial attitudes towards diverse epistemic standpoints. Note that lack of attentiveness could sway us towards a wrong epistemic path, and this could further derail attempts to focus on our epistemic perspectives as the primary and the most significant quest towards decolonization.

If the above virtues are significant for the inculcation of epistemic virtues in higher education for purposes of decolonising knowledge in Africa, how then do we teach them? Several scholars have argued that epistemic virtues can be taught in schools and that there are suitable pedagogical strategies for educating about intellectual virtues (Battaly 2006; Baehr 2013). Others have suggested that there are no appropriate and suitable pedagogical strategies for teaching intellectual virtues or that they areineffective waysof making students lifelong learners (Siegel 1988; Scheffler 1989). Whether epistemic virtues can be taught or not is a debate whose scope is beyond this essay. Hence, I will not delve into this but rather suggest a brief analysis of how the teaching of epistemic virtues can be assimilated into pedagogical strategies in higher education in Africa as a frame for epistemic decolonisation. My proposal is modest and is as follows.

Unless the ethics of epistemic virtue is made a university-wide course in higher education, it will be cumbersome to teach epistemic virtues in the classroom. Even when it is made a university-wide course, depending on how it may be taught, a single course on the ethics of epistemic virtues may not be sufficient for teaching these virtues and making sure students practice them. Hence, an effective way to circumvent this hurdle is that instructors of various scholarly disciplines could incorporate the teaching of epistemic virtues as a pedagogical strategy to teach students about decolonising knowledge as part of their regular topics. One way to advance this strategy is to incorporate a relevant epistemic virtue we wish our students to master as part of the course objectives and to conduct assessment forms that will ensure that students are making important use of that knowledge. To do this effectively, course instructors after indicating the knowledge and skills to be transferred as part of the course objectives may include the relevant epistemic virtue(s) to be transferred as well and make sure that these objectives are read aloud and explained to students at the inception of the course. At the end of the course, the instructor's assessment should be able to determine whether students are engaging with the relevant virtues explored in the course. This is just a rough design to suggest asimple routine way of teaching intellectual virtues that are directed towards epistemic decolonisation in higher education in Africa. It certainly requires details that is beyond the scope of this essay.

## 5 Implication for Development in Africa

The idea of development is a contested subject but when it comes to the issue of the effect of decoloniality on development, one important way of tackling it may involve investigating alternative paradigms to dominant understandings of development. This may include exploring alternative strategies of development different from those that are superimposed on the Global South by hegemonic powers which have over the years failed to propel African development exigencies. Exploring alternative approaches means that Africans, as part of the decoloniality effort, will depart from capitalist and market-driven paradigms inherited from the Euro-modern enlightenment traditions that have kept Africans perpetually subservient to hegemonic dominant approaches.

If this is something to adopt, then the first step in the decoloniality strategy that will propel proper development in Africa is to focus on reorienting the psychological state or the mindset of the colonised because one of the strategies of the coloniser was to force African students to abandon their cultural resources and to embrace the dominant colonial culture as the basis for life successes (Reyhner and Elder 2015). This reinforces the commitment sketched above concerning going beyond the curriculum and pedagogical transformation towards reorienting the mindset of the African student towards self-directedness and intellectual autonomy so that she is able to break away from Eurocentric vestiges and entanglements that lead to an unnecessary desire to emulate foreign cultures and norms that are not contextually relevant to African development needs. By doing this, the student is able to face head-on, through critical reflection, knowledge systems that continue to reproduce power dynamics between the Global North and the South. Additionally, African students will be able to own their knowledge systems while decentering hegemonic knowledge systems and making Africa the center of indigenous and endogenous developmental strategies that will inure to the benefit of the African continent. When students are thought to be intellectually autonomous and curious, they can own their knowledge systems in a manner that reflects their epistemic agency in the creation of local technologies, improvement of local determination of development options and retention of development within their vicinity.

Going beyond the curriculum and pedagogical strategies will ensure that students are taught to recognise other knowledge systems and show openness to new knowledge paradigms in a way that does not suppress their thinking. In this era of globalization, intellectual collaboration is necessary for cross-fertilization and co-production of knowledge where technological inventions and developmental resources are shared between countries. When epistemic decolonization is seen as showing intellectual indebtedness to one another, global advancement won't be seen as a zero-sum game where cultures struggle to survive and win alone. With this done, purveyors of dominant epistemologies will see the need de-superiorize to allow endogenous growth to occur in the Global South. Without these interventions, the clamour for epistemic decoloniality will become another fig leaf which may not lead to development that takes into consideration the local circumstances of the colonised. If curriculum and pedagogical strategies are put in place without the necessary psychological plans to undergird such reforms, the prospects for epistemic decolonization may turn out to be a nine-day wonder which may pose potential danger to human development in Africa.

## 6 Conclusion

The teaching of epistemic virtues has for some time now been neglected and attention rather devoted to the teaching of moral and civic virtues to promote and sustain social growth and justice. Butwithout epistemic justice, social justice cannot take shape because most social systems and structures are constructed upon the knowledge systems that sustain them. It is therefore very crucial to focus on teaching intellectual virtues as the foundational discipline in our quest to reject epistemic inequality and promote epistemic decolonisation through diversity. It is only the teaching of intellectual virtues that bacons both the coloniser and the colonised to see the need to foster epistemic collaboration to end epistemic colonisation and promote a more human-centred approach to knowledge that recognises intellectual equality and fruitful scholarly collaborations between the Global North and the Global South beyond what is currently being paraded as curricula and pedagogical reforms.

## References

Adeleke, T. 2009. *The case against afrocentrism*. Jackson: The University of Mississippi Press.

Allegritti, I. 2002. Renovating Australian Citizenship: A post-liberal approach to citizenship. In *Keynote address at the international conference on 'cultural citizenship: challenges of globalization*. Melbourne: Deakin University, December 6.

Aryeetey, E. 2019. The background story to a statue of Gandhi and the University of Ghana. *The Conversation*. Retrieved from: https://theconversation.com/the-background-story-to-a-statue-of-gandhi-and-the-university-of-ghana-117103. Accessed 15 June 2021.

Asante, M.K. 1988. *Afrocentricity*. Trenton: Africa World Press.

———. 1993. Where is the white professor located? *Perspectives* 31 (6).

Baehr, J. 2013. Educating for intellectual virtues: from theory to practice. *Journal of Philosophy of Education* 47: 248–262.

Baehr, J. 2016a. Introduction: applying virtue epistemology to education. In *Intellectual virtues and education essays in applied virtue epistemology*, ed. Jason Baehr, 1–15. London: Routledge.

———., ed. 2016b. *Intellectual virtues and education essays in applied virtue epistemology*. London: Routledge.

Battaly, H. 2006. Teaching intellectual virtues. *Teaching Philosophy* 29 (3): 191–222.

Berlyne, D.E. 1954. A theory of human curiosity. *British Journal of Psychology* no. 45: 180–191.

Chen, K.-H. 2000. *Asia as method: towards deimperialization*. Durham: Duke University Press.

Danso, S.A. 2018. Moral education and the curriculum: the ghanaian experience. *International Journal of Scientific Research and Management*: 34–42.

de Bruin, B. 2013. Epistemic virtues in business. *Journal of Business Ethics*. 113: 583–595.

Elder, L., and R. Paul. 2012. Critical thinking: competency standards essential to the cultivation of intellectual skills, part 4. *Journal of Developmental Education*. 35 (3): 30–31.

Escobar, A. 2017. *Designs for the pluriverse: radical interdependence, autonomy, and the making of worlds*. London: Duke University Press.

Ezeanya-Esiobu, C. 2019. *Indigenous knowledge and education in Africa*. Los Angeles: Springer.

Fanon, F 1963. *The wretched of the earth*. Trans. Richard Philcox. New York: Grove Press.

Grosfoguel, R. 2007. The epistemic decolonial turn: beyond political-economy paradigms. *Cultural Studies* 21 (2/3): 203–246.

Hester, J.P., and D.R. Killian. 2019. Morality without borders: A vision of humanity as Community. *The Journal of Value-Based Leadership* 12 (2): 1–17.

Horsthemke, K. 2018. Animal rights education. In *The Palgrave Macmillan animal ethics*. series. Cham: Palgrave Macmillan.

Keto, T.C. 1995. *Vision, identity and time: the afrocentric paradigm and the study of the past*. Dubuque, Iowa: Kendall-Hunt.

Maldonado-Torres, N. 2011. Thinking through the decolonial turn: post-continental interventions in theory, philosophy, and critique—an introduction. *Transmodernity: Journal of Peripheral Cultural Production of Luso-Hispanic World* 1 (2).

Marcum, J. 2009. The epistemically virtuous clinician. *Theoretical Medicine and Bioethics*. 30: 249–265.

Maylam, P. 2016. What Cecil John Rhodes said in his will about who should get scholarships. *The Conversation*. Retrieved from: https://theconversation.com/what-cecil-john-rhodes-said-in-his-will-about-who-should-get-scholarships-53172. Accessed 15 Feb 2021.

Mbembe, A. 1999. Getting out of the Ghetto: the challenge of internationalization. *CODESRIA Bulletin* 3 (4): 1–10.

Mbembe, A. 2015. *Decolonizing knowledge and the question of the archive*. Unpublished Speech. Retrieved from: Microsoft Word – Decolonizing the University.docx (wits.ac.za). Accessed 10 Apr 2021.

Mignolo, W.D. 2009. Epistemic disobedience, independent thought and de-colonial freedom. *Theory, Culture & Society* 26 (7–8): 1–23.

———. 2011. *The darker side of western modernity: global futures, decolonial options*. Durham, NC: Duke University Press.

Ndlovu-Gatsheni, S.J. 2012. *Coloniality of power in development studies, and the impact of global imperial designs on Africa*. Pretoria: Department of Development Studies, University of South Africa. Inaugural Lecture Delivered at the University of South Africa, Senate Hall.

———. 2015. Decoloniality as the future of Africa. *History Compass* 13 (10): 485–496.

———. 2018. *Epistemic freedom in Africa: deprovincialization and decolonization*. London: Routledge.

Ngugi wa Thiong'o. 1986. *Decolonizing the mind: the politics of language in African literature*. Nairobi: Heinemann.

Nyamnjoh, F.B. 2019. Decolonising the University in Africa. *The Oxford Research Encyclopedia*.

———. 2020. Decolonising the academy: a case for convivial scholarship. Carl Schlettwein Lecture 14, Basler Afrika Bibliographien, Namibia Resource Centre and Southern Africa Library, Klosterberg 23.

Paul, H. 2011. Performing history: how historical scholarship is shaped by epistemic virtues. *History and Theory* 50: 1–19.

Porter, R.O. 2005. The decolonization of indigenous government. In *For indigenous eyes only: a decolonisation handbook*, ed. W.A. Wilson and M. Yellow Bird, 87–108. Santa Fe: School of American Research Press.

Reyhner, J., and J. Elder. 2015. *American Indian education. A history*. Norman: University of Oklahoma Press.

Santos, B. 2016. *Epistemologies of the South: justice against epistemicide*. New York, NY: Routledge.

Scheffler, I. 1989. *Reason and teaching*. Indianapolis: Hackett.

Sekyi-Otu, A. 2019. *Left universalism: africacentric essays*. New York: Routledge.

Siegel, H. 1988. Rationality and epistemic dependance. *Educational Philosophy and Theory* 20 (1): 1–6.

Tamale, S. 2020. *Decolonisation and Afro-Feminism*. Ottawa: Dajara Press.

Wiredu, K. 1998. Toward decolonizing African philosophy and religion. *African Studies Quarterly* 1 (4): 17–46.

Witt, C., and L. Shapiro. 2021. Feminist history of philosophy. *Stanford encyclopedia of philosophy*. Retrieved from: https://plato.stanford.edu/entries/feminism-femhist/. Accessed on 13 July 2021.

Zagzebski, L. 1996. *Virtues of the mind: an inquiry into the nature of virtue and the ethical foundations of knowledge*. Cambridge: Cambridge University Press.

———. 2013. Intellectual autonomy. *Philosophical issues* 23: 244–261.

**Husein Inusah** is Senior Lecturer at the Department of Classics and Philosophy, University of Cape Coast, Ghana, where he teaches Philosophy. His area of specialisation is epistemology. He currently researches on topics including the regress problem, consensual rationality and epistemic decolonisation. He is the leading author of Understanding and Applying Critical Thinking (Accra: Sub-Saharan Publishers, 2019) and has published several papers in both local and international peer-reviewed journals. His current project is on harnessing the insights of African proverbs to promote the intellectual virtues for epistemic decolonisation and biodiversity conservation in Africa.

# Educational Challenges to Africa's Development: The Imperative of Epistemic Decolonisation

**Victoria Openif'Oluwa Akoleowo**

**Abstract** The colonial experience in Africa, characterised by an exhibition of Eurocentric attitudes which questioned the very humanity of the colonised, upheld 'Whiteness' as the standard of purity and civilisation. It also subjugated the endogenous epistemologies of the colonised to the 'pure' epistemologies and worldviews of the colonialists. This experience occasioned a disruption of the organic trend of Africa's development, truncating its socio-political and economic trajectories and stagnating/destroying traditional African socio-political values and institutions through its imposition of western standards on colonised societies. The resultant effect – an epistemicide against pre-colonial epistemes, suppressing, vilifying and/or partially destroying such epistemes and labelling them as local, uncivilised and traditional. In contrast, the colonial-imposed Eurocentric, western episteme was upheld as modern and civilised, the standard to which all other knowledge systems had to comply. Such Eurocentric hegemony persists to date. This chapter, therefore, builds on the notion of 'colonial legacy' as an insidious challenge to Africa's development. Utilising the analytic and synthetic methodologies, it avers that epistemic decolonisation is an essential factor in development ethics. Epistemic decolonisation, the demand for the dismantling of Eurocentric hegemonies in African educational systems, and its replacement with African-centered epistemes which identify Africa as the heuristic core of the episteme presents as an imperative for justice, a means for Africans to (re)construct their worldviews to reflect themselves as the centre of such worldviews in relationship with others and for the African educational curricula to be (re)constructed to reflect contextual concerns.

**Keywords** Africa · Development · Education · Epistemic decolonisation · Epistemic injustice

---

V. O. Akoleowo (✉)
Department of Philosophy and Religious Studies, Dominican University, Ibadan, Nigeria



B. Okyere-Manu et al. (eds.), *Contemporary Development Ethics from an African Perspective*, Philosophy and Politics - Critical Explorations 27,
https://doi.org/10.1007/978-3-031-32898-5_15

# 1 Introduction

Although colonialism has come and gone, its negative legacies continue to linger and indirectly sustain coloniality/neocolonialism in contemporary Africa. It is especially worrisome that negative colonial superimpositions and the legacies of Eurocentric hegemony are sustained in many contemporary African systems and institutions, including institutions of learning. These superimpositions and legacies include the subjugation of African indigenous epistemologies and worldviews. Studies on the causes of Africa's continued underdevelopment have continually identified that the Eurocentric hegemony which characterised African states during the colonial era continues to persist. As Rodney (1981, p. 240) argues, colonial-era systems and institutions, including legal, educational and religious systems, were established for a particular purpose – to aid in the consolidation of colonial rule. Colonial rule itself was primarily justified on economic grounds as necessary to enable the exploitation of African natural resources. Given that these systems and institutions were not dismantled after colonial rule, they have perpetuated such exploitation covertly long after colonies gained independence. Essentially, they have contributed to the underdevelopment of Africa, while engendering the development of European countries.

In view of the foregoing, this chapter, therefore, examines the notion of 'colonial legacy' as an insidious challenge to Africa's development. It avers that epistemic decolonisation is an essential factor in development ethics. The African continent experienced a form of epistemic injustice through epistemic colonisation. Epistemic decolonisation can, therefore, be conceived as an attempt to right this epistemic wrong. As such, it falls under the moral epistemology of development theory – where moral epistemology concerns itself with moral justification of knowledge systems. It thereafter argues that the current epistemic injustice experienced in African educational systems must be resolved through the dismantling of Eurocentric hegemonies in such educational systems and replaced with African-centered epistemes which identify Africa as the heuristic hard core of the epistemes and are capable of alleviating the epistemic injustice occasioned by the *status quo*. The chapter divides its argument into five sections. The first part attempts a justification of epistemic decolonisation. The second part explores the relationship between indigenous knowledge and development in an attempt to analyse how inflexions and reflections on the environment and immediate needs determine the scope of knowledge production. The third part presents a philosophical exposition of colonial epistemicide. The fourth part, in examining Africa's epistemic framework, illustrates how contemporary African knowledge systems are underpinned by the colonial legacy of Eurocentric knowledge forms. The final part proposes decolonisation of the African knowledge space as a means of reforming and repositioning African educational systems for sustainable developmental purposes.

## 2 The Imperative of Epistemic Decolonisation

An incontrovertible fact about colonial education systems is that they were designed to meet colonial needs. In meeting these needs, the colonialists committed epistemicides against African epistemes by promulgating colonial policies which vilified indigenous African knowledge systems and cultures. African rights to their knowledge systems and cultures were thus, violated. Such injustice, I argue, is best rectified by a decolonisation process that reimagines indigenous knowledge systems as central and valuable, thus, the imperative of epistemic decolonisation.

Proponents of epistemic decolonisation hold that the epistemic justice meted out to African epistemes did not end with the attainment of political decolonisation as one would expect. Rather, it has persisted till date, as evident from the educational curricula in African educational institutions which remain predominantly western and Eurocentric. This phenomenon, the persistence of Eurocentric epistemic hegemony in African education systems, has been referred to as neocolonialism (Nkrumah 1965, 35–36). Decolonial scholars refer to it as coloniality, a state of affairs occasioned by colonial matrixes of power that equate the colonial with modernity (Mignolo and Walsh 2018, 24). As neocolonialism or coloniality, the Eurocentric epistemic hegemony implies a new form of colonial exploitation where the African scholar is deprived of knowledge about his/her indigenous culture.

In explicating this form of exploitation, scholars including wa Thiong'o and Wiredu have averred that the African is barely cognisant of his/her indigenous epistemic concepts and theories. For wa Thiong'o and Wiredu, the colonial imposition of foreign language has resulted in mental colonisation, the inability of the colonised to know, understand and utilise his/her indigenous concepts and theories (wa Thiong'o 1986, p. 16; Wiredu 1998, 17–19). Colonised peoples are thus, doubly disadvantaged – they are alienated from their indigenous epistemes and are also not fully accepted into the western epistemes.

Epistemic decolonisation is further justified by criticisms against Eurocentric notions of learning which hold that the abstract and hegemonic nature of such Eurocentric knowledge system precludes it from promoting interplay of knowledge systems essential for community engagement and development. This abstract and hegemonic nature of Eurocentric knowledge systems results in an educational system that is completely divorced from the social and cultural needs of society; one which consequently produces graduates who lack the requisite skills to fulfil required roles in society (Mignolo 2011).

This chapter, therefore, holds that decolonisation of education presents as a means for Africans to (re)construct their worldview to reflect themselves as the centre of such worldviews in relationship with others and that through critical pedagogies, African educational curricula can be (re)constructed to reflect contextual concerns to make such curricula relevant in contemporary African quests for development.

## 3 Development and Indigenous Knowledge

The concept of development is a multi-faceted phenomenon and as such, remains a contentious one to define. It is defined variously as 'a social condition within a nation, in which the authentic needs of its population are satisfied by the rational and sustainable use of natural resources and systems'(Reyes 2001, p. 1); a 'normative concept referring to a multidimensional process'(McLean and McMillan 2003, p. 148); a process through which the lives of poor people are bettered and as a reproduction of the Western-style economic prosperity (Ewane and Ajagbe 2018, p. 65–66); among other definitions. Extrapolating from the above, development is at equal times a means and an end. As a means, it is an ongoing, never-ending process through which humans arrive at better standards of living, and as an end, it is the actual bettered standard of living (Ekanola 2012, p. 2).

While the above definitions emphasise the social aspect of the development phenomenon, it must be noted that development applies both to the individual and the collective. At the individual level, it is used interchangeably with growth. An in-depth analysis of both concepts leads to the conclusion that development is akin to growth only in the sense that both refer to changes in the individual. However, while growth refers to the process of quantitative changes in the individual's physical body, development refers to the process of qualitative changes in all aspects of the individual's life, inclusive of social, physical and religious.

In its social aspect, development is typically defined in economic terms. As Walter Rodney (1981, p. 4) avers, in this sense, it connotes the capacity to which a society's ability to interact with its environment improves. Rodney's historical analysis of development across the African and European continents notes that this notion of development applied universally prior to the colonial incursion in Africa, contrary to arguments utilised to justify colonialism. For him, all human groups/societies exhibited evidence of increasing prowess in their relations with their immediate environment in the efforts at extracting the necessities for quality living from their immediate environment, ultimately translating to improved conditions of living.

The Marxian model of historical materialism underpins contemporary conceptualisations of development. This model traces societal development through various historical epochs, from primitive communism, through the slave-owning society, feudalism, capitalism, socialism into its eventual resolution in stateless communism. Rodney's analysis, while noting the uneven level of development in pre-colonial African societies, rightly asserts that African societies cannot be qualified as underdeveloped, given that many of them had developed beyond the generally accepted minimum of primitive communalism. While he argues that the social formations across pre-colonial Africa prove difficult to categorise, due to the differing levels of development, contemporary research shows that many pre-colonial African societies, going by the Marxian standard, were at the feudal level of societal development, characterised by an economy based on slavery, forced labour, taxes and tribute (Nzimiro 2011). This further validates Rodney's and this author's shared position that pre-colonial African societies were experiencing their own self-paced, organic developmental processes prior to the colonial incursion.

Education is an incontrovertible feature of development. It helps to unleash the potentials of the human mind. These are potentials typically geared towards mastering nature in one form or the other. As a means of unlocking or developing potentials that help in the mastery of the environment, education is thus, an essential feature of development. As Ozturk (2001, p. 39) argues, education enables a richer understanding of reality and improves the quality of living by encouraging creativity which raises productivity and technological advances; thereby securing social and economic progress. Given, therefore, that education is essential to development, and development connotes an improvement in a people's ability to interact with their environment, it is germane to assert that development starts from local concerns, ditto education. If development starts from the local, and if, as Mafeje (2000) avers, knowledge is first local; then it logically follows that local knowledge is a major determent of developmental progress. What then is this local knowledge, and how does it determine developmental progress?

Local knowledge, more commonly known as indigenous knowledge (IK) is said to comprise 'local, traditional, nonwestern beliefs, practices, customs and world views' (Horsthemke 2004, p. 32). As such, it is an ingrained part of a people's culture, derived from experience, religious beliefs and communal norms. IK is essential to developmental concerns by virtue of its role as the primary repository of a people's dealings with their environment. This implies that IK represents the history of how a people have successfully managed their interactions with their environment and the many innovations that have ensued through which they have been able to extract their sustenance from nature. Given that this analysis of IK is akin to the notion of development as a process, IK emphasises how development is necessarily geared towards surrounding particularities of a people or society. This is in view of the fact that knowledge production and acquisition is ultimately driven by problem-solving challenges.

It is imperative to note that during the colonial era in Africa, and many years into the post-colonial epoch, IK was largely ignored by developmental professionals who vilified it as primitive and static, in comparison with Western formal knowledge systems. The colonial period is particularly replete with accounts of how the Western epistemic system was upheld as the standard of knowledge acquisition. This led to what is now known as the epistemicide of IK systems.

## 4 Colonial Epistemicide

Colonialism, the practice of taking full or partial control of a people and their territory, involved the domination and subjugation of the colonised people by the colonial power(s). It was underpinned by economic profiting, which necessitated the transfer of settlers from the colonial country to the colonised territory. History records various accounts of colonialism and demonstrates the fact that colonialism is not a modern phenomenon. Rather, accounts of colonial experiences dot humanity's historical landscape. Examples of such accounts include Greek and Roman colonisations of the ancient epoch, the Anglo-Saxon, Norse and Anglo-Norman colonisations of the medieval period, and the modern European colonisation (Hurst and Owen 2005; Sarnowsky 2013). These colonial exercises were characterised by certain features: (1) Racial capitalism through which colonised populations were divided and ruled on the basis of their racial characteristics; (2) Colonial settlements in colonies; (3) Colonial policies, underpinned by racial capitalism which regulated the exchanges between the colonials and the colonised, and which were key to capitalist practices vis-à-vis wealth accumulation at the expense of the colonised (Manjapra 2020).

As Lyons and Papadopoulos state, '(the) success of colonial movements often depends on subtle shifts in habits and state of mind'(Lyons and Papadopoulos 2002, p. 11–12). Colonial rule transcended physical conquests to attempts at influencing and ruling the minds of the colonised. The dominant power structures favoured colonial authorities and enabled alterations in traditional socio-cultural practices. Primary among the resultant effects of such power structures was the devaluing of the cultures and traditions of the colonised in favour of the colonisers' cultures and traditions. This *modus operandi*, though common to all accounts of colonialism, was particularly prevalent in the fifteenth-century accounts, the epoch of modern colonialism, through Portugal and Spain's exploration travels for new territories which resulted in the colonisation of territories in Africa, Asia, The Americas and India, up to the nineteenth-century European colonisation of the African continent.

The colonial experience in Africa in particular continues to provoke critical analyses. Initially justified as a civilisation mission, a cursory analysis of the experience leads to the inevitable conclusion that the civilisation rationale was an excuse utilised to obscure the exploitative and demeaning practices of colonialism. Indigenous African cultures, traditions and knowledge systems were relegated and labelled as inferior to those of the colonisers. Colonialism brought the main ills of existential and economic imperialism and Eurocentric epistemic hegemonies. Hegel's seminal work, *The Philosophy of History*, gave philosophical imprimatur to the Eurocentric conception of Africa. In it, Hegel conceptualised Africa as a continent outside of world history, one with races naturally inferior to the whites, given their uncivilised, undeveloped nature and one beyond self-consciousness, untamed, wild and with weak or non-existent moral sentiments. This gave a philosophical justification to racist conceptualisations of Africa, as well as the imperative to colonise Africa in order to civilise it. We must note at this juncture, that this philosophical justification of Eurocentric racist conceptions of Africa has been severally criticised.

Following from the above, the colonial experience involved deliberate destruction of the knowledges and cultures of the colonised (Santos 2016, p. 18). This process consisted of delineations of the global knowledge space between the Global North and South, in a mode that ensured the exclusion of the latter from the group of valid knowledge producers as a producer of defective and invalid knowledges in the first instance, and as belonging to the zone of 'incomprehensible magical and idolatrous practices of sub-human savages' in the second (Santos 2007, p. 51). This phenomenon, known as epistemicide, transcended the devaluing of knowledge systems to a critique of forms of beings, given its destruction of social practices and its disqualifications of physical agents that operated on such social knowledge practices. It privileged western ways of knowing above others, establishing an imperial monopoly on knowledge production. In the process, African indigenous epistemes became subjected to western Eurocentric epistemes for validation. Such validation, 'conferred' solely on the colonised culture's adoption of the western standard, was widely sought for its 'modernising'touch.

Colonial Africa's adoption of Eurocentric epistemic systems ensured that its indigenous epistemes remained constantly maligned and sidelined from global knowledge discourse. Colonial African societies adopted and established western educational institutions which espoused, produced and transmitted Eurocentric epistemes through European languages, in a manner that discouraged critical reflections on the transmitted knowledge (Freire 1993; Fanon 2004; Wiredu 2004, p. 2). As earlier established, African IKs had been vilified as 'inferior' and 'unscientific', thus, it was easy to proffer 'superior' and 'scientific' western educational systems as the alternative. While early enrollment into these institutions was low, economic necessities soon necessitated a higher level of enrollment, birthing generations of Africans who were indoctrinated into the dominant ideology that their indigenous knowledge systems were defective (Mazrui 1979, p. 32–35; Matasci et al. 2020, p. 11 & 16). With high levels of enrollment, these institutions gained wide acceptance from the African populace such that long after political independence, the only changes made in them was the replacement of colonial administrators and teachers by indigenous African administrators and teachers (Ndlovu-Gatsheni 2017, p. 60). Contemporaneously, subsequent generations of Africans pass through these institutions and emerge as hybrid agents, Africans living at the intersection of two or more cultures who often experience difficulties in situating themselves in any of the cultures.

Hall and Tandon (2017, p. 8) aver that Western epistemic hegemony has resulted in an epistemicide against many of the diverse epistemes of the world, arguing that higher educational institutions are complicit in this epistemicide by utilising colonial epistemes and excluding others. They adduce that the creation of walled-in institutions served as a measure of limiting access to knowledge by enclosing it, creating in that sense a form of control over knowledge and those who acquire it (2017 p. 8). In this wise, other forms of knowledge became invalid. Knowledge was restricted to those within the enclaves, and others outside of the enclave 'non-knowers'; knowledge became completely divorced from the 'vast majority' of communal knowledge keepers, being restricted to a small elite (2017 p. 8). Western epistemic hegemony is thus, best conceptualised as an epistemic monoculture that excludes alternate epistemes as invalid. Building on Grosfoguel's epistemicides of the sixteenth century, Hall and Tandon (2017 p. 8–11) enumerate exemplars to show how western Eurocentric epistemic hegemony has alienated and dispossessed indigenous communities from their rich knowledge of indigenous developmental practices. These exemplars, thankfully, also include accounts of how such indigenous communities have realised that their autochthonous epistemes are more pertinent to the realisation of their full potentials. These accounts establish how these exemplars, recognising the inadequacies of the western Eurocentric episteme, resurrected/developed autochthonous, non-Eurocentric modes of creating, sharing, applying, archiving and accessing knowledge.

The epistemic violence occasioned by hegemonic Eurocentric epistemic canons has been rightly recognised as a causal factor in Africa's perennial underdevelopment – the products of these hegemonic epistemes are not only alienated from their indigenous cultures, the knowledge acquired prove irrelevant to development concerns (Spivak 1994, p. 80; Mbembe 2016, p. 32). To redress this, there must be a critical undoing of Western epistemological tyranny which has cognitively usurped the powers of all subaltern nations to work towards complete decolonisation of knowledge. Given the recognition that development starts from the local/personal, the reconstructed epistemes must replace Eurocentric epistemic hegemony with African-centred epistemes, where African concerns drive knowledge production, and where the epistemic universe is constructed to reflect African worldviews as the heuristic hard core.

## 5 Perennial Eurocentric Knowledge Forms and Development in Africa

From the above, the reader is confronted with the contemporary reality of African educational institutions. The institutional, infrastructural, personnel and tradition of research prevalent in these institutions were inherited as colonial relics, and they continue to privilege western standards, symbols and cultures imposed through colonial epistemicide. Of concern to this work is the reality that such educational institutions and their products, which were highly heralded as agentsof change and development, are unable to resolve the persistent developmental challenges bedevilling most African states. If Western education as the standard of modernity is the basis of development, and African states operate colonial, Eurocentric epistemic systems, why are African states perennially confronted with developmental challenges? Why have the different developmental programmes failed? Why have adopted development theories, including the modernisation theory of development, the dependency theory of development, the world-system approach to development and the state theory of development failed? Why has liberal capitalism, heralded as an effective antidote to underdevelopment, failed?

Answers to these questions vary. However, underpinning these answers is the concern that African epistemic systems operate under a form of injustice. As Santos states, the western hegemonic, monocultural way of knowing operating in African educational institutions remains the tool for sustaining 'capitalism, colonialism, patriarchy and all their satellite oppression' (2014, p. 10). Many African universities continue to operate with Eurocentric, western based-curricula which continue to propagate Eurocentric hegemonies, neglecting Afro-centric knowledge bases and systems and excluding subaltern ideas and authors (Heleta 2016). Little, if any, changes have been made to the foundational curricula of earlier established African educational institutions. These educational systems as established by the colonialists were meant to promote colonial economic, social and political interests and were, therefore, specifically designed to achieve these goals (Rodney 1981, p. 240; Bako 2005, p. 5). This reality portends the major challenge to developmental concerns. These concerns derive from the fact that any system designed to meet the needs of colonialism cannot subsequently be adopted to meet the needs of liberating the colonised (Mbembe 2016).

Consequently, Afrocentric researchers have proposed a reversal of colonial epistemicide in order to arrive at authentic African IK systems which are germane to sustainable development. This proposal is premised on two factors namely: (1) Development and education start from the local, and (2) Pre-colonial African societies were not as undeveloped or uncivilised as have been portrayed by justifiers of colonialism. As Rodney, Aime Cesaire, Mahmood Mamdani and Toyin Falola among others have argued, historical accounts of pre-colonial African societies are replete with accounts of African societies' developmental progress, which in some cases compared more favourably than their European counterparts; witness Rodney's account of Cecil Rhodes' encounter with Zimbabwean culture (Rodney 1981, p. 33).

In addition to arguments on favourable, pre-colonial African societal developmental progress, Oloruntoba et al. (2020, p. 4) assert that indigenous African epistemic systems undergirded the developmental processes in pre-colonial African societies. In particular, Rodney's groundbreaking work, *How Europe Underdeveloped Africa*, presents credible research to support the view that African societies also experienced self-paced development prior to the colonial incursion. This provides contrary evidence to the misleading claims of justifiers and adherents of colonialism in Africa, who conceived the African continent as one comprising savage, uncultured, uncivilised and amoral/immoral societies. As Rodney (1981, p. 239) avers, indigenous African education was closely linked with traditional African social life. It was holistic in ensuring the physical, emotional and mental development of the African and, given its close links with African social life, was of direct and immediate relevance to societal challenges. It was formal and informal, formal at specific life stages and for specific purposes; informal in its lack of distinction between practical, daily and intellectual education (1981, p. 239). This was in sharp contrast to the colonial educational system which was formal in all its modes. Given the reality that pre-colonial African societies experienced self-paced developmental progress through their IKS, Afrocentric scholars argue that African perspectives on development must be harnessed to engender contemporary development (Ewane and Ajagbe 2018, p. 65). In precise terms – these African perspectives are to be found in African IKS.

It is trite to note that current models of development are patterned after Occidental realities. These models were implemented on African states with little or no considerations of the contexts, traditions, histories and situations of such African states. However, developmental realities, coupled with the tremendous progress that has been made in China and other Asian countries necessitate a rethink of these dominant models. The high economic growth experienced by China and the Asian Tigers in particular lend credence to the need to integrate IK systems with adopted models of development. Such adopted models are archetypally implemented as universalist models, and this rationale continues to inform and validate conceptualisations of development that equate it with economic and technological advancements as equitable to Western models of development. They also persist as standards for measuring African developmental progress, standing in that sense as non-African parameters to measure African progress and disregarding indigenous African parameters and Africa's self-paced developmental progress across African states (Falola 2005, p. 4; Iwara 2015, p. 120). In view of their failures and, in consideration of the developmental progress of countries that integrated their IKS with Western epistemic ones, these models must now be adapted and integrated with indigenous developmental models to meet the needs and concerns of the adopting country (Amtaika 2017, p. 19–20).

It is necessary to note at this juncture that the notion of development as one referring merely to economic indices is a reductionist one. It is reductionist in the sense that it limits the individual aspect of development, human good, solely to economic flourishing. That conception is fundamentally faulty. The human person comprises of different aspects, of which economic is one. Limiting development to a singular aspect in the reality of the existence of the human is therefore problematic as it ignores or downplays other aspects of the human person. To that extent, this research notes that authentic and sustainable development can only be achieved through a developmental model which not only recognises all aspects of the human, but also acknowledges the need for all aspects to experience improvement in the quality of living. As Anthony Akinwale avers:

> There is no development where the desires and potentials of the human person are unrealised because unduly stifled, and the desires and potentials of the human person by far exceed the range of the economy. The good of the order of humanity is not to be erroneously equated with the good of the economic order (Akinwale 2005, p. 2).

This critique, it must be noted, applies particularly to western concepts of development which emphasise economic and technological progress to which its educational system is geared/targeted. Development transcends the economic or technological aspect, involving full humanisation, the realisation of the need for human flourishing that is essential for other forms of social, political and economic growths. If the above rings true, that development must transcend economic indices to all other aspects of the human person, one is liable to argue that pre-colonial indigenous African epistemic systems evinced a model of such all-encompassing development. This is particularly true in the light of contemporary comparisons between pre-colonial and post-colonial epistemic systems. Kola Babarinde's comparison is apt for this purpose. Babarinde (2014) presents a comparative analysis detailing the different stages of education, gains and modes of transmission.

He acknowledges that the four Eurocentric educational stages have their counterparts in indigenous knowledge systems, but differentiates between the modes of transmitting knowledge as well as the gains and products of these two epistemic systems. Primary among the differences is that of pedagogy, where Eurocentric epistemic systems establish schools divorced from communities and taught using the banking system, a system that leaves no room for critical reflections and prioritises colonial gains while decrying traditional institutions and cultures (Babarinde 2014, p. 157). The Eurocentric colonial epistemic system resulted into ideological conditioning of students, and eventually, identity crises where the African graduate was neither fully African nor European but remained stranded between these cultures with their dissociation from their root cultures and their non-assimilation into western culture. The indigenous pedagogy on the other hand prioritised the knowledge of history and heritage andwas transmitted through practical methods that encouraged critical reflections and subsequently the honing of rational skills. These indigenous epistemic systems give rise to well-rounded citizens capable of meaningful contribution to societal development (Babarinde 2014, p. 160).

## 6 Decolonisation: A Proposal for the Repudiation of Epistemicide

Epistemic decolonisation implies a reflective and inflective exercise, a reflection on existent realities, and an inflective approach to what needs to be done. In this sense, it connotes at the initial start, the systematic critique and removal of biases (Wood 2020, p. 44). This exercise facilitates the diagnosis of challenges and supports critical analysis which enables insights into the solutions of such identified challenges. In Walter Mignolo's words:

> Epistemic decolonisation … is, in the first place, a constant set of processes in which *the means is the end*; and second, the steady set of process understood as epistemic decolonisation is not oriented toward "the deconstruction of Westernmetaphysics" but, rather … to uncovering the illusions of modernity, progress, and development by revealing its darker side, coloniality (Mignolo 2003, p. 456).

Reality is always viewed from particular perspectives. Knowledge is thus, dependent on the perspective from which the knower approaches, the perspective from which the known is known as objective and valid truth, within a paradigm of social reality. By implication, cultures give meaning to the world (Wartenberg 1990, p. 131). Extrapolating from this, education does not occur in a vacuum. The concepts utilised and transmitted during educational processes are derived from contexts/cultures/milieus from which they derive their meanings. As such, knowledge confers power on the knower –the knower assumes an infallible position with access to 'objective' knowledge. This is where the political nature of education comes to the fore, a deduction that is sufficiently analysed in Paulo Freire and Donaldo Macedo's *Literacy: Reading the Word and the World* (1987). Scholars must therefore take cognisance of the ideology driving contemporary educational systems, and must critically question prevalent knowledge hierarchies and epistemologies.

Questions to be asked include: Whose knowledge and whose ways of knowing are given priority? What role do educational institutions play in society? Who legitimises(ed) this role? What power structures result from these roles?

While Hall and Tandon (2017, p. 10) propose knowledge democracy, a phenomenon which recognises the multiplicity of epistemes, its constructions and creations, frameworks and the importance of access to knowledge, as a means of achieving justice and fairness in the epistemic frameworks of indigenous cultures (2017, p. 10), this research maintains that such concerns of justice and fairness can only be alleviated by a decolonisation process through which the epistemic heuristic hard core predominantly reflects African worldviews and concerns.

D. A. Wood identifies two strategies to epistemic decolonisation, the Differential and Revolutionary-socialist approaches (2020, p. 27). The Differential approach emphasises the restoration of the unique African IK systems as different and distinct from the colonisers. This approach is seen in the philosophical currents of poststructuralism, postcolonialism and liberation philosophy, all of which emphasise the notion of difference, and in that sense represent a revolt against globalism's 'sameness'/totalitarianism. This approach is however problematic – it ends up reinforcing what it previously condemned through its uncritical validation of dichotomous epistemes (2020, p. 56, 70).

The Revolutionary-socialist approach comprises ideologies that endorse Marxian-influenced radicalism. As exemplified by Fanonian socio-political ideas, it adopts a critical outlook to knowledge, one which leaves the knower free to explore different epistemes. As such, it presents as, paradoxically, a universalist outlook, one underpinned by the notion that truth, and therefore knowledge, is not the sole preserve of any episteme (2020, p. 104). This approach is in sharp contrast to the epistemic relativism of the Differential approach. While the latter calls for a return back to IK systems, the former recognises that:

> Decolonisation consists of those dialectical processes that undermine all possible and real colonialist realities (for example, structures, agents, actions, things, systems, functions, and mechanisms), thereby simultaneously reducing the quantity and quality of the ways in which said realities have been and/or continue to be colonised. The world comprises temporal struggles between realities that cannot but change through such conflicts. Every particular thing exists in systems of relations where, ontologically speaking, remaining the exact same overtime proves impossible…Since all realities constantly become something or someone new, the goal consists in directing oneself and the world around one toward novel and radically egalitarian alternatives (2020, p. 159).

Toeing the steps of Emmanuel Onyechere Osigwe Anyiam-Osigwe, Anthony Akinwale, Akhona Nkenkana, Louise du Toit and Azille Coetzee, this research advocates for a more inclusive notion of epistemic decolonisation, one which recognises that epistemic hegemonies are not limited to Eurocentric epistemes, but can also occur in African-centred epistemes. Such inclusivity acknowledges that the decolonisation process, while targeted at an epistemography that reflects African concerns, accepts sub- and super-alter disciplines and epistemes based on their usefulness. In this manner, it presents as an amalgam of both approaches in recognising that colonial legacies cannot be wished away, although their hegemonies can be nullified/overthrown.

Various theories have been proffered on practical ways to decolonise Africa's educational systems. These include Freire's 'Critical Pedagogy (CP)', Asante's 'Afrocentricism' and Chimakonam's B, C and D models (Freire 1993, 152–122; Asante 1998, 95; Chimakonam 2016, 514). This research suggests that Freire's CP, in conjunction with Chimakonam's B-model be adopted. The CP advocates that the learning process must be one in which the teacher stimulates the critical consciousness of the learner through a dialogical teaching method. This teaching method must involve the application of the teaching subjects to the learner's immediate environment to encourage a questioning attitude in the learner. Chimakonam's B-model advocates that the preponderance of western theories and ideas must be balanced by the inclusion of African theories and ideas such that there is a semblance of equality between them. This would result in a multi-, intercultural curriculum. In conjunction with the CP, this would open learners to a wide multiverse of ideas and knowledge systems, without undue preference for one or the other.

The weakness of this proposed synthethised mode of decolonising African educational systems lies in the weaknesses of the composing theories. Freire's CP, for example, has been criticised for its utopian and vague nature. Its exposition of the teacher-scholar role is particularly regarded as ambiguous and problematic – ambiguous in the sense that the teacher-scholar is both a facilitator and participant in the learning process; and problematic in its avoidance of the fact that the teacher-scholar is not an equal participant in this process (Ohliger 1995). In addressing these critiques, Akoleowo cites examples of how the CP has been successfully implemented to refute accusations of its utopian and vague nature, while also proffering Michael W. Apple's notion of scholar activism as a mode of resolving the ambiguity of the teacher-scholar's role and reducing the possibility of a subversion of the learning process (Apple 2011; Akoleowo 2021, 446–447). As such, she maintains that:

> The CP…informs of the need to rethink how scholars teach and transmit knowledge, with particular emphasis on the need to integrate local and international knowledge systems, with the local having primacy in the first instance, given its immediate understanding of and relevance to the community (2021, p. 446).

Chimakonam's B-model has also faced its own fair share of criticisms. Of primacy to this work is the criticism that scholars and students will be faced with the challenge of too many courses and texts in the immediacy as it involves the learning of two distinct perspectives to knowledge and a possible third perspective arising from the attempt to gauge/discover what lies between these distinct perspectives (Chimakonam 2016, pp. 520–521). In reaction to this critique, this chapter argues that this model is already in praxis in most African universities where scholars interrogate many subaltern realities. These scholars were trained in the western model of thought and are able to oscillate between this model and other subaltern model, as well as what may lie 'in-between.' Many students are also well-versed in understanding and utilising distinct and varying perspectives to knowledge. However, much of this praxis remains at the personal interest level – scholars teach themselves these varying perspectives which are then introduced to students during class discussions.

In the light of the above, we note that the weaknesses of the component models of decolonisation are not insurmountable. They can and have been resolved. A synthesis of these component theories would, therefore, result in an educational system premised on knowledge democracy; one where learners are introduced to varying knowledge perspectives through a dialogical system of learning where the knowledges acquired from these diverse perspectives can be of benefit to their immediate environment.

## 7 Conclusion

The central argument of this chapter is of twofolds. First, premised on the notion of development as local/personal, it has argued that contemporary models of development have failed in Africa. This failure is accredited to the fact that such models, regarded as universalist, fail to consider the contexts, traditions, histories and situations of African states, and as a result, lack the necessary in-depth knowledge for proffering solutions to developmental challenges experienced in Africa. Second, African educational systems as currently constituted, are alienated from African cultures, and can, therefore, not provide adequate responses to the developmental concerns of African states. Therefore, it is essential that these educational systems be deconstructed and reconstructed such that current Eurocentric epistemic hegemony is replaced with African-centered epistemes which identify Africa as the hard core of the episteme in the quest needed for epistemic justice and sustainable development.

## References

Akinwale, A.A. 2005. *Genealogy and wages of a detrimental preference*. Ibadan: Dominican Institute.

Akoleowo, V.O. 2021. Critical pedagogy, scholar activism and epistemic decolonisation. *South African Journal of Philosophy* 40 (4): 436–451. https://doi.org/10.1080/02580136.2021.2010175.

Amtaika, A. 2017. Socio-economic development theories in Africa: policies and realities. In *Socio-economic development in Africa: challenges and dimensions*, ed. A. Amtaika, 19–54. Austin: Pan-African University Press.

Apple, M.W. 2011. Paulo Freire, critical pedagogy and the tasks of the critical scholar. *Activist Revista e-Curriculum (Pontifícia Universida de Católica de São Paulo)* 7 (3): 1–21.

Asante, M.K. 1998. *The afrocentric idea*. Philadelphia: Temple University Press.

Babarinde, K. 2014. Education in pre-colonial, colonial and post-colonial Africa. In *Sustainable development in pre-colonial, colonial and post-colonial Africa*, ed. L. Popoola, O. Olaniyan, and O. Olayide, 155–164. Ibadan: University of Ibadan Centre for Sustainable Development.

Bako, S. 2005. *Universities, research and development in Nigeria: time for a paradigmatic shift*. Maputo: CODESRIA.

Chimakonam, J.O. 2016. Can the philosophy curriculum be Africanised? An examination of the prospects and challenges of some models of Africanisation. *South African Journal of Philosophy* 35 (4): 513–522.

Ekanola, A.B. 2012. MDGs and the neglect of Anyiam-Osigwe's third dimension of the human person: a bane of inclusive development in Africa. *Caribbean Journal of Philosophy* 4 (1): 1–17.

Ewane, F., and S. Ajagbe. 2018. Indigenous knowledge and the development debate in Africa. *International Journal of African Development* 5 (1): 64–81.

Falola, T., ed. 2005. *The dark webs: perspectives on colonialism in Africa*. Durham: Carolina Academic Press.

Fanon, F. 2004. *The wretched of the earth*. New York: Grove Press.

Freire, P. 1993. *Pedagogy of the oppressed*, 30th Anniversary Edition. New York: Continuum.

Freire, P., and D. Macedo. 1987. *Literacy: reading the word and the world*. 1st ed. Oxfordshire: Routledge and Kegan Paul Ltd.

Hall, B.L., and R. Tandon. 2017. Decolonization of knowledge, epistemicide, participatory research and higher education. *Research for All* 1 (1): 6–19. https://doi.org/10.18546/RFA.01.1.02.

Heleta, S. 2016. Decolonisation of higher education: dismantling epistemic violence and eurocentrism in South Africa. *Transformation in Higher Education* 1 (1): 1–8. https://doi.org/10.4102/the.v1i1.9.

Horsthemke, K. 2004. Indigenous knowledge: conceptions and misconceptions. *Journal of Education* 32: 31–48.

Hurst, H.R., and S. Owen, eds. 2005. *Ancient colonizations: analogy, similarity and difference*. London: Duckworth.

Iwara, E.I. 2015. Cultural hegemony and Africa's development process. *African Journal of Political Science and International Relations* 9 (4): 120–130. https://doi.org/10.5897/AJPSIR2014.0749.

Lyons, C.L., and J.K. Papadopoulos. 2002. Archaeology and colonialism. In *The archaeology of colonialism*, ed. C.L. Lyons and J.K. Papadopoulos, 1–23. Los Angeles: Getty Publications.

Mafeje, A. 2000. Africanity: a combative ontology. *CODESRIA Bulletin* 1: 66–71.

Manjapra, K. 2020. *Colonialism in global perspective*. Cambridge: Cambridge University Press.

Matasci, D., M.B. Jerónimo, and H.G. Dores. 2020. Introduction: historical trajectories of education and development in (post) colonial Africa. In *Education and development in colonial and postcolonial Africa: policies, paradigms, and entanglements, 1890s–1980s*, ed. D. Matasci, M.B. Jerónimo, and H.G. Dores, 1–28. Cham: Palgrave Macmillan.

Mazrui, A. 1979. Churches and multinationals in the spread of modern education: a third world perspective. *Third World Quaterly* 1: 30–49.

Mbembe, A. 2016. Decolonising the university: new directions. *Arts & Humanities in Higher Education* 15 (1): 29–45. https://doi.org/10.1177/1474022215618513.

McLean, I., and A. McMillan, eds. 2003. *Concise Oxford dictionary of politics*. 2nd ed. Oxford: Oxford University Press.

Mignolo, W.D. 2003. *The darker side of renaissance: literacy, territoriality and colonization*. Michigan: The University of Michigan Press.

———. 2011. *The darker side of western modernity: global futures, decolonial options*. Durham: Duke University Press.

Mignolo, W.D., and C.E. Walsh. 2018. *On decoloniality: concepts, analytics, praxis*. Durham\London: Duke University Press.

Ndlovu-Gatsheni, S.J. 2017. The emergence and trajectories of struggles for an 'African University': the case of unfinished business of african epistemic decolonization. *Kronos* 43 (1): 51–77.

Nkrumah, K. 1965. *Neo-colonialism: the last stage of imperialism*. London: Thomas, Nelson & Sons Ltd.

Nzimiro, I. 2011. Feudalism in Nigeria. In *Towards a marxist anthropology*, ed. S. Diamond, 337–364. Berlin\New York: De Gruyter Mouton.

Ohliger, J. 1995. *Critical views of Paulo Freire's works, compiled for Iowa Community College summer seminar*. Madison: Basic Choices, Inc.

Oloruntoba, S.O., A. Afolayan, and O. Yacob-Haliso. 2020. Introduction: African knowledges, decolonization and alternative futures. In *Indigenous knowledge systems and development in Africa*, ed. S.O. Oloruntoba, A. Afolayan, and O. Yacob-Haliso, 1–14. Cham: Palgrave Macmillan.

Ozturk, I. 2001. The role of education in economic development: a theoretical perspective. *Journal of Rural Development and Administration* XXXIII (1): 39–47. https://doi.org/10.2139/ssrn.1137541.

Reyes, G.E. 2001. Four main theories of development: modernization, dependency, world-system, and globalization. *Nómadas. Revista Crítica de Ciencias Sociales y Jurídicas* 4 (2): 1–16.

Rodney, W. 1981. *How Europe underdeveloped Africa.* Revised ed. Washington D.C: Howard University Press.

Santos, Bde S. 2007. Beyond abyssal thinking: from global lines to ecologies of knowledges. *Review* XXX (1): 45–89. https://doi.org/10.4324/9781315634876-14.

———. 2014. Epistemologies of the south: justice against epistemicide. Oxon: Routledge.

———. 2016. Epistemologies of the south and the future. *From the European South* 1: 17–29.

Sarnowsky, J. 2013. British isles, medieval colonization. In *The encyclopedia of global human migration*, ed. I. Ness, 1–8. Hoboken: Blackwell Publishing Ltd.

Spivak, G.C. 1994. Can the Subaltern speak? In *Colonial discourse and post-colonial theory: a reader*, ed. P. Williams and L. Chrisman, 1st ed., 66–111. New York: Harvester/Wheatsheaf.

wa Thiong'o, N. 1986. *Decolonising the mind: the politics of language in African literature*. London: James Currey Ltd.

Wartenberg, T. 1990. *The forms of power: from domination to transformation*. Philadelphia: Temple University Press.

Wiredu, K. 1998. Toward decolonizing African philosophy and religion. *African Studies Quarterly* 1 (4): 17–46.

———. 2004. Introduction: African philosophy in our time. In *A companion to African Philosophy*, ed. K. Wiredu, 1–27. Oxford: Blackwell Publishing Ltd.

Wood, D.A. 2020. *Epistemic decolonization; a critical investigation into the anticolonial politics of knowledge*. Cham: Palgrave Macmillan.

**Victoria Openif'Oluwa Akoleowo** holds a doctorate in Philosophy from the University of Ibadan. She is a Senior Lecturer at the Department of Philosophy and Religious Studies, Dominican University, Ibadan, Nigeria, as well as Coordinator of the Philosophy Unit of the same department. She is also an Associate Lecturer at Saints Peter and Paul Major Seminary, Ibadan. Her teaching and research interests include African Philosophy, Feminist Philosophy, Philosophy of Education, and Business and Professional Ethics. She has widely published in these areas.

# Part VII
# Politics and African Development

# “A Model Without Plenty”? A Critical Assessment of the “Winner Takes All” Concept in Zimbabwean Politics 1980–2021

**James Hlongwana**

**Abstract** Zimbabwe’s governance system between 1980 and 2021 has been characterised by politics of inclusivity and exclusivity with attendant economic and political consequences. The economic blizzards which bit Zimbabwe after 2000 receded following the establishment of a government of national unity in 2009.The promising situation was by no means an outcome of fortuity, but a consequence of the competent hand of inclusive politics at the wheel of governance that facilitated speedy recovery. In spite of ZANU-PF’s celebration of the 2013 and 2019 general election victories and rule under the guidance of the“winner- takes- all” model, this article argues that Zimbabwe has not seen an improvement in its economic and political fortunes. On the contrary it has experienced resurgence in liquidity crunch, unprecedented unemployment, introduction of a surrogate currency and street demonstrations. In this regard, the paper argues that Zimbabwean politics and economics have gone into the doldrums. In view of the challenges emanating from the “winner- takes- all” political paradigm, the paper advocates the adoption of coalition democracy in Zimbabwe because it will arguably promote national unity and macro-economic fundamentals that favour economic development.

**Keywords** Coalition · Democracy · Development · Election · Model · Winner

## 1 Introduction

The “winner- takes- all” model is a political paradigm in which the party that garners the highest number of votes in an election solely forms a government (Miller 2009). The aim of this political system is to create a manufactured majority in order to produce an effective working parliamentary majority for the government while at

J. Hlongwana (✉)
Department of History, Archaeology and Development Studies, Great Zimbabwe University, Masvingo, Zimbabwe



B. Okyere-Manu et al. (eds.), *Contemporary Development Ethics from an African Perspective*, Philosophy and Politics - Critical Explorations 27,
https://doi.org/10.1007/978-3-031-32898-5_16

the same time overshadowing small political parties (Norris 1977). It can be argued that the focus of the proponents of this model is efficient governance not representation of all minority views. Also, the argument proffered in favour of this political system is that the leading parties in parliament and government are able to implement their policies without the need to engage in post-election negotiations with coalition partners. In this regard, cabinet can pass legislations without contestation from members of the opposition political parties during their term of office (Gilens and Benjamin 2014).

This article discusses the applicability of the "winner- talks- all" model in Zimbabwe's political environment. Further, the paper views coalition democracy as an alternative political paradigm for Zimbabwe. The article is a product of a multi-pronged methodological approach that was used to collect data. Interviews with informants were conducted to ensure that this study captured experiences and thoughts about the Zimbabwean political dilemma. To solicit data from the interviewees, personal semi-structured questions were asked (Kale 2002). This was through qualitative research interviews which placed emphasis on the interviewee's thoughts. Further, textual analysis of sources such as books, theses, journal articles and other sources was undertaken to compliment the aforementioned sources. The data was subsequently analysed qualitatively.

## 2 Theoretical Underpinning

This article is given shape and impetus by Liberalism Theory and *Ubuntu* ethics. The argument advanced by liberalism theory is that maldistribution of power causes conflict which in the end undermines human flourishing in the society (Keohane 1991). The theory is desirable not because it reflects human environment but because it is the political configuration mainly suitable to providing solutions to economic and political challenges bedevilling human society (Homes 1984). According to the liberal thought, human society is made up of individuals whose conduct is motivated by interests and endeavour to form individual organisations to promote their political ambitions. In this context, politics simultaneously restrains and advances the purpose and possibilities of governments (Haas 1964). Closely related to the above in terms of rendering theoretical relevance to the paper is the *Ubuntu* ethics. *Ubuntu* defines a person in terms of his relationship with other people in the society (Forster 2007) where observance of communal ethos of African culture is central to the survival of the community. In this regard, the enhancement of the traditional African ethics would curb conflicts and ultimately promote development in the society (Nicolson 2008). However, it is important to note that the *ubuntu* ethics has been undermined by colonialism which worsened ethnic differences in Africa (Van der Merwe1996). Consequently, *ubuntu* ethics has been made to function in homogenous indigenous communities(ibid). Commenting on the failure by political players to adopt power sharing practices to achieve stable societies, Manning argued that disproportionate accrual and exercise of power destroys political equilibrium thereby ushering an era of disharmony in society (Manning 1976). What emerges from the above discussion is that the stability of the state is a consequence of a balanced relationship between or among political parties which influence the country's political order. Some of the insights which have been raised in this section will be integrated in the discussion below.

## 3 The Winner- Takes- All Model and Its Problems in Zimbabwe

The winner- takes- all model was used in colonial Rhodesia and later adopted by the Zimbabwean government after the 1985, 2013 and 2019 elections respectively. After the 2013 general elections which ended the era of a Government of National Unity in Zimbabwe, ZANU-PF under Robert Mugabe, guided by the winner- takes-all model, excluded the MDC formations from central government despite their control of a significant number of seats in the country (Biti 2014). In spite of the compelling arguments in support of the paradigm, the model's professed virtues have hardly engendered political and economic stability in Zimbabwe since 2013. Zimbabwe, in its current state, is a country that needs reconciliation and national healing to stop further polarisation and ultimately to achieve economic prosperity (Simango 2021). Since 2013 when ZANU PF re-assumed sole control of the Zimbabwean state, the economy has been performing badly and there are fears that the economy could be heading towards a recession. The generality of the Zimbabwean society are slowly losing hope in government's ability to turn around the country's economic fortunes (Danje 2021). Mass dissatisfaction with the country's leadership in politics and economics has steadily gone up since 2013, thereby reversing the positive trend of the power -sharing period between 2009 and 2013. In this instance the growing displeasure is directed at the ruling ZANU PF party and its members. The general impression emerging is that the government seems to be running out of ideas to stem the unfolding economic crisis which has left many living from hand to mouth (Muchenje 2021). Analysts argue that there has been no sign of economic revival since the beginning of the Second Republic (Tukuza 2019). If anything, the general populace is going through the pain of severe inflation with prices going up almost on daily basis. This has pushed some retailers and service providers to demand payment in the United States dollars or pegging prices against parallel market foreign currency rates, thus driving prices beyond what many ordinary people can afford (Sithole 2020).

Also, the country witnessed a resurgence of long queues at filling stations amid increases in the price of fuel at the pump (Chidoko 2018). The fuel shortage is attributed to limited foreign currency reserves in the country. Further, several companies have been liquidated since the advent of the Second Republic in 2017, throwing thousands of people out of employment (Zvinoira 2019). The company closures are happening at a time when the economy is facing several challenges, including debilitating liquidity crunch, low capacity utilisation and lack of cheap financing among other constraints. Indeed, the situation in Zimbabwe in 2020 was reminiscent of the 2008 socio-economic environment prior to the signing of the Government of National unity in 2009.The analysis relates closely with the argument advanced by the liberal theorists that governance which is devoid of inclusive politics compromises stability and development (Keohane 1991). It is against this background that the paper interrogates the usefulness of the "winner- takes- all" model.

## 4 Towards a Coalition Democracy

Coalitions have been defined as a collection of government parties (Busse 1999). Office-seeking and spatial ideological convergence have been proffered as the major reasons for coalition formations (ibid). Office-seeking parties endeavour to form an alliance of parties with a minimum number of seats over the majority in the legislature (Robert 1984). In this regard, the party with the highest number of seats in parliament will dictate the political direction that the country takes and office seeking politicians sheepishly support policy pronouncements by the majority government. However, it has been noted that coalition governments are also a result of spatial ideological convergence. Here, parties create coalitions with ideologically 'closest' partners. In these 'spatial proximity' paradigms, policy interests rather office-seeking motivates coalition formation (Michael 1990). While unstable coalitions have been seen in countries such as Italy, Belgium, Poland and others, by and large coalition democracy has diminished internal political strife, for example in countries such as Germany, Israel, Finland and many other countries in Western Europe (Pridharm 1987). Therefore, political stability is a result of constant compromise and avoidance of contentious policies by coalition partners. It can thus be argued that economic development in the aforesaid countries is inextricably linked to coalition democracy- induced national unity.

Joint governance has been practised in Zimbabwe since the colonial period. Rather than the "winner takes all" model in which the party that obtains the highest number of votes assumes sole administration of the country (Liu and Wu 1997), supporters of coalition democracy argue that other considerations are more important in governance, including the fairness of the outcome for minor parties which are not excluded from the governance of the country (Norris 1977).

As a result of the guerrilla war which had started in 1966 and had escalated to affect every aspect of life in Rhodesia, Ian Smith, then Prime Minister, devised a strategy to stop the war by engaging politicians who were based in Rhodesia. This consideration led to the 1978 general elections which culminated in the country being renamed Zimbabwe-Rhodesia. The elections pitted Abel Muzorewa of the United African Council, Reverend Ndabaningi Sithole of ZANU, Sithole and Chief Chirau of Zimbabwe United People's Organisation (Hull 1978). In an effort to accommodate the political parties that participated in the elections, the Internal Settlement partners adopted proportional representation as the country's guiding model. The agreement was called the "internal settlement' to emphasise that it had been reached with moderate African nationalist leaders inside Rhodesia as opposed to the militant Patriotic Front movements under Robert Mugabe and Joshua Nkomo who were the leading guerrilla combatants against the Rhodesian government from Mozambique and Zambia (Ngara 1978). However, it soon emerged that the aim of the political agreement was to entrench white minority rule in Rhodesia by co-opting fringe African politicians in a government in which whites continued to exercise enormous political power. Because the "Internal Settlement" excluded key players in the Zimbabwean question, it did not usher an era of stability; the liberation war escalated leading to the Lancaster House Conference of 1979 where the Rhodesian belligerents agreed to stop fighting in preparation for independence in 1980.

Also, inclusive politics were pursued in the 1980 independence general elections as a strategy to manage a polarised society (Sithole and Makumbe 1997). Robert Mugabe, in the interest of promoting national unity, announced a policy of reconciliation and assured the nation that whatever government he would form would adhere to the letter and spirit of the constitution and would respect the rule of law (Machakacha 2010). In the spirit of reconciliation, Mugabe formed a government of national unity and his cabinet had ministers from Joshua Nkomo's ZAPU and Ian Smith's Rhodesian Front (Tshuma 1997). The Policy of Reconciliation and the government of national unity were dictated by the desire to achieve stability in a country that was emerging from war and to dispel whatever fears the white community might have had about the new political order in Zimbabwe (Massiwa and Chigejo 2003). Since colonial policies had made the Rhodesian economy an appendage of foreign and white capital and to encourage white Zimbabweans to remain in the country, it was essential to assure them that the sins of the past would not be visited upon them under the new dispensation. As a result of inclusive politics, Zimbabwe experienced economic prosperity during the early days of independence.

Further, an interparty unity agreement was signed in 1987 between ZANU and ZAPU in order to stop a dissident war in Matebeleland and the Midlands provinces. By 1987, the war had claimed approximately 20,000 lives and some politicians, for example Ian Smith, put the figure at 30000 (Smith 1997). The Ndebele were arguably targeted for killing because they were suspected of supporting and harbouring the dissidents (Mahaka 2018). In relation to the above argument, it has been opined that Gukurahundi was Mugabe's creation to liquidate Joshua Nkomo's ZIPRA as it posed a serious post war security threat. Mugabe's failure to condemn the massacres gave credence to the school of thought that it was a genocidal war for ZANU PF's political expediency. Furthermore, Mugabe's complicity in the conflict is vindicated by the deployment of the Shona- speaking North Korean trained 5$^{th}$Brigade in Matabeleland and Midlands provinces. This lends weight to the allegation that the military operation was a decoy by Mugabe to engage in ethnic cleansing and achieve hegemonic political control. It is further postulated that the ethnic dimension was used by Mugabe to achieve wider political imperatives of a socialist one-party state (Moyo and Mazuru 2012). However, Mugabe is known for having described the Gukurahundi period as "a moment of madness", a tacit acceptance that what transpired was uncalled for and unacceptable. Nevertheless, implicit in the above assertion is the argument that the instability in the two provinces should be explained in terms of Mugabe's blunders. Without shooting down the credibility of the foregoing analysis, this paper argues that it is morally and historically wrong to blame Mugabe alone for the outbreak of the post-independence war. Based onNkomo's reaction to the post- independence political arrangements, this study asserts that Nkomo cannot be exonerated from culpability in the post liberation war crisis. Had he accepted the post of president which was eventually given to Canaan Banana, ZIPRA combatants and the entire Ndebele population could have warmed towards the Mugabe government in 1980 and prevented the risk of civil war that was witnessed (Hlongwana et al. 2012). However, his refusal meant that something was wrong and consequently former ZIPRA cadres and the Ndebele people in general got ruffled, thereby increasing the possibilities for conflict. However, it is important to note that the conflict in Matebeleland and Midlands was not resolved militarily but diplomatically. The former war allies, after protracted negotiations, resolved to bury the hatchet and formed a government of national unity. The immediate result of the agreement was the cessation of hostilities in the southern and western regions of Zimbabwe.

Zimbabwe also embraced a government of national unity in 2009 following a political crisis that was caused by the disputed 2008 Presidential Elections in which the late Morgan Tsvangirai, the leader of the Movement for Democratic Change (MDC), claimed to have been robbed of victory by the now late Robert Mugabe. Conflict escalated when Morgan Tsvangirai withdrew from the presidential re-run citing unprecedented levels of violence and intimidation in the race. Justifying his decision to withdraw his candidature from the presidential race, Tsvangirai argued that the political situation had become so dangerous that it was no longer possible to hold a credible election (Hlongwana and Muguti 2016). The resulting political stalemate prompted SADC and AU to find a solution to the Zimbabwean crisis. Consequently, Thabo Mbeki, the then President of South Africa, was tasked with mediation in the Zimbabwean problem. After prolonged negotiations, a Government of National Unity was established with Mugabe as the executive President and Tsvangirai as the Prime minister. Remarkably, the Government of National Unity brought peace and socio-economic stability in the country. Rival political parties, in the spirit of reconciliation and rebuilding Zimbabwe, worked together especially in the historic constitution- making process. The economy dramatically recovered following the adoption of the United States dollar as a unit of exchange in the country (Muguti et al. 2012). It can thus be argued that Zimbabwe has in the past successfully experimented with coalition democracy.

## 5 Coalition Democracy as a 'Magic Wand' for Zimbabwe

Given the fact that each time this country resorts to power sharing it experiences political stability and prosperity, this study proposes that Zimbabwe should embrace coalition democracy as its political model.

The main quality invoked by the admirers of coalition democracy is that it promotes electoral justice as it allows representation of all shades of opinion and ensures the smaller parties' representation in parliament and government (Chitauro 2021). Drawing evidence from the 2009 Government of National Unity where the MDC formations had representation in parliament and the executive, one can argue that this arrangement engendered a sense of national unity across the country. In that regard, inclusivity guarded against the possibility of wasted votes which has been cited as the underlying cause of voter apathy in Zimbabwe. Citizens contribute to forming a government and an opposition and confer legitimacy to governors who will represent their interests and preferences when they vote (Chitauro 2021). Thus, the elections are not just a race that some gain at the expense of others but a means by which voters participate in creating a representative authority (Cincea 2013). In accordance with coalition democracy, power is dispersed in parliament which means that all groups in society will exert influence on policy making at all levels (ibid). The supporters of such parties, especially finding their own positions reflected in those articulated by elected members of deliberative bodies are more motivated to take part in electoral politics.

(Miller 2009). This analysis resonates well with the common good approach concept which regards individuals as part of a larger community. Such political accommodation promotes solidarity (Wiredu 1998) and the determination to work together for the development of the community.

Many political scientists have argued that coalition democracy is not only more democratic than the "winner takes all" but it is also an effective mechanism for managing and accommodating ethnic and other cleavages in plural societies (Horowitz 1983) as is the case in Zimbabwe. For example, voting patterns in Zimbabwe since independence in 19 80 have shown that the electorate's choice is informed by ethnic and class interests (Sithole and Makumbe 1997). The Ndau in south eastern Zimbabwe and the Ndebele in the southern region have tended to be influenced by tribalism in voting. Even Mugabe who ruled Zimbabwe for 37 years benefitted from the majority Shona tribal group in Zimbabwe. The Ndau, for example, have repeatedly shown dislike for ZANU PF by voting into parliament politicians from the opposition and from their own ethnic political party (Zhavairo 2021). One notable politician who was elected into the legislature ahead of ZANU PF candidates was Reverend Ndabaningi Sithole. It is important to note that the failure to win the Chipinge parliamentary seat derailed ZANU PF's idea to create a one-party state in Zimbabwe (Moyo 2014). The reasons for the popularity of the late Ndabaningi Sithole were varied: he belonged to the Ndau ethnic group and also, he was the founding President of the Zimbabwe African National Liberation Army (ZANLA), a military wing of ZANU which successfully fought against the Rhodesia government. Furthermore, the Ndau who accused Robert Mugabe of high jacking the liberation struggle from its founding father, Sithole, would not vote Mugabe's ZANU PF party into the legislature (Kadembo 2008). ZANU PF's determination to beat Sithole in the political race was evidenced by the careful selection and deployment of respected individuals from Chipinge district such as William Ndangana, a former guerrilla commander, Chief Musikavanhu, Dr. Vhuso Moyana, a historian and ambassador and several other accomplished Ndau men to compete with Sithole in every parliamentary election. However, the Ndau electorate consistently elected Ndabaningi Sithole into parliament much to the chagrin of ZANU PF (Laakso 2004). It is postulated that in response to the defeats that were handed over to ZANU PF by the Ndau people in Chipinge, the ZANU PF government got frustrated and shelved developmental projects including vibrant land redistribution exercise in Chipinge district (Mutondoro et al. 2016).

Similarly, the Ndebele people in Matabeleland, the southern region of Zimbabwe, have demonstrated since independence in 1980 voting patterns which are influenced by tribalism. From the late Joshua Nkomo ZAPU, to the revived version of the party under Dumiso Dabengwa to Weshman Ncube's MDC, there remains a reading of local politics through an ethnocentric prism in spite of protestations by the beneficiaries of ethnic politics in the region (Phiri 2019). Related to the above argument, Joshua Nkomo, prior to joining ZANU PF, used to win all seats in Matebeleland (Sithole and Makumbe 1997). In addition to being influenced by ethnic nationalism, the Ndebele have issues to settle with the ZANU PF- led government ranging from Mugabe's proposal for one man one vote in the 1980 which gave him advantage over Nkomo, the Gukurahundi question to the marginalisation of the Ndebele region by Mugabe's administration (Janssen and Meldrum 2018).

Also, Zimbabwean electorate is divided between rural and urban. Rural areas are predominantly ZANU PF while urbanites have demonstrated their support for the MDC since its formation in 1999 (Motsi 2018). It is important to note that in an agrarian economy the land is an important means of production and those who seem to subscribe more to the interests of the peasant communities are guaranteed of the rural vote. In relation to the foregoing analysis, Boone and Wahman refer to rural areas as captive constituencies for incumbent regimes (Boone and Wahman 2013). Accordingly, the much- hyped 'Command Agriculture', Presidential inputs scheme and, indeed, the land reform are all meant to increase ZANU PF's popularity in the country side (Chidoko). Moreover, ZANU PF carefully reminds rural folks of their heroic participation in the liberation struggle and that it was them (rural communities) who bore the brunt of the war. The communities in fact provided intelligence, food, shelter and different forms of assistance to the liberation combatants. This comradeship is shrewdly manipulated by ZANU PF to win votes. .

While rural communities tend to gravitate towards ZANU PF, urbanites support the MDC-Alliance. Economic challenges as a result of the adoption ofthe Economic Structural Adjustment Programme (ESAP) in 1991 were the major cause of concern in urban areas (Maposa et al. 2010). The country's economy fell following the post-independence massive social policies in education and heath which constituted a serious burden on the treasury (Mlambo 1997). The resulting poor economic performance compelled the Zimbabwean government to borrow money from the World Bank (Willems 2004). However, the implementation of ESAP boomeranged as it produced unintended consequences such as shortages of basic commodities, closure of industries and loss of jobs (Mlambo 1997). Resultantly, the ZANU PF led government became unpopular especially amongst urban people whose savings had been eroded by inflation (Brett 2017). Also, the government's participation in the Democratic Republic of the Congo (DRC) War in 1998 and the payment of War Veterans' gratuities which had been unbudgeted for further caused inflation in the country (Vehnamaki 2001). While the economy was performing poorly and the government seemed to lack a solution to the country's quagmire, there arose an opposition political party, the Movement for Democratic Change (MDC) in 1999 which promised to revive the economy. These developments compelled the ZANU PF led government to adopt a radical land policy in order to win support from landless peasants. Again, as alluded earlier, these government policies further destroyed economic achievements which the ZANU PF led government had posted in the first decade of independence. Thus, the urban population saw salvation in the MDC forming a government in Zimbabwe.

Another important virtue of coalition democracy is that it is most suitable for societies which are in the process of developing a democratic culture (Moyo 1992). Western liberal democracy is a relatively new phenomenon and therefore the adoption of coalition democracy presents a chance for people to participate in electoral processes without the fear of losing to dominant political parties or to vote rigging. While liberation struggle war fighters promised democracy, at independence in 1980, however, they became reluctant to surrender their hard won independence to democracy arguing that it was the gun that brought independence and not the pen (Mail& Guardian 2008). The determination hedge against democracy was also given a boost by bi-polar politics of the time which gave rise to authoritarian leadership in Africa, Zimbabwe included. Under these circumstances, this paper argues that participation in opposition political activity was akin to subversion as political opponents were targeted for victimisation as evidenced by the cases of Zimbabwe's violence during the 2002 and 2008 general elections (Hlongwana and Muguti 2016). Consequently, Zimbabwe has not only witnessed imperfect political representation in governance but also concentration of power in one political party and, undeniably, state capture which has undermined economic development. This lends credence to the liberal argument that there is a close link between democracy and prosperity (Moravcsik 1992). What emerges from the above discussion is that collective governance engenders a sense nationhood which, in the final analysis, will become a seed bed for conditions which nourish humanity.

## 6 Conclusion

This paper attempted to critique the “winner- takes- all” model in the context of Zimbabwe’s political environment. The model was defined and its universal virtues were highlighted as well. One of the arguments presented in favour of this paradigm is that elections are decisive mechanisms to elect office bearers and those elected enjoy substantive power to implement policies on behalf of citizens. However, it emerged that the model is fraught with weaknesses and as such it was cited as one the underlying causes of instability in ‘young democracies’ such as Zimbabwe. Related to this assertion is the argument that Zimbabwe under the guidance of this model has experienced unprecedented levels of corruption, unemployment, inflation, poor service delivery and loss of confidence in the country’s leadership. Concomitantly, disillusionment has led to sporadic mass street demonstrations which have resulted in the loss of life and property. It is against this background that the paper proposed the adoption of coalition democracy to be the guiding political model for Zimbabwe. In contrast, proponents of coalition democracy argue that the electoral system should promote processes of conciliation and coalition- building within parties above a minimum threshold of who should be included in parliament in rough proportion to their level of electoral support. As a result, the composition of parliament reflects the main divisions in the social composition of the electorate so that all citizens have voices articulating their interests in the legislature. In this regard, parties in government craft policies based on a consensus among the coalition partners. An important plus for coalition democracy is the fact that it reduces the number of wasted votes as all votes are considered and this leads to a fair allocationof votes obtained by the competing candidates and the percentage of assigned seats. Therefore, even though it generates an assortment of parliamentary parties, coalition democracy has a series of advantages that largely compensate for the deficiencies and which bring it closer to the ideal of electoral equity. In this view the “winner takes all” over- rewards the ‘winner’, producing an elected dictatorship where the government can implement its programmes without the need for consultation and compromise with other parties in parliament. The most compelling virtues of coalition democracy include the ability to cater for political diversity, motivate citizens to participate in electoral processes and ultimately engender a sense of national unity. In summation, the paper argues that coalition democracy will be a panacea to Zimbabwe’s political and socio-economic ills.

## References

Biti, T. 2014. *Rebuilding Zimbabwe: lessons from a Coalition government*. Centre For Global Development.

Boone, C., and M. Wahman. 2013. Unequal representation in single member district elections. *Paper presented for presentation at the annual meeting of european consortium for political research*. Bordeaux, September 4–7.

Brett, E.A. 2017. *State failure and success in Uganda and Zimbabwe: the logic of political decay and reconstruction in Africa*. Crisis states research centre working paper no 78, p. 76.

Busse, A.R. 1999. Coalition formation and regime divide in Central Europe. *Working paper series* No. 5 November.
Chidoko, M. 2018. Interview. Mashava, Masvingo, Zimbabwe, May 15.
Chitauro, Z. 2021. Interview. Mbizo, Kwekwe, Zimbabwewe, June 20.
Cincea, E. 2013. Proportionality or majoritarianism? In search of electoral equity. *Epoca* 11 (8).
Danje, L. 2021. Interview. Great Zimbabwe University, Masvingo, Zimbabwe, May 15.
Doran, S. 2019. Mugabe complicity in Gukurahundi. *Newsday*, May 18.
Forster, D. 2007. Identity in relationship: the ethics of ubuntu as an answer to the impasse of individual consciousness. In *The impact of knowledge systems on human development in Africa*, ed. C.W. Du Toit. Pretoria: Research Institute for Theology and Religion.
Gilens, M., and I. Benjamin. 2014. Testing theories of American politics: Elites, interest groups and average citizens. *American Political Science Association* 12 (3): 564–581.
Haas, E.B. 1964. *Beyond the Nation State: functionalism and international organisation*. Stanford: Stanford University Press.
Hlongwana, J., and T. Muguti. 2016. Mere paper covering the cracks? The case of South Africa's mediation role in Zimbabwe 2008–2013. In *Myths of peace and democracy? Powers building pillars of hope, unity and transformation in Africa*, ed. M. Mawere and N. Marongwe, 195–229. Oxford: Langaa Books.
Hlongwana, J., R.S. Maposa, and T. Moyo. 2012. Sithole, Nkomo, Muzorewa and the birth of Zimbabwe: a reconsideration of autobiography as a literary mode of national history. In *African cultures and literatures*, ed. G. Collier, vol. 41, 321–339. New York: Matatu.
Homes, S. 1984. *Benjamin constant and the making of liberalism*. New Haven: Yale University Press.
Horowitz, D. 1983. Democracy in divided societies. *Journal of Democracy* 4 (4): 12–19.
Hull, G. 1978. The political economy of Zimbabwe. Implications for internal settlement. *Africa Today* 25 (2): 27–44.
Janssen, B., and A. Meldrum. 2018. Zimbabwe's Matabeleland massacre haunts monday's elections. *Associated Presstime*, July 28.
Kadembo, E. 2008. Dynamic positioning for survival in political marketing warfare Mugabe's manoeuvrings out of crises in Zimbabwe. *Journal of Politics and Law* 1 (1): 21–32.
Kale, D. 2002. *Interviews*. London: Sage Publications.
Keohane, R.O. 1991. International liberalism reconsidered. In *Economic identity to modern politics*, ed. J. Dunn, 78–89. Cambridge: Cambridge University Press.
Laakso, L. 2004. Opposition politics in independent Zimbabwe. *African Studies Quarterly* 7 (2&3): 1–19.
Liu, E., and J. Wu. 1997. Report on proportional representation, provisional legislative council. *Secretariat Research and Library Service Division*.
Machakacha, P. 2010. national healing and reconciliation in Zimbabwe: challenges and opportunities. Zimbabwe monograph series no. 1.
Mahaka, B. 2018. MDC alliance invokes sithole's name in Chipinge. *Daily News*, July 15.
Mail & Guardian. 2008. Zim 2008 election taken by Gun, Not Pen. August 10.
Manning, D.J. 1976. *Liberalism*. New York: St Martin's Press.
Maposa, R.S., J. Hlongwana, and D. Gamira. 2010. Aluta Continua ?: A critical reflection on the Chimurenga within third Chimurenga among the Ndau people in Chipinge district of South-Eastern Zimbabwe. *Journal of African Studies and Development* 2 (6): 192–200.
Massiwa, M., and O. Chigejo. 2003. *The Agrarian reform in Zimbabwe: sustainability and empowerment of rural communities*. Harare: IDS University of Zimbabwe.
Michael, L. 1990. Government coalition and intraparty politics. *BJPS*: 489–507.
Miller, J. 2009. Does proportional representation boost turnout? A political knowledge-based examination. Working paper presented at the comparative study of electoral systems conference, University of Toronto, September 6.
Mlambo, A.S. 1997. *The economic structural adjustment programme: the case of Zimbabwe 1990–1995*. Harare: University of Zimbabwe Publications.
Moravcsik, A. 1992. Liberalism and international relations theory. *Centre for European Studies*. Paper no. 92-6.
Motsi, C. 2018. Why rural vote is heart, soul of Zimbabwean democracy. *The Herald*, September 20.

Moyo, J. 1992. *Voting for democracy: electoral politics in Zimbabwe*. Harare: University of Zimbabwe Publications.
Moyo, S. 2014. Regime survival strategies in Zimbabwe after independence. *Journal of International Relations and Foreign Politics* 2 (1): 32–43.
Moyo, T., F. Sibanda, and M. Mazuru. 2012. Angles of telling on reality: representations of the Gukurahundi period in selected Zimbabwean Fiction in Shona, Ndebele and English. In *African cultures and literatures*, ed. G. Collier, 45–53. New York: Matau.
Muchenje, F. 2021. Interview. Great Zimbabwe University, Masvingo, Zimbabwe, May 15.
Muguti, T., B. Tavuyanago, and J. Hlongwana. 2012. Untenable marriages: situating governments of national unity in Africa's political landscape since 2000. *International Journal of Developing Societies* 1 (4): 149–158.
Mutondoro, F., K.M. Chiweshe, and R. Gaidzanwa. 2016. *The intersection of women, land and corruption in Zimbabwe: case study of women in Chisumbanje and Chinyamukwakwa villages in Zimbabwe*. Transparency International Zimbabwe.
Ngara, J. 1978. The Zimbabwe revolution and the internal settlement. *Marxism Today*.
Nicolson, R. 2008. Introduction. In *Persons in community: African ethics in a global culture*, ed. R. Nicolson. Scottsville: University of Kwazulu Natal Press.
Norris, P. 1977. Proportional, majoritarian and mixed systems for contrasting political institutions. *Special Issue of the International Political Science Review* 18 (3): 297–312.
Phiri, M. 2019. Ethnic politics on the Zimbabwean Campaign Trail: do voters really care. *African Argumentation*, February 19.
Pridharm, G. 1987. Coalition behaviour and party systems in western Europe: a comparative approach. *Parliamentary Affairs* 40 (7): 374–387.
Robert, A. 1984. *The evolution of cooperation*. New York: Basic Books.
Sibanda, G. 2019. Expanding economy driving fuel demand. *The Herald*, March 11.
Simango, M. 2021. Interview. Gwenzi, Chipinge, Zimbabwe, May 2.
Sithole, P. (2020) 'Addressing inflation: consumer watchdog'. Newsday, June 19.
Sithole, M., and J. Makumbe. 1997. Elections in Zimbabwe: the ZANU PF hegemony and its incipient political system. *African Journal of Political Science* 2 (1): 118–129.
Smith, I. 1997. *Bitter harvest: the great betrayal and the dreadful aftermath*. London: Blake.
Tshuma, L. 1997. *A matter of (In) justice: law, state and the agrarian question in Zimbabwe*. Harare: SAPES Books.
Tukuza, P. 2019. Confidence levels plummet. *Daily news*, May 4.
Van der Merwe, W.L. 1996. Philosophy and the multi-cultural context of (post) apartheid South Africa. *Ethical Perspectives* 3 (2): 1–15.
Vehnamaki, M. 2001. Diamonds and warlords: the geography of war in The Democratic Republic of the Congo and Sierra Leone. *Nordic Journal of African Studies* 11 (1): 48–74.
Willems, W. 2004. Peasant demonstrators, violent invaders: representations of land in Zimbabwe. *World Development* 32 (10): 1771–1779.
Wiredu, K. 1998. Democracy and consensus in African traditional politics: a plea for a non-party polity. In *Philosophy from Africa*, ed. P.H. Coetzeu and A.P.J. Rou. Johannesburg: International Thomson.
Zhavairo, R. 2021. *Interview*. Mbizo, Kwekwe, Zimbabwe. June 20.
Zimbiro, S. 2018. Total undeterred by forex crisis. Zimbabwe Independent. 28 September to 4 October.
Zvinoira, T. 2019. Interview. Mbizo, Kwekwe, Zimbabwe, June 20.

**James Hlongwana** is a Senior Lecturer at the Department of History, Great Zimbabwe University, Zimbabwe. He holds a PhD in History, MA in History, BA Hons in History, BA Gen and Dip-Ed. He has published book chapters and articles in refereed journals. He has presented papers at international conferences in Zimbabwe, Namibia, South Africa, Italy and Finland. His research interests are largely in politics and borderland histories.

# Zimbabwean Politics and Development: An *Ubuntu* Perspective

**Tobias Marevesa and Esther Mavengano**

**Abstract** Zimbabwe has been in deep political and economic crises for the past three decades, a scenario that has persisted even after the demise of the late president Robert Gabriel Mugabe. The political terrain in Zimbabwe has been characterised by political conflicts, political violence, alleged elections rigging, abuse of human rights, lawlessness, among other undesirable traits which are detrimental to development. The international community had to intervene to bring sanity and peace to Zimbabwe. The imposed sanctions by Britain and its allies came as a punitive measure to force the Zimbabwean government to observe human rights and the rule of law. Unfortunately, this move instigated untold suffering of the generality of the people of Zimbabwe. The chapter interrogates the protracted and nuanced political conflict and sanctions in Zimbabwe in the context of development in the post-coup society.The chapter explores the essentials of *Ubuntu/Unhu* philosophy as an ethical framework which helps to frame arguments for a possible 'rebirth' of the nation after the demise of the late president Mugabe in order to pave way for the national development. Thus, the virtues of *Ubuntu/Unhu/ Vumunhu* are utilised in this study in the context of transition politics and the reconstruction process in post-Mugabe society vis-à-vis the effects of the imposed sanctions. The chapter argues that political conflict and sanctions should be carefully examined to unpack the complex dynamics of present-day Zimbabwean politics. It can be concluded that

T. Marevesa (✉)
Philosophy and Religious Studies Department, Simon Muzenda School of Arts, Culture and Heritage Studies, Great Zimbabwe University, Masvingo, Zimbabwe
e-mail: tmarevesa@gzu.ac.zw

E. Mavengano
Alexander von Humboldt Postdoctoral Research Fellow at TU (Techische Universistat Dresden), Dresden, Germany

Institute of English and American Studies, Department of English, Dresden, Germany

Research Institute for Theology and Religion, College of Human Sciences, UNISA, Pretoria, South Africa
e-mail: emavengano@gzu.ac.zw



B. Okyere-Manu et al. (eds.), *Contemporary Development Ethics from an African Perspective*, Philosophy and Politics - Critical Explorations 27,
https://doi.org/10.1007/978-3-031-32898-5_17

political stasis and sanctions require immediate solutions to pave way for national development in post-coup Zimbabwe. It is also recommended that the use of sanctions as a punitive measure should be revised by the international bodies because it is not the intended people who are punished but the generality of innocent Zimbabweans.

**Keywords** Sanctions · Political conflict · *Ubuntu/Unhu/Vumunhu* philosophy · Development · Post-coup Zimbabwe

## 1 Introduction

Zimbabwe has been plunged into deep and troubling political and economic crises for more than three decades from the 1990s to the present day in the post-Mugabe period. This development has continued even after the demise of late president Robert Mugabe. The political landscape in Zimbabwe has been daunted by political conflicts, political violence, allegations of election rigging, abuse of human rights, lawlessness, among other unwelcome practices which are detrimental to development (Marevesa 2019). This environment attracted the imposition of illegal sanctions by the West which came as a punitive measure against the Zimbabwean government for not observing human rights. Regrettably, the act amplified poverty and generated untold suffering for the common Zimbabweans. There is a need for academic conversations that quiz the vexed contributions of political conflict and sanctions in generating the economic and political stasis that hamper development even in the contemporary post-Mugabe society. Ndlovu-Gatsheni and Ruhanya (2020) posit that Zimbabwean transitional politics are troubled with the problematic Mugabe–Mnangagwa, party-state and party-nation entanglements that manifest in the nationalist matrix of power. This observation is important in debating the fate of Zimbabwe in the present context when the country needs visible reforms that will turn around existing the economic state. Thus, the focus of this chapter is to interrogate and examine nuanced political conflict and sanctions that are detrimental to development in the perceived 'new dispensation.' The study is framed by the following vexing questions that demand careful consideration:

Why is Zimbabwe facing a crisis of change in the post-Mugabe era?
How can Zimbabwe reposition itself in the post-coup era towards development?
Why is the subject of sanctions still relevant in present-day Zimbabwe and does it give respect for human dignity?

In considering these questions, there is a need to pose and reflect on the legacy of the Mugabe regime or Mugabeism according to Ndlovu-Gatsheni and Ruhanya (2020), in nationalist politics. The above research questions guide in delineating the problematic link between Mugabe and post Mnangagwa leaderships, the political environment and development in Zimbabwe.

## 2 Ubuntu Paradigm in the Context of Post-Coup Zimbabwe

The *Ubuntu/V/umunhu* sensibilities are utilised in this study to interrogate political conflict and sanctions in the context of development for the post-Mugabe society in Zimbabwe. *Ubuntu* lens brings into conversation the conceptualisation of African/ Zimbabwean humanity and humanist vistas vis-a-vis the longstanding culture of exclusionary and toxic politics in Zimbabwe. According to Tutu (2004: 25), central to *Ubuntu* philosophy is the view that "[a] person is a person through other persons and none of us comes into the world fully formed." Translated into *isiZulu* as *Umuntu Ngumuntu Ngabantu* (Broodryk 2006), and in ChiShona the philosophy of *Unhu/Vumunhu* is hinged on the view that *Munhu Munhu nevanhu*" (Chemhuru-Hapanyengwi and Makuvaza 2014). *Ubuntu* is a humanist philosophy that privileges respect, cooperation, reciprocity, sharing, peace-building, forgiveness among people from diverse national, linguistic and ethnic backgrounds (Mukusha 2013). Scholars such as Samkange and Samkange (1980), Broodryk (2006), Shizha (2010), Mavengano (2020) among others describe *Ubuntu or V/umunhu* in the Shona language as a philosophy about African conception of human beings that speaks about pertinent humanist values such collaboration, intercultural brotherhood, kindness, sympathy, respect for human dignity, reciprocity and solidarity. These are germane ethics since they articulate values that condemn dichotomisation or othering logics based on cultural, political, linguistic or ethnic differences. This study invokes *Ubuntu* ethics to critique, political conflict and sanctions in Zimbabwe and highlight the imperatives of a united Zimbabwean humanity for the sake of developing the nation after the departure of Robert Mugabe.

## 3 Political Conflict and the Problematic Legacy in the Post-Mugabe Era

This segment predominantly dwells on political conflict in Zimbabwe from the beginning of 2000 to the forceful military removal of Mugabe in November 2017. According to Ndlovu-Gatsheni and Ruhanya (2020) the political conduct and practices around elections are essential in the in/stability, peace-building or lack thereof and development of every nation. To generate a new political culture in Zimbabwe, it is fundamentally important to rethink the historical development of political conflict which has taken the country into the current economic quagmire and political doldrums. Ndlovu-Gatsheni (2009), Raftopoulos (2009), Nyambi (2013), Marevesa (2019) and Mavengano (2020) are some of the scholars who observe that the elections in Zimbabwe have been characterised by political violence since the formation of the Movement for Democratic Change (MDC) hereafter in 1999, which posed a momentous threat to Mugabe's presidency in Zimbabwe. The formation of a new party came amidst the frustration with the ruling party's arrogance, political intolerance, authoritarianism and mismanagement of the economy (Marevesa 2019).

The grave antagonism from MDC met resistance and pugnaciousness from the ruling party, the Zimbabwe African National Unity Patriotic Front (hereafter, ZANU PF) which had tested and enjoyed power for almost two decades in Zimbabwe without a serious opposition party insight. This view also resonates with Moyo and Mavengano (2021) who state that the present culture of political violence, toxic politics and indolence in Zimbabwe is traceable to the formation of MDC. Yet, some scholars such as Chung (2007) and Mhanda (2011) earlier on refute this claim and point out that political violence is traceable to the days of the liberation struggle when ZANU members were fighting each other. Mhanda (2011) who was a party of *Dare reChimurenga* which was a governing authority during the liberation struggle, explains how he became a victim of political violence, both during and after the war perpetrated by his (ZANU PF), party members. These arguments speak about the enduring history of political conflict and 'rule by violence' in Zimbabwe (Ndlovu-Gatsheni and Ruhanya 2020:2). From 2000, the Tsvangirai-led party, MDC turned out to be a permanent rival for ZANU PF, particularly during elections. The Mugabe-led government in 2000 held a referendum on a draft constitution which was expected to grant the government officials immunity from prosecution and also permit the government to grab land without compensation to the landowners who were dominantly the white community. The electorate voted against the proposed draft constitution which infuriated Mugabe and his party ZANU PF. In response to this political humiliation, the Mugabe government lashed out at white farmers who were suspected to support the MDC party (Mavengano 2020). The war veterans and ZANU-PF youth invaded white-owned farms and grabbed the land. This situation further ruined the diplomatic relations between Zimbabwe and the international community especially the West that felt the farm invasions and land redistribution programme were ZANU-PF's hit back strategies. As a result, Zimbabwe was ostracised (Ndlovu-Gatsheni 2009). Farm invasions earned the term *jambanja,* a warrior tradition or a demonstration by war veterans reclaim the land of course through violence. Chung (2007), Mhanda (2011) and Magosvongwe (2014) state that Britain and particularly the former Prime Minister Tony Blair had violated the Lancaster House agreement and failed to pay compensation so the war veterans justified their *jambanja* actions to repossess the land which was lost by the indigenous people to whites during the colonial period.

This political conflict worsened during 2008s harmonised presidential and parliamentary elections when Mugabe's leadership had lost credibility, legitimacy and international support. The 2008 presidential election results showed that ZANU PF had suffered a historic defeat when MDC candidate Morgan Tsvangirai emerged as a winner in the national elections for the first time in the historical record of Zimbabwe since independence in 1980. Nonetheless, Ndlovu-Gatsheni (2011) and Nyambi (2013) note that the 2008 presidential elections were condemned and discredited because of the hostile political environment that was generated by the fight between ZANU PF and MDC. There were allegations about vote-rigging, intimidation, displacement and violence which led to the contestation of the election results, MDC accusing the ruling party of tampering with the results before they were announced by the Zimbabwe Electoral Commission (ZEC). Although the

MDC-Tsvangirai (MDC-T thereafter) leader Morgan Tsvangirai gained 47.9% and Mugabe closely followed with his 43.2% score the outcome pleased neither of the two contenders (Marevesa 2019). This amplified the political conflict and violence between these parties. Ndlovu-Gatsheni (2011, 18) states that after the publication of the election results that the MDC–T candidate had won, but could not gunner the 50% plus one threshold that was a precondition of the new electoral law for one to become an absolute winner and constitutionally a run-off was obligatory. On the other hand, ZANU PF felt humiliated which prompted it to be more aggressive in its bid to remain at the helm of power in Zimbabwean politics. The unwelcome election encounters with the MDC-T provoked ZANU PF to take a radical stance against the opposition parties and particularly became more brutal with the MDC-T which was assumed an arduous challenger and its support base in the urban centres (Mavengano 2020).

The political conflict and clampdown deepened towards the run-off of the presidential elections in June 2008 because Mugabe and the ruling party were not ready to hand over power or share it with the opposition party. ZANU PF adopted punitive and violent mechanisms against the electorate for its allegiance with the opposition party MDC-T (Mavengano and Hove 2019). Some members of the MDC-T party went into hiding, as the date for the re-run of the presidential elections approached, the political violence intensified. Thousands of the opposition members were intimidated, displaced and some lost their lives (Nyambi 2013). The intensity of violence and aggression led Morgan Tsvangirai, the presidential candidate for the MDC-T then to withdraw his candidature allowing Robert Mugabe of ZANU PF to "run a one-horse race." Mugabe 's violence and aggression against the opposition as well as running for the election alone was against the ethics of international democracy The results of the presidential elections came out and Mugabe was declared an outright winner but the civil society, local and international human rights organisations, as well as the West, condemned Mugabe's leadership and ZANU PF for autocracy, coercion, persecution, vote-rigging, human rights abuse and restriction of political participation which is against the respect of human dignity (Raftopoulos 2009; Nyambi 2013, Ndlovu- Gatsheni 2013; Mandaza 2016; Mavengano and Hove 2019, and Mavengano 2020). Mugabe initially was arrogant and deaf to the outcry but he later succumbed to the pressure from regional and international communities giving birth to the Global Political Agreement (GPA) in Zimbabwe from 2009 to 2013, which appeared to bring sanity after a decade of socio-political and economic crises (Ndlovu-Gatsheni and Ruhanya 2020). The Global Political Agreement was a power sharing agreement which was signed among the major political parties in Zimbabwe which was facilitated by SADC (Raftopoulos 2009). The Zimbabwean economy improved and the politics of the land briefly transformed into a friendlier environment. Unfortunately for the Southern African country, the GPA was ephemeral and Zimbabwe plunged back into economic and political crises immediately after its end in 2014. The deterioration of the Zimbabwean economy worked against ZANU PF and Mugabe which caused factionalism and ructions within the ruling party. This scenario continued until the fall of Robert Mugabe from power through the military intervention in November 2017. Factionalism was intense at this point probably because the majority of people were disgruntled due to the daunting economic environment. The disgruntlement was now visible even from within the ruling party it is most likely that this one of the several reasons which eventually resulted in the coup of 2017. The ousting of Robert Mugabe as a president of Zimbabwe and the ascendancy of Emmerson Mnangagwa into power was greeted with wild enthusiasm throughout the country (Roger 2017). Yet, it is evident that there is a crisis of change in the post-Mugabe era (Moyo and Mavengano 2021). Ndlovu-Gatsheni and Ruhanya (2020)) are cynical of the Mnangagwa government's ability to bring change and develop the post-Mugabe society. They contend that the current regime is born of a military coup even if it attempts to 'civilianise' itself through appointing an unelected civilian figure as president and organise elections to cover its illegitimate footprints, the fact remains that the regime is "a progeny of violence" (ibid, 2020:20). It is from this historical background that this study argues that the prospects for economic and political transformation is are hinged on nuanced dynamics that include redefining Zimbabwean humanity from *Ubuntu* philosophy, revisit political practices, and a desire to create a friendly economic and socio-political environment that fosters unity, collaboration, respect, empathy, solidarity among other *Ubuntu* ethics in post-coup politics.

## 4 Sanctions an Impediment to the Development or Mere Scapegoating?

Helliker and Murisa (2020) note that despite of Mnangagwa's mantra 'Zimbabwe is open for business,' the country's economic performance is badly affected by sanctions that were imposed by the West in 2003 through the Zimbabwe Democracy Economic Recovery Act (ZIDERA) and later renewed in 2018. The imposed sanctions led to the isolation of the Zimbabwean government and limited the possibilities for capital formation. Zimbabwe remains illegible for market access. Gono (2008:91) defines sanctions as "mechanisms which are employed by countries and international organisations to persuade a particular government or group of governments to change their policy by restricting trade, travel, investment or other commercial activities." Marevesa (2019:132) also observes that concerning Zimbabwe, "sanctions, were widened to include other elements such as diplomatic, cultural and sporting isolation." The sanctions imposed on Zimbabwe are considered illegal by the ruling party because they were not sanctioned by the international body, the United Nations Security Council, but rather imposed by Britain and her allies (Marevesa 2019). According to Moyo (2014), the imposed sanctions curtailed the Zimbabwean government's access to international finance and aid. This negatively impacted on the livelihoods of many Zimbabweans. The economy deteriorated and common citizens languish in poverty. In addition, health service delivery, education, among other critical ministries, were hugely affected by limited access to financial aid. On one hand, the MDC-T views the sanctions as restrictive measures to punish ZANU PF's despotic and dictatorial practices, lawlessness and violation of human rights while ZANU PF views sanctions as a reality which is affecting all Zimbabweans (Moyo 2014; Marevesa 2019) ignoring how ordinary citizens suffer under the heavy burden of sanctions. These views on sanctions speak about the dissonance and political conflict around the subject of sanctions in Zimbabwe. The ruling party condemns what it perceives as the illegality of the sanctions whereas the MDC-T regards sanctions as a necessary evil against ZANU PF's autocratic behaviour. The MDC-T views the narratives about sanctions as regime' survival strategies or divergent discourses constructed by the ruling party. The Zimbabwean government was forced to 'look East' for economic survival since the sanctions imposed by the West affected financial relations, trade and financial flows. This threw the county into the deep end (Marevesa 2020). The 'look East' was a foreign policy which was adopted by the Zimbabwean government to counter the sanctions which were imposed by the west. It could be argued that the dissonance is caused by a lack of compassion, power greed and disunity. The international community needs to find other means of punishing Governments that are abusing human rights and other oppressive means because innocent people are hard hit by sanctions. Ethically these sanctions are against human dignity and solidarity. The Zimbabwean Government should demonstrate the love for its people, collaboration, respect, empathy, solidarity among other Ubuntu ethics by making some meaningful political reforms for sanctions to be lifted in Zimbabwe. Apparently, for the 'second republic' or the post-Mugabe government to make developmental strides, there is need to speak together against sanctions from a common position as Zimbabweans not ZANU PF or Movement for Democratic Change-Alliance but rather a common identity that is Zimbabwean. Although there is political polarisation between the major political parties in Zimbabwe there is need for them to come together and demonstrate respect and empathy for each other and make some reforms which the international community is demanding so that the sanctions can be removed.

## 5 Ubuntuism in Troubled Politics of Transition

This study is positioned in the context of exclusionary logics and political deadlocks vis-a- vis social and economic progress in post-coup Zimbabwean society. Zinyama (2012) posits that Zimbabwe's trajectory in the post-2000 is marred by political bigotry, violence, polarisation and killings which have sadly affected the general welfare of the public. Mugabe's reign left a legacy of authoritarianism and human rights violations (Mavengano and Hove 2019). The political conflict has negatively impacted on efforts towards development, peace and nation-building. This disquieting situation came against the background that Zimbabwe in the 1980s to mid-1990s was a jewel of Africa,' a term that speaks of the economic fortune and the value the nation earned across Africa due to its stable economy, good education, flourishing Agricultural sector immediately after independence, together making the country admirable and significant to the continent (Marevesa 2020). According to Human Rights Watch (2005), the status of socio-economic and political paralysis in

Zimbabwe can be traced to violations of civil and political rights in the early 1990s. Nyambi (2013), Magosvongwe (2014), Mangena (2015), Mhiripiri and Ureke (2018) and Mavengano (2020, 2021) also concur with this view and mention that Zimbabwe has gone through prolonged multiple crises since the commencement of its contentious farm occupations and land redistribution programme in the late 1990s. During Mugabe's leadership, the ruling party had a culture of muffling rebellious voices of the political opponents, civil societies and government workers who protest against the regime (Zinyama 2012; Nyambi 2013; Ndlovu-Gatsheni 2009, 2011; Mavengano and Hove 2019, Mavengano 2020). Ndlovu-Gatsheni and Ruhanya (2020:1) also provide a detailed history of a state of stasis in Zimbabwean politics. Similarly, Moyo and Mavengano (2021) bemoan what they described as toxic politics and crisis of change or change in crisis in Zimbabwe. It is evident that the above scholarly views concur that Zimbabwe's political landscape is tension-filled.

The ascendancy of Mnangagwa to power in November 2017 through military coup and the subsequent July 2018 harmonised elections triggered hope to the disgruntled and disenchanted population in Zimbabwe which expected to witness the re-birth of the country with new political culture and practices that would bring development to a nation that has been economically deteriorating for more than two decades. It is ironic that November is regarded in Zimbabwe as a scared month when ancestors are perceived to be resting known as *mwedzi waMbudzi* (the month of the goats) (Zimoyo 2020). The implication is that anything that has to do with spiritual and ancestral world such as payment of lobola, weddings, tombstone unveiling, inauguration of chief among others are would be suspended because the ancestors would be resting. Yet, the demise of Mugabe which marks the ascendancy of Mnangagwa to the helm of power, this is against the Unhu philosophy that it is a taboo culturally in Zimbabwe to carry out such important occurrence. It is probably the reason why Mnangagwa's ruler ship is having so many challenges that it does not have the blessing of the ancestors. Ndlovu-Gatsheni and Ruhanya (2020) offer an extended critique of the Zimbabwean politics of transition and conclude that Mnangagwa regime remains entangled in Mugabe legacy of political conflict, development inertia and economic instability. The post-coup society is fraught with multiple challenges that require prompt political and economic reforms. This raises vexed questions about what can be done to save the beloved nation which is the thrust of the next sections.

## 6 Dialoguing in the Spirit of Ubuntu for Development and Nation-Building

It is generally agreed by the majority of scholars such as Raftopoulos (2009), Marevesa and Mavengano (2022) that the post-coup society is in a limbo state politically which is a troubling scenario that leaves Zimbabweans lamenting about the fate of their adored motherland. Yet, numerous reform pathways could be taken and reverse the fate of the nation in the post-Mugabe period. This study proposes dialogue as a panacea to political conflict in Zimbabwe. There is a need for a dialogue that includes key stakeholders such as the civil societies, politicians from both the ruling party and opposition camps, the judiciary, the academia, the international community, the church and the traditional leadership. Such a composition of important players can revert the current political impasse and bring the country back on a developmental trajectory. The dialogue should be guided by sincerity, quest for reunion, justice, inclusivity, understanding and benevolence which are all salient virtues of *Ubuntu/Unhu/Vumunhu* philosophy. It is critical in Zimbabwe to have meaningful dialogue that brings peace and development such as Political Actors Dialogue (POLAD) advanced by the Church. However, this dialogue is not inclusive enough to deal with national issues (Muromo 2021). This study encourages all stakeholders in Zimbabwe to have the nation at heart, burry their differences and build Zimbabwe by advocating for a facilitated dialogue with a neutral facilitator a situation which is similar to what led to the birth of the GPA.

Most significantly, the stakeholders should adopt a new language of healing the nation. This refers to a manner of languaging nation–building, unity, and forgiveness, aspects that are critical for national development. How language is put to use is essential in the nation-building process. Power relations and conflict are constructed in political discourses by politicians (Weiss and Wodak 2003). This view is insightful and relevant to the contemporary conversations about transition politics and reconstruction process because, for Fairclough (1998), language can be utilised to shape and influence thoughts, values, beliefs and perceptions of reality. What this means is that language is an important instrument that can be employed to generate new political thinking and attitudes in Zimbabwe. It is critical in changing existing exclusionary beliefs and toxic political practices that were previously constructed during the Mugabe era and inherited into the post-Mugabe era. Bratton and Masunungure (2018) suggest that stakeholders participating in dialogue should not also align themselves with political parties because such biases disrupt progress towards peace-building. This simply means that key players involved in dialoguing the nation should be above partisanship and any other forms of biases. Furthermore, ordinary citizens make a very influential and strong constituency that can bring about political healing (Bratton and Masunungure 2018). The role of the academics cannot be overstated since they are a formidable and versatile force in bringing expertise for conflict resolution thereby paving way for development.

Having mentioned the significance of appropriate languaging for the unity of purpose, there is a need to examine the role of the church and traditional leaders in the reconstruction programme. The church and traditional leadership are also significant institutions that can play a substantial part in bringing sanity and heal the fractured country. The teachings of the church should promote tolerance, justice, love, peace, freedom and understanding which resonate with *Ubuntuism.* The church's potential in political negotiations should be explored during the political dialogue. The church organisations such as the Zimbabwe Catholic Bishops' Conference (ZCBC), and Catholic Commission of Justice and Peace (CCJP) and the Evangelical Fellowship of Zimbabwe (EFZ) can be useful in conversations about nation-building, reconciliation and peace-building (Chiwara et al. 2013). The church has proved to be an effective peace broker in previous political conflicts, for instance, during *Gukurahundi*, the historical conflict between ZANU PF and Zimbabwe African Patriotic Union (ZAPU) in the 1980s (Chiwara et al. 2013). The church mediated in the dialogue and eventually a peace agreement was signed between ZANU PF and ZAPU on 22 December 1987 that brought peace and unity, bringing Mugabe and Nkomo working together.

There is a consorted effort by the Mnangagwa government to show a disjuncture between his leadership and that of his predecessor. No one seems to refute the idea of change or the need to transform the economy and politics of the day in Zimbabwe. However, transitional politics in Zimbabwe should not only be verbalised but rather radical political actions should speak of this turnaround. Ethos of *Ubuntu* are very essential in this regard. Zimbabwean politicians from both the ruling party and opposition camp need to dialogue in the spirit of honesty, mutual respect, peace, unity, inclusivity, nation-building, collaboration and patriotism. These virtues would take the country towards reconstruction and development paths after decades of degeneration. Politicians should desist from blame game and construction of self-aggrandisement discourses that do not bring development and change to the livelihoods of the suffering common citizens. While Mnangagwa's government is at pain to detach itself from Mugabe's misgovernance, mere scapegoating, hypocrisy and disdain for the West will not solve the multiple problems faced by Zimbabweans. Although the anti-sanctions campaigns are necessary and relevant, politicians and the government need to resolve political conflict. This will allow Zimbabweans to speak in unison against economic sanctions and work together towards development. Ndlovu-Gatsheni and Ruhanya (2020) make very insightful comments about the Mnangagwa-led government which is warned against hiding behind the sanctions rhetoric. They go on to point out that current monetary policies and overall macroeconomic turnaround strategies are premised on 'austerity for prosperity' almost a replica of the structural adjustment programme that left thousands of Zimbabweans languishing in poverty during the Mugabe era. In other words, there are no radical economic policies as expected by the generality of Zimbabweans to bring national development.

The contemporary political and economic landscape in Zimbabwe also demands a shift from egocentric and corrupt political culture. Mavengano and Hove (2019) are also critical of elitism which has been part of the political and economic culture in Zimbabwe where the few in positions of power enjoy the national cake at the expense of the majority. This undesirable culture is a barrier to a thriving national economy and a hindrance to the development of the nation. There is also need to be politically and economically accountable rather than constructing a single narrative around the failures in government performance. It is also critical to promote national unity and inculcate *Unhu* ethos of forgiveness, compassionate, mutuality among others for the prosperity of the entire population. Moyo and Mavengano (2021) propose a multi-party transitional government that will make vital economic and democratic reforms with the intention to depart from toxic political culture inherited from Mugabe era. In addition, another troubling issue is that both the ruling ZANU

PF and opposition parties are riddled with factionalism, a situation that negatively impacts on national politics and national development. The opposition parties in Zimbabwe, especially the MDC-A, always cry foul during elections and lobby for the international community and civil society to intervene. Yet, the opposition camps in Zimbabwe are partly to blame for the unfavourable economic situation. The role of the opposition parties remain marginal and mere politicking. The opposition parties should stop the blame game and start working to develop the nation. The function of opposition parties should receive scholarly attention in conversations about transition politics and development in Zimbabwe. In addition, opposition parties need to embrace a patriotic approach in dealing with local political conflict since inviting sanctions is ignoring the interest and welfare of ordinary Zimbabweans. Mutual commitment to political dialogue is a fundamental aspect that possibly will take Zimbabwe towards re-building and reconciliation.

## 7 Reflections

From the above discussion, it is apparent that the post-coup Zimbabwean society remains a troubled land due to the prolonged political conflict and dissonance on the issue of sanctions. This can be addressed if the ethos of *Ubuntu*are to be adhered to. The second aspect is that a new political culture is to be generated to promote peace, collaboration, economic reforms and democratisation practices. The study highlighted the complex indexes of political transition in the post-Mugabe era and a daunting task of changing the political culture from Mugabe's reign. The study also observed that Mugabe-Mnangagwa entanglement can be resolved through political dialogue that brings together key players such as the church, politicians, and citizens, among others, for inclusivity and justice. Meaningful development is possible if political conflict is resolved. Clearly, the nation should speak in unison against sanctions that retard the rate of development. The birth of a new nation remains a delusionary narrative as long political conflict and sanctions define the Zimbabwean land.

## 8 Concluding Remarks

The nation that emerged after the fall of Mugabe from power is still struggling to generate new political culture that fosters development and peace-building in Zimbabwe. Despite the Mnangagwa government's discourses of newness embedded in terminologies like 'Second Republic' and 'New Dispensation', the rebirth of the nation is problematic due to the crisis of change as well as the economic sanctions imposed by the West. In addition, despite the efforts made by the Zimbabwean government to re-engage with the international community and also speak against the sanctions, the West has remained deaf and adamant on this issue. The West makes unpalatable demands to the Mnangagwa government for it to lift sanctions. This has caused a diplomatic impasse as the Zimbabwean government views these conditions as unwelcome interference with internal politics of a sovereign state. The ambiguities, paradoxes and ironies of an emerging society in Mnangagwa era are embedded in the problematic lack of disjuncture in the political practices of the Second Republic from Mugabe's policies. The continuous prevalence of political impasse, persistent culture of political intolerance and the sanctions speak against the narrative of a 'new dispensation,' when the newness is invisible and vague. The return to constitutionalism and respect for human rights is necessary to foster nation-cohesion and development (Tofa 2020). It was also highlighted that national leaders from the ruling party and opposition parties should dialogue and function on a partnership basis. This promotes unity, cooperation and humanism which are important ethics that generate a peaceful national environment and foster national development. In addition, new languaging in national narratives is critical to bring peace between the warring parties. This aspect is significant if a new nation is to be born in Zimbabwe. These reforms may facilitate democratic avenues and dismantle Mugabeism logic through an environment that promotes the re-birth of a nation which had been tormented and fragmented for decades. The fuzzy borderline between Mugabe's iron fisted rule and that of his successor, Mnangagwa, is quite disturbing. The disjuncture between the political rhetoric of newness in post-coup society and the unfolding disquieting actual practices cannot be overstated. There is need to emphasise the importance of unity in order to expedite national development in a country that has been rocked by political and economic instability. Both the ruling party and opposition politicians should adopt dialogic approach to pave way for the rebirth of the nation. The government of Zimbabwe also needs to desist from window dressing narratives about its so-called commitment to political dialogue and re-engagement, yet on the ground nothing speaks to that effect. There is a troubling disjuncture between what the New Dispensation claims to represent and what is taking place on the ground. Furthermore, the discussion in this study has shown that the sanctions narrative cannot be entirely used to account for the deterioration of socio-economic domains. There are complex problems intertwined in the political culture, political practices and attitudes that require a careful analysis and rethinking to pave way for national development.

## References

Bratton, M., and E.V. Masunungure. 2018. *Zimbabwe's Presidential race tightens one month ahead of July 30 voting*. Afrobarometer Dispatch No 223. http://afrobarometer.org/sites/default/files/publications/Dispatches/ab_r7_dispatchno223_zimbabwe-presidential-racetightens.pdf

Broodryk, J. 2006. *Ubuntu African life coping skills: theory and practice. Paper presented at CCEAM conference*. Cyprus: Lefkosia.

Chemhuru-Hapanyengwi, O., and N. Makuvaza. 2014. Hunhu: In search of an indigenous philosophy for the Zimbabwean education system. *Journal of Indigenous Social Development* 3 (1): 1–15.

Chiwara, A., T. Shoko, and E. Chitando. 2013. African traditional religion and the church: catalysts for national healing in Zimbabwe in the context of the global political agreement. *Southern Peace Review Journal* 2 (1): 34–54. (Special issue with OSSREA Zimbabwe Chapter).

Chung, F. 2007. *Re-living the second Chimurenga: memories from the liberation struggle in Zimbabwe successes*. Harare: Weaver Press.

Fairclough, N. 1998. *Discourse and social change*. Cambridge: Polity Press.

Helliker, K., and T. Murisa. 2020. Zimbabwe: continuities and changes. *Journal of Contemporary African Studies* 38 (1): 5–17.

Human Rights Watch, World Report. 2005. http://wwww.hrw.org

Magosvongwe, R. 2014. *Land and identity in Zimbabwean fiction writings in english from 2000 to 2010: a critical analysis*. Cape Town: University of Cape Town.

Mandaza, I. 2016. *Zimbabwe in transition: The political economy of the state in Zimbabwe: The rise and fall of the Securocrat State SAPES Trust*. University of California.

Mangena, T. 2015. *Counter-discourse in Zimbabwean literature*. PhD Thesis. Leiden: Leiden University.

Marevesa, T. 2020. The government of national unity and national healing in Zimbabwe. In *National healing, integrations and reconciliation in Zimbabwe*, ed. Ezra Chitando, Kelvin Chikonzo, and Nehemiah Chivandikwa. Routledge\Taylor and Francis: London.

———. 2019. *Social identity complexity and conflict-resolution in Luke and Zimbabwe*., Published PhD. Thesis. Pretoria: University of Pretoria.

Matsikidze, R. 2013. *Alternative dispute resolution in Zimbabwe: a practical approach to arbitration, mediation and negotiations*. Harare: Molhurst Printers and Publishers.

Mavengano, E. 2020. *A comparative stylistic analysis of selected Zimbabwean and South African fictional narratives 2000–2015 published*. Ph.D. Thesis. Mafikeng: North West University.

Mavengano, E. 2021. Metaphor and representation of COVID-19 pandemic: A cognitive linguistic perspective. In *Covid-19 and the dialectics of global pandemics in Africa: Challenges, opportunities and the future of the global economy in the face of Covid-19*, ed. M. Mawere, B. Chazovechii, and F. Machingura. Langaa, RPCIG, Cameroon. https://www.africanbooks-collective.com/books/covid-19-and-the-dialectics-ofglobalpandemics-in-africa.

Mavengano, E., and M.L. Hove. 2019. Kaka country: an intertextual reading of nation dysfunction in Bulawayo's we need new names and Jinga's one foreigner's ordeal. *Literator* 40 (1): a1595. https://doi.org/10.4102/lit.v40il.1595.

Mavengano, E., and L.M. Hove. 2020. The translingual subjects: shaping identities and deconstructing rainbowism in *one foreign ordeal*. *Literator* 41 (1): 1–11.

Mavengano, E., and T. Marevesa. 2022. A critical discourse analysis of Media landscape and political conflict in Zimbabwe. In Emerging trends in strategic communication in the Sub Saharan Africa, ed. I. Mhute, H. Mangeya, and E. Jakaza, 224–240. London: Routledge Publishers.

Mhanda, W. 2011. *Dzino: memories of a freedom fighter*. Harare: Weaver Press.

Mhiripiri, N.A., and O. Ureke. 2018. Theoretical paradoxes of representation and the problems of media representations of Zimbabwe in crisis. *Critical Arts* 32 (5–6): 87–103.

Moyo, T., and E. Mavengano. 2021. A déjàvu of orwellian proportions: re-reading animal farm in the context of Zimbabwean politics of change. In *Cultures of change in contemporary Zimbabwe, social political transition from Mugabe to Mnangagwa*, ed. G. Ncube, O. Nyambi, and T. Mangena. London: Routledge.

Moyo, N.E. 2018. Dismantling the system of Mugabeism (1st ed.) ISBN 978-3-00-059459482-3.

Moyo, S. 2014. Regime survival strategies in Zimbabwe in the 21st century. *Journal of Sociology and Social Work* 2 (1): 21–49.

Mukusha, J. 2013. *Ubuntu/unhu*: A philosophical reflection. In *Ubuntu/Unhu philosophy: A brief Shona perspective*, ed. J. Mapara and B. Mudzanire, 32–44. Harare: Bhabhu Books.

Muromo, L. 2021. Polad is here to stay. *News Day*, September 14. www.newsday.co.zw

Ndlovu-Gatsheni, S.J. 2009. *Do Zimbabweans exist:? Trajectories of nationalism, national identity formation and a crisis in postcolonial state*. New York: Peter Lang.

Ndlovu, S.J. 2008. Patriots, puppets, dissidents and the politics of inclusion and exclusion in contemporary Zimbabwe. *East African Science Research Review* 24 (1): 81–108.
Ndlovu-Gatsheni, S.J. 2011. *The Zimbabwean nation state project: the historical diagnosis of identity and power-based conflicts in a postcolonial state*. The Nordic Africa Institute: Uppsala.
Ndlovu-Gatsheni, S.J. 2013. *Decoloniality in Africa: a continuity search for a new world order. The Australasian Review of African Studies* 36 (2): 22–50.
Ndlovu-Gatsheni, S.J., and P. Ruhanya, eds. 2020. *The history and political transition of Zimbabwe: from Mugabe to Mnangagwa*. Palgrave: Macmillan.
Noyes, A.H. 2020. *A new Zimbabwe? Assessing continuity and change after Mugabe*. RAND Corporation.
Nyambi, O. 2013. *Nation in crisis: alternative literary representations of Zimbabwean Post-2000*. Stellenbosch University.
Raftopoulos, A. 2009. *Cognition and perception: How do psychology and neural science inform philosophy?* MIT Press.
Roger, S. 2017. Bob's out, the croc In. In: *Continuity or change in Zimbabwe? Africa Spectrum* 52 (3): 81–94.
Samkange, T.M., and S. Samkange. 1980. *Hunhuism or ubuntuism: a Zimbabwe indigenous political philosophy*. Salisbury: Graham Publishing.
Shizha, E. 2010. Rethinking and reconstituting indigenous knowledge and voices in the academy in Zimbabwe: a decolonisation process. In *Indigenous knowledge and learning in Asia/Pacific and Africa: perspectives on development, education, and culture*, ed. D. Kapoor and E. Shizha. New York: Palgrave Macmillan.
Tofa, M. 2020. The rise and demise of the "new dispensation". In *Gender, protests and political change in Africa. Gender development and social change*, ed. A. Okech. Cham: Palgrave, Macmillan.
Weiss, G., and R. Wodak. 2003. Introduction: theory, interdisciplinarity and critical discourse analysis. In *Critical discourse analysis: theory and interdisciplinary*, ed. G. Weiss and R. Wodak, 1–34. Hampshire: Palgrave Macmillan.
Zimoyo, T. 2020. *The sacred month of Mbudzi*. November 21, www.herald.co.zw
Zinyama, T. 2012. The complexity of democratic transition: the Zimbabwe case, 1999 to 2011. *International Journal of Humanities and Social Science* 2 (12): 136–145.

**Tobias Marevesa** is a New Testament Lecturer at the Department of Philosophy and Religious Studies, under the Joshua Nkomo School of Arts and Humanities at the Great Zimbabwe University, where he teaches New Testament Studies and New Testament Greek. He holds a PhD from the University of Pretoria in South Africa. He is a Research Fellow at the Research Institute for Theology and Religion, College of Human Sciences, UNISA, South Africa. His areas of interest are New Testament studies and politics, Pentecostal expressions in Zimbabwean Christianity, culture, human rights and gender-based violence. He has also published in the area of New Testament studies and conflict-resolution in the Zimbabwean political landscape. He has attended and presented a number of papers in both regional and international conferences and has published articles in reputable international journals.

**Esther Mavengano** is a Lecturer who teaches Linguistics and Literature at the Department of English and Media Studies, Great Zimbabwe University. She holds a PhD in Linguistics and Literary Studies. She obtained her PhD in December 2020 from the University of North West in South Africa. She is a Research Fellow at the Research Institute for Theology and Religion, College of Human Sciences, UNISA, South Africa, and a Georg Forster Postdoc Research Fellow at Alexander von Humboldt, Germany, TU (Techische Universistat Dresden) Institute of English and American Studies, Department of English. Her areas of interests are Language Planning, Sociolinguistics, Curriculum Studies, Politics, Translingual Writing, Discourse Analysis, Stylistics, Zimbabwean and South African literature, Anglophone literature and English as a Second Language. She has published in these areas.

# Integrity, Public Accountability, Ethical and Exemplary Leadership Models as Imperatives for Resolving the Problem of Leadership in Africa

**Peter Wilfred Naankiel, Robert Odey Simon, and Ghulam Abbas**

**Abstract** The problem of governance, mismanagement and inefficacious leadership models and practices of most contemporary African leaders calls for finding both individual and collective lasting solutions. This study sets out to proffer sustainable ideological and pragmatic solutions to leadership issues, if imbibed and sustained. Drawing from intuition and secondary data, the study employs qualitative approach to discuss, with ample examples, how integrity criterion and public accountability of ethical and exemplary leadership models (IPACEEL Models in short form) could aptly address the leadership issues in contemporary Africa. It concludes that institutionalising the IPACEEL Models would ideologically and pragmatically resolve most leadership issues, such as bad governance, mismanagement, and underdevelopment, in Africa. The study recommends IPACEEL Models to governments of all levels and non-governmental institutions in Africa as well as other parts of the world.

**Keywords** Africa · Leadership problem · Integrity · Accountability · Exemplary models

P. W. Naankiel (✉)
Department of History and International Studies, Federal University of Lafia, Lafia, Nigeria

R. O. Simon
Ebonyi State University (EBSU), Ebonyi, Nigeria

G. Abbas
Department of Animal Production, Riphah College of Veterinary Sciences (RCVetS), Lahore, Pakistan


B. Okyere-Manu et al. (eds.), *Contemporary Development Ethics from an African Perspective*, Philosophy and Politics - Critical Explorations 27,
https://doi.org/10.1007/978-3-031-32898-5_18

# 1 Introduction

A call for more studies projecting new ideologies and models has been made to bridge the gap in the dearth of research examining leadership theories in sub-Saharan Africa and the assumptions of implicit leadership theory regarding the attributes, traits and skills needed for effective leadership in organizations (Javidan et al. 2006). In agreement with this assertion, Fadare (2018, p. 1) says 'any research that explores the full range of leadership theories and their practical application in societies other than where they were developed would make a significant contribution to existing knowledge available in this area of organisational leadership.' In view of the foregoing, this study proposes what it calls 'Integrity and Public Accountability Criteria of Ethical and Exemplary Leadership Models' (IPACEEL Models henceforth) as a duo intellectual means of resolving African leadership issues. What this study proposes is duo in that it involves integrity and public accountability criteria of ethical leadership model and integrity criterion and public accountability of exemplary leadership model.

Leaning on the foregoing scholars' observations, this study observes that the problems of governance, mismanagement and inefficacious leadership models and practices in contemporary Africa call for both individual and collective lasting solutions, such as through a scholarly research of this kind. In other words, given the dearth of research work putting forth models for addressing leadership issues in post-colonial Africa, this study is an attempt in that direction to bridge the knowledge gap, theorise leadership challenges and models in Africa and contribute to the extant theoretical and practical knowledge on leadership in Africa. It is hoped that the scholarly contributions of this study would cause some desired change in contemporary African society and beyond. With a recourse to a good number of studies, an exposition of the proposed combined models will be made and a logical and empirical conclusion drawn in the end. Following the exposition and the findings, the models shall be recommended for adoption and sustained practice.

# 2 The Problem of Governance and Management of Resources

The misdeeds of African leaders since the attainment of independence from the colonialists have been lamented by scholars (e.g. Robert 2020; Prah 2009). Robert (2020) radically blames the colonialists and the post-independence African leaders and elites for the misfortunes of contemporary Africa and Africans. Prah (2009) regrets the inability of African indigenous leaders to have had any development headway after 50 years of their respective independence. He observes that the development approach and paradigms employed so far are inefficacious; stressing that 'Africans need to go back to fundamentals.' Being so, it is obvious that new approaches and paradigms have to be evolved, made operational and sustained across ages. Prah recalls the voice of Frantz Fanon, who had intellectually prophesied that the post-colonial African leadership was not adequately re-constructed to be able to make developmental headway in all senses of the word.

Fanon (1963) has observed that no meaningful development was evidentially possible in the mission of the new ruling groups that had inherited colonial power. He foresaw the inability of the new indigenous leaders to take over Africa and make any development headway. Prah (2009) agrees that Fanon's prophecy had come to pass, because 'so far, what the post-independence leaders show to the masses, as leadership, aptly justifies Fanon's earlier view about their inadequacies and incompetence in the mission.' Most African nations are yet to make development headway because of the kind of elites and leadership these nations have had since their respective independence. As Gasper (2016, p. 3) points out, the streams in development practice are from: diverse areas of socio-economic development policy, planning and management, both within countries and in the relations between countries; other partly institutionally separate, partly overlapping, and practice worlds, inclusive of human rights activism and practice; emergency relief, conflict response and humanitarian intervention; migration and refugee issues; and work on business ethics, labour conditions, and corporate social responsibility.

The significant influence of leadership models or styles on leadership efficacy or otherwise has been affirmed (Yiing et al. 2009). In other words, the kind of leadership practised by the leaders of a given nation or organisation largely determines the efficient or otherwise leadership obtained in that given nation or organisation. Pointing at changes in the social environment, such as contestable access to new political positions or perceptions of new resources, as the cause of conflicts, Otite (1999) has observed that conflicts arise from the pursuit of divergent interests, goals and aspirations by individuals and/or groups in particular social and physical environments, as in Nigeria and most other parts of Africa. Many scholars agree that the errors of boundary demarcation by the colonialists still ignite conflicts among African peoples in contemporary times (Meredith 2006, p. 1; Alao et al. 2012, p. 10). Alao et al. (2012), p. 10) observe that issues of boundary and the administration of resources along the boundary line are bound to last for long wherever they obtain until the government proffer lasting solutions to them. This paper argues that the sustenance of the hostility is a result of the failure of the indigenous government of African nations to do away with the negative legacies of their colonial predecessors. The failure of these governments continuously manifests in the mismanagement of resources in Africa, especially in Nigeria.

Again, some other scholars have agreed with Meredith (2006), as they maintain that the colonial creation, captured above, has ushered in sustained division rather than unity between and among the disparate and antagonistic ethnic groups of the ex-colonies (Alani 2003, p. 80; Alozieuwa 2016, p. 8). Alozieuwa (2016, p. 12) also observes that the violent conflicts posing severe security challenges to Nigeria over the years are the aftermaths of the Nigerian Civil War. What this later observation implies is that Nigerian indigenous political and military leaders failed to correct the wrongs of their colonial predecessors. Correcting the wrongs would have rightly averted the rise of the common security challenges traced to the Nigerian Civil War.

Population explosion (high population density) in Africa in particular and the world at large is one of the major causes of the problems of natural resources management and recurrent conflicts over resources (Bisong and Apologun 2014, p. 37).

Mismanagement is another chronic challenge to natural resources management and the conflict over them. Mismanagement issues include corruption, misuse, reckless exploration and exploitation of the resources, bad leadership and followership, obnoxious policies, incompetence and lack of leadership charisma, negligence, negative attitude, inequitable distribution of assets, and bitter contestation for and conflicts over natural resources (Bisong and Apologun 2014, p. 38; Besong 2017, pp. 159, 162). Others revolve around negative human versus non-human relations. These include humans' misdeeds against the environment; diversion of attention and funds for environmental and human resources management; industrial hazards and pollution; deforestation, forest depletion and the extinction of some mammals and other animal species; reckless mining, causing health challenges and environmental degradation; and issues of biosphere and the threat to the ozone layer (Bisong and Apologun 2014, p. 38; Besong 2018, p. 4–5). As to the foregoing, we argue that the ability to duly manage both human and natural resources proves the kind of leadership styles exerted by the leaders of a nation. When resources are well managed, the possible conflicts over them are often prevented and easily resolved with expertise, experiential knowledge and skills. Doing so involves making recourse to socio-cultural norms and values, morality and acceptable and conventionalised ethical principles of the culture. In what follows hereunder, norms, values, ethics, morality, ethics and African ethical principles shall be concisely discussed.

## 3 Norms, Values, Ethics, Morality and Ethics: Some Clarifications

All societies, whether traditional or modern, had evolved, learnt and shared guidelines for behaviour by its members Nwauzor 2014, p. 103). These guidelines are so internalised that they become pervasive. Cultural behaviour pervades all parts of a people's life. Aseka (2010) avers that African minds are products of unique 'culture edifices' and 'cultural streams' that rose from environmental conditioning and long standing cultural traditions. Within the African cultural streams are psychological and moral characteristics pertaining to African identity, personality and dignity (Nwauzor 2014; Robert et al. 2016). Among others, Haralambos et al. (2004) reiterate the fact that all societies have had norms governing their behaviours and ways of life, inclusive of dress code. Basically, norms attract punishment for deviance and reward for continuity (Nwauzor 2014).

Value has been conceptualised by various scholars, with some sharing a single viewpoint but for approach and perspective variances. The conception of the society by the functionalists as integrated value-consensus, co-operation, harmony and order ensured in the society (Haralambos et al. 2004, p. xi; Ifeanacho 2010, p. 152) revolves around ethics. Ifeanacho (2010, p. 152) succinctly captures it that the value system in any society states in normative terms the premium placed over things, modes of reasoning and behavioural patterns. Members of a society generally share norms which define acceptable male and female apparel and appropriate dress for different groups (Haralambos et al. 2004, p. xi; Ifeanacho 2010, p. 152). Values go beyond all situations and affect what people do. Like most aspects of culture, the value system is the non-material, which unlike culture and norms, varies according to society over time.

Values are important in modulating social, though they are not exclusively preserved for maintaining social order alone. Certain social forces attenuate the perception and importance attached to the value system of a society. Colonialism, urbanisation and modernisation are some events that had modified cultural traits and values in Nigeria and most other parts of Africa (Robert 2020; Nwauzor 2014, p. 104). African values (ethics) and norms, inclusive of aesthetics, are parts of the basics of African philosophy. Okolo (2005, p. 10) describes African philosophy as a part to a systematic, coherent discovery and disclosure of the African as a being in the African world. He adds that through this knowledge or disclosure of himself and his world by critical reflection, the African grasps reality. That is, through this, the African attains the truth about man and cosmos in its entirety (Okolo 2005, p. 10).

Ethics, as a philosophical concept, lacks a single general definition. However, the varied conceptions by legion scholars (philosophers) all centre on morality. According to Sharma and Hyland (1991, p. 22), ethics is the study of human conduct and of how mankind ought to behave. It is 'an enquiry into how men ought to act in general, not as means to a given end' (Lacey 1972, p. 60). Ethics is also known as axiology: 'axios' (worthy or value), while 'logos' (theory). Thus, ethics is derived from the two Greek words: 'axios' and 'logos'. It is thus the theory of value and the investigation into that which is worthy. The question of right and wrong in human behaviour is the fundamental concern of ethics– the studying of moral values. It should be noted that the Latin word 'mores,' meaning 'concerning habits, customs, ways of life, etc.', corresponds to the Greek word 'ethical.'

The Greek word *ethike,* from which the English word ethics is derived, means character '*he ethike*'. Ethos, popularly known as ethics *(ethike),* Aristotle calls 'the study (or science) of character' (Gbadegesin 1991, p. 79). To philosophers, ethics simply means a philosophical study of morality, while morality is understood as a set of social rules, principles and norms that guide or are intended to guide the conduct of people in a society, and as beliefs about right and wrong conduct as well as good or bad character (Omoregbe 1993; Danjuma 2021). Even though morality is the subject matter of ethics, it is most often used interchangeably with ethics. Both morality and ethics are terms used interchangeably to refer to the same moral phenomenon, human conduct. In Islamic moral philosophy, the word used for 'ethics', namely, *akhlaq,* means character. The implication here is that ethics or morality is conceived in terms essentially of character.

Essentially, what most African languages have as the equivalent of ethics or morality is character. African indigenous ethics is said to be the norms, principles and moral codes, which regulate the conduct and actions of individuals in African societies (Udokang 2014, 266). The principles are built on African traditional ways of life, including African values, norms, customs, worldviews and conventions. The concepts of good, bad (or evil), right and wrong feature prominently in African moral thought, as they do in the moral systems of other peoples and cultures, inclusive of Western cultures (Mbiti 1969; Omoregbe 1993; Ozumba 1995). Beliefs and presuppositions of a people about right and wrong conduct, good and bad character, remain substantially or generally intact. They continue to constitute the moral framework within which the members of the society function (Danjuma 2021).

## 4 African Ethical Principles

African societies have undoubtedly evolved ethical systems, ethical values, principles, rules, intended to guide social and moral behaviour. African norms, precepts, principles and moral codes, which regulate the conduct and actions of individuals in African societies, are what constitute African indigenous ethics (Udokang 2014, 266). The ethics of a society is rooted in the ideas and beliefs about what is right or wrong, and what is a good or bad character, among others. It is also embedded in the conceptions of satisfactory social relations and attitudes held by the members of the society. It is rooted in the forms or patterns of behaviour that are considered by the members of the society to bring about social harmony and co-operative living, justice and fairness (Danjuma 2021). Generally, a people's ethical principles are rooted in their culture, worldview, norms and values, beliefs, customs and traditions, conventions, articulated and popularised ideas, and experiences.

Essentially, both morality and ethics are terms used interchangeably to refer to the same moral phenomenon– human conduct. The various societies found in traditional Africa routinely accept that personhood is the sort of thing which has to be attained, and is attained in direct proportion as one participates in communal life through the discharge of the various obligations defined by one's area and status. The carrying out of these obligations transforms one from the 'it-status' of early childhood, marked by an absence of moral function, into 'the person-status of later years, marked by a widened maturity of ethical sense— an ethical maturity without which personhood is conceived as eluding one' (Menkiti 1984, 176). African ethical principles, like African ethics itself, are characterised by character, humanism, personhood, brotherhood, religion, familyhood, social life or sociality, welfarism, solidarity, unison rather than individualism, and obedience to elders, seniors and constituted authorities.

Moral principles and rules may emerge from or are evolved by a particular human society. Even so, they are principles that can (and do) apply to all human societies in as much as they respond to basic human needs, interests and purposes. Good character is the essence of the African moral system, the linchpin of the moral wheel. A character-based ethics has common justification. For all that a society can do, regarding moral conduct, is to impart moral knowledge to its members, making them aware of the moral values and principles of that society. In general, society satisfactorily fulfills this duty of imparting moral knowledge to its members through moral education of various forms, including, as in African societies, telling morally freighted proverbs and folktales to its younger members (Robert and Anura 2018).

Therefore, African leaders, who are conscious of keeping the ethical principles of the land and possess the leadership criteria spelt out, are bound to be able to efficiently handle leadership issues that work against good governance, national development, and public accountability and ethical and exemplary leadership, built on integrity, ethical leadership criteria and outstanding leadership qualities. The otherwise leaders continuously present sustained challenges to the wellbeing of citizens and the development of African nations and their resources, as in Nigeria and all nations of East Africa (Robert 2020; Besong 2017; Mulugeta 2008; Khadiagala 2008; The Economist 2006; Deng 2005; Asiwaju 1996). Be it so, this study argues that bad leadership has remained one ageing challenge to development, progress, peace and the wellbeing of Africa and Africans over the years. These phenomena are commonly challenged by bad leadership. Meanwhile, they (development, progress, peace and the wellbeing) obtain where and when there is good leadership.

Good leadership offers good governance and allows these phenomena to thrive, while bad leadership offers the opposite and continuously battle with leadership, development and nationhood issues. Corruption is the worst evil of every government characterised bad leadership and bad governance to the state and its citizenry. Corruption causes a rise in the cost of governance, bad leadership and governance, underdevelopment, recurrent conflicts, insecurity and heinous crimes against the state and its citizenry (Besong 2017; Robert and Anura 2018). Corruption is affirmed to have generally caused incalculable damage to the social and political development of Nigeria as well as many other African nations (Odo 2012).

## 5 Commonly Theorised Leadership Styles and African Leaders

Although there are over five commonly theorised leadership styles, as Burns (1978, pp. 19–20) has demonstrated, leadership styles can be broadly divided into two: transactional leadership and transforming leadership (Burns 1978, pp. 19–20). Transactional leadership describes the leadership practice in which one leader takes initiative of making contact with others for the purpose of an exchange of valued ways of leadership and governance (Burns 1978, p. 19). Next, transforming leadership is that which involves one or more persons engaging with each other in such a way that leaders and followers raise one another to higher levels of motivation and morality (Burns 1978, p. 20). This work advocates the combination of these two styles for more efficient and productive results.

In analysing leaders' traits in relation to their leadership behaviour, Burns posits that while leaders may be born, leadership behaviour might not necessarily be inborn but learnt, because great leaders lead and at the same time teach their followers. In doing so, they lead and teach their followers 'truth and mutual actualisation' (Burns 1978, p. 449). Additional to transactional and transformational leadership are three others (laissez-faire, authoritarian and democratic leadership styles), which are all associated with traditional groups and organisations (Burns 1978, pp. 20; Fadare 2018, 2). Given the foregoing, the traits are what this study advocates to be the parameters for determining the suitability of aspiring leaders, as they were in Ancient Athens. The study posits that with such traits, the ideal leader is well-behaved, virtuous, altruistic, morally upright, ethical, accountable and democratic. Athenian sortition, the root of modern democracy and good leadership styles, had involved systemic and procedural tests for personality traits that constitute worthwhile leadership traits (see Courant 2017, 2). Sortition refers to the democratic system or process of selecting representatives by lots or lottery, based on three principles: equality, impartiality and representativeness (Courant 2017, 2). The impartiality was got through the lottery system of picking out members of popular jury. Representativeness depended on the population through a representative sample. Impartiality and representativeness were based on and demonstrated equality.

For Bass (1985), transformational leadership comprises charisma or idealised influence, inspirational leadership, individualised consideration, and intellectual stimulation. Bass and Avolio (1994) posit that the four I's (i.e., intellectual stimulation, individualised consideration, idealised influence, and inspirational motivation) are the mechanisms for the transformational leadership style to produce better outcomes than the transactional leadership style. Again, Bass (1985) has argued that it is impossible to attribute the way people behave only to a simple performance–reward relationship or cost–benefit formulation. Additional to performance–reward relationship or cost–benefit formulation are unconventional variables that influence the behaviour of people in a nation or an organisation, and also account for excellent management or running of public or organisational affairs (Bass 1985). Bass (1985) has held that leaders of traditional organisations set goals, monitor and reward performance, whereas leaders of exceptional organisations do not set these but inspire employees to transcend themselves and do more than what is required of them.

Bass' above view tells of what makes the difference between developed and underdeveloped nations, following the differences in the leadership deeds of their leaders. African leaders practise only transactional leadership and set goals without reasonable monitoring and performance–reward. Corruption continuously erodes monitoring and performance–reward systems, ethics, morality, virtuous living and leadership, and gives no room for public accountability and exemplary and ethical leaders of high integrity (Robert 2020; Besong 2017; Odo 2012). For Burns (1978, p.142), transforming (transformational) leadership is of four categories. The first is intellectual leadership, which involves the use of analytical and normative ideas. Next is revolutionary leadership, which involves effecting a complete change to an entire system. Reform leadership is the third category, which involves moral leadership dealing with issues of strategy and conflict (Burns 1978, p. 170). The fourth is heroic leadership, involving a leader that rises as a solution provider during times of major crises. Transforming leadership is the unlike of transactional leadership, as it possesses and exhibits unique attributes that the transactional leadership lacks. Transforming leadership has a moral element, which engender the desire to transform both the society and the citizenry.

Commenting on transformational leadership, Yukl (1999, p. 285) has pointed out that emotions, ethics, and moral behaviour are important elements of transformational leadership. Meanwhile, the transactional leadership lacks these elements and rather exhibits the opposites of these elements and others noted earlier. Yukl (2013, p. 286) claims that the followers of transformational leaders accord them trust, admiration, loyalty and respect, which make the leaders able to influence and motivate their followers. Being motivated, the followers become mindful of the significance of completing tasks, as they must have got encouraged by the leaders to transcend their own self-interests for that of their nation or organisation (Yukl 2013, p. 286). This has been the case in contemporary Africa, where the substitution of alien ethical principles for African indigenous ones had long ago brought widespread moral laxity and violations of indigenous ethical principles that efficaciously guided actions of past Africans, including the leaders (Akintona and Oluwadolapo 2019, p. 13; Udokang 2014, p.266).

The violation of indigenous ethical principles results mainly from the abandonment of our indigenous (native or African) ethical principles for Western ethical principles, which have largely influenced us (Danjuma 2021; Akintona and Oluwadolapo 2019). By so doing, most of the contemporary Africans seem to be accepting the racial claims by most Western philosophers that Africa has no indigenous ethics (Danjuma 2021, p. 1). As Danjuma (2021, pp. 1–2) rightly observes, the increasing rate of moral decadence in contemporary African society calls for revisiting, indigenous ethics, so as to address the rising ethical issues. Thus, revisiting African ethics in the political arena would do us a whole lot of good. That involves having ethics based parameter for leadership in Africa. Retracing or revisiting our indigenous African ethics and ethical principle would free us from mindless and needless imitation of West. The imitation causes and compounds the nationhood problems confronting Africa over the years. As Akintona and Oluwadolapo (2019, p. 13) rightly note,

> Westernisation is mistaken for civility and modernisation; the adoption of Western principles as ideals; and the abandonment of African indigenous moral values have done more harm than good to African development and the moral fabric of our dear continent and nations.

On their part, Spreitzer, Perttula & Xin (2005, p. 221) theorise that traditional or cultural values of individuals moderate the relationship between all dimensions of transformational leadership and leadership effectiveness. They affirm that there is likely to be some degree of cultural value differences in the effectiveness of different dimensions of transformational leadership (Spreitzer et al. 2005, p. 221). However, they argue that for Asian and North American leaders, individuals' traditional cultural values moderate the relationship between four (intellectual stimulation, articulating a vision, appropriate role model, and expectations of high performance) out of six specified dimensions of transformational leadership on leadership effectiveness with the two other dimensions being growing up goals and individualised support (Spreitzer et al. 2005, p. 212). Essentially, of interest to us here is Spreitzer et al.'s (2005), p. 221) theoretical assertion that traditional or cultural values of individuals moderate the relationship between all dimensions of transformational leadership and leadership effectiveness. This assertion implies that African cultural values of individuals moderate the relationship between all dimensions of transformational leadership and leadership effectiveness, which good leadership and governance and meaningful remain a yet-to-achieve sustained struggle. This is so because African values have been put in bad light and continuously violated.

The foregoing discourse on leadership styles suffices for further details. The discourse is done in view of the fact that the thrust of this study is leadership models as mechanisms for solving the ageing leadership issues in Africa. The discourse is a critical reflection on extant viable theoretical models on attributes, traits and skills required for efficient leadership (Javidan et al. 2006; Fadare 2018). It suffices to say that the discourse is an attempt to 'explore some leadership theories and their practical application in societies [African societies] other than where they were developed' (Fadare 2018, p. 1). Having done that, we will now move on to the main preoccupation of our study, IPACEEL Models.

## 6 Theorised Leadership Styles as Performance Determinants: Some Perspectives

To avoid the redundant use of leadership, we use leadership once with 'styles', and 'performance' to serve as an adjective to both 'styles', and 'performance'. 'Peculiarity' is used likewise to describe the distinct style and performance of every government or leader respectively. Every government has its peculiarly adopted leadership style(s). This does not mean that every government evolves its own new leadership style(s). Additional to some randomly selected extant general or commonly shared leadership style(s), models and practices that a government might evolve its own critically thought-out or craft new ones. It could only rely on the extant or commonly shared ones or its own drawn out leadership style(s), models and practices. Every leadership style triggers as well as determines a peculiar performance that characterises every given government. This applies to the management of every organisation. Effective leadership styles determine leadership performance (Fadare 2018, 2; Amirul and Daud 2012).

Any government adjudged good, or affirmed to be characterised by good governance, performs well either minimally or maximally. Amirul and Daud (2012) attribute effective leadership and high performance by Malaysian government-linked companies to the leadership styles used by the leaders. This reality lends credence to the thinking that if African leaders evolve, use and maintain worthwhile or effective leadership models, good leadership, good governance and significant development would be easily attained in Africa. To paraphrase the words of Immanuel Kant (Kant 1795, p. 1) on his proposed condition for perpetual peace, the practical politicians in Africa have to stop disregarding the theoretical warnings or admonitions of the theoretical politicians in Africa. Also, on Kant's line of thought, the up and doing African philosopher, who has lots of good dreams, has to be listened to and be given favourable avenues to realise his/her 'sweet dreams' (Kant 1795, p. 1).

Premised on the presumption of the culturally endorsed implicit leadership theory, Javidan et al. (2006, p. 72) have argued that it is fallacious to presume that because a leader is successful in one country, the same leader will be successful in other countries. Culturally endorsed implicit leadership theory is an extension of the implicit leadership styles. The leadership styles considered effective by individuals in organisations may differ on the basis of the set of beliefs the people hold in terms of the attributes, skills, behaviours, and other stereotypes that are accepted as contributing to or impeding outstanding leadership (Javidan et al. 2006, p. 72). It is important to note that what Javidan's (Javidan et al. 2006, p. 72) view implies is that there are inherent leadership challenges in each nation, which are peculiar to the given nation and its leaders. So, that a particular leader could surmount the challenges s/he must have faced in one nation does not really mean that s/he could also surmount such challenges in another nation. Well, on one side, Javidan et al. (2006) are right on the ground of the peculiarity of the leadership challenges in each nation alongside the inherent factors that limit the possibility of surmounting the challenges.

On the other, they are not right in that the importation of the experience, motivation and factors behind the successful leadership in one nation into the leadership practice(s) and styles of the other country would ultimately guarantee success in the other country too. The importation would bring to place what this study calls *blended leadership* practice and *harmonised leadership* styles. A *blended leadership* practice is one which involves a selective socio-cultural and political borrowing from a source to a target, towards attaining maximum leadership results from a mindful combination of two or more leadership practices, the borrowed practice(s) and the original practice(s) in the leaders' home nation or own organisation. Combined worthwhile practices are certainly bound to trigger efficient or better leadership performance. The combination entails several leadership styles with a view to attaining quality, efficient and productive leadership, good governance, and significant human and resources development and management.

## 7 Postulations and Orientations of IPACEEL Models

At this juncture, we argue that ethical leadership is the base of every worthwhile leadership style, while unethical leadership is the bane of every unworthy leadership style. Ethics, as the element of worthy leadership values, is supreme and takes centre stage in all the elements and attributes for effective leadership. This reality is implicitly reiterated, depicted and analysed by scholars (e.g. Burns 1978; Bass 1985; Bass and Avolio 1994; Yukl 1999; Spreitzer et al. 2005; Javidan et al. 2006; Yukl 2013) in both theoretical and empirical discourses on leadership styles, models and efficiency or performance as well as leadership issues across nations of the world. The foregoing brief explanation offers an insight to understanding our theoretical construct, IPACEEL Models.

Basically, this study theorises that ethical leadership parameter is the basis of exemplary leadership. Ethical leadership is the leadership practice of a certified ethical leader, who had met and continuously meets the integrity criterion. Both integrity and accountability are core features of ethical and exemplary leadership. There can be no ethical leadership without these features, which is why every leadership aspirant must meet these criteria in order to attain the leadership position(s) they vie for. We argue that any leadership that is ethical is exemplary and vice versa. Ethical leadership is built and rests on ethics, morality and natural as well as common law. Thus, ethical leadership is worthwhile, accountable, productive, responsible, responsive and excellently good. Such leadership is exhibited by good leaders. This leadership produces and offers good governance, development, satisfaction, freedom, rule of law, support and basic needs of the citizenry for the common good of all and for the sake of the nation. By producing these, it is indeed exemplary.

An ethical leader is virtuous and a virtuous leader is ethical. Given that integrity is a virtue, the virtuous leader is one who has high integrity and moral uprightness, for which s/he exhibits public accountability and offers good governance. With these attributes, the ethical leader leads with the fear of God; remains or at least aims at remaining virtuous; has respect for nature (including natural law and the environment alongside all the non-humans in it); and manages human and natural resources well, as a servant rather than a leader. An ethical leader, who upholds his/her integrity above materialism and position, remains virtuous, exemplary and followers-focused at all times and everywhere he/she leads. Such a leader alone is the one who deserves to lead. Given the foregoing, we further assert that the possession of high integrity and moral uprightness makes the leadership charisma of an individual to be outstanding.

Thus, it is imperative for leaders to acquire these skills and attributes. Where they have not acquired them through learning processes before vying for or attaining leadership positions, they should get equipped with them through specially designed and sustained learning programmes for acquiring and testing for being knowledgeable in them. The possession of high integrity and moral uprightness is the driving force of discipline, self-control, contentment, non-covetousness, philanthropy and other virtues. Since integrity is not inborn in individuals, the individual has to be educated, socialised, trained, instructed, indoctrinated, conditioned and compelled to acquire it through these learning processes (education, socialisation, training, instruction, indoctrination, criteria conditioning and compulsion) (Ocheje 2020). Individuals who neither possess nor acquire integrity as such are bound to be leaders who practice and exhibit leadership that lacks the essentials of good leadership. They have little or nothing good or worthwhile to offer their subjects, the led.

Finally, based on the theoretical postulations and pedagogical orientations of IPACEEL Models, we maintain that for contemporary African leaders (as well as leaders of any other parts of the globe) to be able to resolve the lingering chronic leadership issues, they ought to base all leadership criteria, styles, measures and deeds on ethical and exemplary leadership practices, styles and parameters. These begin with the integrity and accountability test stage of pre-leadership evaluation to the public accountability practical stage. The test for integrity and accountability also involves testing for other commonly affirmed virtues. Essentially, ethical leadership styles and models allow for effective leadership styles and their application.

They are the conditions for producing good leaders, who are virtuous, exemplary, accountable and of high integrity and moral uprightness, and do offer good leadership and governance to their nations and citizenry. We further aver that to get ideal leaders, who are ethical, exemplary, accountable and of high integrity, in Africa and beyond, IPACEEL Models have to be judiciously understood and put into practice, while continuously modifying its tenets, scope and characteristics ethically, morally, legally, conventionally and collectively from time to time. However, we reject any form of pirating, defilement and unjust modification of the IPACEEL Models.

Not considering these models worthwhile or rejecting them as what could resolve leadership issues implies the disposition of sentiments and subjectivity. These models apply to both secular and traditional politics, whereby these requisite conditions are to endlessly serve as worthwhile parameters for determining and practising worthwhile (ethical) leadership in Africa and beyond. Electorates and 'king-makers crew' ought to have these internalised in their mind besides spelling them out in written leadership documents. They have to insist on these at all times. When guided by these requisite parameters, their choice for leaders that would rule them must be informed by the tenets of IPACEEL models. King-makers crew here refers to all who make up the fortunate few (elites of various class and magnitude) that choose or pronounce leaders. They play leadership selection roles beyond what the electorates, being the masses, do in choosing leaders. Often times, this crew frustrates the right choice and deeds of the electorates in most African nations in particular and in some other nations of the globe in general. Members of this crew most often compromise standards, upon indulging in bribery and corruption scandal, and present and/or impose the wrong persons on the masses as the right candidates/leaders. Consequently, these persons offer no good leadership, since they lack the requisitions, qualities and qualifications.

## 8 IPACEEL Models: Towards Resolving Leadership Issues

Given the foregoing, we argue in this section that most of the leadership issues confronting Africa could be addressed with critically thought out and tactically crafted models, which ought to be imbibed and sustained across ages. Leadership is crucial to all spheres. That is why right leadership is needed in Africa as well as every continent. Planning and management are two of the most essentials of development streams. IPACEEL Models place emphasis on these essential development streams, as the base of the other streams. The streams of theorising leadership and development are also based on planning and management. On the streams of theorising, Gasper (2016, p. 3) notes,

> The streams of theorising which are brought into dialogue with the demands and dilemmas of practice come from, besides academic moral philosophy and critiques of mainstream economics, also theology, various humanist ethics, human rights theory and jurisprudence, feminist theory and care ethics, environmental philosophy, well-being research, and additional perspectives generated within professional and practical ethics.

Gasper's words above justify the attempts of this study to theorise leadership in Africa, as to resolve the leadership issues bordering on resources management. Resources management by leaders, for which good leadership and governance are among the core requisitions, entails as well as begins with planning and management. To have good leaders, who would be capable of rightly leading a nation and its populace, planning is imperative. This is followed by the management of resources. For worthwhile planning and management, chronic challenging leadership issues ought to be resolved diplomatically with lasting approaches, paradigms and result-oriented measures, which undoubtedly include theories or models. Given the foregoing, this paper argues that democratisation and development processes targeted at efficient performance and significant results must be based on public accountability, integrity, ethical leadership and exemplary leadership.

Prospective leaders must be subjected to passing rigorous tests to prove their level of integrity, public accountability capability, character and exemplary leadership dispositions evidenced in their proven charisma, prowess and dexterity, life styles, personality traits, background, and so on. With these criteria, good governance and efficient resources management is possible. Therefore, all the criteria have to be met by a candidate. Again, the democratisation and development processes ought to be transparent as to allow for public accountability. The development agenda and projects of African leaders must be based on development ethics (Gasper and Truong 2010). The leaders ought to be ethical. If otherwise, unethical and unaccountable, they are deficient and unfit for execution and practice. Testing, proving and practising what IPACEEL models point out and demand above follow what obtained in sortition and characterise and obtain in true democracy of modern and post-modern eras. Also, the ethical leadership aspect of our model rests on development ethics. This aspect of the model demands that leadership in Africa and even beyond be based on ethics and ethical principles. Africa has always had ethics and morality from time being. It is a question of turning to these non-material aspects of African culture in these critical moments of Africa's existence.

The entirety of the ethical base of resolving African leadership issues rests on sustained practice of African ethics and rooting all political activities in African ethical principles and norms and values. The abandonment as well as abuse of African ethics and ethical principles in the political arena is what manifest ethical deviance as leadership issues (see Ozumba 1995, p.55). Using these paradigms would mean that 'Africans have gone back to the fundamentals' (Prah 2009; Fanon 1963). Be it so, the viability and application of IPACEEL Models will manifest. The prospects of IPACEEL Models will reveal themselves and prove the worth of the duo models, as the productive results of using the paradigms rooted in ethical and exemplary leadership practices and styles. Once African leadership is solidly built on African values, norms, customs, worldviews and conventions (Udokang 2014, p. 267), the lingering leadership issues on the continent will be easily resolved sustainably. It should be recalled that African indigenous ethics refers to the norms, principles and moral codes, which regulate the conduct and actions of individuals in African societies (Udokang 2014, p. 266). Also recall that African ethical principles, like African ethics itself, are characterised by the quality of individual's character, religion (Udokang 2014, p. 268), morality cum moral values (Mbiti 1969, p. 175), the doctrine of humanism, and family-hood, brotherliness, and communalism (Akintona and Oluwadolapo 2019, p. 13).

Having said the above, we argue that the chronic issues of leadership in Africa could be addressed by institutionalising integrity criterion and public accountability of ethical and exemplary leadership models as the first criteria to be compulsorily met before qualifying for any significant leadership positions in Africa. These criteria constitute and ought to compulsorily serve as the first stage criteria, upon which other socio-cultural and political criteria have to be based. It is until an emerging African leader fully passes these first-stage criteria that s/he could be granted the next stage of leadership screening. Then, the rigidly followed screening processes continue stage-by-stage to the last stage of mass or collective determination of the prospective leadership candidate as the most fit for the given leadership position(s). Chronic leadership issues in contemporary Africa include lack of integrity and public accountability, bad governance and mismanagement of resources, which allow for corruption, underdevelopment, impoverishment of African nations and populace, conflicts, insecurity and continuous erosion of African ethics and cultures, and the looting and wiping out of African belongings – resources.

Next, we argue that issues of governance transcend to and as well influence issues of resources management across all human societies. This is because efficient management of resources depends on the kind of governance obtained in a particular area. Good governance undoubtedly paves way for efficient management of resources. We also argue that the management of non-human resources depends on the management of human resources. Where and when there is good governance, human resources are bound to be well-managed. And, when human resources are well-managed by the leaders, the human resources, in turn, join force with the leaders to manage the non-human resources well. Conversely, where and when human resources are not well-managed, bad governance is what is responsible for the backdrop. The mismanagement of resources in society causes a lot of issues. Some of the issues are developmental issues. For example, conflicts arise over control and share of natural resources. The conflicts arise over clash of interests in controlling and sharing the resources. Conflicts threaten as well as shatter development. Thus, mismanagement causes conflicts that threaten and as well shatter significant development.

## 9 Conclusion

This study is an attempt to theorise ways of resolving leadership issues in Africa, which include issues of managing both human and natural resources. The focus is on the leadership issues arising from mismanagement of resources and the failure to duly handle factors responsible for bad governance, unethical leadership and mismanagement of resources. Issues of governance and resources management are discussed in fair details. Commonly affirmed leadership styles are discussed in relation to the IPACEEL Models. An exposition of IPACEEL Models is made, with ample descriptive illustrations. The theoretical views of the IPACEEL Models are presented descriptively and logically.

From the angle of African ethics and ethical principles, the base of ethical and exemplary leadership, the viability of these models is justified by several literatures. In all, the study's ethical leadership models double as a leadership style and model and serve as the base of all worthwhile leadership styles. Unethical (unworthy) leadership styles and models are otherwise, counterproductive and lack the capacity for effective leadership, good governance and efficient management of resources. IPACEEL Models are recommended to governments of all levels and non-governmental institutions in Africa as well as other parts of the globe in general, as viable theoretical and intellectual means of resolving leadership issues.

## References

Akintona, E.O., and D. Oluwadolapo. 2019. Developing ethical principles from indigenous moral values. In *African moral character and creative thinking principles*, ed. J.I. Unah and G. Fasiku. Ile-Ife: Obafemi Awolowo University Press.

Alani, B.I. 2003. Ethnic politics and democracy in Nigeria's history. *Nigerian Forum* 24 (3–4).

Alao, D.O., et al. 2012. Resolving resource conflict in Nigeria: a case of akwa-ibom and cross river states. *Arabian Journal of Business and Management Review (OMAN Chapter)* 2 (3).

Alozieuwa, S.O. 2016. The Ombatse crisis in Nigeria: background, recent developments and possible solutions, *Journal of Interdisciplinary Conflict Science* 2 (2).

Amirul, S.R., and H.N. Daud. 2012. A study on the relationship between leadership styles and leadership effectiveness in Malaysian GLCs. *European Journal of Business and Management* 4 (8).

Aseka, E.M. 2010. *Culture and dress: need for a national dress code.* Retrieved June 5.

Asiwaju, A.I. 1996. Borderlands in Africa: a comparative research perspective with particular reference to Western Europe. In *African boundaries: barriers, conduits and opportunities*, ed. P. Nugent and A.I. Asiwaju, 266–272. London: Pinter.

Bass, B.M. 1985. *Leadership and performance beyond expectation.* New York: Free Press.

Bass, B.M., and B.J. Avolio. 1994. *Full range leadership development: manual for the multifactor leadership questionnaire.* Palo Alto: Mind Garden.

Besong, E.N. 2017. How corruption deteriorates poverty in Nigeria. *International Journal of Engineering and Information of Systems (IJEAIS)* 1 (9): 152–164.

———. 2018. *An application of innocent asouzu's noetic propaedeutic pedagogy to the resolution of environmental problems.* Unpublished MA Thesis submitted to the department of philosophy. Calabar: University of Calabar.

Bisong, P.B., and S.S. Apologun. 2014. The noetic propaedeutic pedagogy as a panacea to environmental degradation. *Canadian Social Science* 10 (4): 37–46.

Burns, J.M. 1978. *Leadership.* New York, NY: Harper & Row.

Courant, D. 2017. Thinking sortition modes of selection, deliberative frameworks and democratic principles. *PSA 67th Annual international conference, 'Politics in interesting times' technology & innovation centre, University of Strathclyde*, Glasgow. April 10–12.

Danjuma, C. 2021. *A critical discussion of indigenous ethical principles with western principles.* Unpublished semester course (Phil 413: Classics in ethics) assignment paper submitted the course lecturer, Department of Philosophy. Lafia: Federal University of Lafia,.

Deng, L.B. 2005. The challenge of cultural, ethnic, and religious diversity in peace-building and constitution-making in post-conflict Sudan. *Civil Wars* 7 (3): 244–257.

Fadare, S. 2018. Leadership styles and effectiveness among sub-Saharan African employees. *The Journal of Values-Based Leadership* 11 (2): 11. https://doi.org/10.22543/0733.62.1219.

Fanon, F. 1963. *The wretched of the earth*. New York: Grove Press.

Gasper, D. 2016. In *Development ethics (Entry for encyclopedia of global bioethics)*, ed. H. ten Have. Cham: Springer.

Gasper, D., and T.-D. Truong. 2010. Development ethics through the lenses of caring, gender and human security. In *Capabilities, power and institutions: towards a more critical development ethics*, ed. S. Esquith and F. Gifford, 58–95. PA: Pennsylvania State University Press, University Park.

Gbadegesin, S. 1991. *African philosophy: traditional yoruba philosophy and contemporary African realities*. New York: Peter Lang.

Haralambos, M., M. Holbon, and R. Heakd. 2004. *Sociology: themes and perspectives*. 6th ed. London: Harper and Collins.

Ifeanacho, M.J. 2010. *Fundamentals of sociology*. Port Harcourt: Chibest Publishing Company.

Javidan, M., P.W. Dorfman, M.S. de Luque, and R.J. House. 2006. In the eye of the beholder: cross cultural lessons in leadership from project GLOBE. *The Academy of Management Perspectives* 20 (1): 67–90.

Joda, T.H. 2010. *Anti-corruption handbook for Nigerian youths*. Kaduna: Joyce Graphic Printers and Publishers.

Kant, I. 1795. *Perpetual peace: a philosophical sketch*. Available online with other publication details missing.

Khadiagala, G.M. 2008. *Eastern Africa: security and the legacy of fragility (Africa program working paper series)*. Johannesburg: International Peace Institute. www.ipinst.org.

Lacey, A.R. 1972. *A dictionary of philosophy*. Oxford: OUP.

Mbiti, J.S. 1969. *African religions and philosophy*. London: Heinemann.

Menkiti, I.A. 1984. Person and community in african traditional thought. In *African philosophy: an introduction*, ed. R.A. Wright, 3rd ed. Lanham: University Press of America.

Meredith, M. 2006. *The state of Africa: a history of fifty years of independence*. London: Free Press.

Mulugeta, A. 2008. Promises and challenges of a sub-regional force for the Horn of Africa. *International Peacekeeping* 15 (2): 175–184.

Ndaliman, A.H., and M. Anwalu. 2011. *Socio-economic development programs in Nigeria: the Obansanjo era (1999–2007)*. Kaduna: Pyla-mak Services Limited.

Nwauzor, A.A. 2014, February. Changing values in contemporary Nigeria. *Education Research International* 3 (1).

Ocheje, D.O. 2020. *Philosophy of education*. 2nd ed. Abuja: Yinkus and Sons Ent.

Odo, L.U. 2012. *The impact and consequences of corruption on the Nigerian Society and economy*. Being a paper presented at the 57th Annual Congress of the Historical Society of Nigeria, held at Ibrahim BadamasiBabangida University, Lapai, Niger State, October 28-31.

Okolo, C.B. 2005. *Problems of African philosophy and one other essay*. Nsukka: Celta Nigeria Ltd.

Omoregbe, J.I. 1993. *A systematic and historical study*. 2nd ed. Lagos: Joja Educational Research and Publishing Ltd.

Otite, O. 1999. Aspect of conflict in theory and practice in Nigeria. In *Community conflicts in Nigeria: management, resolution and transformation*, ed. O. Otite and I.O. Albert, 137–151. Ibadan: Spectrum Books.

Ozumba, G.O. 1995. African ethics. In *Footmarks on African philosophy*, ed. A.F. Uduigwomen, 52–61. Lagos: Obaroh and Ogbinaka.

Prah, K.K. 2009. African languages, African development and African unity. An address presented at the *Centre for Black and African Arts and Civilisation (CBAAC)* organized *Public Lecture*, Abuja, 7th May.

Robert, O.S. 2020. Classical and contemporary leadership misdeeds thwarting Africa's development: Nigerian case. *International Journal of Academic Multidisciplinary Research (IJAMR)* 4 (1).

Robert, O.S., and F. Anura. 2018. Poetic appraisal of state custodians' Sins against the state: Philip Umeh's 'Ambassadors of Poverty'. *International Journal of Academic Pedagogical Research (IJAPR),* 2, 2, February, pp. 9–18, ISSN: 2000-004X.

Robert, O.S., E.N. Besong, and G.A. Dibie. 2016. Retracing our socio-cultural norms/values for a better african society. *Mediterranean Publications International Journal of Humanities and Social Sciences (IJHSS) 2* (4).

Sharma, A.P., and J.T. Hyland. 1991. *Philosophy of education for Nigeria.* Kaduna: Gbabeks Publishers Limited.

Spreitzer, G.M., K.H. Perttula, and K. Xin. 2005. Traditionality matters: an examination of the effectiveness of transformational leadership in the United States and Taiwan. *Journal of Organizational Behavior* 26 (3): 205–227.

The Economist. 2006. The horn of Africa: the path to ruin. August 10, pp. 4–6.

Udokang, E.J. 2014. Traditional ethics and social order: a study in African. *Philosophy. Cross-Cultural Communication* 10 (6): 10.3968/5105. www.aau.org/aur-hiv-aids/ws/.../hiv_africa_sociocultural.pdf.

Yiing, L.H., K. Zaman, and B. Ahmad. 2009. The moderating effects of organizational culture on the relationships between leadership behaviour and organizational commitment and between organizational commitment and job satisfaction and performance. *Leadership & Organization Development Journal* 30 (1): 53–86.

Yukl, G. 1999. An evaluation of conceptual weaknesses in transformational and charismatic leadership theories. *Leadership Quarterly* 10 (2): 285–305.

———. 2013. *Leadership in organizations.* Upper Saddle River: Prentice-Hall.

**Peter Wilfred Naankiel** is a published multidisciplinary scholar, with over 40 scholarly publications. He is a Lecturer at the Department of History and International Studies, Federal University of Lafia, Lafia, Nasarawa State, Nigeria. He has been teaching, researching and writing for over 15 years. His research interests include Social, Political and Public Service History, Security, Gender and International Studies, and Jurisprudence and Human Rights. He is happily married with children.

**Robert Odey Simon** is an erudite Ebonyi State University (EBSU) linguist, is a consultant, researcher, writer, editor and scholar, with over 50 international and scholarly publications to his credit. This Bekwarra-born multidisciplinary post-graduate scholar concentrates on themes in Languages and Linguistics, Philosophy, Religion, Feminism and Gender Studies, Education, Media Studies, Politics, Leadership and Development, Sociology, Psychology, History and International Relations, among others. Robert has worked with several research firms and schools, including tertiary institutions. He has been teaching English Language and Literature in both tertiary and secondary institutions for over 14 years.

**Ghulam Abbas** is a Lecturer and an Assistant Professor at the Department of Animal Production, Riphah College of Veterinary Sciences (RCVetS), Lahore, Pakistan. This scholar holds PhD in Poultry Science, MSc (Hons) in Animal Breeding and Genetics, and Poultry Science and BSc in Animal Husbandry, all from UAF, Pakistan. His core research area is Poultry Science, where he aims at contributing to making Pakistan a major poultry producer. He is the Assistant Director of Graduate Studies, and Member of Graduate Admissions Committee, and Board of Faculty, RCVetS. He is a registered Faculty and Member of Tibb Council, Pakistan.